Soviet Foreign Trade

Glen Alden Smith

The Praeger Special Studies program—utilizing the most modern and efficient book production techniques and a selective worldwide distribution network—makes available to the academic, government, and business communities significant, timely research in U.S. and international economic, social, and political development.

Soviet Foreign Trade

Organization, Operations, and Policy, 1918-1971

PRAEGER SPECIAL STUDIES IN INTERNATIONAL ECONOMICS AND DEVELOPMENT

Praeger Publishers   New York   Washington   London

PRAEGER PUBLISHERS
111 Fourth Avenue, New York, N.Y. 10003, U.S.A.
5, Cromwell Place, London S.W.7, England

Published in the United States of America in 1973
by Praeger Publishers, Inc.

© 1973 by Praeger Publishers, Inc.

Library of Congress Catalog Card Number: 72-83573

Printed in the United States of America

To Kari and Mike

In past years much has been written and said
about the dangers of a Soviet economic offensive that
reportedly was begun following the death of Stalin
in 1953. Unfortunately a good many of these reports
have been based on isolated instances and selected
short-term statistics. Furthermore, most of them
have been based on the assumption that all actions
taken by the Soviet Union are designed solely for
the purpose of defeating the capitalist West and expanding Soviet influence around the world. More recently there has been much discussion of a rapid increase in East-West trade in the near future. In
many cases these forecasts are based more on optim-
ism than on fact.

If the countries of the West are to maximize
their East-West trade relations or take actions to
counter any possible threat posed by a Soviet foreign trade expansion, it is essential that these actions be based on an objective analysis of the nature
of the Soviet foreign trade system, its operations,
and its policies. Although certain limited aspects
of this problem have been studied, no comprehensive
analysis of Soviet foreign trade organization and
operations has previously been available in English.
The major purpose and contribution of this book,
therefore, is to present an objective analysis of
Soviet foreign trade organizations, operations, and
policies for the period from 1918 to 1972, including
an analysis of various long-term trends in Soviet
foreign trade.

In preparing this study extensive use has been
made of Soviet sources, primarily in Russian. Since
most businessmen interested in trade with the Soviet
Union are unfamiliar with Russian, it is hoped that
the rendering of this information in English will
assist improved East-West trade relations. It should
be pointed out, however, that this did not involve
a mere translation from Russian into English but required a sifting of available data to separate the

relevant from the irrelevant, promises from deeds, and fact from propaganda.

This study analyzes the Soviet foreign trade organizations, operations, and policies for a period of 54-year period, and cross-references are made to indicate the relationships between topics at different chronological points. The book begins with an analysis of major Soviet foreign trade policies. The following two chapters discuss the organizations responsible for Soviet foreign trade operations and the control of Soviet foreign trade, respectively. Chapter 4 analyzes various financial aspects of this trade, and Chapter 5 presents a study of Soviet foreign trade promotion organizations and operations. The next two chapters consider the special nature and importance of Soviet trade with the socialist countries and the developing countries. Western restrictions on trade with the Soviet Union are briefly described in Chapter 8. The final two chapters present a forecast of actions that the Soviet Union can be expected to take and suggestions for actions to be taken by the West under various circumstances.

At all stages in this work I was greatly assisted by my mentors and colleagues in both business and Russian studies. A special debt of gratitude is owed Gayton Germane of Stanford's Graduate School of Business, whose many suggestions regarding substance and form were of inestimable value. Special thanks are also extended to Anatole Mazour, Arthur Kroeger, Philip Buck, and Gundar King. The resources of the Hoover Institute and Library at Stanford University were relied upon heavily, and I am indebted to the continual assistance of the Institute's research personnel. Last, I would like to thank Mary Newman for her untiring efforts in preparing the figures and tables included in this book.

It is also a pleasure to express my belated thanks to the Ford Foundation, whose financial assistance during the initial stages of this study made this book possible. However, the conclusions, opinions, and other statements in this publication are mine and are not necessarily those of the Ford Foundation.

To my children, Kari and Mike, I am deeply indebted for the infinite patience they showed and the

deprivations they endured during the last months of
this book's preparation.

Glen A. Smith
June 28, 1972

CONTENTS

LIST OF TABLES

LIST OF FIGURES

Figure		Page

Soviet Foreign Trade

1

SOVIET FOREIGN
TRADE POLICY

The foreign trade policies of the
Soviet Union are of two types--general
policies applicable to all Soviet foreign
trade and exemptions from the general
policies and special policies designed
for trade with specific areas. After a
consideration of the conditions that surrounded the adoption of these policies,
this chapter will discuss the development
and application of both the general and
the special aspects of the following policy topics: the monopoly of foreign
trade, socialist development and autarky,
comparative advantage as a policy, trade
relations with other countries, and tariffs. The primary Soviet foreign trade
policy is the monopoly of foreign trade.
It will be shown that the major advantages of such a policy are protectionism,
austerity, planning, efficiency, fiscal
gain, and the use of foreign trade for
political purposes. Socialist development theory required economic isolation
of the Soviet Union. The import and export policies used to achieve this autarky will be described. Major depar-
tures from this policy in the postwar
period will be discussed, and an explana-

tion of the dumping of Soviet goods will
be given. A discussion of comparative advantage will examine the separate policies
followed by the Soviet Union for socialist
nations, capitalist nations, and developing countries. The discussion of trade
relations with other countries will be
limited in this chapter to the problems
of recognition, the status of trade representatives abroad, relations with former Russian territories, and an introduction to postwar relationships. A more
detailed discussion of the latter topic
will be included in separate chapters on
trade with specific areas. This chapter
will conclude with an analysis of Soviet
tariff policy.

From its inception the Soviet Union has followed foreign trade policies that differ considerably from those of the capitalist countries. To
understand these policies it is necessary to examine
the circumstances that surrounded their adoption.
Prior to the Bolshevik Revolution of 1917, Tsarist Russia was basically an agricultural country.
There was some industry and it was developing gradually, but it was still quite small. This produced
an anomaly. Although Marx had written about a revolution of the proletariat, the industrial workers
of the world, the revolution had taken place in a
country with little industry and a small proletarian
class. To the Bolsheviks this lack of a true proletarian basis was only a temporary situation and one
that goaded them into a long-term program of industrialization. The goal of this program has always
been to catch up with and surpass the industrial
production of the leading capitalist countries. For
most countries such a goal would probably be un-
attainable; however, it must be remembered that the
Soviet Union possesses natural resources that probably exceed those of the United States. To reach
their goal, the Soviets felt it necessary to overcome the existing inertia and develop a self-propelling economy. Labor had to be freed from the
farms so that it would be available for industrial

work. This required tractors, which at first had
to be imported. Factories had to be built. Under
capitalistic conditions it is possible that these
factories would have been for consumer goods. The
Soviets, however, planned for capital-goods industries that could utilize the local resources and
create further means of production. To spur development of this self-propelling economy, it was necessary to rely on foreign trade. Thus, the various
policies followed regarding foreign trade always
took into consideration the stage of growth of the
internal economy. In all cases the policies followed a uniform strategic pattern, although tactical means of applying these policies varied from
period to period. The application of these policies in the weaker, earlier stages of development
reflected the great need for imports. After the
First Five-Year Plan had been completed, the internal economy had reached such a stage that the Soviets
could hold more closely to their established policies. Despite changes in the Soviet government
since the death of Stalin in 1953, it appears that
these policies are still in effect and will continue
until the economic and political goals of the Soviets
are achieved.

Even more important than the program of rapid
industrialization were the means used to fulfill its
requirements. The Soviet Union is a socialist state.
As such the state is supreme in all matters economic, including foreign trade. But the state is
not merely an overseer and controller of economic
functions; it is also a very active participant.
As a result the scope of Soviet economic policies
is broader than that of capitalist countries. In
capitalist countries policies regarding trade promotion, finance, tariffs, and other matters are designed merely to assist the independent businessman; but in the Soviet Union such policies are considered an integral part of overall business operations. Furthermore, because these business operations are the responsibility of the state, the Soviets have applied a comprehensive planning scheme.
With all the economic operations within the state
controlled by this plan, it was necessary to consider foreign trade as a planned sector. In addi-

tion to permitting better coordination of all economic planning, this provided some controls useful
in maintaining Soviet trade relations with countries
that outspokenly sought the downfall of the socialist type of government. Thus, in its varied aspects
the socialism of the Soviet Union has played a prom-
inent role in the establishment of foreign trade
policies.

Another important factor in the shaping of foreign trade policies is the fact that the Soviet
Union is the home of militant world Communism. As
such the Soviet Union openly seeks a world Soviet
order. There is ample evidence that foreign trade
has been used as a tool toward this end. As will
be discussed later, special policies were adopted
in trade relations with the countries of the East
prior to World War II so as to bring these countries
within the Soviet fold. The same strategy was repeated in South America in the 1930's and after
World War II in the countries of Eastern Europe and
the developing nations.

MONOPOLY OF FOREIGN TRADE

Lenin, in his The Immediate Tasks of the Soviet Government, written in 1918, stated:

> First of all we must accomplish the
> simple things, properly organize what is
> available, and then prepare for the more
> intricate things. Consolidate and regu-
> late the State monopolies (in grain,
> leather, etc.) which have been introduced
> already, and by that pave the way for the
> State monopoly of foreign trade. Without
> this monopoly we shall not be able to save
> ourselves from foreign capital by paying a
> tribute.[1]

This monopoly of foreign trade was declared by
the decree of April 22, 1918, which stated in part:

> All foreign trade is nationalized.
> Commercial transactions involving pur-

chases and sales of all kinds of products
(of the extractive industries, manufacturing industries and agriculture) from and to
foreign states and from and to individual
trading enterprises abroad are to be conducted on behalf of the Russian Republic
by specially authorized agencies. All commercial import and export transactions with
foreign countries outside of these agencies
are prohibited.[2]

At the time of this proclamation, the monopoly
of foreign trade had no real meaning, for there was
no foreign trade. With the beginning of trade with
Estonia and England in 1920, the People's Commissariat of Foreign Trade was organized and made responsible for all foreign trade transactions. As
stated in the decree of April 22, 1918, trade by all
other organizations was forbidden. The monopoly of
foreign trade now meant a state monopoly of all foreign trade operations exercised exclusively by the
Commissariat of Foreign Trade.

The institution of the New Economic Policy in
the Soviet Union brought about a basic change in
the monopoly of foreign trade. In accordance with
this policy it was decided that other organizations,
such as cooperatives, state trusts, syndicates, and
mixed Soviet-foreign companies, should be allowed to
engage in foreign trade activities. Article I of
the decree of March 13, 1922, formally reaffirmed
that "the foreign trade of the R.S.F.S.R. is a monopoly of the state."[3] This decree, however, provided
that other organizations could carry on foreign trade
under specific authorizations to be issued by the
Commissariat of Foreign Trade.

By this means the monopoly of foreign trade
was converted from a state monopoly of foreign trade
operations to a state monopoly of foreign trade control. B. L. Krassin emphasized this point by stating: "The regulation of foreign trade as a monopoly
does not mean that all commercial operations are
carried out by organs of the People's Commissariat
for Foreign Trade, but involves the transaction of
such operations under their control."[4] M. Ya. Kaufman later described this as a change "from a monopoly
of a department to a monopoly of the state."[5]

Under these new conditions the monopoly of foreign trade was formalized further by the 1923 and
1936 constitutions of the USSR. The dominant role
of the Commissariat of Foreign Trade was emphasized
in article 17 of the Criminal Code of the Soviet
Union, which states:

> All persons and bodies on the territory
> of the USSR may participate in foreign trade
> only through the agency of the state as per-
> sonified by the People's Commissariat for
> Foreign Trade. Independent operations on
> the foreign exchange market are permissible
> only in cases specifically mentioned in law,
> and under control of the People's Commis-
> sariat for Foreign Trade.[6]

In 1930 monopoly export and import corporations
were established under the jurisdiction of the Commissariat of Foreign Trade, and all other foreign
trade organizations were liquidated. Once again all
foreign trade operations were concentrated in the
hands of the government, and there was a state monopoly of foreign trade operations. According to Soviet
law, however, these corporations were considered to
be autonomous economic organizations and not state
organs. As a result the state monopoly of foreign
trade continued to be defined as a monopoly of foreign trade control. As before, this monopoly was
exercised by the Commissariat of Foreign Trade.
Beginning in 1957 new centrifugal forces brought
about a number of changes in Soviet foreign trade
organization. In that year monopoly corporations
specializing in foreign aid were transferred to the
State Committee for Foreign Economic Relations of
the Council of Ministers. Subsequently other corporations were transferred to other state committees
and to other ministries, and various other organizations were authorized to conduct foreign trade operations. Despite these changes the concept of the
state monopoly of foreign trade remained essentially
unchanged. In 1967 V. S. Pozdniakov remarked that
" . . . the state monopoly continues to be the basis
of the legal regulation of Soviet foreign trade and
the determination of its legal forms of organization."[7]

Although the Ministry of Foreign Trade maintains many controls over the foreign trade activities of other state organs, it would appear that today the monopoly of foreign trade is exercised by the Council of Ministers of the USSR.

When the Soviets speak of the monopoly of foreign trade, they are usually referring to the monopoly of foreign trade control. Since 1930, however, a state monopoly of foreign trade operations has also been a basic policy of the Soviet Union. From 1930 to 1957 this monopoly, like the monopoly of foreign trade control, was exercised exclusively by the Ministry of Foreign Trade through its monopoly corporations. There has been no change in this aspect of the Soviet monopoly of foreign trade except that it is now exercised by various state organs.

Protectionism

A basic premise on which the monopoly of foreign trade was founded was protectionism. The Soviet Union had as its goal industrial production surpassing that of the West. To achieve this both the older and the newly established industries needed protection from outside competition. The Soviet leaders, probably quite correctly, felt that outside competition would not only stifle growth in Russian industry but would also bring with it the destruction of the Soviet socialist system.

The conventional method of protection, and the one used by Tsarist Russia, was a high tariff wall. The Bolsheviks were convinced that the capitalist nations and individuals would stop at nothing in destroying the Soviet Union and hence would break through such a tariff wall. Lenin emphasized this point, stating:

> No tariff policy can be really effective in an era of imperialism, an era of enormous discrimination between poor countries and very rich countries. In such circumstances any rich industrial country can completely defeat tariff protection. To do so it need only introduce an export

> bounty on the goods exported to Russia on
> which we levy a duty. Any industrial coun-
> try has more than enough money to finance
> such a bounty, and consequently any indus-
> trial country can, with absolute certainty,
> defeat our home industries.[8]

He further declared that it would be impossible "to
make Russia an industrial country, without protecting it, not by means of a tariff policy, but solely
through a monopoly of foreign trade."[9]

Not everyone was in agreement with Lenin. The
economist Kondratiev, for example, proposed that the
principle of comparative advantage be adhered to.
He claimed that "for purposes of weakening the autarky it is necessary to strengthen those industries
at home which are most profitable to us, are economically most efficient from the point of view of
the international division of labour."[10] Preobreshen-
sky considered it quite legitimate to curtail or dis-
continue entirely the production of certain goods in
fields where the foreign engineering industry was
able to offer Russia more advantageous prices. These
men, along with Trotsky, who claimed that the Soviet
economy would be controlled by the world economy,
were in the minority. The majority feared that, on
the basis of comparative advantage, Russia would remain a granary for Europe and industry would never
be developed. To develop such industry it was necessary to provide protection until Russian industry
could compete on an equal basis with other world industries.

Stalin also considered protection to be the primary duty of the monopoly of foreign trade and referred to it as "the shield and breast-plate of our
young socialist industry."[11] He further clarified
this point when he stated:

> . . . for the workers, the abolition
> of the monopoly of foreign trade would mean
> a refusal to industrialize the country, to
> build new factories and plants and to en-
> large the old ones. That would mean an in-
> undation of the U.S.S.R. with goods from
> capitalist countries, a decrease in indus-

try because of its relative weakness, an
increase of unemployment, a decline in the
standard of living of the masses, a weakening of the economic and political positions.
For peasants this would mean the transformation of our country from an independent
one into a semi-colonial one with an impov-
erished peasantry. Speaking of workers and
peasants I must say that a demand to abolish the monopoly of foreign trade would produce laughter and hostility.[12]

Today the Soviet Union is one of the strongest
nations in the world. Its capital-goods industries
are well developed and the Soviet Union is a net exporter of machines and equipment. In various industries the Soviet Union would appear to have a comparative advantage with no further need for protection.
There is still, however, a structural imbalance in
the Soviet economy; and the monopoly of foreigh trade
continues to serve as a protective umbrella over the
less-developed industries.

Austerity

A second major pillar supporting the principle
of monopoly of foreign trade was the need for austerity in the economic development of the country.
This austerity was the result of three important
factors. First, the Soviet leaders had based this
economic development on rapid industrialization.
Second, products immediately available for export
were limited despite the richness of Russia's natural resources. As a result there was little foreign
exchange available for the purchase of imports.
Third, because of the past relative poverty of the
Russian people, there was a large pent-up demand for
consumer goods.
In accordance with long-term goals of the Soviets, it was desirable that the limited resources
available be applied to the purchase of industrial
machinery, raw materials, and similar items that
would help in the industrialization of the country.
If foreign trade was left on a free trade basis, it

was feared that a large quantity of nonessential consumer goods would pour in at the expense of broad,
long-range economic benefits. This not only would
impair the program of industrialization but also
would result in a mortgaging of future crops to pay
for such imports. It was felt that as a result the
West would interfere in internal matters and Russia
would eventually become a labor colony for the capitalists.[13] Tariffs, as mentioned above, were not
considered adequate protection. A. P. Rozengolts in
1934 stated that "had there been no foreign trade
monopoly we should have had silk stockings and similar articles."[14]

Similarly, it was felt that under free trade
certain commodities might be exported although they
were urgently needed at home for industrial development. As a result the monopoly of foreign trade was
given the task of regulating imports and exports so
that only that trade benefiting the industrialization
program would be allowed.

The absence of an adequate consumer goods industry in the Soviet Union, combined with import restrictions, resulted in constant pressure being applied to the monopoly of foreign trade to allow more
consumer goods to be imported. Although Malenkov
and subsequent leaders made some concessions, there
has been no wholesale satisfaction of consumer wants.
Even the Fiat automobile plant is affected by the
austerity policy, and a good portion of the output
is being exported despite the extremely strong domestic demand for automobiles. Until the Soviet leaders feel that they have achieved their industrialization goals, it is very likely that pressures for consumer-goods imports will have no more than a token
effect.

Planning

The subject of planning is related to Soviet
austerity. At the time the monopoly was declared,
there was little, if any, planning. The first formal attempt at planning was introduced by the State
Planning Board (Gosplan), established in 1921. Planning reached its climax with the initiation of the

First Five-Year Plan in 1928. All phases of the internal economy were then controlled by one centralized overall plan. This plan included the disposi-
tion of all resources, the capital to be applied,
and the quantities of each item to be produced. To
be at all effective this type of planning requires
economic near-isolation, physically or by controls.
Free trade would lead to a situation in which the
state would not be able to control completely the
internal trade operations. M. N. Sobolev states
that because of this, "free foreign trade represents
in itself a principle which is not harmonious with
all the economic form of life of the Soviet Union."[15]
Thus, although planning was not an original reason
for establishing the monopoly of foreign trade, it
became one of its most important justifications.
Since 1928 the foreign trade of the Soviet Union has
been carefully planned as a sector of the total econ-
omy--the sector that can be said to "balance the
books" and thus maintain the needed near-isolation
of the internal economy. Without the monopoly of
foreign trade, such planning would have been of little value.

Efficiency

Soviet writers such as M. M. Zhirmunski and
J. D. Yanson claim added efficiency as one of the
basic reasons for and advantages of the monopoly of
foreign trade. It is important to point out that
this advantage results only from the monopoly of
foreign trade operations and not from foreign trade
control. During the period of the New Economic
Policy the monopoly was one of control alone, and
operations were carried on by various organizations
that competed with each other to some extent. In
this case there was no efficiency accruing from the
monopoly. The specialization in trade organizations
that culminated in the establishment of the monopoly
foreign trade corporations did provide the opportunity for increased efficiency. Since each corporation dealt in only one commodity or group of commodities, extreme specialization was made possible.
On the one hand, this specialization resulted in

efficiencies and lowered overhead costs; but, on the
other hand, the formation of monolithic corporations
produced bureaucracy unabated by competition, and as
a result efficiency was probably greatly reduced and
overhead costs increased. Since there was no competition of buyers of Soviet export goods, it is also
probable that the monopoly of trade operations contributed to inefficiency in Soviet industries. It
would appear that the shifting of monopoly operations
from the Ministry of Foreign Trade to other organizations in the 1960's offered increased specialization
and coordination and has tended to improve efficiency.

Fiscal Gain

Another advantage attributed to the monopoly of
foreign trade operations is that of fiscal gain.
Such an advantage was obtained in three ways. By
eliminating the middleman, profits accrued to the
state. However, because the costs of monopoly operations were so high, it is possible that larger
profits could have been obtained by other means from
free traders. Two more important means were "by . . .
concentrating purchases, thus making it possible to
secure lower prices and more favourable terms generally, and . . . concentrating sales, thereby securing
more favourable prices and terms and abolishing competition between the Soviet exporting bodies."[16]
Although these statements may be valid, they do not
constitute an important advantage of the monopoly of
foreign trade operations. If free trade had resulted
in trade at or above the 1913 level, an application
of a high tariff on such trade would have produced
much greater fiscal gain than was achieved by economies of foreign trade monopoly operation. For this
reason it can be said that fiscal gain was merely a
by-product of the monopoly of operations, and such
gain did not influence either the monopoly or the
trade volume in any visible manner.

Political Use of Foreign Trade

History is replete with examples of the use of
foreign trade by a nation for political gain. In

modern capitalism, with its separation of business and state, such activities are usually limited to programs of governmental assistance to foreign trade. The monopoly of foreign trade in the Soviet Union provides that country with a weapon that can be used directly and most effectively for political reasons. Furthermore, this weapon is just one of an arsenal that includes coordination of trade, propaganda, political actions, agitation, and cultural ties. Traders of capitalist countries operate on the basis of economics and for a profit. As a result they operate only where and when a profit can be realized. The only means of using these traders for political purposes is by means of subsidies that make certain trade appear profitable. The Soviet Union, on the other hand, seeks no profit and trades to obtain commodities it needs, or to gain political advantage, or both.

The uses of foreign trade as a political tool will be discussed in detail in later sections. In the West these actions have included the shifting of trade in order to influence state loans and credits; cuts in trade resulting from raids on trade delegations and granting of amnesty to defectors; switching of trade from fascist to democratic countries; and the use of trade to force political recognition of the Soviet Union. In the developing countries trade and aid have been used as tools to separate these countries from the West and from China. Trade was also an important tool in gaining control over Eastern Europe; and trade with socialist countries, particularly China, has varied in direct relation to the warmness of political ties.

ISOLATION AND INTEGRATION

A second major policy that has differentiated Soviet foreign trade from that of the West is that of closely relating foreign trade to the autarkic development of the Soviet economy. As Zhirmunski stated, "The explanation of the nature of Soviet export trade must be sought, not in comparison with the foreign trade of capitalist countries, but in the specific tasks of a state which is building socialism in the midst of capitalist encirclement."[17]

To achieve this goal of autarky, the Soviet Union
has followed special import and export policies and
a policy of integrating the economies and the foreign
trade of the bloc countries of Eastern Europe.

Import Policy

During the prewar period the Soviet Union imported only those goods that could be used in the
rehabilitation or development of industry, the mechanization of agriculture, and other fields of socialist development. The "import policy has at all
times been guided by singleness of purpose: at all
stages of our socialist construction the structure
of imports was made completely subservient to the
vital tasks in hand."[18] These "vital tasks" increased at a rapid rate and finally resulted in the
First Five-Year Plan, inaugurated in 1928. The grand
scale of this plan called for ever-increasing imports
until a peak of $569 million was attained in 1931.
This First Five-Year Plan built up an economic base
that was then able to produce much of the machinery
and equipment needed to fulfill the "vital tasks."
As a result imports of heavy lifting apparatus, electric, furnaces, welding equipment, pumps, diesel
engines, locomotives, and tractors were completely
discontinued. Industrial raw materials were now
being produced in the Soviet Union, so imports of
cotton, fertilizers, tanning materials, and materials
for the textile, building, and foods industries were
eliminated.[19] As a result the import volume of the
Soviet Union declined from its 1931 peak to a low of
$120 million in 1936.
It is clear from these data that the Soviet import policy has been based on two main considera-
tions--what is needed for socialist development and
what the Soviet Union itself can produce. The difference between these quantities is the amount to be
imported--no more and no less. In the early years
the Soviets could not and did not produce very much
and were forced to rely on imports. As an adequate
economic base was built, Soviet production increased,
reliance on imports was greatly reduced, and the
autarkic trend became very noticeable.

Since World War II, and particularly following
the death of Stalin, Soviet imports have expanded
greatly over prewar levels, reaching $11.7 billion
in 1970. This increase does not indicate a change
in policy--imports are still determined by socialist
needs. Rather, this increase reflects changes in
Soviet priorities. Consumer goods are now imported
to satisfy some small part of pent-up demand. Further development of the Soviet economy requires new
technology, which is imported in the form of machines,
equipment, and complete plants. Political activities
in the developing countries have brought about some
priority changes; the most important change resulted
from the "building of socialism" in Eastern Europe.
It should be noted that in 1970 fully 65 percent of
Soviet imports were from socialist countries, 11 percent came from developing countries, and only 24 percent were from the developed countries of the West.

Export Policy

According to the import policy, only those goods
needed in the socialist development are imported.
The export policy states that exports will be "in
the quantity necessary for the flow of imports or
for the payment of obligations on imports of the
past year."[20] For this reason the exports of the
Soviet Union in any particular year have closely
paralleled the volume of imports for the same period.
As imports increased up through the First Five-Year
Plan, exports also increased. When imports dropped
off after this period, so did exports. Similarly,
after World War II exports increased at roughly the
same pace as imports. The structure of exports at
any given time was determined by what might be called
the principle of socialist comparative advantage.
In the overall planning of the Soviet economy, an
analysis was made of all the needs of Soviet industry
and of the resources available to meet these needs.
Within the limits set by the volume of foreign exchange needed to cover imports, an analysis of the
available resources was made to determine the comparative advantage of each commodity to the overall
plan. If a particular resource could be applied more

TABLE 1

Soviet Foreign Trade Volume
(in millions)

Year	Exports 1921 Rubles	Exports 1936 Rubles	Exports 1950 Rubles	Exports 1961 Rubles	Exports U.S. Dollars	Imports 1921 Rubles	Imports 1936 Rubles	Imports 1950 Rubles	Imports 1951 Rubles	Imports U.S. Dollars
1913	1,520	6,658	5,297	1,192	782	1,375	6,023	4,792	1,078	708
1914	956	4,188	3,332	750	492	1,098	4,809	3,826	861	565
1915	402	1,760	1,400	315	207	1,139	4,987	3,968	893	586
1916	502	2,199	1,750	394	296	2,488	10,899	8,672	1,951	1,415
1917	488	2,138	1,701	383	239	2,449	10,726	8,534	1,920	1,012
1918	8	36	28	6		105	461	367	83	
1919	0	0		0		3	14	11	2	
1920	1	6	5	1		29	126	100	23	
1921	20	89	70	16		211	923	734	165	
1922	82	357	284	64		270	1,182	940	212	
1923	218	955	760	171	98	143	627	499	112	64
1924	337	1,476	1,175	264	171	260	1,139	906	204	132
1925	608	2,664	2,120	477	313	827	3,621	2,881	648	425
1926	724	3,174	2,525	568	348	689	3,017	2,400	540	355
1927	746	3,267	2,600	585	397	758	3,321	2,642	595	390
1928	803	3,519	2,800	630	414	453	4,175	3,322	748	233
1929	924	4,046	3,219	724	476	881	3,857	3,069	691	454
1930	1,036	4,539	3,612	813	534	1,059	4,638	3,690	830	545
1931	811	3,553	2,827	636	418	1,105	4,840	3,851	867	569
1932	575	2,518	2,004	451	296	704	3,084	2,454	552	363
1933	495	2,168	1,727	389	255	348	1,525	1,214	273	179
1934	418	1,832	1,458	328	215	232	1,018	810	182	120
1935	367	1,609	1,280	288	189	241	1,057	841	189	124
1936		1,359	1,081	243	270		1,352	1,076	242	269
1937		1,729	1,376	310	344		1,341	1,067	240	267
1938		1,332	1,060	239	265		1,423	1,132	255	283
1940		1,412	1,084	244	271		1,446	1,151	259	288
1942		399	318	72	79		2,756	2,192	493	548

18

Year								
1943	373	297	-67	74	8,460	6,728	1,514	1,682
1946	3,288	2,615	588	654	3,896	3,075	692	769
1950		7,178	1,615	1,795		5,824	1,311	1,450
1955		13,704	3,084	3,426		12,244	2,755	3,061
1956		14,460	3,254	3,615		14,448	3,251	3,612
1957		17,524	3,943	4,381		15,748	3,544	3,937
1958		17,188	3,868	4,297		17,408	3,917	4,352
1959		21,764	4,897	5,562		20,292	4,566	5,073
1960		22,248	5,006	5,998		22,512	5,066	5,628
1961			5,398				5,245	5,827
1962			6,328	7,031			5,810	6,455
1963			6,545	7,272			6,353	7,058
1964			6,915	7,683			6,963	7,736
1965			7,350	8,167			7,248	8,053
1966			7,957	8,841			7,123	7,914
1967			8,687	9,652			7,683	8,536
1968			9,571	10,634			8,469	9,409
1969			10,490	11,654			9,294	10,326
1970			11,520	12,800			10,565	11,738

Notes: Prior to 1924 the exchange rate of the ruble was determined in the open market. In 1924 the ruble was valued at 0.774234 grams of pure gold, or U.S. $0.515. In 1936 it was revalued at 0.176766 grams, but at the same time the American dollar was devalued. Therefore the 1936 ruble is valued at U.S. $0.1989 after 1936 and U.S. $0.117 before 1936. In 1950 the ruble was revalued at 0.222168 grams of pure gold, or U.S. $0.25. For conversion to the pre-1936 dollar, the 1950 ruble was valued at U.S. $0.148. In 1961 the ruble was revalued at 0.987412 grams of gold, or U.S. $1.11.

Sources: Compiled from data in Scientific-Research Institute of the Monopoly of Foreign Trade, Foreign Trade of the USSR for 20 Years: 1918-1937 (Moscow: V/O Mezhdunarodnaya Kniga, 1939), p. 6*; USSR, Ministry of Foreign Trade, Foreign Trade of the USSR for 1956 (Moscow: Vneshtorgizdat, 1958), pp. 7-10; for 1957, pp. 7-10; for 1959-63, pp. 10-11; for 1964, p. 10; for 1966, p. 10; for 1968, p. 10*; J. D. Yanson, Foreign Trade in the USSR (London: Victor Gollancz, 1934), pp. 45, 54; Nikolai A. Voznesensky, The Economy of the USSR During World War II (Washington, D.C.: Public Affairs Press, 1948), p. 43; M. M. Zhirmunski, Soviet Export (Moscow: Mezhdunarodnaya Kniga, 1936), pp. 18, 29; Foreign Trade, No. 11 (1957), p. 70; No. 4 (1958), p. 70; No. 5 (1971), p. 21; No. 5 (1971), p. 57.* (Note: Sources indicated by * are in Russian.)

advantageously directly in industry, this was done.
The exports, then, were those resources that provided
the greatest relative advantage in exchange for the
needed imports or technical assistance.[21] The development of the Soviet economy and the reshuffling of
priorities have resulted in some marked changes in
the composition of exports. In 1938 grains, timber,
textile raw materials, and furs accounted for over
two-thirds of Soviet exports. By 1968 these commodities represented only 20 percent of exports. Conversely, machines and equipment, metals and ores,
fuels, and industrial goods increased from 20 percent
of exports in 1938 to 67 percent in 1968. Obviously
grain, timber, and textile raw materials had become
more important domestically and could not as easily
be made available for export. In the case of grain
this is borne out by the abortive virgin lands program of Khrushchev and the large grain purchases
that have been made from Canada, the United States,
and other countries. At the same time the Soviet
foreign aid program is a reflection of the growing
availability of industrial products.

                              Dumping

     Strict adherence to balancing imports with ex-
ports was the major cause for alleged dumping in
1930, 1957, and 1963. In the 1930's the major Soviet
exports were highly competitive and their prices
fell rapidly. Taking 1929 as 100, the export price
indexes in 1931 were wheat, 45.4; rye, 41.8; flax,
43.4; petroleum, 51.5; and timber, 49.6.[22] Import
prices did not decline so severely. As a result the
physical volume of exports had to be increased
sharply. Thus, the "Soviet export policy . . . [was]
designed first and last to get the business and . . .
Soviet prices [were] . . . , as a rule, just low
enough--but always low enough--to get the business
and not, if the Soviets can help it, any lower."[23]
There is no question that there was sharp price competition. Whether this resulted in dumping is a
moot question. In any case the Soviet Union was not
following a policy of dumping but a policy of importing what they needed and exporting what was needed
to pay for the imports.

TABLE 2

Composition of Soviet Exports
(in percent)

	1938	1958	1968
Machines and equipment	2.2	18.5	21.6
Ores, metals, and metal products	4.4	21.5	18.5
Oil, coal, and other fuels	8.9	15.2	16.1
Industrial goods and raw materials	4.4	12.3	10.3
Grains and food products	28.9	8.9	8.4
Timber and timber products	20.3	5.6	6.4
Textile raw materials	10.6	6.8	4.5
Chemical products, fertilizer	4.4	3.6	4.1
Consumer goods	0.9	3.6	2.7
Furs	9.8	0.8	0.5
Other products	5.2	3.2	6.9
	100.0	100.0	100.0

Sources: Compiled from data in USSR, Ministry of Foreign Trade, Foreign Trade of the USSR for 1959-63 (Moscow: Vneshtorgizdat, 1965), pp. 24, 26, 28-56; for 1968, pp. 19-34.*

A soft aluminum market during the recession of
1957-58 resulted in new charges of dumping. Alcan
Aluminium reacted to this weakened market by cutting
production back 60,000 tons per year in January 1958
and by cutting the world price two cents per pound
in March 1958.[24] In announcing the price reduction
Alcan's president said, "We believe this price reduction at this time, when important segments of the
aluminum smelting industry are idle, and when there
is a widespread public demand for lower prices, will
be a constructive force in improving the national
and world economy and will be beneficial to companies,
fabricators, and the industry as a whole."[25] At the
same time Alcan asked the British Board of Trade to
impose an antidumping tariff so as to protect the
British market from Russian dumping of aluminum.[26]

In 1957 English imports of aluminum dropped
41,000 tons. Since Alcan controlled 88 percent of
this market, it could well expect to suffer most of
this loss. In fact, however, Alcan sales to England
dropped 52,000 tons. Since Soviet sales had increased
12,200 tons during this period (a little more than
the difference between 41,000 and 52,000 tons), a
ready-made scapegoat was at hand. It is true that
the Soviets were selling in England at a price approximately two cents a pound under the world price,
but the statement of Alcan's president would make it
appear that the world price had been held artificially
high despite slackening demand. In such a case the
Soviets could be accused of severe price competition
but not of dumping.[27]

Even if the Soviet aluminum sales to England
are classed as dumping, there is no evidence to support the idea that the Soviet Union was following a
policy of dumping for the purpose of disrupting
Western markets. On the contrary, it seems that the
Soviets were following their basic import and export
policies. A postwar complication to these policies
was the inconvertibility of currencies, especially in
the sterling bloc. An analysis of Soviet trade statistics indicates that Soviet purchases, especially
of raw materials, from the British Commonwealth in
1957 resulted in a severe Soviet balance-of-payments
deficit in relation to the sterling bloc. To obtain
the needed sterling currency, the Soviet Union sharply

increased its sales of petroleum, timber, manganese,
ferroalloys, aluminum, and tin to Great Britain.
The increases in sales of these commodities over the
1956 level amounted to 185 million rubles, or somewhat more than one-fourth of all Commonwealth sales.
It appears that there were no price reductions on
the first four items; but, since the Soviet Union
had not established itself in the tin and aluminum
markets in Great Britain, it was necessary to offer
price concessions to obtain the sales. Since the
increased sales of these two items alone accounted
for 87 million rubles, it can be seen that the Soviet
Union was following its policy of exporting to obtain
the means of paying for needed imports.[28]

At Senate hearings in 1963 Senator Kenneth Keat-
ing claimed: "Khrushchev has threatened to bury us
on more than one occasion. It is now becoming increasingly evident that he would also like to drown
us in a sea of oil. The Soviets are dumping oil at
bargain prices throughout the world . . . for political and military reasons."[29] Once again the reaction would appear to be based more on emotion and
politics than on fact. Soviet crude oil exports in
1955 were only 3.8 million tons, most of which went
to socialist countries. By 1961 these sales had
grown to 23.4 million tons--about 4 percent of total
world sales. More important, 40 percent of this
amount went to Italy, Japan, and West Germany and
another 15 percent went to other nonsocialist nations.[30]

During this buildup the American oil industry
tried to get the U.S. government to take some action.
Finally in 1961 the State Department instructed am-
bassadors to discourage foreign governments from increasing imports of Soviet oil and entered into international consultations on the "Soviet crude oil
problem."[31] These efforts were generally unsuccess-
ful, and in 1964 France agreed to at least triple
its imports.[32] Other nations followed the same pattern; and by 1968 Soviet crude oil exports totaled
59.2 million tons, with half of this total going to
Western countries. The United States was successful,
however, in coercing other NATO nations to cut off
shipments of 40-inch pipe needed for a Soviet pipeline to the West. The United States argued that such

a pipeline would allow the Soviet Union to apply political and military pressure on free world customers.[33]

Soviet oil production was burgeoning, and crude
oil now had a greater comparative advantage as an
export commodity. As in the case of aluminum and
tin, the markets were tightly held by producers that
maintained artificially high prices. To enter these
markets the Soviets were forced to use the only tool
available to them--price concessions. The monopoly
corporation Soyuzneftexport claims that its prices
are normally pegged to Platt's Oilgram Price Service
but allows that it gives discounts where those prices
are not considered realistic. This happened in Germany, where in 1961 Soviet crude oil was priced at
$1.70 per barrel, compared with a world price of
$2.50. In Japan, Idemitsu Kosan Co. received a 20
percent discount on a six-year supply contract.[34]
This stiff price competition gave the Soviets what
they needed, the wherewithal to pay for needed imports. Again there is little evidence of intentional
dumping. The major oil producers probably cried
"dumping" because they were forced to make overdue
cuts in price to meet Soviet competition. They used
the security issue as Pavlov used a bell.

Autarky

As mentioned above, the import and export policies of the Soviet Union were based on the principle
of autarky, or economic isolation from the capitalist
world. Litvinov stated in 1934: "In distinction
from other countries, we, with a great increase of
our own output, do not aspire to autarky and do not
resist advantageous import of foreign goods."[35] The
actions of the Soviet Union, however, belie this; and
statements made by such Soviet writers as Rozengolts
and Zhirmunski do not coincide with such claims regarding autarky.

Lenin, in a speech to the Eighth Congress of
Soviets in December 1920, declared:

The resumption of trade relations will
enable us to make large purchases of indis-

pensable machinery. We must bend all our
energies to this end . . . to introduce a
more equitable exchange of commodities so
that we shall be able to buy as quickly as
possible the necessary machinery for our
extensive plans of rehabilitating the national economy. The quicker this is done,
the greater will be our chances of achieving
economic independence of the capitalist
world.[36]

Later, at the Fourteenth Congress of Soviets,
Stalin reemphasized this desire for autarky by announcing:

We must build our economy in order
that our country will not become an appen-
dage to the capitalist system, in order
that we will not be included in the overall
system of capitalist development as a second class undertaking, in order that our
economy will grow not as a second class undertaking of capitalism but as an individual economy in its own right, based primarily on the internal market which is
based on the union of our industry with the
peasant economy of the country.[37]

From these statements it is clear that the Soviet intention has always been the establishment of
an economy that is completely independent of and
isolated from the economy of the capitalist world.
According to V. Boyeff, by 1935 the Soviet Union had
"become a country economically independent and no
longer required large imports in order to fulfill
[its] economic plans."[38] The very definite trend
toward this independence or autarky in the period
prior to World War II can be seen from an analysis
of the statistics of Soviet foreign trade. (See
Table 1.) It can also be seen in the relationship
of exports to total industrial and agricultural production. In a growing economy it is usual for exports to expand from year to year, keeping a somewhat similar ratio to production. In the Soviet

Union exports increased as a percentage of production until a peak of 3.5 percent was reached in 1930. Subsequently production increased rapidly while exports were contracted, so that the ratio dropped to 2.5 percent in 1932, 1.8 percent in 1934, and 0.8 percent in 1936.[39]

Immediately following World War II the Soviet economist N. Voznosensky declared: "The U.S.S.R. will continue in the future to maintain economic ties with foreign countries in accordance with the tested line of the Soviet Government devoted towards the attainment of the technical-economic independence of the Soviet Union."[40]

Despite vastly increased trade turnover this policy has remained steadfast, and in 1959 Undersecretary of State C. Douglas Dillon reported:

> The Soviet Union in its trade with the West is today motivated by the same autarkic considerations as in the Thirties. This is borne out most forcefully by the fact that the second-ranking industrial power of the world exports to the West at about the level of Denmark--roughly $1 billion a year--and that these exports are more characteristic of those you would expect from an underdeveloped or semideveloped country than from an industrial giant.[41]

This same situation prevails today. In 1969 Soviet trade turnover with nonsocialist countries totaled $6.8 billion, almost exactly the turnover of Denmark; and total turnover was only $22 billion, slightly more than that of the Netherlands.

The autarkic economy after the war, however, was different from that of the prewar period in that it became an autarky of the Soviet bloc as a whole. The countries of Eastern Europe adopted Soviet-style economies, including the idea of autarky. As time passed, the Soviet Union guided a transformation from the autarky of an individual country to an autarky of the socialist world. At the same time the Soviets were carrying out their plans for integrating the economies of this socialist world.

Soviet Bloc Integration

Economic integration of the socialist world is a postwar strategic policy that has gone through three overlapping tactical stages since 1947. During the first stage (1947-55) the individual economies of Eastern Europe were tied to the Soviet economy by a series of bilateral agreements and actions. In June 1947 the Soviet Union refused Marshall Plan assistance and announced its own Molotov Plan of development credits for Eastern Europe. Within a short period the Soviet Union had also negotiated bilateral trade and scientific-technical collaboration agreements, organized mixed companies in each of the countries of Eastern Europe, introduced the ruble as the bloc clearing currency, and assisted each of these countries to establish Soviet-style ministries of foreign trade and monopoly foreign trade corporations. By 1951 these bilateral links were fairly well forged, but the emphasis on bilateralism did not wane until after the unrest in Eastern Europe in 1953 and the liquidation of the mixed companies in 1955.

In the second stage (1949-59) emphasis was gradually shifted toward developing intrabloc trade. The Soviet Union urged the people's democracies to enter into a network of bilateral trade and scientific-technical collaboration agreements between each other and the USSR. In January 1949 the Council for Mutual Economic Assistance (Comecon) was organized to provide some coordination of economic planning, technical assistance, and foreign trade. Although the Soviet Union was the senior member of this partnership, it did not enjoy absolute powers--especially after the death of Stalin in 1953. During this period the Soviets guided the bloc slowly toward eventual integration by means of the soft sell. Near the end of this stage, the Soviet Union urged a multilateral clearing system and a bloc bank, but it was unable to maneuver these integration measures through Comecon channels.

Following the split with the People's Republic of China in 1959, the Soviet Union refocused its attention on the socialist development of the Comecon nations of Eastern Europe and of Mongolia. This resulted in the current stage (1959-72), which is char-

acterized by overt and intensive Soviet actions aimed
at achieving rapid and total integration of the economies of the Comecon nations (including Mongolia,
which became a member in 1962). A blueprint for integration, entitled "Fundamental Principles of the
International Socialist Division of Labor," was pressured through Comecon in 1962. In the same year the
Soviets finally convinced other Comecon members of
the advantages of a multilateral clearing system, a
bloc bank, and a collective bloc currency. In 1964
and 1965 they were successful in setting up coordinated planning within Comecon for the 1966-70 Five-
Year Plan. To increase specialization and cooperation in the production of machine tools, the Soviets
called for Comecon discussions on this topic in February 1966. In 1970 the Soviet-planned International
Investment Bank began operations. Beginning in 1968,
the Soviet Union made a major push for total integration. Rumania, which has opposed integration
measures and refused to participate in the International Investment Bank, once again blocked the Soviet
plan. In July 1971, however, a somewhat watered-
down, 15- to 20-year integration plan was announced
for Comecon. It is expected that Soviet pressures
will continue until the USSR achieves its long-range
goal of total integration for the bloc.

TRADE RELATIONS WITH
OTHER COUNTRIES

The policies discussed heretofore have all
proved to be rather long-range and stable policies
that were always visible despite tactical variations.
The policies in regard to relations with other countries have also been quite stable; but, since they
were applied only step by step, they often gave the
appearance of unstable and short-range policies.
Above all, it must be remembered that the Soviets
were attempting to convert old, backward Tsarist
Russia into a powerful country, economically and
technically advanced. Foreign trade was merely one
of the tools used in this conversion. In this con-
nection Boyeff remarked, "The U.S.S.R. requires not
just any kind of foreign trade relations with other

countries, but only such relations as will contribute
to the fulfillment of the national economic plan."[42]
It is this philosophy that has always characterized
Soviet trade relations with the developed countries
of the West.

On the other hand, the Soviet Union is the home
of militant international Communism. Foreign trade
is an effective weapon in the fight for political
control in various areas. Prior to World War II
this was shown in the relations with certain countries
of the East, where the Soviet Union followed a policy
of granting special advantages to foster foreign
trade. Following the war such a policy was extended
to cover the new nations of Asia and Africa. A policy akin to plunder and control was also followed
in the so-called people's democracies during the
same period. It is this writer's opinion, however,
that militant world Communism had little if any effect on the nature of trade with the West or on the
policies governing such trade. However, as the Soviet
Union approaches its avowed goal of production su-
premacy, it is entirely possible and even probable
that promotion of world Communism will become the
primary objective of Soviet foreign trade.

In recent years the Soviet Union has made a
number of foreign trade policy pronouncements that
superficially sound like those of a proponent of
free trade. In 1964 one Soviet author announced
that "the Soviet Union, like all socialist countries,
is a consistent advocate of greater international
trade."[43] Two years later the directives of the
23rd Congress of the Communist Party for the 1966-
70 Five-Year Plan echoed this idea and added that
the USSR is opposed to all limitations, discrimina-
tions, and barriers to the widening of trade ties.
These directives then enumerated the basic principles
of Soviet foreign trade as being complete equality
on all sides, respect of states and national sovereignty, noninterference in the affairs of other countries, mutual benefit, and conscientious fulfillment
of all obligations.[44] Actual events have cast doubt
on these principles, and in any case the Soviet
Union followed three separate policies. These three
policies were clearly differentiated in 1971 in party
statements regarding the 1971-75 Five-Year Plan.

These policies are the following:

> Economic, scientific, and technical
> ties of the Soviet Union with other social-
> ist countries, aimed at further strengthen-
> ing the community and consistently promoting
> the economic integration of the [Comecon]
> countries shall be improved and extended in
> every way.
> Development of stable external economic,
> scientific, and technical ties with develop-
> ing Asian, African, and Latin American coun-
> tries shall be continued on terms of mutual
> benefit and in the interest of strengthening
> their economic independence.
> Economically justified commercial,
> scientific, and technical contacts with in-
> dustrially developed capitalist countries
> which show willingness to develop co-opera-
> tion with the Soviet Union in these spheres,
> shall be extended.[45]

Recognition

One of the major tasks that faced the new Soviet
government in 1918 was obtaining diplomatic recognition. During 1920 and 1921 the Soviet Union signed
peace treaties with the Baltic states of Estonia,
Latvia, Lithuania, Finland, and Poland, all of which
had formerly been a part of Tsarist Russia. Peace
treaties that were based on mutual recognition,
equality, and sovereignty were also concluded with
Persia (Iran), Afghanistan, Turkey, Mongolia, and
the Khorezm and Bukharan People's Soviet Republics.
By this means the Soviet Union won de jure recognition. Since these were all rather minor countries,
this de jure recognition proved of little importance.
What the Soviets actively sought was such recognition
by the major countries of the West, and toward this
end they adopted a policy of using trade to obtain
recognition.

Trade agreements of various types were concluded
during this period with England, Germany, Norway,
Austria, Italy, and Sweden. All of these agreements

clearly specified that they were made on the basis
of nonrecognition. Although trade relations with
these countries could be carried on without recognition, the Soviet Union actively sought such recognition for other purposes. In 1922 the Soviet Union
turned to the other isolated country of Europe--Ger-
many--and offered economic advantages provided Germany would recognize Soviet Russia de jure. This
recognition was granted in the Rapallo Treaty of
April 16, 1922. Czechoslovakia followed on July 5,
1922, with de facto, not de jure, recognition.[46]
Denmark, on April 24, 1923, also recognized the
Soviet Union de facto.[47] Under the pressure of offers of greatly increased trade, de jure recognition
was granted first by Great Britain on February 2,
1924, and in following months by Italy, Norway,
Austria, Sweden, and Greece.[48] Immediately trade
with Italy, Austria, and Greece increased by large
amounts; but trade with the other countries did not
rise appreciably because of this recognition.[49] The
United States refrained from granting any sort of
recognition until 1933, but the Soviet Union had
achieved its goal of recognition by the major European
powers.

Status of Trade Representatives

Since the foreign trade of the Soviet Union was
a monopoly of the state, the Soviet government considered that its representatives abroad were representatives of the state and thus entitled to diplomatic privileges. Western countries, with their
division of business and government, objected that
this would provide Soviet traders with a privileged
position in relation to that of capitalist traders.
Realizing this opposition, the Soviet Union made it
a policy to include in all trade treaties a recognition by the other country of the monopoly of foreign
trade and a granting of diplomatic privileges to the
representatives of this state monopoly.[50]

Germany, in its temporary trade agreement of
May 6, 1921, was the first country to recognize the
monopoly. This agreement provided that each country
could send a trade delegation of eight members to

the other and that these members would enjoy diplomatic immunity.[51] The trade agreement with Norway, concluded on September 2, 1921, stated in Article XI(A): "The Monopoly of foreign trade--as far as Russia is concerned--belongs to the Government of the Russian Socialist Federal Soviet Republic, which works through the Commissariat of Foreign Trade and its organizations."[52] The same recognition was offered by Italy in its trade agreement of February 7, 1924. The Soviets won their major victory when they were able to include similar language in the Anglo-Soviet trade agreement of August 8, 1924. Article 2 of this agreement stated:

> Taking into account that the monopoly of foreign trade in the Union of Soviet Socialist Republics belongs to the Government, and that this Government may engage in trading operations either directly through the Trade Representative of the Union or through any body or authority under its control, or otherwise, both parties agree on the following: the Trade Representative and his assistants . . . shall be members of the Union Embassy in London and shall, as such, enjoy all the privileges and immunities appertaining thereto, including extra-territoriality for their offices in the Embassy.[53]

Following this victory the Soviets were able to include similar provisions in all trade treaties with other countries and would make no concession on this point.[54]

It has been alleged many times that under the protection of diplomatic immunity the Soviet trade representatives have engaged in various political activities within the country to which they were assigned. Such activities were given as the reason for the 1923 German police raid on the trade representatives' offices, the 1927 British raid on the offices of Arcos Ltd., the 1927 expulsion of Soviet trade representatives from Vienna, and the ousting of Yuzhamtorg officials from Argentina in 1931 and from Uruguay in 1935. That these activities are not just a thing of the past can be seen by the actions of

England and Belgium in late 1971. In September 1971,
Oleg Lyalin, an intelligence officer posing as a member of the Soviet trade delegation in England, defected to the West, providing England with a list of
other agents. The English reacted by expelling 105
Soviet officials--many from the trade delegation.
Three weeks later, on October 18, 1971, a related
defection in Belgium produced a list of another 37
intelligence types and another mass expulsion. These
were major incidents--but it is not expected that
they were the only ones in recent times.

Relations with Former
Russian Territories

The Baltic countries of Latvia, Lithuania, and
Estonia were formerly part of Imperial Russia; and
as such they were considered as a class apart by the
Soviets. Trade relations with these countries were
based on peace treaties concluded in 1920 that also
included some questions of trade. When regular
trade agreements were concluded in 1927, 1928, and
1929, these Baltic states were given special privileges in regard to licenses and other matters. It
was further agreed that all such privileges were not
to be granted to other countries under the most-
favored-nation (MFN) treatment.[55] Trade with Lithuania never did amount to very much. Latvia and Estonia became excellent trading partners; but, after
the First Five-Year Plan was completed in 1932, trade
with these two countries dropped to an insignificant
amount.[56]

Under the pressures of war and the fear of growing German influence in the Baltic states, trade
treaties were concluded with these countries in 1939.
The treaty signed with Estonia on September 29, 1939,
promised an increase in trade of four and one-half
times.[57] The Lithuanian pact called for a "considerable extension of trade" and the Russo-Latvian
trade pact indicated a threefold increase in that
trade.[58] Actually these pacts were part of a soft-
ening-up technique that resulted in mutual assistance
pacts, the stationing of Soviet troops in the Baltic
countries, and then, in 1940, the assimilation of
these countries into the Soviet Union.

In the south several areas of Imperial Russia
declared their independence during the revolution.
The Soviet Union followed a policy of regaining these
territories by first converting them into People's
Soviet Republics and then absorbing them into the
Soviet Union. In Armenia, Azerbaijan, and Georgia,
this process was completed by 1922. The khanates
of Khiva and Bukhara took two years longer, and
Tanna Tuva was not absorbed until 1944. The foreign
trade of these areas was insignificant; and, since
it was entirely with Russia, it can be considered
more as intraregional trade. In Transcaucasia this
trade was handled by the Russian Commissariat of Foreign Trade.[59] In Khiva, Russian-controlled local
organizations handled the foreign trade, whereas the
mixed Russian-Bukharan Trading Corporation (Russobukh)
and the Tanna Tuva Central Cooperative handled trade
in their areas.[60] In all cases control over trade
activities was ensured by the granting of various
privileges. In Tanna Tuva one of the most important
of these privileges was the right to export to or
import from the Soviet Union without the necessity
of obtaining licenses.[61]

Trade, Aid, and National Liberation

In 1920 Lenin laid down the basic strategy to
be followed in gaining control of the independent
underdeveloped nations of the Middle East and Central
Asia. Foreign trade was one of the tools to be used
to achieve this goal. For this reason a special
policy was applied to trade with Turkey, Persia, Afghanistan, and the Sinkiang province of China. This
policy included the elimination of import license
requirements, special trade financing, permission to
trade freely on the territory of the Soviet Union,
reduced prices, and a special lower tariff.[62] That
these privileges were offered as political bait can
be seen in the fact that they were soon revoked by
the Soviets because they proved disadvantageous.
Trade with these countries began in 1921, and a real
trade push started in 1923. At first the trade
balance favored the Eastern countries, but after a
few years the Soviets revoked most of the earlier
privileges and the balance of trade shifted to the

Soviets' favor. Afghanistan reacted with its own
monopoly of foreign trade in 1925, and Iran followed
suit in 1931. Trade with these countries peaked in
1930 and subsequently dropped to an insignificant
level as the Soviets apparently lost interest in this
area. A preview of things to come was an $8 million
credit for machinery and equipment to help Turkey in
its first industrialization program in 1934.[63]

Soviet foreign trade with the underdeveloped
countries in the years following Stalin's death has
frequently been referred to as an economic offensive
for political purposes. Actually the Soviets have
had various reasons for their trade and aid ties
with these countries, and these reasons have been reflected in changing policies. (See Chapter 7 for a
fuller discussion of this topic.) One very important
reason was that a number of these countries had much-
needed raw materials, such as cotton, wool, rubber,
hides, and jute, or much-desired foodstuffs, including
sugar, cocoa, rice, fish, oranges, and tea. Immediately following World War II the demand for these
commodities resulted in a policy of buying goods
from selected underdeveloped countries on a strictly
cash basis. In 1948 the Soviet Union was buying
cotton from Egypt, cocoa from Ghana, wool and food
from Iran, tea and hides from India, jute from Pakistan, and rubber from Malaya. This policy faced
one serious problem. These countries were willing
to sell to the Soviet Union, but they were reluctant
to buy Soviet exports. As a result the Soviet Union
had to generate foreign exchange elsewhere, and, as
shown earlier, in the case of rubber from Malaya
this resulted in the charges of dumping of aluminum
and tin in England in 1957 and 1958. To circumvent
this problem the Soviet Union determined that it had
to develop an export market in the Third World.

Beginning in 1952 the Soviet Union participated
in a number of industrial exhibits and fairs in underdeveloped countries, and at the Moscow Economic Conference that year the Soviets paid special attention
to delegates from the developing nations. This sig-
naled a switch from a policy of purchases for cash to
one of paying for purchases with the export of Soviet
machines, equipment, and other items. This policy
was implemented by a rapidly increasing use of barter

arrangements and was amplified in 1953 with the addition of an aid program with long-term credits for complete plants, roads, and sports stadia. By permitting repayment in local commodities, the Soviets had found a means of penetrating a market that had earlier belonged to the West.

Following the split with China, the Soviet Union faced new problems. On the one hand, they now had a surplus of machines and equipment to dispose of. On the other hand, they faced political competition with China in the Afro-Asian area. Aid programs were now beefed up, not just to pay for needed imports but also to insure markets for the Soviet machine-tool industry and to win Afro-Asian nations away from Chinese influence. Following the second Afro-Asian Solidarity Conference the conflict with the Chinese ebbed to a battle more of words than of rubles; and domestic needs for scarce technicians, capital goods, and materials required cutbacks in the aid program. In 1966 the aid policy reverted to tied aid in support of the basic import policy. If aid brought the Soviet Union such commodities as rubber, oil, copper, tin, zinc, iron ore, or cotton, it was good. If not, it should be curtailed.

In the early 1960's the Soviet foreign trade policy called for developing trade relations with all the newly independent nations. An intensive trade expansion and propaganda program was carried on in Africa. At this time trade was also encouraged by adoption in 1964 of a special lower tariff applicable only to goods from underdeveloped countries.

Although the major changes in policies regarding the underdeveloped countries can be explained in economic terms, this does not mean that politics was not involved. On the contrary, the Soviet Union's foreign policy has made national liberation of the underdeveloped countries a high-priority objective. When trade could support this goal, it was used.

Today Soviet trade policy regarding the underdeveloped countries is little changed from the mid-1960's. A 1971 policy statement announced: "Development of stable, external economic, scientific, and technical ties with developing Asian, African, and Latin American countries shall be continued on terms of mutual benefit and in the interest of strengthening their economic independence."[64]

Cold War Trade Policies

The basic foreign trade policies of the Soviet
Union described above have remained relatively unchanged during the years following World War II.
When the United States and other Western countries
applied restrictions on trade with the Soviet bloc
in 1948, the Soviet Union merely reverted to its policy of autarky, and trade volume was sharply reduced
until a low in trade turnover was reached in 1950.

In 1951 the Soviets evidently realized that the
second postwar Five-Year Plan (1951-55) could not be
fulfilled unless foreign trade volume was increased.
Within the framework of the basic policies, the Soviet Union at this time adopted a policy of circum-
venting (and, if possible, doing away with) Western
restrictions on East-West trade and of promoting increased trade with nonbloc countries. In July 1951
the English language journal Soviet News began a
series of articles on improving trade relations between the East and the West. In October 1951 invita-
tions were extended to Western businessmen to attend
the Moscow Economic Conference in April 1952. On
November 6, 1951, Beria called for increased trade
with the United States, Great Britain, and France.[65]
Subsequently the Soviet Union carried out a continuing
campaign to get the West to drop all restrictions on
trade with the East so that they could buy urgently
needed advanced technology. That these efforts were
successful can be seen in the fact that beginning in
1954 Western Europe gave up many trade restrictions
in favor of trade profits. From a low of $553 mil-
lion in 1950, Soviet trade with nonbloc countries
doubled to $1,075 million in 1954. Trade with the
developed countries then quintupled from $1 billion
in 1955 to $5.2 billion in 1970.

The Soviet policy regarding trade with the countries of the West (and Japan) has remained fairly
constant since the 1950's. The most important consideration was obtaining needed imports. Political
changes, rebuffs by the United States, and even ex-
pulsions of trade delegates and others have not in-
terfered with this basic policy. This current prag-
matism is reflected in a 1971 policy announcement
that stated: "Economically justified commercial,

scientific, and technical contacts with industrially
developed capitalist countries which show willingness
to develop co-operation with the Soviet Union in
these spheres, shall be extended."[66]

Relations with Nonbloc
Socialist Countries

Soviet policy regarding trade relations with
the members of Comecon has been fairly consistent
and, for the most part, is founded in the economics
of the socialist division of labor. Their policy
for trade with other socialist countries, on the
other hand, has been erratic and has been dominated
by political considerations.

Immediately following World War II, Yugoslavia
was a good friend and ally of the Soviet Union and
trade relations were very amicable. Then in 1948
Yugoslavia was drummed out of the Cominform and this
trade dried up completely. Yugoslavia's relations
with the West increased gradually, reaching a high
pitch in 1954. This was clearly unacceptable to the
Soviet Union; in the fall of that year the Soviets
backed down and called for "normal" relations. A
policy of increasing trade was now inaugurated toward
the goal of rapprochement. Following the split with
China this policy was intensified so as to keep Yugoslavia from joining the Chinese. Cordial relations
were finally restored in 1962, and then Soviet policy
switched to using trade to woo Yugoslavia into an
integrated socialist economy. These efforts have
evidently been at least partially successful, for
Yugoslavia announced that while retaining its ties
with the West it would participate to some extent in
the grandiose integration plan announced in August
1971.[67]

Soviet trade policy with China has also been
the victim of politics. This trade began immediately
after the People's Republic of China was formed and
increased rapidly over the next decade, reaching a
peak of $2.1 billion in 1959. In that year political
relations between these countries reached a breaking
point. Although most aid programs were cut off
abruptly, trade continued--but at a rapidly decreasing

rate. By 1970 this trade had been cut to an insignificant $45 million.

At the time that Russia and China were splitting
up, Russian relations with Cuba were beginning. The
Soviet Union had been importing sugar from Cuba
since 1953, but Cuban-American relations in 1960 set
the stage for increased Soviet influence. To gain
this influence the Soviet Union openly used foreign
trade. From a beginning of $179 million in 1960
this trade grew to $1.2 billion in 1970. That this
trade is essentially political can be seen from the
fact that no attempts have ever been made to include
Cuba in the integration of the socialist world.

The Soviet policies regarding trade with Albania,
North Korea, and North Vietnam are not so easy to
categorize. Albania allied itself with China during
the de-Stalinization period; and when China split
with Russia, Albania followed suit. Soviet policy
in this case seems to have been one of noe policy
whatsoever. The Sino-Soviet rift also determined
Soviet policy on trade with North Korea. To counter
Chinese influence, the Soviet Union, beginning in
1960, stepped up its trade with North Korea. On the
other hand, China seems to have had no effect on Soviet trade with North Vietnam. It would appear that
the war in Vietnam was the main influence here; and,
as the United States stepped up its reactions in
1965, Soviet trade (not including military hardware)
began to increase.

Although all of these countries are classified
by the Soviets as socialist, it is interesting to
note that only Yugoslavia has been invited to participate in the socialist world--and even this participation was on a very restricted basis.

COMPARATIVE ADVANTAGE
AS A POLICY

As mentioned earlier, the theory of comparative
advantage and the international division of labor
were denounced in the early days of the Soviet state
as being contrary to the principles of socialism.
In the 1950's, however, certain younger Soviet economists began suggesting that the Soviet Union would

gain if its foreign trade was based on comparative
advantage; and during 1957 and 1958 various articles
in the journal Foreign Trade called for more international trade based on the international division
of labor.[68] It would appear that the Soviet Union
had made an about-face and had adopted comparative
advantage as a way of life after this. In 1964, for
example, a group of economists stated, "Foreign trade
is regarded as economically justified if the economy's
needs for a particular product are satisfied at a
lower cost to the economy through foreign trade than
if the output of this product is developed at home."[69]
Konstantinov would appear to reconfirm this in 1971,
when he stated:

> It is not always possible or economi-
> cally justifiable for each country to make
> the whole range of its own requirements.
> An excessive extension in the range of prod-
> ucts may reduce the economic efficiency of
> social production. Consequently, it becomes
> increasingly important to make a balanced
> switch to a complex interaction between the
> national economies, a consistent development
> of international specialization and cooper-
> ation in production, strengthening of eco-
> nomic ties and the development of foreign
> trade.[70]

An economic analysis of the fields of production
in which the Soviet Union enjoys a comparative advantage that might be the basis of international
trade is beyond the scope of this work; however, a
brief comment should indicate the potential importance
of this topic to Soviet foreign trade policies. A.
Bergson, R. Bernaut, and L. Turgeon, in their study
of Soviet prices, have shown that between 1928 and
1950 the prices of industrial products as a whole
rose 569 percent. Price rises below this average
were primarily for finished goods and semimanufactures, while price rises above the average were for
coke, lime, turpentine, brick, iron ore, and lumber.[71]
All of these latter items are products close to the
extractive stage. This indicates that while emphasis on industrialization has brought economies of

scale and economies resulting from improved technique
and improved management, the costs of raw materials
have increased. A similar situation exists in agriculture, as was pointed out by Khrushchev's "virgin
lands" program. To avoid higher raw material costs,
the Soviet Union could turn to imports of needed
items in exchange for manufactured goods.

Comparative advantage, or the "socialist division of labor," is the philosophy behind the economic
integration of Comecon discussed earlier. Bulgaria,
Rumania, Hungary, and especially Mongolia are less
developed than the Soviet Union. In relation to
these countries the Soviet Union has a comparative
advantage in machines and equipment, processed fuels,
and industrial goods; these are the major Soviet exports to these countries. The Soviet Union has a
comparative disadvantage in foodstuffs, tobacco and
spirits, and less-sophisticated clothing and consumer
goods; it imports these commodities from the poorer
members of Comecon. On the other hand, Czechoslovakia, the German Democratic Republic, and Poland
are more economically advanced and the comparative
advantages are reversed. As a result the Soviet
Union supplies these countries with ores, fuels,
food products, and timber products and receives in
return high-technology machines and equipment and
quality consumer goods.

Soviet trade with the developing countries is
both politically and economically motivated. Although some of the commodities imported from these
countries are not essential or even useful, this
trade adheres to the principle of comparative advantage. For example, the Soviet Union supplies India
with complete plants, other machinery, industrial
products, and petroleum products--all goods in which
the Soviet Union has a comparative advantage. In
return the Soviets receive foodstuffs, jute, wool,
hides, and unsophisticated clothing and consumer
goods--products in which the Soviet Union has a comparative disadvantage.

Although the Soviets rely on marginal utility
in their trade with the West, they do not follow a
pure policy of comparative advantage. One reason
for this is that the Soviets take into consideration
not only the direct costs and savings of such trade

but also the effect of this trade on the development
of the economy. Therefore, although the Soviet Union
has a decided comparative disadvantage in automobiles,
it has refused to import them and instead has imported
an automobile plant. Even when this plant was completed, comparative advantage was ignored and the new
cars were exported--mainly because they had more
marginal utility as an earner of hard currency. On
the other hand, Soviet exports of petroleum would
seem to be based on both marginal utility and comparative advantage, and imports from the developed
countries are universally those in which the Soviet
Union has a comparative disadvantage.

This threefold policy would seem to indicate
that the Soviet Union fully accepts the idea of comparative advantage and utilizes it without hesitation when it can control the outcome. Conversely,
it indicates that local resources, even of a marginal
nature, are to be exploited in preference to becoming
reliant on supplies from the developed countries of
the West. It is entirely possible, however, that
the benefits received from a partial use of comparative advantage in recent years may lead, in the not
too distant future, to a revision of policy toward
fuller use of this principle. Since such a revision
would necessarily require a complete reversal of
many policies, it is quite probable that any changes
would be made only gradually.

TARIFF POLICY

Lenin early complained that no tariff would be
high enough to protect Soviet industry because it
was not merely competitive industry but also the
symbol of an opposing economic ideology. Following
suit, Soviet economists deprecated the idea of having
tariffs; and for several years it seemed an open
question as to whether the Soviet Union should or
should not use tariffs. When trade was resumed in
1920-21, there was no effective tariff law. In 1921
it was decided that a tariff was needed, and a special
commission was set up by the Council of Labor and
Defense to prepare one.[72]

The first Soviet tariff became effective on
June 13, 1922.[73] Actually this tariff was merely a
reedition of the 1903 Imperial Russian tariff. In
some cases, such as coffee and tea, the duties were
designed for revenue purposes only. For other commodities the duty was high so as to forbid the import
of luxuries and to protect industries. In some cases,
cotton for example, the duty was both protective and
fiscal in nature.[74]

The 1922 tariff consisted of four separate tariffs. The first two were the European import and
export tariffs. These tariffs were applied to all
trade between the Soviet Union and all European
countries, as well as colonies and dependencies of
these countries, the United States, South America,
and Japan. A third tariff was the Asiatic tariff
"for goods coming through the ports on the Caspian
Sea and across the Asiatic land borders from the
Black Sea to the East to a point where the borders
of the U.S.S.R., Mongolia, and North China intersect
and coming from those countries bordering on the
Caspian Sea and on the specified land borders."[75]
The claimed reason for this special customs treatment
was that the Asiatic peoples and their trade were
oppressed by European capitalists and were not in a
position to compete with Europe. As a result the
Asiatic tariff provided customs duties lower than
the European tariffs.[76] The fourth tariff was for
trade through the port of Murmansk.[77]

The tariff was expanded in 1924 and 1926. A
completely new tariff was prepared in 1927 and yet
another in 1930. The changes were mostly in nomenclature and in the amount of duty to be charged for
each item. The trend of these changes was toward
even stronger protection. These tariffs continued
the principles of no import duty on agricultural
machines and fertilizer, industrial raw materials
and semimanufactures not produced in the Soviet Union,
books for schools and institutions, or pharmaceuti-
cals; no export duty on manufactured goods or agricultural and food exports; low duties on raw materials and semimanufactures if needed; high protective
tariffs on goods produced in the USSR; and very high
export duties on scarce raw materials.[78]

After 30 years of no change in tariff policies,
a new import tariff went into effect on October 1,

1961, and a new customs code was adopted on July 1,
1964.[79] The 1961 tariff, on the surface, was a total
reversal of previous policy. Supported by the growing strength of the Soviet economy and the volume of
trade with bloc partners and developing countries,
the Soviets now dropped all pretense of protectionism
and affected a free-trade stance by considerably lowering tariff rates. This tariff follows the standard
two-column format, with one set of duties for goods
from countries granting the Soviet Union most-favored-
nation (MFN) treatment and another set of duties for
goods from all other countries.

This new tariff policy was clearly designed to
convince trading partners that the Soviet Union was
a low-tariff, free-trade nation interested in encouraging broader trade ties and to convince these countries to extend MFN privileges reciprocally to the
Soviet Union. In the tariff applicable to the MFN
nations, over half of the items—particularly machines and raw materials—are duty-free and less than
one-fifth of the items—mainly consumer goods—have
duties over 5 percent. For non-MFN nations only
four items are duty-free, half have duties between
10 percent and 15 percent, and 30 percent have duties
over 15 percent.[80]

In this writer's opinion the major purpose of
the Soviet tariff system is to provide a basis for
tariff negotiations with other countries. In the
earlier period the monopoly of foreign trade provided
effective protection against unwanted imports. Today
the monopoly controls the inflow of goods nullifying
any beneficial effects of lowered tariffs. Support
for this position can be found in the peculiar Soviet
handling of goods from non-MFN nations. Purchasing
organizations are provided funds to pay for import
duties, but only at the MFN rate. If imports are
made from a non-MFN nation, the supplier theoretically
must absorb the duty by adjusting the price down-
ward.[81] This, of course, may prove disadvantageous
to the Soviet Union; but at the same time it provides
a great pressure on other nations to grant the Soviets MFN treatment. Despite these pressures the
United States still has not granted the Soviet Union
MFN treatment.

On December 21, 1964, the Soviet Council of
Ministers decreed that as of January 1, 1965, all

imports originating in the developing countries of
Asia, Africa, and Latin America would be subject to
a further liberalized tariff.[82] By this action the
Soviets reverted to an expanded version of the special
Asiatic tariff. Details of this new tariff have not
been publicized; but it would appear that the MFN
privileges have been extended, particularly in the
area of foodstuffs and consumer goods. Again, this
action would appear to be totally political in origin,
since the purchases from these countries will be determined by factors other than tariffs.

SUMMARY

     Soviet foreign trade policy differs from that
followed in capitalist countries in many significant
ways. The most important of these policies has been
the monopoly of foreign trade instituted on April 22,
1918. In accordance with this policy, all foreign
trade of the Soviet Union is strictly controlled by
the Ministry of Foreign Trade. As a strategic policy
the Soviet Union also has a monopoly of foreign trade
operations, although at various times this monopoly
has been relaxed for tactical reasons. The primary
purpose of the monopoly of foreign trade has always
been that of protecting and supporting the industrialization program of the Soviet Union. Other
major purposes of the monopoly have been austerity
to assist the development program, planning, the
gaining of political advantage, and efficiency.
Another claimed purpose is that of fiscal gain, but
it appears that this purpose was of little importance.
     The import and export policies of the Soviet
Union limit imports to those goods that contribute
to socialist development and exports to those necessary to pay for the needed imports. In the early
days this policy was interpreted to include imports
only of equipment and materials vitally needed by
the Soviet Union. In recent years this interpretation had been broadened to include the import of certain consumer goods needed as a part of the Soviet
industrial incentive program. In 1930, 1957, and
1963 a close adherence to these policies resulted in
claims of Soviet dumping. Associated with the import

and export policies is the Soviet policy of self-sufficiency or autarky. In the period following World War II this autarky has been expanded and is now an autarky of the Soviet bloc as a whole and the foundation for the Soviet policy of integrating the economies of the bloc countries.

The Soviet Union has followed various policies in its trade relations with other countries. In the earlier years trade was used to gain recognition for the USSR. The special status of trade representatives then became a major policy. Territories that had formerly been a part of Imperial Russia were accorded special privileges prior to World War II, as were developing nations following the war. Recent Soviet policy regarding trade with the West has mainly been one of reacting to Western restrictions and attempting to remove these barriers.

Comparative advantage was rejected by the Soviets at first, but a modified version of this principle has been accepted in recent years. The bloc economies now follow comparative advantage almost without question. In relations with the West, comparative utility is used; but comparative advantage is applied only where beneficial to the idea of socialist development.

The tariff policies of the Soviet Union have also come about-face. At first they were supposedly protectionist, whereas today they would appear to be free trade in nature. At all times, however, the tariff policy appears to be politically oriented, since imports are determined by factors other than tariffs.

2

ORGANIZATION FOR
OPERATIONS

To carry out foreign trade operations in accordance with the policies discussed in the last chapter, the Soviet Union has organized various types of foreign trade organizations. The discussion of these organizations will be divided according to five historical periods. These are the period of war Communism (1917-21), period of the New Economic Policy (1922-28), period of the Five-Year Plans (1928-39), World War II and the postwar period to the death of Stalin (1940-53), and the period of post-Stalin expansion (1954-71). The Soviet Union conducted little foreign trade before the end of the first period, at which time all trade was concentrated in the hands of the People's Commissariat of Foreign Trade. As will be shown, the period of the New Economic Policy was one of experimentation. During this period foreign trade operations were conducted by various state and cooperative organizations. The development, changing nature, and relative importance of these organizations will be discussed. The period of the Five-Year Plans was one of specialization and concentration. The multitude of organizations developed in the preceding period were eliminated and re-

placed by specialized monopoly foreign trade
corporations. A detailed discussion will
indicate the nature and scope of these corporations. The monopoly foreign trade corporations are still the basic foreign trade
operations organizations. Decentralization
and further specialization of these corporations, the development of foreign aid corporations, and the reemergence of cooperatives in foreign trade during the post-
Stalin period will be detailed.

PERIOD OF WAR COMMUNISM

When the Bolsheviks came to power in November
1917 they had no effective organization for carrying
on foreign trade operations. The Russians themselves
had not been foreign traders; the bulk of Russia's
foreign trade had been conducted by foreigners--es-
pecially Germans.[1] Since the Bolsheviks were opposed
ideologically to external economic control, new forms
of trading were inevitable.

Such new forms of trading did not develop until
active foreign trade operations were resumed in 1921.
Prior to this time the Foreign Trade Council was supposedly responsible for organizing and coordinating
purchases through its member organizations, state
purchasing commissions, cooperatives, and trading
firms. Since there was no trade, this responsibility
was not exercised.

The People's Commissariat of Foreign Trade soon
emerged as a state trading organization. When it
was established in June 1920 this commissariat was
given the sole right to handle foreign trade, although it could permit other organizations to carry
out actual operations. On March 17, 1921, it was
ordered that all purchases abroad were to be made
only by the representatives of the commissariat.[2]
Five months later, on August 9, 1921, the People's
Commissariat of Foreign Trade was empowered to carry
on its own independent purchasing operations. This
decree transformed the commissariat "into a commercial institution charged with establishing the price
of sale and purchase of merchandise."[3] Now the com-

missariat had an organization for handling foreign
trade operations both within and outside Russia.
With this organization foreign trade operations were
"concentrated in the hands of the People's Commissariat of Foreign Trade itself to the exclusion of
all other organizations. The monopoly of foreign
trade thus bore a strictly centralized character."[4]

PERIOD OF THE NEW
ECONOMIC POLICY

This centralization of the monopoly of foreign
trade was just being completed when the New Economic
Policy went into effect. This policy was, in effect,
a controlled retreat from the complete centralization
of the earlier period. In 1922 a new policy declared
"that the machinery of Russia's foreign trade must
combine unity of the controlling centre with a variety of organizations performing the actual buying
and selling operations in the foreign market."[5] This
variety included state export and import offices
(gostorgi), joint stock companies, specialized import-export corporations, trading arms of trusts,
syndicates, cooperative organizations, and mixed companies.

State Export and Import
Offices (Gostorgi)

During the period of war Communism, the commercial section of the Commissariat of Foreign Trade of
the RSFSR handled what little trade there was. In
1922, however, this section was converted into a
state corporation—the State Export-Import Office
(gostorg) of the RSFSR.[6]
The State Export-Import Office of the RSFSR was
empowered "to perform all operations connected with
the purchase abroad, import into Russia, and subsequent sales of goods, and the purchase within Russia
and her allied Republics, export and sale abroad of
various goods, either on its own account or on a
commission basis on behalf of State bodies, cooperatives, private firms, and private individuals."[7] At

the Foreign Trade Conference in July 1922, it was
decided that the State Export-Import Office "shall
act as a legal entity, and shall have its own commercial apparatus and its own systems of accounting.
Its Board shall be nominated by the Collegium of the
Commissariat, and shall conduct its activities in accordance with the directions and instructions of the
Collegium."[8]   In setting up the State Export-Import
Office, the Soviets laid the foundation for future
foreign trade corporations and for the contention
that foreign trade operations are conducted by legal
entities and not by the state.

   Shortly after the State Export-Import Office of
the RSFSR was established, gostorgi were set up in
the Ukraine (Ukrgostorg), White Russia (Belgostorg),
and the Transcaucasian Republic (Zakgostorg).[9]   Later
gostorgi were established in Uzbekistan (Uzbekgostorg)
and Turkmenistan (Turkmengostorg).[10]   Thus, there
was a separate State Export-Import Office for each
republic.   Each of these "offices" was an autonomous
state enterprise with at least 51 percent of its
capital provided by the Commissariat of Foreign Trade
and the balance supplied by the republic government.[11]
Although these State Export-Import Offices were basically owned and controlled by the Commissariat of
Foreign Trade, they were not generally considered to
be a part of the commissariat itself.   On the other
hand, the State Export-Import Offices were considered as a part of the republic in which they were established, and thus operating revenues were included
in the republic's budget.[12]

   Even after the formation of the USSR, the activities of the State Export-Import Offices were
geographically limited to the republics in which
they were organized.   The operations of the State
Export-Import Office of the RSFSR were so large and
spread over such a wide area that regional offices
were established.   These regional offices were, to
some extent, autonomous and were responsible directly
to the authorized local representatives.   They were
found in the Northwest (Sevzapgostorg), Siberia
(Sibgostorg), Southeast (Yugvosgostorg), Middle Volga
(Sredvolgostorg), Far East (Dalvosgostorg), Kirghiz
(Kirgostorg), Central Asia (Sredasgostorg), and the
Crimea (Krimgostorg).[13]

FIGURE 1

Soviet Foreign Trade Internal Operations Organization, 1922-25

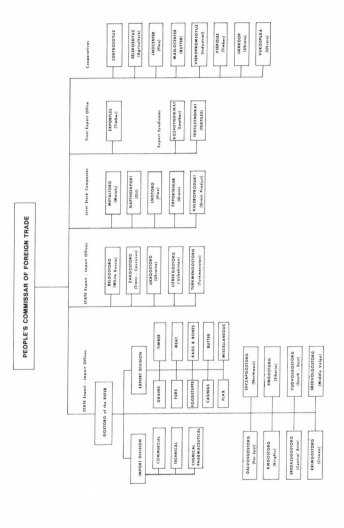

Source: Prepared by the author.

The State Export-Import Offices were universal
in nature, dealing in all goods and commodities involved in Soviet foreign trade. Their operations,
however, were conducted by specialized divisions
and sections, each having specialists in a particular
type of goods.[14] The State Export-Import Office of
the RSFSR, for example, had three import sections and
ten export sections. Imports were handled by the
Commerical Section, the Technical Section, or the
Chemical-Pharmaceutical Section. The export sections
were for grain, furs, foodstuffs, casings, flax,
timber, meat, rags and bone, butter, and miscellaneous.[15]

The regional offices of the RSFSR gostorg were
subdivided by product specialist offices along the
same lines as the parent office. The Northwestern
State Export-Import Office (Sevzapgostorg) had sections for technical commodities (wood distillation
products, coal products, ammonia, and other chemicals), timber, sundry goods (game, fish, mushrooms,
and handicrafts), drugs (medicinal herbs), meat,
waste products, and foodstuffs.[16] This organization
varied, of course, in accordance with the products
or the import needs of the particular region.

By 1925 the State Export-Import Office system
had a virtual monopoly on foreign trade operations.
At the same time it was an extraordinarily diversified, cumbersome, and inefficient organization. The
joint-stock corporations, syndicates, and trusts
involved in foreign trade, on the other hand, were
narrowly specialized, tightly organized, and highly
efficient. Efficiency finally won out, and at the
end of 1925 Soviet foreign trade operations were reorganized.

The major effect of this reorganization of operations was the establishment of specialized export
and import corporations.[17] The establishment of
these new corporations posed the question of what
was to be the role of the State Export-Import Offices
now that a large portion of their operations had
been taken away from them and they were placed in a
less favorable position in comparison with the specialized corporations. One result of this change
was the conversion of the State Export-Import Offices
into bodies dealing chiefly in secondary commodities

and new items of export.[18] A second result was the
formation of the Council of State Export-Import Offices. This council coordinated the activities of
the republic offices, handled all relations with organizations abroad, and in general protected the
remaining interests of the State Export-Import Offices in the overall foreign trade organization of
the Soviet Union.[19]

In 1930 the move toward specialization was completed with the establishment of monopoly export and
import corporations. At that time all trading activities within the Soviet Union were transferred to
such corporations and the State Export-Import Offices
were gradually liquidated.

Specialized Export-Import
Corporations

Along with the State Export-Import Offices, the
New Economic Policy also gave birth to three organizational forms that later served as the nucleus of a
completely specialized foreign trade structure.
These three forms were joint-stock companies, syndicates, and export-import offices of trusts.

The most important of these three forms was the
joint-stock company. The decree of March 13, 1922,
authorized the establishment of Soviet-owned trading
corporations that would operate primarily within the
Soviet Union. Immediately following this decree
three corporations were founded. The Metals Trading
Company (Metalotorg) was organized and owned jointly
by the People's Commissariats of Foreign Trade,
Transport, and Agriculture; the Supreme Economic
Council; and the Revolutionary Military Council.
The Petroleum Export Company (Naptheexport) was owned
by the People's Commissariat of Foreign Trade, the
State Fuel Board, and the Azerbaijan and Georgian
Petroleum Administrations. The owners of the Flax
Trading Company (Lnotorg) were the Flax Board, Yaro-
slav Flax Works Trust, Vitebsk Textile Works Trust,
Viaznikov Flax Works Trust, Ekaterinburg Textile As-
sociation, and the Rykov works.[20] Later the Grain
Products Company (Khleboprodukt), the Export Grain
Company (Exportkhleb), and the Export Flax Company

(Exportlen) were founded.[21] These companies operated only within the USSR, preparing and processing
exports of their specialty. Although the State Export-Import Offices operated as universal companies,
usually they were not permitted to trade in the
specialized commodities handled by these companies.

In April 1923 the six major timber trusts were
authorized to conduct operations abroad.[22] For this
purpose an export company (Exportles) was established.
In the same manner various textile enterprises organized their marketing into the Textile Syndicate
(Textilsyndikat) and a number of leather firms joined
together to form the Leather Syndicate (Kozhsyndikat).

By 1925 the State Export-Import Offices had
grown so large and unwieldy that their efficiency
was impaired. On the other hand, the several joint-
stock companies and specialized export offices of
trusts and syndicates had proved to be efficient
operators. As a result the Soviet government considered it necessary to move away from universal trading
organizations and toward more specialized forms.
The form chosen was the specialized foreign trade
corporations. These corporations, like the ones
described above, were to be owned by the producing
and purchasing organizations having an interest in
the exports or imports of these companies. In this
manner the producers and users would have a closer
contact with the practical work of foreign trade.[23]

The Metals Trading Company (Metalotorg) now became the Metals Import Company (Metaloimport). Similarly, the Flax Trading Company (Lnotorg) became
the Flax Export Company (Lnoexport) and the Leather
and Textile Syndicates became import firms (Kozhim-
port and Textilimport). The Grain Products Company
(Khleboprodukt), the Export Grain Company (Exportkhleb), the Export Flax Company (Exportlen), and the
Timber Export Office (Exportles) all retained their
names and their functions. Contrary to the trend,
the Petroleum Export Company (Naptheexport) was converted into the Petroleum Syndicate (Napthesyndikat).
During the next five years a number of other specialized export and import corporations were formed.[24]

The functions of the specialized export corporations were limited to the collection, preparation,
and processing of exports and the distribution of

TABLE 3

Joint Stock Companies and Specialized Export and
Import Corporations, 1922-30

Company	Products	Dates[a]	Monopoly Corporation[a]
Avtopromtorg	Motor vehicles	1929-30	--
Elektroimport	Electrical equipment	1926-30	Elektroimport
Exportkhleb	Grain	1922-30	Exportkhleb
Exportles	Timber	1922-30	Exportles
Exportlyon	Flax	1922-30	Exportlyon
Khimimport	Chemicals	1926-30	Khimimport
Khleboprodukt	Grain	1922-30	Khleboprodukt
Kozhsyndikat Kozhimport	Leather	1922-26 1926-30	Kozhimport
Lnotorg Lnoexport	Flax	1922-26 1926-30	Lnoexport
Manganoexport	Manganese	1929-30	Mangano Export
Metalotorg Metalo Import	Metals	1922-26 1926-30	Metalo Import
Mezhdunarodnaya Kniga	Books	1928-30	Mezhdunarodnaya Kniga
Naptheexport Napthesyndikat	Petroleum	1922-26 1926-30	Soyuzneftexport
Promexport	Industrial goods	1926-30	Soyuzpromexport
Selkhozimport	Agricultural implements	1926-30	Selkhozimport
Textilsyndikat Textilimport	Textiles	1922-26 1926-30	Textilimport

[a]Specialized export and import corporations converted to monoply foreign trade corporations in 1930.

Sources: Compiled from A. A. Santalov and Louis Segal, Soviet Union Year Book (London: George Allen and Unwin, 1928), pp. 239-44; (1929), p. 249; Jacques Jeramec, Le Monopole du Commerce Extérieur en Russie Sovietique (Paris: Librairie Générale de Droit et de Jurisprudence, 1928), p. 92; Great Britain, Commercial Counsellor to His Majesty's Embassy in Moscow, The Organisation of Foreign Trade of the Union of Soviet Socialist Republics (London: HM Stationery Office, 1931), p. 23; M. N. Sobolev, ed., Economics and Policies of Foreign Trade (Moscow: Narkomtorga SSSR i RSFSR, 1928), p. 107*; 50 Years of Soviet Foreign Trade (Moscow: Mezhdunarodnieye Otnosheniya, 1967), p. 51.*

imports. From the very beginning these corporations
attempted to achieve a monopoly position. This
meant that within their field they were required to
satisfy the needs of all union, republic, and local
industries. Since the areas covered by these corporations were so broad, the State Export-Import Offices
were gradually squeezed out of the market and rele-
gated to transactions in secondary goods.

During this same period (1925-30) a number of
trusts were authorized to establish special export
or import offices that operated independently. The
only restrictions on these trusts were that they
could buy and sell only those items produced or used
by the trust itself and that they could not import
for resale purposes. By 1930 there were 12 such
trusts involved in foreign trade: the Match Trust
Export Bureau, Rubber-Asbestos Combine Export Bureau,
Coal Combine Export Bureau (Ugleexport), Fish Trust
Export Office (Ryboexport), Eastern Coal Export
(Vostugleexport), Medium Machine Trust Export Bureau
(Exportmashina), Paper Trust Import Office (Soyuzbu-
maga), Rubber-Asbestos Combine Import Bureau, Construction Trust Import Office (Orgstroi), Auto Import
Office (Autosoyuz), Ship Imports (Sudoimport), and
the Movie Trust Foreign Trade Film Office (Intorg-
kino).[25]

The specialized corporations and the export-
import offices of the trusts proved quite efficient,
and they continually obtained a larger share of the
export and import business. Their operations, however, were not as efficient as they could have been,
since they did not maintain a monopoly position in
their particular specialty and there was no true competition. The resultant overlap of operations and
responsibilities led to the creation of the monopoly
foreign trade corporations in 1930. At that time
the export-import offices of the trusts and some of
the specialized corporations were liquidated or
transformed into monopoly foreign trade corporations.
Many of the corporations created during the period
from 1922 to 1930 were continued but in a monopoly
position, and still more new corporations were organized.

Cooperative Organizations

In January 1920 the Supreme Economic Council in
Paris decided to end the blockade of Soviet Russia
and renew trade through cooperative organizations.[26]
The most important of these organizations was the
Central Consumers Union (Centrosoyuz), founded in
1898.[27] It was not until 1921, however, that the
Soviet government gained control over the domestic
and overseas assets of Centrosoyuz and the Soviet
organization was recognized by the International
Congress of Cooperatives.[28]

Immediately after being admitted to the International Congress of Cooperatives, the Soviets took
steps to effect trading by their cooperatives. On
March 13, 1922, the Central Consumers Union was
authorized to carry on foreign operations.[29] Centro-
soyuz-England, Ltd., was reopened in April 1922 as a
Soviet-owned company. Later in the year Centrosoyuz
G.m.b.H. in Berlin reopened, and in November 1922
Centrosoyuz America, Inc. commenced operations. In
1923 Centrosoyuz-France became active again.[30]
Other offices of the Central Consumers Union were
active in China and in Latvia and Estonia.

On May 9, 1923, the Council of Labor and Defense
extended the right to trade abroad to the Agricultural Cooperative Union (Selskosoyuz) and other cooperative organizations.[31] On June 10, 1923, the
Agricultural Cooperative Union established an office
in London, incorporated as Selskosoyuz-England,
Ltd.[32] Within a short time this cooperative organization had offices in Berlin, Paris, Riga, New York,
and several Far Eastern cities.[33] By 1925 eight
different cooperatives were actively engaged in
trading abroad. In addition to the Central Consumers
Union and the Agricultural Cooperative Union, these
organizations were the Central Union of Flax Growers
(Lnocenter), the Central Butter Union (Maslocenter),
the Industrial Cooperative Union (Vsekopromsoyuz),
the Timber Association (Vsekoles), the Ukrainian
Union of Cooperatives (Ukrkoop), and the Ukrainian
cooperative Vukospilka.[34] Most of the latter cooperatives operated only in England and Germany. Despite this diversity of organizations, in 1925 the
cooperatives were responsible for only 10 percent of

Soviet foreign trade; and Centrosoyuz and Selskosoyuz handled 80 percent of this cooperative trade.[35]

The functions of the cooperatives in the foreign trade field were to sell the produce of the member cooperatives and to purchase the needs of these co-operatives. The cooperatives were permitted to con-duct their own negotiations but were required to ob-tain trade representative approval on all transac-tions.[36] Although the cooperatives were considered to be public and not state organizations, they were directly under the control of the People's Commis-sariat of Foreign Trade on matters regarding foreign trade.

The establishment of the monopoly corporations in 1930 spelled the end of active participation by the cooperatives in foreign trade. For a while they carried on some activities, but in general they were no longer of any importance in foreign trade.[37] By 1936 Centrosoyuz America, Inc. and Selskosoyuz Amer-ica, Inc. had become inactive.[38]

Soviet Companies Abroad

After two months of trade negotiations, on May 31, 1920, the British government authorized Leonid Krassin to open a Soviet commercial office in Eng-land.[39] This office was established on June 18, 1920, as the All-Russian Cooperative Society (Arcos), Ltd. The claimed objectives of the company were "to act as representatives of cooperative organizations car-rying on business in Russia and elsewhere and to pro-mote and develop the business of general import and export merchants."[40] In fact Arcos carried out the functions normally conducted by the commercial oper-ations section of a Soviet trade representative.

Following the pattern of the State Export-Import Offices, Arcos operated as a universal trading com-pany. To handle a wide range of commodities, it was organized into eight commodity offices and three sup-porting offices. As the functions of these offices increased, they were spun off as subsidiary corpora-tions. Thus, in June 1923 the shipping office became Arcos Steamship Company.[41] Later the same year the book department was reorganized as Kniga, Ltd.; at

the end of 1924 the financial operations of Arcos
were incorporated as the Arcos Bank, Ltd.; and the
insurance section was transformed into the Black Sea
and Baltic Insurance Company, Ltd.[42] In August 1924
the Russian Oil Products Company was established to
handle all of the oil trade between the Soviet Union
and England.

On May 13, 1927, the English police raided the
Arcos offices for political reasons.[43] The Soviets
protested this raid and immediately curtailed trade
with England. In April 1930 the operations of Arcos
were resumed, but the fiction of an independent corporation appears to have been abandoned and operations were carried out as a trade representation.[44]

Trade with the United States was initially handled by Arcos-America, Inc. (formerly a branch of
Arcos Ltd.), the Products Exchange Company (Prodexo),
and Allied America Corporation. In May 1924 Arcos-
America and Prodexo were merged and incorporated as
the Amtorg Trading Company. This new company was
then made the exclusive agent in the United States
for the State Export-Import Offices.[45] From the beginning Amtorg acted in the capacity of an unofficial trade representative. It not only carried on
commercial activities in its own name but also acted
as a consular agent for the Soviet Union and as an
information clearinghouse and controlled the activities of other Soviet concerns operating in the United
States.[46] In addition to Amtorg and Allied America,
the Soviets also established the All-Russian Textile
Syndicate, Inc. as a branch of the Textile Syndicate
and Amkino as a branch of Intorgkino.[47]

In November 1925 Amtorg opened a branch in
Buenos Aires, Argentina, to handle the purchase of
hides. In 1927 the Comintern opened a Latin American
campaign and set up special revolutionary sections
to conduct operations there.[48] Concurrently, on
October 1, 1927, the Buenos Aires branch of Amtorg
was incorporated as the South American Trading Company (Yuzhamtorg) and a branch was opened in Monte-
video, Uruguay.[49]

The Yuzhamtorg venture was not very successful.
After an Argentine police raid on August 1, 1931,
Yuzhamtorg moved to Uruguay and was reincorporated
there.[50] But since politics were as important as

trade to this firm, its actions led Uruguay to break
diplomatic relations with the Soviet Union in 1935;
Yuzhamtorg was then liquidated.[51]

All of the Soviet corporations described above
were basically commercial enterprises. In all cases
the owner was the Soviet government, presumably in
the form of the People's Commissariat of Foreign
Trade, which organized them. In England, Arcos acted
as the commercial section of the trade representation
and reported directly to the trade representative.
In the United States and in South America, Amtorg
and Yuzhamtorg operated as both the commercial and
the regulatory sections of a trade delegation, since
no trade representatives as such were assigned. As
a result these corporations reported directly to the
Commissariat of Foreign Trade.

Mixed Companies

Ideologically the Soviet government could not
tolerate foreign control over any phase of the Russian economy. On the other hand, the Russians lacked
the capital needed for various foreign trade operations. This rasied the question of what part, if
any, foreign capital could play in the development
of Soviet foreign trade. The Germans, who had controlled Russian trade prior to World War I, proposed
joint investments of Soviet and foreign capital.[52]
On March 13, 1922, a decree instructed the Commissariat of Foreign Trade to establish such "mixed"
companies.[53]

The mixed companies were basically joint investment corporations established outside the USSR. Although in a majority of the cases the Russians invested
nothing, they held at least 50 percent of the ownership
and control was thus always in Soviet hands.[54] The
board of directors would consist of representatives
of all owners. The chairman of the board and chief
policy-maker was always a representative of the
People's Commissariat of Foreign Trade. The managing
director was invariably appointed from the foreign
group.[55]

There were three basic types of mixed companies:
universal trading companies, specialized trading

FIGURE 2

Soviet Foreign Trade Internal Operations Organization, 1925-30

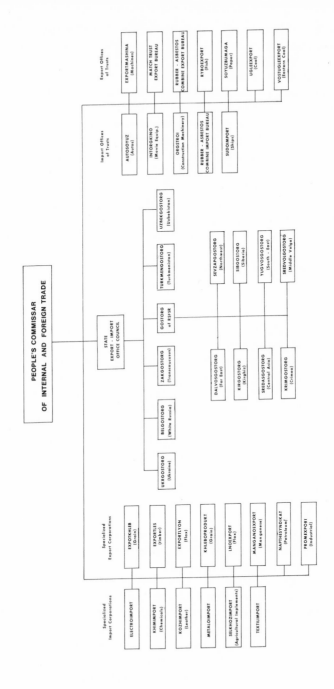

Source: Prepared by the author.

companies, and producing and transportation companies. The universal trading companies handled a wide range of goods and were usually restricted to trade between the USSR and the country in which the company was established. Examples of this type of company were the Russian-Austrian Trading Company (Russavstorg), the Russian-Austrian Trading Company, Inc. (Ratao), the Russian-German Trading Company (Russgertorg), the Russian-Turkish Trading Company (Russoturk), and the Russian-Persian Trading Company (Shark).[56] Specialized trading companies dealt in one product or a small group of related products. Examples are Egg Export and Rasso, which handled fur trade with England.[57] Most of the mixed production companies were engaged in the exploitation of the northern timber resources.

The total volume of trade of the mixed companies was never very large, exceeding 5 percent of total trade only in 1925.[58] If the mixed companies had specialized in goods of secondary importance, it is entirely possible that they would have grown considerably. The goods in which they did specialize were also handled by other state and cooperative organizations. As a result there was a degree of conflict. The Soviet government naturally favored its own enterprises and applied various pressures on the mixed companies. These pressures, more than anything else, probably explain the extremely poor showing of the mixed companies.

The original premise of the mixed companies was that they would be used to attract foreign capital. In trade relations with various countries of the Near and Far East, however, the attraction of foreign capital could hardly have been the reason for the establishment of mixed companies. The pattern of the creation of such companies in Iran, Turkey, Bukhara, and Mongolia clearly indicates that these mixed companies were used as a means for gaining economic control over these countries. It should be noted that this pattern was repeated in Eastern Europe and China following World War II.

Closely related to the mixed companies were the German and American firms that traded with the Soviet Union on a concession basis. The most important of these was the West-Oestliche Warenaustauschgesell-

schaft, or Vostvag, which was granted a concession
as a universal trading company on May 8, 1923.[59]
Other concession companies were limited in either
the commodities handled or the length of the concession or both. Such firms in Germany were the Dantzig
Trading Company, or Dava Britipol (an eight-month
universal concession), the North-Western Trading
Agency Bureau (a one-year egg concession), Ruben
and Billifeld (fish), and A. Roesch (agricultural
products).[60] The U.S. firms included Allied America,
Simon Sootha (furs), and Sitingen-Schild. The volume
of concession trade was always quite small, reaching
a peak of 4 percent in 1928.[61] With the advent of
the monopoly foreign trade corporations in 1930, all
concessions were canceled.

PERIOD OF THE FIVE-YEAR PLANS

By 1930 it became clear that new organizational
forms were needed in the field of foreign trade.
Within the Soviet Union the introduction of the
First Five-Year Plan in 1928 had wrought various
changes. Private trading that had been developed
under the New Economic Policy was eliminated. The
drive to collectivize farms was begun in 1929, necessitating a change in the internal procurement organization. In all phases of the economy an intensifi-
cation of centralization and control became the rule.

At the same time the world market situation was
deteriorating into the depression of the 1930's.
Exporting countries had difficulty in disposing of
their commodities, especially grain. As a result
competition became more intense. One Soviet author
reported: "The general accentuation of competition
in the world markets, and, in particular, the in-
tensification of the struggle of the capitalist
world against Soviet exports, demanded in this new
stage that the monopoly of foreign trade should be
organizationally so constructed as to increase its
capacity for manoeuvring in foreign markets in the
conditions of the world economic crisis."[62]

FIGURE 3

Soviet Foreign Trade External Operations Organization, 1922–30

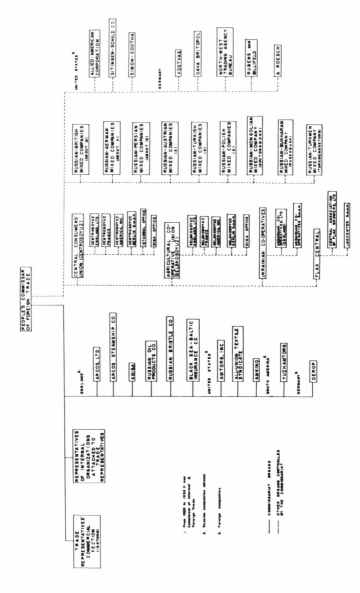

Source: Prepared by the author.

Monopoly Foreign Trade
Corporations

The 17th Congress of the Communist Party considered these changes in the internal and external conditions of foreign trade and decided on a complete reorganization of the foreign trade operations structure.[63] On February 6, 1930, Anastas Mikoyan, then commissar of internal and foreign trade, issued Decree 358, which established a series of monopoly export and import corporations.[64] With this one decree the confused maze of foreign trade organizations was eliminated and replaced by a simplified structure.

"The object of the reform is to create an organ, under the form of a monopoly office, which will have as its aim the export and import operations of articles of one type or relevant to one branch of the economy."[65] Since the new corporation had a monopoly over its group of commodities, and since there were monopoly corporations for all fields of foreign trade activity, secondary organizations such as the State Export-Import Offices and the cooperative organizations were no longer needed within the Soviet Union. At the same time the trade representatives abroad were given the exclusive right to handle all transactions for the monopoly export and import corporations. As a result all Soviet foreign trade organizations abroad, with only a few exceptions, were gradually liquidated.[66] The exceptions were Amtorg Trading Company in the United States and Yuzhamtorg in South America, where no trade representatives had been appointed, and the Russian Oil Products Company, Arcos Steamship Company, and the Black Sea and Baltic Insurance Company in England. Arcos Ltd. continued to exist on paper, but it did not carry on operations as a corporation. The Soviet Union now had two basic organizations for foreign trade operations. Within the country all operations were handled by the specialized monopoly corporations. Abroad all operations were conducted exclusively by the various trade representatives.

The establishment of monopoly export and import corporations was merely the final step along the path of specialization. The basic framework for these new corporations was the series of specialized cor-

FIGURE 4

Soviet Foreign Trade Operations Organization, 1930–38

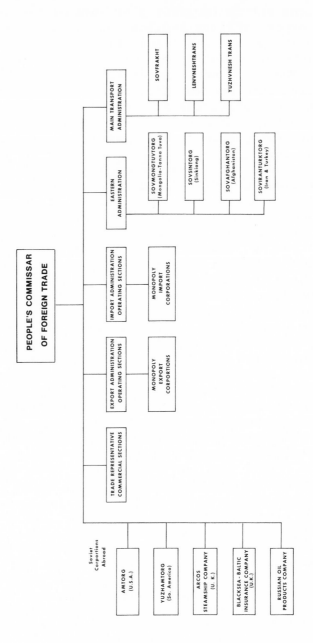

Source: Prepared by the author.

porations set up in 1925, plus some of the state
trust export offices and some of the syndicates.
Of the 16 specialized corporations, 13 were converted
into monopoly corporations without even a change of
name. The Petroleum Syndicate (Napthesyndikat) was
converted into the monopoly corporation Soyuzneftexport; the Industrial Products Company (Promexport)
became Soyuzpromexport; and the Automobile Trading
Company (Avtopromtorg) was liquidated. In addition
23 new monopoly corporations were added to the list
in 1930. The basic difference between the specialized
corporations of 1925-30 and the monopoly corporations
established in 1930 was that the new corporations
had a complete monopoly over their fields, whereas
their predecessors may have had a monopoly in certain areas but usually had some form of competition.
Now, for any given commodity one organization alone
would have the responsibility. In this way duplica-
tion of effort and wasteful competitive practices
were eliminated.

In many ways the organization established in
1930 resembled that of 1920 and 1921. All trade was
now centralized and handled strictly by government
bureaus. In 1921 these activities were conducted by
the specialized offices of the People's Commissariat
of Foreign Trade; in 1930 they were handled by the
specialized monopoly corporations. These corporations were autonomous from the commissariat but at
the same time were within the commissariat's jurisdiction. This position can be seen in the standardized bylaws of the monopoly corporations:

1. All-Union Corporation _____ is
founded to realize, on a monopoly basis,
export operations and the sale on foreign
markets of _____ [goods specified for
this corporation].
2. The Corporation appears as an independent economic entity, possessing the
rights of a juridical person and operating
on a self-supporting basis.
3. The Corporation is within the jurisdiction of the People's Commissariat of
Foreign Trade of the USSR and operates on
the basis of plan directives and under the
control of the latter.

TABLE 4

Monopoly Foreign Trade Corporations, 1930-39

Corporation	Products Handled	Date
Antiquariat	Antiques	1930-34
Avtomotoexport	Motor vehicles	1936-37
Elektroimport	Electrical plant and equipment	1930-39[b]
Exportkhleb	Grain	1930-[c]
Exportles	Timber	1930-[c]
Exportlyon	Flax	1930-[c]
Intourist	Tourism	1930-[c]
Khimimport	Chemicals and equipment	1930-39[b]
Khleboprodukt	Grain	1930-39[b]
Kinoexportimport	Movies and equipment	1930-39[b]
Koverkustexport	Carpets	1930-35
Kozhimport	Leather and hides	1930-39[b]
Kustexport	Handicraft goods	1930-39[b]
Lecktlekhsyryo	Medicinal herbs	1930-36
Lnoexport	Flax	1930-39[b]
Manganoexport	Manganese	1930-39[b]
Mashinoimport	Machines	1934-[c]
Masloexport	Butter	1930-39[b]
Metaloimport	Metal goods and equipment	1930-39[b]
Mezhdunarodnaya Kniga	Books	1930-[c]
Mineralsilikatexport	Minerals, silicates, matches	1934-36
Novoexport	New articles of export	1930-39[b]
Plodoexport	Fruits and vegetables	1930-36
Promsyryoimport	Industrial raw materials	1935-58
Pticieexport	Game and poultry	1930-39[b]
Pushnoexportsyndikat	Furs	1930-39[b]
Raznoexport	Miscellaneous goods	1930-[c]
Raznoimport	Miscellaneous goods	1930-[c]
Rudoexport	Ores	1930-39[b]
Rybokonservexport	Fish	1934-36
Ryboplodexport	Fish	1934-35
Selkhozhimport	Agricultural machines	1930-39[b]
Sovexportfilm	Movies	1930-[c]
Soyuzintorgkino	Movies	1936-39
Soyuzkinoexport	Movies	1934-39
Soyuzmetimport	Metals	1934-38
Soyuzneftexport	Petroleum	1930-[c]
Soyuzprodexport	Food products	1930-36
Soyuzpromexport	Industrial products	1930-[c]
Soyuzpushnina	Furs	1930-[c]
Soyuzugleexport	Coal	1934-39
Stankoimport	Machine tools	1930-[c]
Tabakexport	Tobacco	1934-39
Tekhnoexport	Technical products	1934-[c]
Tekhnopromimport	Engineering goods and equipment	1930-[c]
Textilimport	Textiles and textile equipment	1930-35
Torgsin	Special store for foreigners	1930-35
Tzvetmetimport	Nonferrous metals	1930-39[b]

Corporation	Products Handles	Date
Regional Corporations		
Sovafghantorg	Afghanistan	1931-34
Soviranturktorg	Iran and Turkey	1937-39
Sovmongtuvtorg	Mongolia and Tanna Tuva	1931-45
Sovsintorg	Sinkiang	1931-47
Vostgostorg	Eastern countries	1930-31
Vostokintorg	Sinkiang	1939- c
Transport Corporations		
Dalvneshtrans	Freight forwarding, Far East	1935-51
Inotrans	Freight forwarding	1935-36
Iransovtrans	Transport to Iran	1939-51
Lenvneshtrans	Freight forwarding, Leningrad	1935-51
Sovfrakht	All transportation operations	1931- c
Sovirantrans	Freight forwarding, Iran	1935-37
Vneshtrans	Freight forwarding	1930-35
Yuzhvneshtrans	Freight forwarding, south	1935-51

[a]Converted from specialized foreign trade corporation in 1930.

[b]Liquidation date not reported; corporation not reactivated after World War II.

[c]Corporation reqctivated after World War II and in operation in December 1971.

Sources: Compiled from Pavel A. Cherviakov, Organization and Technique of the Foreign Trade of the USSR (Moscow: Vneshtorgizdat, 1958), pp. 42-43*; Great Britain, Commercial Counsellor to His Majesty's Embassy in Moscow, The Organisation of Foreign Trade of the Union of Soviet Socialist Republics (London: HM Stationery Office, 1931), pp. 9, 23-25; Jacques Jeramec, Le Monopole du Commerce Extérieur en Russie Sovietique (Paris: Librairie Générale de Droit et de Jurisprudence, 1928), p. 92; A. A. Santalov and Louis Segal, Soviet Union Year Book (London: George Allen and Unwin, 1928), pp. 239-44; (1929), p. 249; (1930); Soviet Union Information Bureau, The Soviet Union (Washington, D.C.: The Bureau, 1929), pp. 70, 71, 77*; Scientific-Research Institute of the Monopoly of Foreign Trade, Trade Relations of the USSR with Countries of the East (Moscow: V/O Mezhdunarodnaya Kniga, 1938), pp. 24, 82, 104-05*; A. M. Smirnov and N. N. Liubimov, Foreign Trade of the USSR (Moscow: Vneshtorgizdat, 1954), pp. 84-85*; M. N. Sobolev, ed., Economics and Policies of Foreign Trade (Moscow: Narkomtorga SSSR i RSFSR, 1928), p. 107*; A. Stoupnitsky, Statut International de l'URSS-- Etat Commerçant (Paris: Librairie Générale de Droit et de Jurisprudence, 1936), pp. 100-01; J. D. Yanson, Foreign Trade in the USSR (London: Victor Gollancz, 1934), pp. 151-52; M. M. Zhirmunski, Organization and Technique of Soviet Exports (Moscow: Vneshtorgizdat, 1935), p. 44*; and Soviet Export (Moscow: Mezhdunarodnaya Kniga, 1936), p. 52.

4. The Corporation is responsible for
its operations and liabilities on its property, on which in accordance with existing
legislation can be charged a penalty. The
Corporation is not liable for claims against
the State, its organs or other organizations. The State is not liable for the
operations and liabilities of the Corporation.[67]

These rules in no way imply that the property
of these companies does not belong to the state;
however, although these corporations report directly
to the operating sectors of the Export and Import
Administrations of the Commissariat of Foreign Trade,
the commissariat preferred to refer to them as autonomous organizations separate from the commissariat,
which was occupied with the functions of regulation.
    The functions of the monopoly corporations cov-
ered all phases of foreign trade operations. Specifically, these functions were to import or export
goods of their specialty, prepare operating plans,
expand foreign trade in their specialty, study conditions of foreign markets, help in the planning of
production, and earn a profit.[68] Goods for export
were obtained from the manufacturers on the basis of
contracts based on the overall economic plan for the
year. These contracts stipulated the quantity, quality, assortment, manner of packing, price, manner of
delivery, terms of payment, and mutual penalties to
be imposed if the contract was violated.[69] The
monopoly export corporation then either turned the
goods over to a freight forwarding agency or loaded
the goods on ships chartered through the Soviet
Freight Office (Sovfrakht). All of these arrangements were also covered by annual contracts concluded
between these agencies and the monopoly corporations.
    On July 27, 1935, the Council of People's Com-
missars authorized the monopoly corporations to conclude agreements with foreign firms either in the
Soviet Union or abroad.[70] Rosengoltz stated: "The
transfer of foreign trade transactions to the USSR
is an organizational expression of the stronger position which the Soviet Union has attained in foreign
trade."[71] Actually, in 1935 the Soviet Union reached
its lowest volume of foreign trade since 1924, and

the change appears to have been more a reflection of autarky than of strength. The actual effect of the decree of July 27, 1935, was a wholesale transfer of foreign trade operations to the Soviet Union proper. From January 1, 1935, to July 1, 1936, the move was so great that foreign trade personnel abroad were reduced from 1,233 to 398.[72] Stores of goods at strategic points abroad were liquidated, and sale by sample and by previous experience replaced sale by sight. This change reduced the cost of storage-- and thus enhanced the profitability of Soviet exports. As a result Soviet trade during these last prewar years was on what might be considered a more or less normal basis.

Along with the establishment of the monopoly export and import corporations, two transport monopoly corporations working in foreign trade were established in 1930. These firms were the Foreign Transportation Corporation (Vneshtrans), which handled freight forwarding, warehousing, and loading and discharging of ships, and the Soviet Freight Corporation (Sovfrakht), which was responsible for the chartering of foreign and Soviet ships. Although all other foreign trade organizations abroad were abolished at this time, Sovfrakht established subsidiary firms abroad: the Anglo-Soviet Shipping Company in London, Gesellschaft für die Befrachtung von Seeschiffen m.b.H. Sovfrakht in Hamburg, and A/S Sovfrakht in Oslo.[73] In 1935 these transportation organs were reorganized. Vneshtrans was divided into five separate monopoly corporations, each operating in a specific geographic area: the Leningrad (Lenvneshtrans), Southern (Yuzhuneshtrans), and Far Eastern (Dalvneshtrans) Foreign Transportation Corporations; the Foreign Transportation Corporation (Inotrans); and the Iranian-Soviet Transportation Corporation (Iransovtrans). The Foreign Transportation Corporation was liquidated in 1936. In August 1937 Iransovtrans was absorbed by the Soviet-Iranian-Turkish Trading Corporation (Soviranturktorg), and in February 1938 Dalvneshtrans was closed.[74] Sovfrakht continued its operations as before, but its subsidiary firms abroad were liquidated.

The 1935 reorganization of foreign trade operations also resulted in the liquidation of some monop-

oly corporations and the changing of goods handled
by others. In this manner the activities of weak and
unprofitable corporations were combined with those
of stronger firms. Specialization was maintained,
but efficiency and profitability of operations apparently became more important factors.[75] The organizational structure existing at the outbreak of
World War II was now crystallized. One series of
organizations, the monopoly export and import corporations, handled practically all of the trade of
the Soviet Union, both in the USSR and abroad. Trade
representatives, for the most part, did not handle
commercial transactions but served as commercial
attachés.

The organizational structure of the various ex-

When first established in 1930, the monopoly
corporations were not authorized to set up branches
and offices within the USSR and were required to
carry out their transactions through the State Export-
Import Offices.[76] This situation was quickly recti-
fied. The State Export-Import Offices were eliminated and the monopoly corporations opened offices
in the republics, regions, and districts.[77] These
local organs were given the responsibility for carrying out all operating tasks in their areas and
were guided by plans sent down from corporation headquarters. The activities of these local offices
were directly under the control of the authorized
local representatives of the Commissariat of Foreign
Trade, and the exact allocation of corporation plans
was ordered by these representatives and not the corporation itself.

The organizational structure of the various export and import corporations varied with the products
handled and other factors. Generally speaking, however, these structures were quite similar and can be
illustrated by the organization of the Mineralsilikat-
export Corporation. This firm was divided into
three operating offices--matches, minerals, and sili-
cates. Each of these specialized offices handled
all matters regarding its product or products. For
example, the match division prepared all types of
plans regarding the export of matches, cooperated
in the planning of the match industry itself, set
standards for the various types of export matches,
handled the sale of matches abroad, studied the

match market abroad, supervised the transportation
and storage of matches, worked toward a reduction of
all expenses in their operations, and kept all the
accounts for the match exports.[78] Overall supervision
for the monopoly corporations was through the chairman or president of the corporation and his deputies.[79] The chairman was appointed directly by the
People's Commissariat of Foreign Trade. He was personally responsible for all of the operations and
liabilities of the corporation. The chairman appointed the heads of all the major departments and
was responsible for the appointment of all other
personnel. Each department head was completely responsible for all the activities within his department. In this way functional direction was eliminated
and unity of leadership was obtained.

The monopoly corporations described above operated in all of the Western countries. For the Middle and Far East special monopoly corporations were
established along geographic rather than product lines.
Each of these corporations had a monopoly over the
trade of all types of goods within its territory.

Trade Representatives

From 1921 to 1935 the trade representatives assigned to various countries were the primary commercial representatives of the Soviet Union. The overall organization of these offices will be described
in the next chapter. The commercial operations handled by the trade representation were the responsibility of an import and an export office, which
subdivided into various product offices according to
the country. In addition the commercial section had
special staff offices responsible for transport, finance, legal matters, and accounting.[80]

The establishment of specialized corporations
within the Soviet Union in 1925 was reflected in the
trade representations by the establishment of specialized offices corresponding to these corporations.
These specialized offices, although in no way connected with the specialized corporations, were manned
by personnel appointed by the corporations. In this
manner the specialized offices were, to a degree,

made functionally responsible to the corporations
while line responsibility remained with the trade
representative.[81] In 1934 this functional control
was eliminated and replaced by one-man authority.

The decree of July 27, 1935, which authorized
the monopoly corporations to conduct their operations
either at home or abroad, had a profound effect on
the trade representations. Immediately direct sales
by the monopoly corporations assumed a larger proportion of total sales, and the commercial operations
of the trade representations were greatly diminished.[82]
Shortly thereafter the trade representatives ceased
to play a significant role in foreign trade operations.

WORLD WAR II

During World War II most of the foreign trade
monopoly corporations apparently were inactive. Although presidents and vice-presidents were occasion-
ally appointed to these corporations during this period, it appears that the appointments were in name
only. For example, K. V. Shevelev was appointed
president of Soyuzneftexport while he was still serv-
ing as a member of the Buying Commission in the
United States. Most of the foreign trade operations
during the war were conducted by the trade representative in Great Britain and the Buying Commission of
the USSR in the United States. This Buying Commission of the USSR was established in Washington, D.C.,
shortly after the signing of the lend-lease agreement on June 11, 1942.[83] This commission, an official organ of the Soviet government, conducted the
work of organizing supplies on the basis of the lend-
lease agreement. At the peak of its operations the
Buying Commission had a staff of about 3,000 in Washington.[84] On May 4, 1946, the U.S. government re-
quested the Soviet Union and 14 other governments to
liquidate their buying commissions.[85] Within a year
the Buying Commission staff was reduced to about 300
and transactions were being transferred to Amtorg,
which had remained dormant during the war.

The war in the West resulted in more attention
being paid to the trade of the border states of the

East.   In October 1939 Soviranturktorg was liquidated
and an Eastern Trading Company (Vostokintorg) was
set up to handle trade with Iran.[86]   At first this
company limited its operations to Iran; but in July
1940 Sovafghantorg in Afghanistan was liquidated and
its functions were assumed by Vostokintorg.[87]   In
December 1939 the Soviet Union reactivated the
Iranian-Soviet Transport Company, which had been
liquidated in 1937, and renamed it Sovirantrans.[88]
During the war years this company handled a considerable volume of the transit trade from the United
States to the Soviet Union via Iran.[89]

POSTWAR PERIOD TO THE
DEATH OF STALIN

Following World War II the Soviet Union entered
a totally new phase of foreign trade operations.
The monopoly foreign trade corporations were reactivated, and trade was resumed with a number of countries.   A difference in this trade did develop, however, that seemed to reflect a growing Soviet aware-
ness of the advantages of comparative advantage.   Of
much more significance, though, was the reorientation
of trade to the Soviet-occupied countries of Eastern
Europe and China.   For this trade the Soviet Union
established new Soviet-owned companies in these countries and resurrected the mixed companies of the
New Economic Policy period.

Monopoly Foreign Trade
Corporations

At the end of the war, in 1945 and 1946, the
activities of the monopoly foreign trade corporations
were resumed.   All of the corporations reported in
1938 were reactivated, with the exception of the
Union Coal Export Corporation (Soyuzugleexport),
which was liquidated in 1939, and the corporations
Soviranturktorg and Sovafghantorg mentioned above.[90]
During this period there was a considerable amount
of reshuffling of products between corporations,
with the apparent purpose of improving operations.[91]

The new commodity lists were confirmed in the statutes reissued for each corporation between September and December 1948.[92]

Beginning in 1951 six new foreign trade corporations were established to handle specific commodities. Three of these corporations were for imports: the Food Trading Company (Prodintorg), the Ship Importing Company (Sudoimport), and the Transportation Machine Importing Company (Transmashimport), which was dissolved in 1955. The establishment of these companies reflected specific economic needs of the Soviet Union. The Food Trading Company (Prodintorg), established in January 1952, handled the importation of sugar, tea, cocoa, coffee, fruits, conserves, dairy products, and fish products.[93] It is important to note that this company was established over a year before Stalin's death. This is a definite indication that at this time the Soviet government was interested in more than talking about the importation of consumer foodstuffs. The other two import companies specialized in transportation equipment. At this time the Soviet Union was very interested in building up its merchant marine.

The other three companies were organized for export operations: the Union Chemical Export Company (Soyuzkhimexport), the Machine Export Company (Mashinoexport), and the Auto Export Company (Avtoexport). These companies in part reflected the change of the Soviet Union from an importing to an exporting nation. Soyuzkhimexport, which had a mysterious beginning in 1947, was reorganized in September 1951 to handle exports of chemicals and medicinal goods.[94] Mashinoexport exported power plants, electrotechnical equipment, transport equipment, and complete plants for the metallurgical, chemical, food, and other light industries.[95] Avtoexport exported not only cars and trucks but also tractors and all types of road building equipment.[96]

In October 1944 the People's Republic of Tanna Tuva was absorbed into the Soviet Union. As a result, on April 26, 1945, Sovmongtuvtorg, which had served both Tanna Tuva and Mongolia, became Sovmongoltorg.[97] Two years later, on May 16, 1947, Sovsintorg, which conducted trade with the Sinkiang province of China, was liquidated and its functions taken

FIGURE 5

Soviet Foreign Trade Operations Organization, 1952

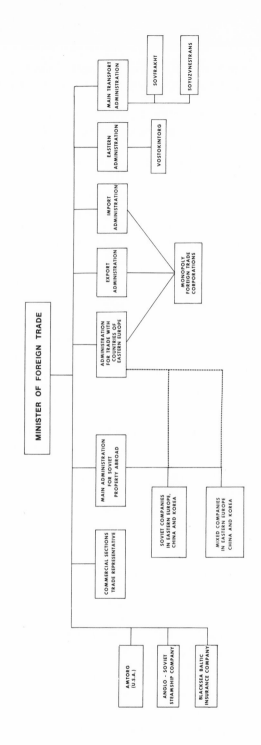

Source: Prepared by the author.

over by Sovmongoltorg.[98] In September 1951 the operations of Sovmongoltorg were merged with those of
Vostokintorg and the Eastern Trading Company (Vostokintorg) was formed.[99] By this action the Soviets
returned to the form first established in 1930, when
Vostgostorg handled all trade with the East. In
August 1947 the Far Eastern Trading Company (Dalintorg) was established. Nothing is known about this
company except that it seemingly handled the export
of Sakhalin coal.[100] In September 1951 Dalintorg
was converted into the Union Chemical Export Company
(Soyuzkhimexport).

A similar unification of activities occurred in
the foreign trade transportation companies. In 1945
the Far Eastern (Dalvneshtrans), Leningrad (Lenvneshtrans), and Southern (Yuzhuneshtrans) Foreign Trade
Transport Companies were reactivated.[101] Their activities appeared to be similar to those of the prewar period. In June 1951 these three companies and
the Iranian-Soviet Transport Company were merged into
the All-Union Foreign Trade Transport Company (Soy-
uzvenshtrans).[102] This merger returned the Soviets
to the conditions of 1930, when Vneshtrans handled
all freight forwarding operations and Sovfrakht chartered all ships. An exception to this unification
was the Auto Foreign Transport Company (Avtovnesh-
trans), which was established in February 1952 to handle trucking operations between the Soviet Union and
Mongolia and Sinkiang.[103]

Following World War II there has been no clear-
cut distinction between importing and exporting corporations, and most perform both tasks. Because of
this and as a result of the regional organization
established in 1953, it would appear that the monopoly foreign trade corporations of this period reported
to departments of the Ministry of Foreign Trade on a
functional basis. Thus, one corporation might have
had relations with each of the import administrations,
both of the export administrations, all four regional
administrations, and the various staff offices.

Soviet Organizations Abroad

The Soviet companies that existed abroad in 1938
continued after the war, although their operations

have been curtailed. In the United States, Amtorg Inc. became inactive during the war, when the Buying Commission handled all purchases. In 1946 both of these organizations were headed by the same man.[104] Because of the restrictions placed on American exports to the Soviet Union, this organization did not resume active operations and remained as a skeleton organization during this period.[105]

In Great Britain the Black Sea and Baltic Insurance Company continued its insurance operations for the Soviet Union and also for the people's democracies. In 1938 the Arcos Steamship Company became the Anglo-Soviet Steamship Company. This company was apparently still operating in the postwar period. The Russian Oil Products Company sold its assets to the Regent Oil Company in 1948 and was then liquidated.[106]

As a result of World War II, a new form of Soviet company abroad came into existence in China, East Germany, and the Eastern European countries. These companies were owned by the Germans and Japanese at the end of the war and seized by the Soviets as reparations, according to their interpretation of the Yalta and Potsdam Agreements. Relatively little is known about these companies other than that they existed. In East Germany, for example, in 1947 the Soviets reportedly owned outright at least 27 percent of the industrial capital.[107] In July 1950 the Soviets announced: "Guided by the principles of the development of friendly relations between the people of the USSR and the German people, and with the aim of assisting the further development of the economy of the German Democratic Republic, the Soviet Government turned over, by a protocol signed in May of this year, 23 enterprises to the possession of the German people."[108] In the spring of 1952 the Soviets turned over another 66 enterprises to the East Germans. Among these enterprises were the Neptune Shipyard, the B.M.W. automobile plant, the Bitterfeld electro-chemical combine, and the Krupp railway car factory.[109] When reparations payments by the German Democratic Republic were canceled on January 1, 1954, still other companies were turned over to the Germans.[110]

In Hungary these Soviet corporations, which accounted for 5 percent of Hungarian industrial capital, were given special privileges and exemptions

that almost amounted to extraterritoriality.[111] The
most important of these firms were 23 textile mills
that had been seized from the Germans. In September
1952 the Soviet government reportedly turned over to
the Hungarians 69 such enterprises.[112] Austrian
firms had similarly been confiscated and were returned only under pressure a month after a peace
treaty had been signed with that country.[113] Such
companies are known to have existed in China, Manchuria, and Korea.[114]

It is interesting to note that these companies
were all industrial or mining firms and not trading
firms. A good portion of the production of these
firms, however, was sent to the Soviet Union. According to the special privileges held by these companies, the Soviet Union handled their trade. The
foreign trade firms involved in this work were the
monopoly foreign trade corporations of the Soviet
Union. For this reason all of these Soviet companies
abroad were under the direct control of the Main Administration for Soviet Property Abroad of the Ministry of Foreign Trade. It appears that all these
companies had been turned over to the local governments by the end of 1955, when the Main Administration for Soviet Property Abroad was abolished.

                        Mixed Companies

Another organizational form used by the Soviet
government to gain control over segments of another
country's economy was the mixed company, which had
been used earlier during the period of the New Economic Policy. Immediately after World War II the
Soviets proposed a mixed Polish-Soviet company to
operate the Polish coal mines. "The Soviet 'contribution' to the company was to be the expulsion of
Germans from the coal fields."[115] Because of strong
Polish objections, the Soviets withdrew the proposal
and offered to accept "coal reparations" from Poland
instead.

In 1946 or 1947 two Soviet-Yugoslav mixed companies were established: an airline (Justa) and a
river shipping company (Juspad). According to an
agreement signed June 8, 1946, each country was to

contribute 50 percent of the capital of these companies. The Yugoslavs later complained that, in the
case of Justa, the Soviets overvalued their contribution of airplanes and grossly undervalued the Yugoslav contribution of an airport. In the case of Juspad, the Soviets did not pay in more than 10 percent
of their share of the capital. Furthermore, these
companies reportedly operated against Yugoslav interests. Juspad, for example, charged Yugoslavia twice
what it charged the Soviet Union for river transport.
Likewise, Justa secured all the profitable air routes,
to the detriment of the Yugoslav National Airline,
JAT. In 1949 these companies were liquidated at the
request of Yugoslavia. At that time the Soviets
withdrew their investment at a higher-than-original
value and left Yugoslavia with a deficit.[116]

During World War II Soviet troops were stationed
in northern Iran. By treaty these troops were sup-
posed to have been withdrawn by March 1946. At that
time the Soviets linked the formation of two mixed
companies to such a withdrawal. As a result the
Iranian premier, Ahmad Ghavan, initialed an agreement
to form these companies.[117] The most important of
these companies was the Soviet-Iranian Oil Company,
which was to have exclusive exploitation rights in certain areas of northern Iran. The Iranian investment
was to be the resources, and the Soviets were to contribute equipment and personnel.[118] During the following year opposition to Soviet penetration increased, and the proposed agreement on the Soviet-
Iranian Oil Company was defeated almost unanimously
by the Iranian Majlis. The other Soviet-Iranian
mixed company was Iranryba, which was actually formed
and conducted fishing operations in Iranian waters.
On January 31, 1953, the term of the agreement on
Iranryba expired and the company was liquidated.[119]

Of much more importance than the above mixed
companies were those formed in Rumania, Hungary,
Bulgaria, and East Germany on the basis of German
reparations. The Soviet Union determined that all
assets held by the German government, German companies, or German individuals at the end of the war
were legitimate war trophies. At first the Soviets
dismantled and shipped quantities of these capital
goods to the Soviet Union. It soon became apparent

TABLE 5

Mixed Companies Organized Abroad by the Soviet Union after World War II

Company	Type of Operation or Product	Date Formed		Date Transferred to Local Government
Rumania				
Sovrombank	Bank	August	1945	September 1954
Sovromgaz	Natural gas	March	1949	September 1954
Sovromkhim	Chemicals	August	1949	September 1954
Sovromles	Timber	March	1946	September 1954
Sovrommetal	Metals	August	1949	September 1954
Sovromneftmash	Petroleum equipment	--		September 1954
Sovrompetrol	Petroleum	July	1945	December 1955
Sovromsig	--	August	1949	--
Sovromstroi	Construction	August	1949	September 1954
Sovromsudostroi	Shipbuilding	--		September 1954
Sovromtractor	Tractors	August	1949	September 1954
Sovromtransport	River Transport	July	1945	September 1954
Sovrommugol	Coal	August	1949	September 1954
Hungary				
Dunaveld Timfeld Ipar	Aluminum industry construction	--		June 1954
Malaj	Petroleum refinery	April	1946	--
Masobal	Aluminum and bauxite	April	1946	June 1954
Masolai	Petroleum	July	1946	June 1954
Masovlet	Airline	May	1946	June 1954
Meskhart	Steamship company	March	1946	June 1954
Soviet Trade Industry Bank	Bank	--		June 1954
Bulgaria				
Gorubso	Mining	February	1946	November 1955
Korbso	Shipbuilding	--		September 1954
Sovbolstroi	Construction material	--		September 1954
Tabso	Airline	May	1949	September 1954
East Germany				
Vismut				
China				
Sovkitmetal	Nonferrous mining	March	1950	January 1955
Sovkitneft	Petroleum exploration	March	1950	January 1955
Sovkitsudostroi	Shipbuilding	--		January 1955
Skoga	Airline	March	1950	January 1955
Korea				
Sokao	Airline		1949	August 1955
--	Maritime transport	--		May 1955
--	Petroleum reprocessing	--		May 1955
Mongolia				
Sovmongmetal	Metal ores	--		August 1957
Finland				
--	Artificial fibers	April	1947	--
Iran				
Iranryba	Fishing		1946	January 1953

Sources: Compiled from Buletinul Oficial (Bucharest, 1949), Nos. 5, 54; Durzhaven Vestnik, No. 71 (Sofia, March 23, 1946); No. 120 (May 28, 1949); Magyar Kozlony, Hivatalos Lap (Budapest, 1946), Nos. 100, 164, 166, 177; Monitorul Oficial, Nos. 186, 188, 245 (Bucharest, 1945); No. 101 (1946); Margaret Dewar, Soviet Trade with Eastern Europe: 1945-1949 (London: Royal Institute of International Affairs, 1951), p. 80; United States, Congress, House of Representatives, The East European Economy in Relation to the European Recovery Program, Preliminary Report 20 pursuant to H. Res. 296, a resolution creating a Special Committee on Foreign Aid, 80th Cong., 2d sess., 1948, p. 40; Foreign Trade, No. 4-5 (1946), p. 40; No. 5 (1950), p. 9; No. 12 (1951), p. 41; No. 10 (1954), pp. 5-6; No. 2 (1955), p. 3; No. 8 (1955), p. 26; No. 10 (1955), p. 30.*

that further plundering of capital goods would crip-
ple the countries of Eastern Europe and make them
dependent on outside aid. To avoid this the Soviet
Union ceased such shipments and reorganized these
assets into wholly Soviet-owned companies, as described in the last section, and, more important,
into mixed Soviet-local companies.[120]

In practically every case the Soviet investment
in these mixed companies was the assets it had seized
from the Germans, whereas the local investment usually
included plant, materials, and capital. In this manner the Soviet Union gained control over additional
sectors of the economies of these countries. The
Soviet Union claims, however, that only the initial
mixed companies were based on reparations and that
subsequent companies resulted from investments of
Soviet capital equipment.[121] From the Soviet point
of view, "the creation of mixed companies follows
the aim of widening the economic collaboration between the USSR and the countries of the democratic
camp and the rendering of aid in the development of
their economy."[122] Furthermore:

> The participation of the Soviet Union
> in mixed companies, organized on a parity
> basis in a number of countries of the peo-
> ple's democracy, represents in itself a
> new, profitable form of collaboration for
> the People's Democratic countries. Pro-
> duction of the mixed companies goes for the
> needs of the internal market and exports
> of the People's Republic. At the same time
> these countries receive from the USSR needed
> industrial equipment and means of transport.
> The mixed companies serve as an example for
> other enterprises of the people's democracy
> in the job of socialist organization of
> work, rationalization of use of equipment
> and the introduction of new production
> methods.[123]

The first of these mixed corporations were
formed in Rumania. On May 8, 1945, a Soviet-Rumanian
protocol to the trade agreement of the same date was
signed. This protocol contained the principles for

the organization of mixed companies for the management of the metallurgy, petroleum, timber, air transport, and other transport industries and for the
banks.[124] On July 17, 1945, an agreement forming
the Soviet-Rumanian Oil Company (Sovrompetrol) was
signed.[125] Shortly thereafter similar agreements
were signed for the Soviet-Rumanian Transport Company (Sovromtransport), the Soviet-Rumanian Civil
Aviation Company (TARS), and the Soviet-Rumanian
Bank (Sovrombank).[126] Subsequently 11 more Soviet-
Rumanian companies were formed.

Sovrompetrol was reportedly established on a
parity basis, with the Soviets contributing existing
installations and shares in Rumanian petroleum companies that had been seized as reparations. The
Rumanian contribution consisted of shares in certain
companies that the government held, all new resources,
and 50 percent of the profits due Rumania until the
Rumanian investment equaled the Soviet investment.[127]
The company was organized as a corporation according
to Rumanian laws. The chairman was Rumanian, the
vice-chairman was Russian, the general manager was
Russian, and the assistant general manager was Rumanian.[128] The operating control, therefore, was in
the hands of the Russians, just the reverse of the
situation in the 1920's. Initially Sovrompetrol
controlled about 60 percent of the Rumanian petroleum
industry, the remaining percentage being controlled
by British and American interests. Sovrompetrol,
however, being listed as a domestic corporation, received preference with regard to taxes and pricing.[129]
The Soviets also forced through certain Rumanian subsidies to Sovrompetrol that were not available to
the other companies. As a result Sovrompetrol eventually forced these other interests out of the Rumanian petroleum industry.

In Hungary and Bulgaria a similar situation
existed. In Hungary 11 mixed companies were established, and four were established in Bulgaria. In
April 1947 the Hungarian government exempted the
Soviet-Hungarian mixed companies from taxes on income,
property, and the transfer of property.[130] As in
the case of Sovrompetrol, the ownership was reportedly on a parity basis and the officers were divided
equally between Russians and Hungarians, although the

position of direct control was always filled by a
Russian.[131] In February 1947 a small mixed company
for the manufacture of artificial fibers was established in Finland, based on reparation claims.[132]

Mixed companies were also established in China
in March 1950.[133] Originally only three such companies (for oil exploration, nonferrous mining, and
civil aviation) were reported; however, a fourth company for shipbuilding was also established.[134] At
least three mixed companies were established in
Korea, but no announcements were made concerning
them.[135]

Beginning in March 1954 the Soviet Union liquidated its interests in all of these mixed companies.
In all cases the Soviet share was given to the country as a loan to be paid back over a period of years
in either cash or goods. The last of these transfer
agreements was signed on December 13, 1955, when the
Soviets transferred their shares of Sovrompetrol to
the Rumanian government, thus ending a decade of
Soviet control of this company.[136] Even though the
Main Administration for Soviet Property Abroad, which
had controlled the operations of these companies,
was liquidated following these transfers, the Soviet
Union retained its interests in at least one Soviet-
German mixed company.[137] Also, the Soviets did not
transfer their holdings in the Soviet-Mongolian Metal
Company (Sovmongmetal) until August 1957.[138] The Soviets have given no explanation for these transfers
other than that local personnel were qualified at
that time to take over operations. It would appear
that the transfer resulted at least partially from
unrest in these countries and a growing resentment
toward Soviet exploitation. By this time other controls, especially the Council for Mutual Economic Assistance, had proved effective, so that the Soviets
could actually profit by selling their interests in
the mixed companies.

As in the case of the Soviet-owned companies in
Eastern Europe, these mixed companies were industrial
corporations, transportation organizations, and
banks. By forming these mixed companies the Soviet
Union was able to expand its control over the basic
industries and transport of these countries. In
this manner they were also able to influence directly

the foreign trade policies and practices of these
countries.

PERIOD OF POST-STALIN
EXPANSION

Since the death of Stalin in 1953, there have
been a number of changes in the foreign trade operations organization of the Soviet Union. The monopoly
foreign trade corporation (V/O, or All-Union Association) is still the primary organization; however,
there has been a great proliferation of these firms,
a new type of firm engaged primarily in foreign aid
operations has been developed, and today not all
these corporations are under the jurisdiction of the
Ministry of Foreign Trade. The operations areas of
the Ministry of Foreign Trade have also been greatly
expanded; and now the monopoly foreign trade corporations report functionally to one or more of four
export, three import, and five regional administrations. A number of domestic organizations have been
empowered to carry on certain foreign operations
either independently or in conjunction with the monopoly foreign trade corporations, and several new
Soviet-owned or mixed companies have been set up
abroad.

State Committee for Foreign
Economic Relations

In 1953 the Ministry of Foreign Trade was reorganized. Included in this reorganization was the
establishment of the Administration for Scientific-
Technical Collaboration.[139] Originally its functions
were limited to coordinating the activities of the
Scientific-Technical Collaboration Commissions organized by the Soviet Union in each of the countries
of Eastern Europe. In early 1955 this administration
was converted into the Main Administration for Economic Relations with Countries of the People's Democracy.[140] In addition to overall coordination and
direction of Soviet economic and technical assistance
policies in the bloc countries of Eastern Europe and

Asia, this administration assumed operational control
over the bloc portion of the Soviet Union's newly
developing foreign aid program.[141] This foreign aid
program began in February 1950 with a $300 million,
10-year credit to the People's Republic of China for
the purchase of industrial and railway equipment.
Following the unrest in Eastern Europe in 1953, the
Soviet Union extended this program with a series of
five-year credits to all the other bloc countries.
In 1955 and 1956 shipments of goods covered by this
tied aid to the bloc countries constituted almost
100 percent of all aid shipments made by the Soviet
Union.

Soviet aid to developing countries began in
1953 with a long-term credit to Afghanistan. In 1957
aid shipments to these countries accounted for almost 15 percent of total aid shipments. The bulk of
these shipments were made to India for the construction of the Bhilai steel mill. Small shipments were
also made to Afghanistan and the United Arab Republic.
More important, the Soviets had committed themselves
to build the Aswan Dam; and the stage was set for
ever-increasing foreign aid shipments. Because of
the similarities in erecting complete steel mills in
Poland and India and because of the priority placed
on improving Soviet relations with the developing
countries, a new organizational form was needed. In
mid-1957 the foreign aid activities relating to the
developing countries were combined with those of the
Main Administration for Economic Relations with Countries of the People's Democracy. The importance of
this change can be seen in the removal of the Main
Administration from the Ministry of Foreign Trade
and its reorganization as the State Committee for
Foreign Economic Relations of the Soviet Council of
Ministers.[142]

The State Committee for Foreign Economic Relations has almost the same stature as a ministry.
The chairman of the committee is appointed by the
Supreme Soviet. His deputy and other members of the
committee are appointed by the Council of Ministers.[143]
Organizationally the committee is divided into functional or staff departments and operations departments. The largest operations department is the Department for Economic Collaboration with Socialist

Countries. This department is subdivided into country groups. Relations with the developing countries
are handled by the Departments for Economic Collaboration with Countries of the Near and Far East, Countries of Africa, and Countries of Southeast Asia.
Like the Socialist Countries Department, these three
departments are divided into country groups. The
major staff departments are the Main Supply Administration, Legal Department, Currency-Finance Administration, Planning Department, and Department for Work
with General Contractors. There is also a special
committee for work with Comecon.[144] In those countries with which the Soviet Union has economic or
technical assistance agreements, the State Committee
for Foreign Economic Relations is represented by missions that are part of the Soviet diplomatic presence
in these countries.[145]

Officially the main functions of the State Committee for Foreign Economic Relations are to develop
measures for widening and strengthening the collaboration of the USSR with other socialist countries; to
develop measures for widening economic ties of the
USSR with developing countries; and to guarantee fulfillment of Soviet obligations for economic collaboration and technical cooperation with other socialist
countries and the developing countries.[146] In practice the committee directly manages a special sphere
of foreign commodity exchange--the delivery of equipment and materials, as well as the performance of
technical services in the building of industrial enterprises and other facilities abroad. It handles
the supplying of complete industrial plants; supplies
Soviet specialists and technicians to supervise and
carry out the construction of turnkey projects; and
trains local personnel to operate the completed
plant.[147] In carrying out its operations the committee works closely with the State Planning Office
(Gosplan) on plans requiring equipment, supplies,
and project-investigative work; with the Ministry of
Finance and the State Bank (Gosbank) on projects requiring credits; with various industrial ministries
in recruiting specialists and acquiring needed technology; and with the Ministry of Foreign Trade on
general matters of export.[148] Above all the State
Committee for Foreign Economic Relations is a planning

FIGURE 6

Organization of the State Committee for Foreign Economic Relations, 1971

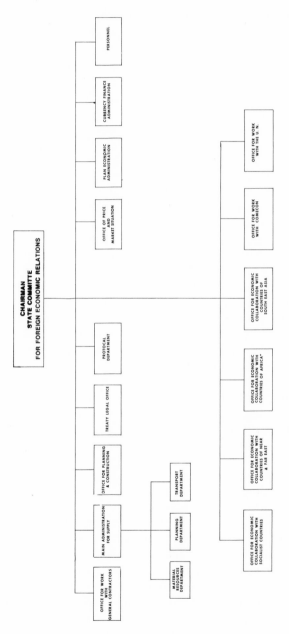

*Includes the United Arab Republic and the Arab countries of North Africa

Sources: Based on Pavel A. Cherviakov, Organization and Technique of the Foreign Trade of the USSR (Moscow: Vneshtorgizdat, 1962), pp. 60, 228*; K. Voronov, "Current Organization of Foreign Trade of the USSR," Foreign Trade, No. 8 (1966), p. 49.*

and operations organization and not a control organization. Unlike the Ministry of Foreign Trade, the
committee does not have the power to issue rules and
regulations binding on all organizations. Rather,
the committee and its subsidiary organs are obligated
to observe the rules and regulations of the Ministry
of Foreign Trade regarding the shipment of goods
abroad and all customs rules.[149]

Foreign Aid Corporations

Prior to 1955 the export of industrial equipment was conducted exclusively by the Technical Export
Company (Tekhnoexport). In April 1955 the Technical
Industry Export Corporation (Tekhnopromexport) was
established to handle the technical aid involved in
the construction of industrial and other enterprises
abroad.[150] It appears that these two corporations
reported only to the Main Administration for Economic
Relations and had no contacts with the export and
import administrations. When the State Committee
for Foreign Economic Relations was established, these
two foreign aid corporations were transferred from
the Ministry of Foreign Trade to the jurisdiction of
the State Committee.

Although these original foreign aid corporations
were universal in nature they evidently proved successful. Shortly after its establishment the State
Committee for Foreign Economic Relations created two
new corporations. The Industrial Machine Export Company (Prommashexport) was organized in July 1957
specifically to construct plants for the machine
tool, automobile, and agricultural machinery industries. The Heavy Industry Export Corporation (Tyazhpromexport) was established in December 1957 to build
plants for the ferrous and nonferrous metallurgy,
coal, and petroleum industries.[151] At the end of
1971 there were seven foreign aid corporations engaged in providing technical assistance, construction
of turnkey operations, training of local personnel,
and export of equipment and materials needed for such
construction. Each of these corporations is specialized and handles technical assistance for only a
limited number of industries.[152]

FIGURE 7

Organization of Tekhnopromexport, 1971

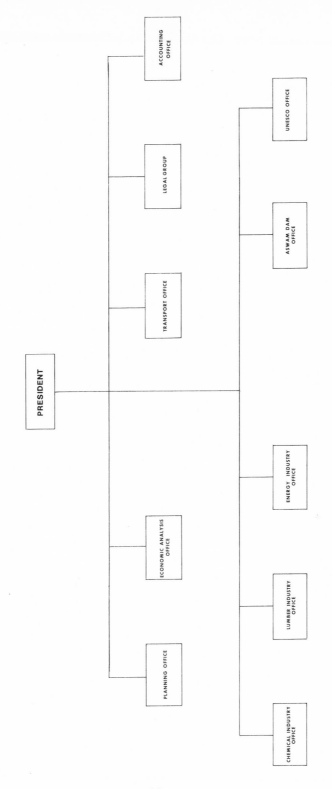

Source: Based on Pavel A. Cherviakov, Organization and Technique of the Foreign Trade of the USSR (Moscow: Vneshtorgizdat, 1962), pp. 61, 231-32.*

TABLE 6

Foreign Aid Corporations, 1953-71

Company	Industries Handled	Date Founded
Neftekhimpromexport	Petroleum exploration Construction of refineries	1964
Prommashexport	Machine-building plants Chemical industry Radio-technical plants Food industry Auto repair shops	1957
Selkhozpromexport	Agricultural and water reclamation projects Agricultural storage facilities Agricultural processing facilities	1965
Tekhnoexport	Pharmaceutical industry Light industries Ports Schools and sport stadia	1932
Tekhnopromexport	Chemical industry Energy industry Lumber industry	1957
Tsvetmetpromexport	Nonferrous metal plants Coal and gas plants	1969
Tyazhpromexport	Iron and steel industry Ore mining Coal industry	1957

Sources: Compiled from Foreign Trade, No. 7 (1957), pp. 33-38; No. 12 (1957), pp. 42-43; No. 1 (1965), pp. 49-50; No. 2 (1965), pp. 51-52; No. 8 (1969), pp. 13-14*; Pavel A. Cherviakov, Organization and Technique of the Foreign Trade of the USSR (Moscow: Vneshtorgizdat, 1962), pp. 229, 232, 339.*

Initially these foreign aid corporations operated only in Eastern Europe. In late 1958 the Soviets reported that Prommashexport, Tekhnopromexport,
and Tyazhpromexport operated only in the people's
democracies, whereas Tekhnoexport conducted operations in other countries.[153] Despite this claim, in
1956 and 1957 representatives were authorized to
sign documents for Tekhnopromexport in Afghanistan,
Burma, Egypt, India, Indonesia, Syria, Yemen, and
Yugoslavia.[154] Subsequently these and newer foreign
aid corporations carried out operations in the many
developing countries with which the Soviet Union had
foreign aid agreements.

Since the foreign aid corporations are under
the jurisdiction of the State Committee for Foreign
Economic Relations, the committee appoints the presidents and provides general policy guidance. These
corporations report functionally to the four regional
Departments for Economic Collaboration of the State
Committee. The foreign aid corporations have a fairly
standardized organizational form. At the staff level
there are five to seven "functional" offices: Planning, Economic and Market Analysis, Transport, Legal,
Accounting, Foreign Exchange, and Cost Calculations.
The line organization consists of offices specialized
by branch of industry. Tekhnopromexport, for example,
has specialized offices for the energy industry, the
chemical industry, and the lumber industry. Because
of its singular importance there is an Aswan Dam Office separate from the Energy Industry Office.
There is also a UNESCO Office, since Tekhnopromexport
handles all of the Soviet Union's aid through UNESCO.
Each of the operating offices is headed by a director
and an assistant director. Depending upon the needs,
there are a chief engineer, senior experts, experts,
senior engineers, engineers, economists, administra-
tors, and others. The other foreign aid corporations
have essentially the same structure. Tyazhpromexport
has a special office for the construction of steel
plants in India but prefers to call it an administration rather than an office.[155]

Monopoly Foreign Trade
Corporations

At the end of World War II, 18 monopoly foreign
trade corporations were reactivated. By the end of
1971 there were 57 of these corporations. As discussed in the last section, seven of these firms are
classified as foreign aid corporations reporting to
the State Committee for Foreign Economic Relations.
Eight report to special State Committees of the
Council of Ministers, the Merchant Marine Ministry,
the Meat and Dairy Ministry, and the Central Union of
Consumers. The remaining 42 monopoly foreign trade
corporations are under the jurisdiction of the Ministry of Foreign Trade. These 42 corporations handle
more than 90 percent of all Soviet foreign trade.

This proliferation of monopoly foreign trade
corporations is a reflection of changes that have
taken place in the Soviet Union and the world since
the end of World War II. The most dramatic of these
changes was the growth of Soviet foreign trade turnover from $548 million in 1938 to $24.5 billion in
1970. Closely related to this growth has been the
integration of Eastern Europe into a socialist trading bloc and the development of socialist countries
in Asia and Cuba. Since 1953 there has also been a
rapid expansion of trading activities with almost all
of the developing countries of Southeast Asia, the
Near East, Africa, and Latin America. At about the
same time the Soviet Union modified its policies and
stepped up production and importation of certain
consumer goods. Intertwined with this rapid growth
in foreign trade is the Soviet Union's rapid industrial development, which has provided an increasing
range of goods available for export and an increasing
need for imports of advanced technology. The original
postwar monopoly foreign trade corporations were unable to meet the increased demands; as a result
firms were set up to handle new areas of trade and,
as needed, corporations were subdivided into more
specialized operations.

Industrial development of the Soviet Union called
for increasing imports of machines, equipment, even
complete plants. Initially these imports were handled by Mashinoimport and Tekhnopromimport. In 1954

TABLE 7

Monopoly Foreign Trade Corporations, 1971

Corporation	Product, Service, or Area	Date Orga- nized
Almazyuvelirexport	Diamonds, jewelry, silver	1970
Aviaexport	Airplanes and helicopters	1961
Avtoexport	Automobiles, trucks, motorcycles	1956
Avtopromimport	Automobile industry machines and equipment	1966
Dalintorg	Trade between Far Eastern region and Japan	1964
Elektronorgtekhnika	Computers and electronic components	1971
Energomashexport	Power and electrotechnical equipment	1966
Exportkhleb	Grains, beans, seeds	1930
Exportles	Forest products, cellulose, paper	1930
Exportlyon	Textiles and textile raw materials	1932
Lenfintorg	Consumer goods between Leningrad and Finland	1960
Litsenzintorg	Patents and licenses	1962
Mashinoexport	Mining, textile, printing, petroleum equipment	1952
Mashinoimport	Power, electrotechnical, mining equipment	1934
Mashpriborintorg	Instruments and precision instruments	1959
Medexport	Medical instruments and medicines	1961
Metallurgimport	Foundry and metallurgical equipment	1970
Mezhdunarodnaya Kniga	Books, phonograph records, stamps	1923
Novoexport	Handicrafts, antiques, art work	1965
Prodintorg	Dairy products, beef, cattle, poultry	1952
Prommashimport	Forest products industry equipment	1965
Promsyryoimport	Iron and steel products	1935
Raznoexport	Tobacco, matches, shoes, bicycles	1930
Raznoimport	Nonferrous metals and rubber products	1930
Soyuzkhimexport	Chemicals, perfumes, cosmetics	1951
Soyuzneftexport	Oil and petroleum products	1931
Soyuzplodoimport	Fruits, vegetables, spirits, cocoa, coffee	1966
Soyuzpromexport	Ores, asbestos, fertilizers, minerals	1931
Soyuzpushnina	Furs and fur products	1931
Soyuzvneshtrans	Transportation	1951
Stankoimport	Machine tools	1930
Sudoimport	Ships	1954
Tekhmashexport	Equipment for light industries	1966
Tekhmashimport	Plants for chemical, fiber, and other industries	1959
Tekhnopromimport	Equipment for food and other industries	1931
Tekhsnabexport	Radioactive isotopes and radiation equipment	1963
Traktoroexport	Tractors, agricultural and road machines	1961
Vneshposyltorg	Local sales for hard currency	1961
Vneshtekhnika	Scientific and technical exchange	1971
Vneshtorgbank	Foreign Trade banking	1924
Vneshtorgreklama	Foreign trade advertising	1964
Vostokintorg	Trade with Sinkiang, Mongolia, Afghanistan	1939
Zapchastsexport	Spare parts for motor vehicles	1965

Sources: Compiled from Pavel A. Cherviakov, Organization and Technique of the Foreign Trade of the USSR (Moscow: Vneshtorgizdat, 1962), pp. 337-39*; V. Golovin, "Medexport--New All-Union Association," Foreign Trade, No. 3 (1961), p. 26*; N. Okonechnikov, "The Course of Widening Specialization in the All-Union Associations," Foreign Trade, No. 9 (1966), pp. 10-11*; N. V. Vasiliev, "Each Day Brings New Work," Foreign Trade, No. 10 (1960), p. 29*; V. Vasin, "USSR Exports Airplanes," Foreign Trade, No. 8 (1962), p. 13*; Foreign Trade, No. 11 (1960), p. 48; No. 10 (1961), pp. 40-41; No. 11 (1962), p. 52; No. 1 (1963), p. 52; No. 12 (1963), pp. 54-55; No. 3 (1965), p. 50; No. 6 (1965), pp. 19-21, 54-55; No. 12 (1965), pp. 49-50; No. 7 (1966), pp. 57, 59; No. 10 (1966), p. 57; No. 9 (1970), pp. 63-64; No. 12 (1970), pp. 57-58; No. 5 (1971), pp. 58-59.*

the Ship Importing Company (Sudoimport) was established to import the ships badly needed for a rapidly
expanding Soviet maritime fleet. Later this company
began exporting ships and boats, particularly fully
equipped fishing factories. In 1958 and 1959 the
British firm Courtaulds, Krupp of Germany, and the
American syndicate Intertex International signed
agreements to supply the Soviet Union with entire
plants for cellulose-acetate spinning, rayon tire
cord, acrylic staple fibers, synthetic fibers, and
other textile materials.[156] To handle the importation of these plants and plants for the chemical,
pharmaceutical, sugar, and soap industries, the Ministry of Foreign Trade in 1959 set up the Technical
Machine Import Company (Tekhmashimport).[157] A second
corporation specializing in the import of complete
plants and equipment, the Industrial Machine Import
Company (Prommashimport), was established in June
1965 for the pulp-paper and forest products industries.[158] In 1966 Fiat of Italy agreed to construct
an automobile plant in the Soviet Union. Again a
specialized firm, the Auto Industry Import Corporation (Avtopromimport), was set up to handle all the
imports involved. This same firm negotiated with
Ford, Mack Truck, and other companies in 1970 and
1971 for the gigantic truck complex planned for Kama.
Another specialized industrial import company is the
Metallurgy Import Corporation (Metallurgimport), organized in December 1970 to import the metallurgical,
crushing and grinding, coke, and foundry equipment
needed for the Kama project foundry.[159] The most recent corporation to be organized, however, is not
involved in the importation of entire plants. The
Electronics Technical Corporation (Elektronorgtekhnika)
was set up in February 1971 to handle the importation
of electronic computers and other electronic com-
ponents.[160]

On the export side there were also new corporations. By 1955 auto and truck production totaled
only 445,300 units.[161] Despite strong domestic demand the Soviet Union began exporting these vehicles.
To handle this new and expanding trade the Auto Export Corporation (Avtoexport) was established in
1956.[162] Other, smaller export corporations were
subsequently organized. The Medical Export Corpora-

FIGURE 8

Soviet Foreign Trade Operations Organization, 1971

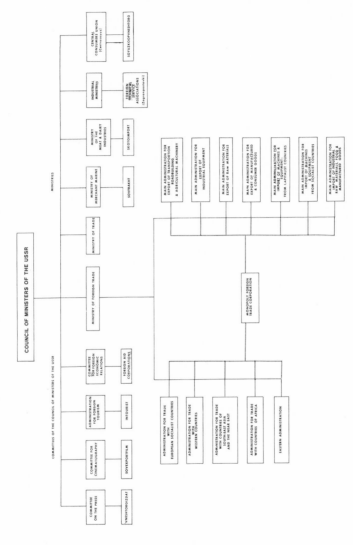

Sources: Prepared by the author from data in V. S. Pozdniakov, State Monopoly of Foreign Trade in the USSR (Moscow: Izdatelstvo "Mezhdunarodniye Otnosheniya," 1969), p. 80*; Alec Flegon, Soviet Foreign Trade Techniques (London: Flegon Press, 1965), p. 31.

tion (Medexport) was formed in February 1961 to handle
medical instruments, medicines, and medicinal raw
materials.[163] In December 1963 the Technical Supply
Export Corporation (Tekhsnabexport) was set up to
trade in radioactive isotopes, radiation equipment
(including X-ray machines), and radiological films.[164]
Because of the growing popularity of Soviet handicrafts, the New Products Export Corporation (Novoexport) began operations in October 1965.[165] The Dia-
mond Jewelry Export Corporation (Almazyuvelirexport)
was organized in September 1970 to export diamonds,
gems, jewelry, silver goods, and similar products.[166]

An example of the trend toward increased specialization can be seen in the evolution of Avtoexport.
When founded in 1956, this firm exported automobiles,
trucks, buses, motorcycles, tractors, road-building
equipment, agricultural machines, agricultural implements, and geophysical, meteorological, and other
laboratory instruments.[167] Later, aircraft were
added to this list. Since the initial volume was
low, this one company could handle these various
items through specialized offices. In November 1959
the precision apparatus, electronic instrument, and
radio-technical instrument lines were split off from
Avtoexport and assigned to the more specialized Machine Instrument Trading Company (Mashpriborintorg).[168]
The tractor, agricultural machine, and road-building
machine lines were then spun off to a new Tractor
Export Corporation (Traktoroexport) in June 1961.[169]
In 1960 and 1961 Avtoexport began displaying airplanes
and helicopters at various fairs and exhibitions.
Then to better handle airplane and helicopter sales,
the Aviation Export Office (Aviaexport) was organized
in October 1961. In 1964 Aviaexport was elevated
from "office" to full corporate status.[170] The spare
parts business of both Avtoexport and Traktoroexport
were split off from these firms and combined into
the Spare Parts Export Corporation (Zapchastsexport).[171]
Today all five of these corporations are in operation
and Avtoexport specializes only in automobiles,
trucks, buses, and motorcycles.

At the 23rd Congress of the Communist Party of
the USSR, increased emphasis was placed on exports
in the machine-technical areas. One result of this
push was the July 1966 reorganization of Mashinoex-

port into a more limited Mashinoexport, the Technical
Machine Export Corporation (Tekhmashexport), and the
Energy Machine Export Corporation (Energomashex-
port).[172] At the same time the fruit, vegetable,
spirits, cocoa, coffee, and tea lines were split off
from Prodintorg and assigned to the newly established
Union Food Import Corporation (Soyuzplodimport).[173]
One reported advantage of this further specialization is that it provides better ties between the
monopoly foreign trade corporations and the providing
or using ministry.[174]

Several other monopoly foreign trade corporations
were established in the early 1960's. The Leningrad-
Finland Trading Office (Lenfintorg) was set up in
1960 to handle trade in consumer goods between the
Leningrad area and Finland.[175] Similarly, the Far
East Trading Office (Dalintorg) was opened in 1964
for trade between the far eastern region of the USSR
and Japan.[176] The fact that these two operations
remain as all-union offices and not full corporations
seems to indicate that the volume of trade handled
is insignificant. Of much greater potential significance was the formation of the License Trading Corporation (Litsenzintorg) in November 1962.[177] This
firm is responsible for acquiring foreign patents
and licenses and for selling abroad licenses and
patents on Soviet inventions.

The monopoly foreign trade corporations are today relatively unchanged from the 1930's. They are
within the jurisdiction of the Ministry of Foreign
Trade, but by Soviet definition they are not part of
the state. Pozdniakov reports: "After 1935, and
at the present time, foreign trade operations are
not carried out by the State but by economic organizations administered by the State which have been
given the right to deal in foreign markets."[178]
Thus, although established by the state, the monopoly
foreign trade corporations are considered autonomous
and the state claims no responsibility for the actions of these corporations. This separation seemingly extends to the presidents and vice-presidents
of these corporations, appointed by the Ministry of
Foreign Trade. These officers are regarded as official persons, and their relationship to the corporation is a state-legal one.[179]

The monopoly foreign trade corporations are set
up to specialize in specific goods and/or services,
and these areas of operations are clearly spelled
out in the charters. Generally these corporations
have a monopoly and no competition is allowed. Certain exceptions do crop up, however, such as duplica-
tion by regional corporations or by organizations
outside the Ministry of Foreign Trade.

A monopoly foreign trade corporation is headed
by a president or chairman. Reporting to the president are a number of functional offices and a series
of operational offices. Each operational office is
responsible for certain categories of goods. Stankoimport, for example, has operations offices for the
import of general machine tools; automated lines;
and foundry, press, and woodworking equipment; and
others for the export and import of rolling mills
and metallurgical equipment; instruments and abra-
sives; and ball bearings.[180] Each of these operational offices has a director, one or two deputies,
and various technicians, commercial experts, foreign
correspondents, and economists.[181] More recently
special offices have also been set up to coordinate
trade with the people's democracies, capitalist
countries, and developing countries.

The functions of the monopoly foreign trade corporations are to plan imports and exports of their
type of goods, to carry out their plan, to ensure
the quality of both exports and imports, to collect
market intelligence for their products, and to study
ways of improving operations. To assist the operations offices each corporation has such functional
offices as Economic Planning, Market Research, Legal,
Transport, Technical, Accounting, Foreign Exchange,
and Personnel.[182]

To carry on their operations the monopoly foreign trade corporations are authorized to set up
local offices in various parts of the Soviet Union
and to hold shares in joint stock companies abroad.
Prodintorg has a Far Eastern office to handle exports
of canned fish and crab from Far Eastern ports; and
Exportles has branch offices in Leningrad, Riga,
Archangel, Nakhodka, and other ports.[183] Overseas,
Soyuzneftexport owns Nafta (G.B.) Ltd., which dis-
tributes Soviet gasoline in the United Kingdom and

FIGURE 9

Organization of Stankoimport

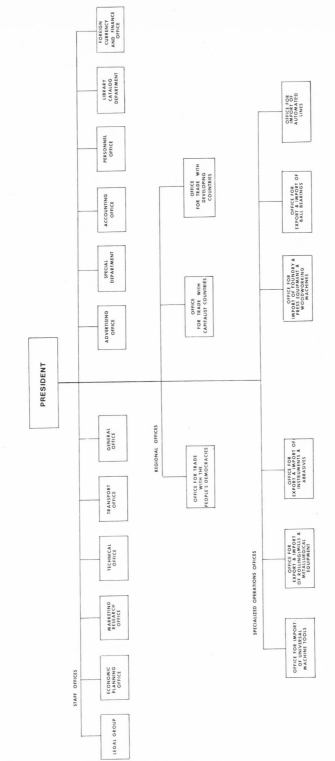

Sources: Based on Pavel A. Cherviakov, Organization and Technique of the Foreign Trade of the USSR (Moscow: Vneshtorgizdat, 1962), p. 38*; Alec Flegon, Soviet
Foreign Trade Techniques (London: Flegon Press, 1965), pp. 46, 48.

is reportedly a partner in the Albatross refinery in
Antwerp, Belgium.[184]

Foreign Trade Activities
of Other Ministries

In 1957 the Council of Ministers of the USSR
became more directly engaged in foreign trade operations when the State Committee for Foreign Economic
Relations was organized under the council. This involvement has increased as new State Committees of
the Council of Ministers have been formed and monopoly foreign trade corporations have been transferred
to these committees and other ministries.

The first such transfer occurred in 1962, when
the Soviet Freight Corporation (Sovfrakht) was reas-
signed from the Ministry of Foreign Trade to the
Ministry of the Merchant Marine.[185] Sovfrakht was
organized in 1932, and for 30 years it handled the
chartering of Soviet and foreign ships and the actual
shipping of goods in foreign trade. This transfer
appears to be a logical result of the rapid growth
of the Soviet maritime fleet. Subsequently a new
firm, the Soviet Fleet Service Corporation (Sovinflot), was established to service foreign vessels
in Soviet ports and Soviet vessels abroad. Now all
matters relating to ocean shipping are under the control of a single ministry.

The second ministry to acquire a foreign trade
organization was the Ministry of the Meat and Dairy
Industries, which inherited the Cattle Importing Office (Skotoimport) in 1964.[186] Skotoimport started
operations in 1934. For 30 years this firm imported
cattle and meat for the Office of the Food Industry
of the RSFSR.

The State Committees established by the Council
of Ministers were the State Committee for Cinema-
tography (1963), State Committee on the Press (1964),
State Committee for Science and Technology, and the
Administration for Foreign Tourism (1964). When
these committees were organized, the Soviet Film Export Corporation (Sovexportfilm), the Foreign Trade
Publishing Corporation (Vneshtorgizdat), and the
joint-stock company Intourist were transferred to the

TABLE 8

Monopoly Foreign Trade Corporations Not Under the Ministry of Foreign Trade, 1971

Corporation	Product or Service	Ministry or Committee	Date Organized
Intourist	Tourism	Administration for Foreign Tourism	1930
Skotoimport	Cattle and meat	Ministry of Meat and Dairy Industries	1934
Sovexportfilm	Movie films	Committee for Cinematography	1930
Sovfrakht	Ocean freight	Ministry of the Merchant Marine	1932
Sovinflot	Servicing of ships	Ministry of the Merchant Marine	
Soyuzkoopvneshtorg	Consumer-goods barter	Central Union of Consumers	1970
Vneshtorgizdat	Foreign trade publications	Committee on the Press	1962
Vneshtekhnika	Technical collaboration	Committee on Science and Technology	1950

Sources: Compiled from V. S. Pozdniakov, "The State Monopoly of Foreign Trade in the USSR," Soviet State and Law, No. 10 (1967), pp. 47, 98; and State Monopoly of Foreign Trade in the USSR (Moscow: Izdatelstvo "Mezhdunarodniye Otnosheniya," 1969), p. 102*; Pavel A. Cherviakov, Organization and Technique of the Foreign Trade of the USSR (Moscow: Vneshtorgizdat, 1962), p. 56*; Foreign Trade, No. 1 (1963), pp. 52-53; No. 7 (1965), p. 50; No. 6 (1967), p. 24.*

103

appropriate committees.[187] Prior to its transfer
Vneshtorgizdat was responsible for publishing books
and magazines on foreign trade and for all foreign
trade advertising. The advertising functions were
spun off in 1964 to the Foreign Trade Advertising
Firm (Vneshtorgreklama), which remained under the
jurisdiction of the Ministry of Foreign Trade.[188]
To carry out its functions abroad, the State Committee for Science and Technology established the Foreign
Technical Corporation (Vneshtekhnika).

The Central Consumers Union had faded from the
international scene in 1930, when it was replaced by
the monopoly foreign trade corporations. Because of
the great consumer push following Stalin's death,
Centrosoyuz was again allowed to engage in foreign
trade in 1953. An interesting aspect of this trade
is that it is entirely on a barter basis. Exports,
for the most part, are agricultural products but also
include consumer goods such as bicycles, watches,
radios, and phonograph records purchased locally with
market funds. The imports are almost entirely consumer goods. At first Centrosoyuz traded in its own
name. For this purpose it had an Administration for
Foreign Relations and offices for foreign trade operations.[189] In 1962 the Union Cooperative Foreign
Trade Corporation (Soyuzkoopvneshtorg) was established
as a monopoly foreign trade corporation to handle this
barter trade. Soyuzkoopvneshtorg is a part of the
Central Union of Consumer Societies and reports to
the latter and not the Ministry of Foreign Trade.[190]

The Ministry of Trade is also involved in barter
operations with foreign countries. Like Centrosoyuz,
the Ministry of Trade restricts its operations primarily to consumer goods. To handle this trade it
has an Import Office for Consumer Goods (Promimport-
torg) and an Import Office for Foodstuffs (Prodim-
porttorg). Unlike Centrosoyuz, the Ministry of Trade
does not have a monopoly foreign trade corporation
assigned, and the import offices must deal through
the corporations under the Ministry of Foreign
Trade.[191]

It has also been reported that the Chief Directorate for the Supply of Consumer Goods (a directorate of Gosplan), the Directorate for Inter-Republican
Trade (Soyuzglavtorg), and the individual Soviet

republics are authorized to engage in some limited form of international trade.192 It is believed, however, that most of this trade is handled through the firms under the Ministry of Foreign Trade.

Because of the increasing volume of machines and equipment in the Soviet export mix, it was only logical that there would be a growing demand for technical and repair services. In 1968 the Ministry of the Aircraft Industry set up a Foreign Aviation Servicing Company (Aviazagranpostavka) to service airplanes sold abroad.193 Today Aviaexport sells the planes and helicopters and Aviazagranpostavka provides the postsales service. Other industrial ministries have followed suit and have set up foreign service companies, or zagranpostavki, which work with the respective monopoly foreign trade corporations to handle postsales service.194 These firms also work closely with Zapchastexport, which deals in spare parts for various equipment.

The Ministry of Finance has also become involved in international trade operations. This ministry's Administration of Foreign Insurance (Ingostrakh) carries out insurance operations for exports and imports. In 1958 Ingostrakh, together with Sovfrakht, organized Garant Versicherungs AG in Vienna. This company specializes in insuring East-West trade and does little if any local insurance business. It is believed that the Black Sea and Baltic Insurance Company in Great Britain is also a subsidiary of Ingostrakh.195

Soviet Companies Abroad

Since the death of Stalin there have been some changes in Soviet companies abroad. Most important has been the liquidation of the mixed companies that had been established in the bloc countries. The Anglo-Soviet Steamship Company continued operations, but apparently as a subsidiary of Sovfrakht. Similarly, the Black Sea and Baltic Insurance Company and the more recently formed Garant Versicherungs AG became arms of Ingostrakh. In 1959 Amtorg came back to life and moved into newer, bigger offices in New York.196

To increase its overseas sales the Soviet Union
organized a number of wholly owned and joint-venture
firms in various countries. Soyuzneftexport established Nafta (GB) Ltd. in England as a distributor
of gasoline. Although the directors of this firm are
Russian, the staff is entirely British.[197] In 1968
Soyuzneftexport also set up a petroleum marketing
company as a joint venture with Belgian investors.[198]
Exportles has joined with a British firm of brokers
to form the Russian Wood Agency, which sells Soviet
timber on the British market. Reportedly this is the
largest company the Soviet Union has abroad.[199]
Avtoexport has a majority interest in Scaldia-Volga,
which sells Soviet cars in Belgium.[200]

To handle the postsales service of a number of
products, the Soviet Union has established a series
of joint-venture service companies. By mid-1971
there were 14 such companies located in 10 countries.
Examples are Technical and Optical Equipment, Ltd.
(precision instruments, cameras, radios) and Umo-
Plant (road-building equipment, excavators) in England; Actif-Auto (farm machines and tractors) in
France; and Scaldia-Volga, which sells and services
cars in Belgium.[201] These companies act as arms of
the zagranpostavki of the industrial ministries, and
it is believed that the ownership is held by these
firms together with the monopoly foreign trade corporations handling the sales.

SUMMARY

The Soviet foreign trade operations organization
has passed through several distinct phases since the
1917 Revolution. The first phase began in 1921, after the trade blockade had been broken. This phase
was characterized by a single state organization
that handled all foreign trade operations, both internal and external. The second phase was the period
of diversification during the first few years of the
New Economic Policy. Foreign trade at this time was
handled by State Export-Import Offices, cooperative
organizations, mixed companies, foreign companies,
private firms, foreign trade representatives, and
Soviet companies established abroad. In 1925 this

diversification was augmented by the establishment
of corporations and offices specializing in the export
or import of certain commodities.

In 1930 the diversification phase was replaced
by the monopoly specialization phase. Foreign trade
corporations were established and given complete
monopoly over the trade operations of specified lists
of commodities. All other foreign trade organizations
were then liquidated; internal foreign trade operations were conducted by the monopoly corporations,
while the foreign trade representatives abroad conducted all external operations.

During World War II the foreign trade organizations were, for the most part, inactive. What trade
there was, was carried out by a Buying Commission in
the United States and trade representatives in Great
Britain and Iran. Following World War II there was
a return to the prewar pattern, with the exception
of the establishment of Soviet-owned and mixed companies in Eastern Europe, China, and Korea.

The death of Stalin brought about the most recent phase. Because of the rapid industrial development of the Soviet Union and a vastly increased
foreign trade volume, there has been a proliferation
of monopoly foreign trade corporations. During this
same period the Ministry of Foreign Trade has lost
its monopoly of foreign trade operations. Reflecting the changed relations with Eastern Europe and
the developing countries of the Third World, there
has been the creation of specialized foreign aid corporations that report to a State Committee of the
Council of Ministers. Other monopoly foreign trade
corporations have subsequently been transferred to
other state committees and other ministries. Furthermore, the Central Consumers Union has reentered
foreign trade, and a number of other organizations
and ministries have in some way become involved in
foreign trade. These recent changes indicate that,
although the system of monopoly foreign trade corporations has proved effective since the 1930's, the
Soviet trade operations organization will remain
flexible to the degree needed to meet organizationally
any internal or external changes.

3

ORGANIZATION
FOR CONTROL

The preceding chapters have discussed
Soviet foreign trade policies and the organizations used to conduct trade according to these policies. This chapter will
describe the control functions of the Ministry of Foreign Trade and the growing importance of the Council of Ministers in
the direction of Soviet foreign trade.
The discussion of the central organization
of the Ministry of Foreign Trade is divided
into six distinct chronological periods,
each of which is identified by the title
of the central organization for that period. These periods were those of the
Foreign Trade Council (1918-20), the People's Commissariat of Foreign Trade (1920-
25), the People's Commissariat of Internal
and Foreign Trade (1925-30), the People's
Commissariat of Foreign Trade (1930-39),
the People's Commissariat (later Ministry)
of Foreign Trade (1940-53), and the Ministry of Foreign Trade (1953-71). The organizational structure, functions, scope
of authority, and reasons for changes in
the central organization are described in
detail for each period. Following a discussion of the Council of Ministers, the
remaining sections of this chapter describe

the authorized local representatives and
the trade representatives or delegations
abroad.

FOREIGN TRADE COUNCIL

Lenin considered a state monopoly of foreign
trade as third among his top priorities in establishing a dictatorship of the proletariat.[1] Accordingly
a commission to frame legislation for the establishment of a state monopoly of foreign trade was established immediately following the signing of the Brest-
Litovsk Peace Treaty with Germany.[2] The legislation
drawn up by this committee was issued as Decree No.
432 of the Council of People's Commissars on April
22, 1918.[3] Its most important provision was the
first article, which nationalized all foreign trade.

This decree also established the Foreign Trade
Council within the People's Commissariat of Trade
and Industry to regulate what little foreign trade
there was. The members of this council were not em-
ployees of the commissariat but were representatives
of other governmental departments. The council was
headed by a president who was, however, a representative of the Commissariat of Trade and Industry.[4]

The decree of April 22, 1918, had great historical and ideological importance and is often referred
to as the "constitutional foundation" of the monopoly
of foreign trade. At the time of its promulgation,
however, it had little if any real effect. The
blockade imposed by the Allied Supreme Economic Council prevented all trade with the Soviet government
until 1920. As a result the Council for Foreign
Trade in the People's Commissariat of Trade and Industry was little more than a paper organization.

PEOPLE'S COMMISSARIAT OF FOREIGN
TRADE (1920-25)

With the resumption of foreign trade in 1920,
it became apparent that the relatively loose, inter-
organizational committee structure of the Foreign
Trade Council was inadequate for present and future

FIGURE 10

People's Commissariat of Trade and Industry, 1918-20

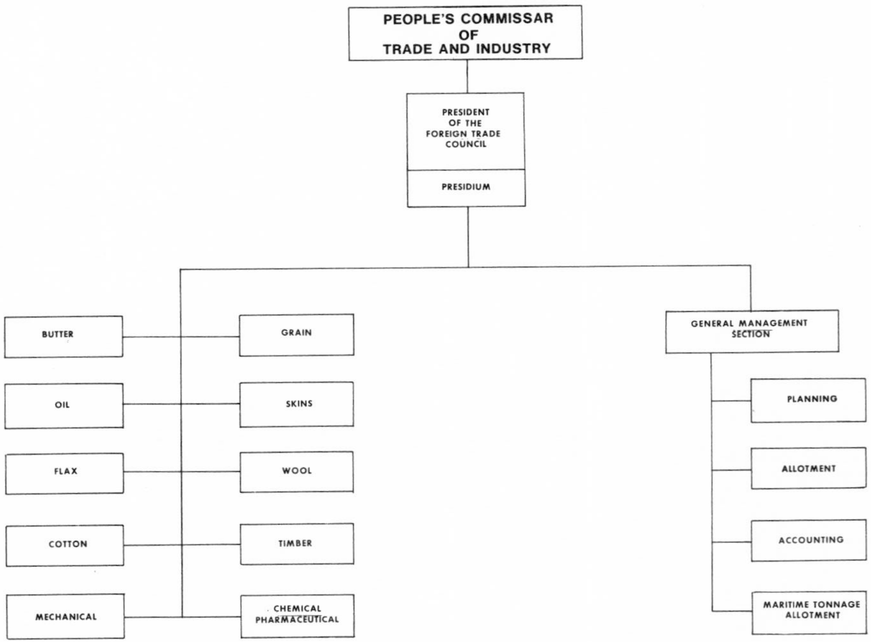

Source: Prepared by the author.

trade activity. As a result the People's Commissariat of Foreign Trade was established on June 11, 1920.

Initially the People's Commissariat of Foreign Trade had a fairly simple organization. Reporting directly to the commissar were five administrations: Export, Import, Transport, Customs-Financial, and Central Administration of Border Guards.[5] There was also a new Foreign Trade Council to handle interdepartmental coordination but not control.[6] Trade expanded rapidly, and a year later the commissariat had grown to 15 central administrations, 42 branches, 14 offices, and 22 agencies.[7]

With the enactment of the New Economic Policy, the bulk of this organization was transferred to the newly formed State Export-Import Offices (gostorgi). The commissariat now became strictly an administrative body concerned with the general direction and regulation of foreign trade activities.[8] To carry out its strictly control functions, the Commissariat of Foreign Trade was organized into three major divisions: the central control staff, the authorized local representatives of the commissariat, and the trade representatives assigned to other countries. The functions of the central control staff were divided among seven administrative boards. The Trading Concerns and Institutions Board directed the activities and coordinated the plans of those organizations authorized to conduct foreign trade activities under the New Economic Policy. A major portion of the regulatory work was conducted by the Regulation Board, which prepared the foreign trade policy of Russia, drew up the export and import program, supervised the execution of this program, determined quotas, and issued export and import licenses. Much of this work was carried on through the authorized local representatives and the trade representatives abroad. The other five boards were Economic-Legal, Financial-Accounting, Transport, Customs, and General Administration.[9]

At the time it was organized in 1920, the People's Commissariat of Foreign Trade had official jurisdiction only over the foreign trade activities of the Russian Socialist Federated Soviet Republic (RSFSR). The USSR was formed on December 30, 1922, and at that time the Commissariat of Foreign Trade became a commissariat of the "whole Union."[10]

FIGURE 11

People's Commissariat of Foreign Trade, 1920-22

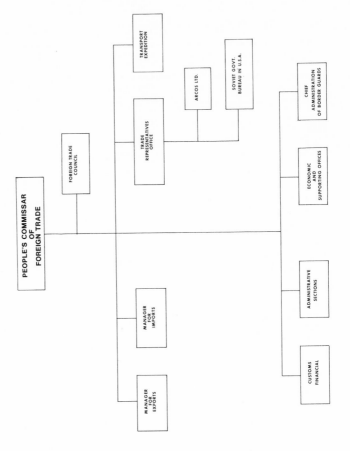

Source: Prepared by the author.

FIGURE 12

People's Commissariat of Foreign Trade, 1922-25

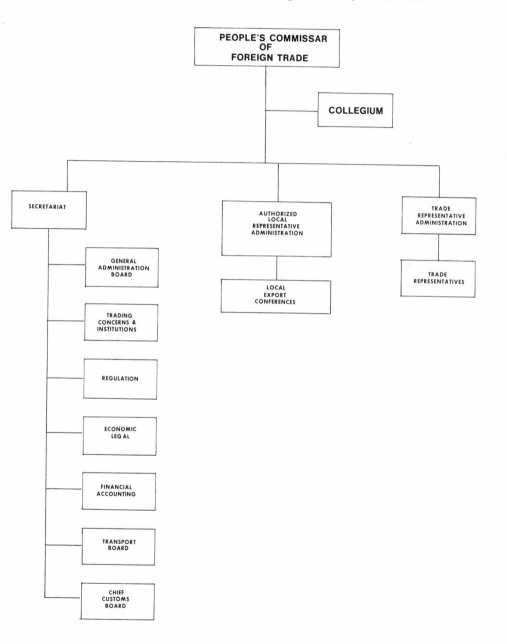

Source: Prepared by the author.

PEOPLE'S COMMISSARIAT OF INTERNAL
AND FOREIGN TRADE (1925-30)

As early as December 1922 a merger of the People's Commissariat of Foreign Trade and the Central Committee for Internal Trade was being planned.[11] By this time the operating functions of the commissariat had been transferred to other organs, and private trading had taken over much of the operations of the committee. Both organizations were now control and regulatory bodies. The interests of both were quite similar and frequently resulted in heated disagreements and watered-down compromises. Furthermore, both bureaus had parallel offices that duplicated each other's work.[12]

To provide harmony between production, consumption, and storage of goods, and the solution of internal and external problems, the Commissariat of Foreign Trade and the Commissariat of Internal Trade (which had been established in 1924) were fused into a joint People's Commissariat of Internal and Foreign Trade in November 1925.[13] This combined commissariat had eight staff administrations and four product administrations. The staff administrations were Administrative-Organization, Economic, Finance, Export-Import, Trade Agreement-Legal, Trade Enterprises and Institutions, Transport, and Customs. The product administrations were Grain-Forage Crops, Raw Materials, Manufactured Products, and Special Orders.[14]

In January 1927 the organization was modified to improve operations. The Export-Import and Trade Enterprises and Institutions Administrations were consolidated into a Foreign Operations Administration, headed by an assistant commissar for foreign trade. The remaining staff and product administrations became a central control staff; and a Trade Regulation Administration, headed by an assistant commissar for internal trade, was established.

The Foreign Operations Administration was divided into an Export Sector, an Import Sector, and special staff offices for economic analysis, planning-licensing, transportation, and trade representatives.[15] The Export and Import Sectors were further broken into subdivisions specializing in products or groups of products. In 1927 there were 14 such groups:

FIGURE 13

People's Commissariat of Internal and Foreign Trade, 1925-30

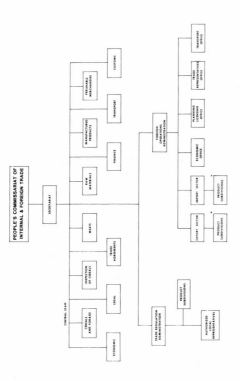

^aProduct subdivisions: mining products, metals, electro-technical, chemicals, foundry, hides and skins, agricultural tools, consumer goods, timber, cereals, raw materials, textiles, perishables, miscellaneous.

Source: Prepared by the author.

metals, electrotechnical, chemical products, foundry, hides and skins, agricultural implements, consumer goods, timber, raw materials, textiles, perishable merchandise, mining products, cereals, and miscellaneous goods.[16]

The basic functions of the Foreign Operations Administration were to regulate and control the foreign trade organizations, to carry out export and import programs, and to issue export and import licenses.[17] The operations of the Customs and Trade Agreement Administrations remained part of the central control staff. Local operations were also excluded, and the authorized local respresentatives were responsible to the Trade Regulation Administration.

PEOPLE'S COMMISSARIAT OF
FOREIGN TRADE (1930-39)

The end of the New Economic Policy and the beginning of the First Five-Year Plan in 1928 brought a number of changes to Soviet internal and foreign trade. As one official put it, "Foreign and internal trade are developing along entirely distinct lines demanding essentially different methods of working. In internal trade, the capitalistic element has been eliminated. . . . Foreign trade, on the other hand, is conducted along capitalistic lines and in the face of international competition."[18] In recognition of these changes, the Commissariat of Internal and Foreign Trade was split into the Commissariats of Internal Trade and Foreign Trade in November 1930.

The Foreign Operations Administration became the framework for the new Commissariat of Foreign Trade. The Export Sector became the Export Administration, but the 14 goods offices were replaced by two operating sectors that controlled the operations of the monopoly export corporations and of the foreign trade representatives abroad. A third sector assumed control over the authorized local representatives. The Import Sector became the Import Administration, which controlled the operations of the monopoly import corporations. The only other office

reported was a Planning-Finance Sector, which handled
overall planning and central accounting. No mention
was made at this time of customs, trade agreement,
and transport functions, which must have been carried
out by this commissariat.[19]

By 1938 the functions of the commissariat had
been expanded and refined and the organization was
given more detail.[20] The Commissariat of Foreign
Trade was now divided into six control administrations and 13 staff offices. The largest and most
important of the control administrations was the Export Administration, which was relatively unchanged
since 1930. In addition to the operating and local
representative sectors, this administration now had
special groups for planning, finance, accounting,
and personnel. The Import Administration was also
little changed from 1930 except for the addition of
special offices for planning-finance and personnel.
The duties of these two administrations were unchanged.

Since the problems of trading with certain countries of the Middle and Far East were considered
different from those of dealing with the West, a
separate trading policy was followed for these countries. Exports to and imports from these countries
were not controlled by the Export and Import Administrations but by a special Eastern Administration.
This administration was divided into groups specialized by country: Mongolia-Tanna Tuva, Sinkiang, Afghanistan, Iran, and Turkey. The remaining three
administrations--Transport, Customs, and Foreign
Trade Schools--are self-explanatory.

The most important of the staff offices was
Planning-Economic. This office had groups for export planning, import planning, production and labor
planning, and economic intelligence. This was the
nerve center of the commissariat. It gathered data
on all the world markets, pieced this information
together with data on the home market, and produced
the overall planning of foreign trade.

Prior to 1935 the trade representatives abroad
were quite important, and their activities were controlled by the Export and Import Administrations.
After 1935 the importance of the trade representatives declined sharply, and the control of these organs was shifted to the Trade Representative Sector

FIGURE 14

People's Commissariat of Foreign Trade, 1930

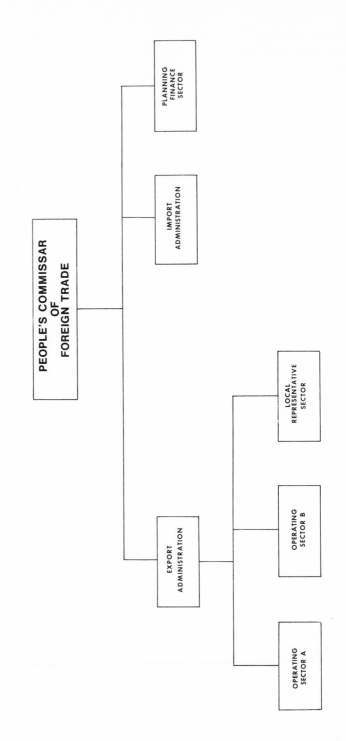

Source: Prepared by the author.

of the staff.[21] In December 1937 the Concessions
Committee of the Council of People's Commissars was
demoted to the Concessions Office of the Commissariat
of Foreign Trade, reflecting the declining importance
of foreign companies in Soviet trade. The remaining
staff offices were self-explanatory functional offices.

It is interesting to note that the Commissariat
of Foreign Trade did not escape the 1937-38 purges.
A. P. Rozengolts, who served as commissar from 1930,
was removed in 1937 and tried for treason. In 1938
Anastas Mikoyan became commissar and held this position until 1949, after which he guided foreign trade
as a deputy premier.

PEOPLE'S COMMISSARIAT (MINISTRY)
OF FOREIGN TRADE (1940-53)

World War II Period

During World War II "all the national economy
of the USSR was put on a war basis. This called for
certain changes in the organizational form and the
methods of work of a number of links in the foreign
trade apparatus."[22] There was no abrupt reorganization; but over a period of seven years, extending
into the postwar period, new administrations were
added to the central organization as needs arose,
existing administrations were divided and regrouped,
and administrations or offices no longer needed were
liquidated.

The most significant wartime change was the
creation of a Trade Treaties Administration, which
was charged with reorienting trading patterns to
meet import needs.[23] Although a wartime creation,
this administration was probably more important in
the early postwar period, when the Soviet Union attempted to reestablish its foreign trade ties. It
was also important in that three of its sectors--the
Balkan countries, Poland-Czechoslovakia, and Hungary-
Austria--were instrumental in the preparation of the
trade treaties that were to bind the Eastern European
countries economically to the Soviet Union. This

FIGURE 15

People's Commissariat of Foreign Trade, 1938

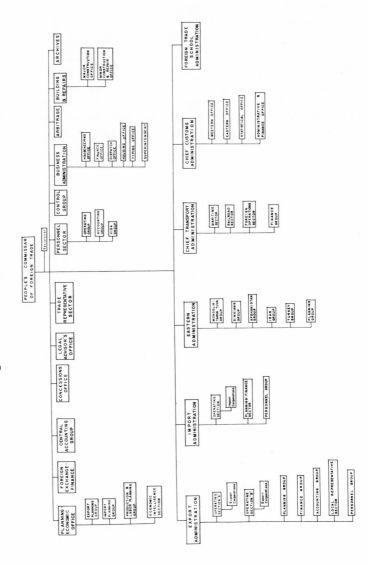

Source: Prepared by the author.

relationship will be discussed in a later section.
It is also interesting to note that a Latin America
Sector was established in 1945, many years prior to
an alleged economic invasion of that area.[24]

During the war the Concessions Office and the
Trade Representatives Sector were liquidated. The
last mention of the Concessions Office was the appointment of a deputy chief in January 1944.[25] No
mention whatsoever was made of the Trade Representatives Sector during this period, nor has it been
mentioned since. In the midst of the war, in January
1943, the Commissariat of Foreign Trade acquired its
oddest addition--the Chief Administration of the
Fur Economy. It appears that this administration
was attached to the commissariat only for lack of a
better sponsor.[26]

Early Postwar Period

The most important change in the foreign trade
control organization during the early postwar period
was the establishment of the Administration for Trade
with Eastern European Countries, the Germany Office,
and the Main Administration for Soviet Property
Abroad.

The Administration for Trade with Eastern European Countries was established in September 1945.
The following month special offices were set up for
trade with Austria, Rumania, Poland, Bulgaria, and
Yugoslavia-Albania. A Hungarian office was established in November 1945. It appears that there was
also a Finnish office during this period. After the
Czechoslovak coup of February 1948, a Czechoslovakian
office was established. The Austrian and Hungarian
offices were combined in 1947; and the Yugoslavian-
Albanian office was liquidated in 1948, following
the dissolution of Soviet-Yugoslav relations. Otherwise, these offices were still operating at the time
of Stalin's death.[27]

No information is available on the functions of
the Administration for Trade with Eastern European
Countries. It is apparent, however, that this organization completely controlled all trade relations
between the Soviet Union and the respective countries.

In all probability it was also the organization that pressured the East European governments to reorganize their foreign trade along the Soviet pattern.

Germany was a case by itself. In November 1945 a special Germany Office was established. Under the terms of the Yalta Agreement, the Soviet Union was entitled to certain reparations from Germany. The administration of these reparations payments was in the hands of the Reparations Sector of the Germany Office. A second division of this office was the Administration for the Operation of Soviet State Corporations in Germany. There is no indication of the type of corporations operating in Germany, but it appears that they included both industrial concerns claimed as reparations and the Soviet monopoly trading corporations.[28]

In addition to the reparations obtained from Germany proper, the Soviet Union interpreted the Yalta and Potsdam Agreements as giving them full reparation rights to all German assets found in other Eastern European countries. At first the Soviets attempted to remove these assets to the Soviet Union. When this did not prove feasible, they organized these assets into Soviet-owned and mixed Soviet-local corporations. (These corporations were discussed in the last chapter.) To control these assets a Main Administration for Soviet Property Abroad was established in April 1946. At the time of its formation, the administration had a Central Accounting Office and a Supply Administration. In the following months special administrations were established to control the enterprises of specific industries. It appears that these administrations controlled the activities of enterprises within their field in all of the Eastern European countries except Germany and Austria. It is important to note that the operations controlled by these administrations were limited to production and internal operations. The foreign trade activities of these industries were controlled by the Administration for Trade with Eastern European Countries and the Germany Office.[29]

Virtually no office or administration in the Commissariat of Foreign Trade emerged unscathed from World War II. The commissariat itself became the Ministry of Foreign Trade on March 15, 1946.[30]

FIGURE 16

Ministry of Foreign Trade as of September 1949

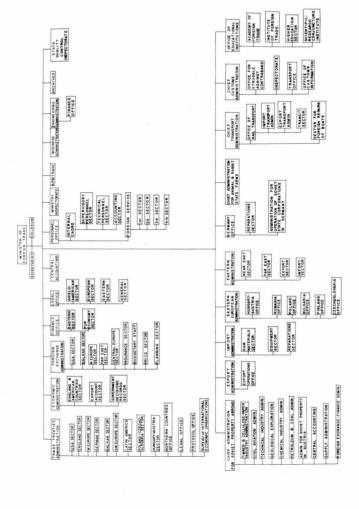

Source: Prepared by the author.

Figure 16 indicates the form of this organization as
of September 1949, the last date that appointments
and transfers of ministry personnel were reported in
the official journal Foreign Trade. Most of the differences from the 1938 organization (see Figure 15)
have been explained above. Other differences can be
explained only by the lack of adequate information.
As an example, in the 1938 organization certain vital
tasks were performed by sections of the Planning-
Economic Office. The 1949 organization does not indicate the presence of similar sections, although it
must be assumed that these functions were being carried on by some specific group.

MINISTRY OF FOREIGN
TRADE (1953-71)

Immediately following Stalin's death on March
6, 1953, the Ministries of Trade and Foreign Trade
were combined into a single Ministry of Internal and
Foreign Trade.[31] It is to be noted that this was a
period of grave crisis in the Soviet government, and
several other ministries were similarly combined.
These combined ministries were headed by deputy
premiers--Anastas Mikoyan, in the case of the Ministry of Internal and Foreign Trade. From this it can
be seen that the move was a temporary one designed
to insure strict control over important sectors of
the government. It was also a period of reorientation of Soviet policies, and the strict control permitted an overhauling of the ministry structure by
Mikoyan. This thesis is borne out by the fact that
six months later, on September 15, 1953, Mikoyan
stepped down and a reorganized Ministry of Foreign
Trade regained its identity.[32]
Today the Ministry of Foreign Trade remains as
the principal agency for the administration and control of Soviet foreign trade. The basic functions
of the ministry are the following:

> Develop and execute measures for the
> widening and improving of trade relations
> with other countries.

Prepare foreign trade plans and carry
out these plans either through ministry
operations or by controlling the operations
of other agencies.

Develop a customs policy and manage
all customs functions.

Guide, control, and regulate the activities of the monopoly foreign trade corporations within its jurisdiction.

Insure the quality of all Soviet exports.

Promote foreign trade in general.

Implement all laws relating to the
monopoly of foreign trade.

Regulate and control the foreign trade
activities of all organizations dealing
abroad--whether or not they are under the
jurisdiction of the Ministry of Foreign
Trade.

To carry out these functions the ministry has a collegium plus a series of export and import administrations, regional administrations, and functional
staff administrations. It also has authorized local
representatives attached to the councils of ministers of the republics; agents at major industrial
and port cities; commercial agencies abroad; and
trade delegations, commercial counselors, and attachés assigned to Soviet missions abroad.[33]

Collegium of the Ministry
of Foreign Trade

In June 1940 the Ministry of Foreign Trade reestablished the collegium that had been used for a
short period under the New Economic Policy.[34] Today
the collegium operates much like a board of directors. The minister of foreign trade is president
of the collegium, and the members are all the vice-
ministers or heads of administrations. The collegium
advises the minister, develops ministry policies,
handles major problems of trade development, supervises the fulfillment of trade agreements and trade

FIGURE 17

Ministry of Foreign Trade, 1971

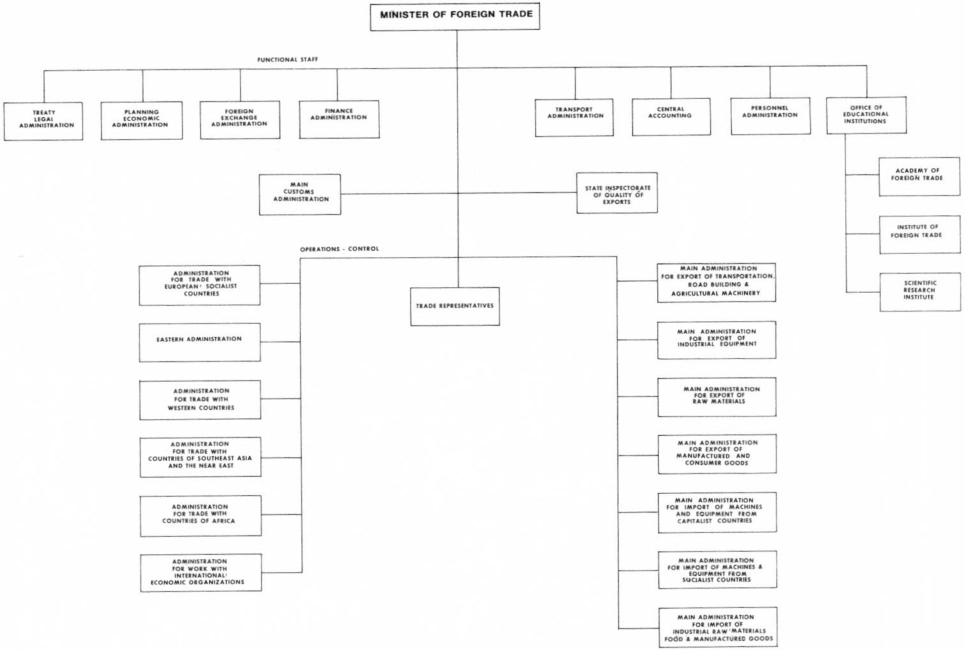

Sources: Prepared by the author from data in A. M. Smirnov and N. N. Liubimov, Foreign Trade of the USSR (Moscow: Vneshtorgizdat, 1954), pp. 77-78*; Pavel A. Cherviakov, Organization and Technique of the Foreign Trade of the USSR (Moscow: Vneshtorgizdat, 1958), pp. 36-37*; Foreign Trade, No. 11 (1958), pp. 51-52*; United States, Department of State, Soviet Political Leaders, Biographical Directory No. 251, July 1957, pp. 53-56; Alec Flegon, Soviet Foreign Trade Techniques (London: Flegon Press, 1965), pp. 30, 32; Cheriakov, Organization and Technique (1962), pp. 40, 44*; V. S. Pozdniakov, State Monopoly of Foreign Trade in the USSR (Moscow: Izdatelstvo "Mezhdunarodniye Otnosheniya," 1969), pp. 76-80*; and "The State Monopoly of Foreign Trade in the USSR," Soviet State and Law, No. 10 (1967), p. 45.

126

plans, and in general controls the operations of the
ministry. It is a staff organ, and its decisions
are usually issued as orders of the minister.[35] The
major contribution of the collegium appears to be in
improving communications and coordination among the
multitude of operational and functional-staff administrations.

Export and Import
Administrations

As part of the reorganization of 1953, the Export Administration was divided into the First and
Second Export Administrations. The First Export Administration regulated and controlled all raw material exports, and the Second Export Administration
performed the same job for the export of machines
and equipment. Likewise, the Import Administration
became the First and Second Import Administrations.
The First Import Administration regulated and controlled all imports of machines and equipment, while
the Second Import Administration did the same for
all other imports.[36]

This organization remained unchanged as late
as 1962.[37] By 1969, however, there were four Main
Export Administrations and three Main Import Administrations. The First Export Administration became
the Main Administration for the Export of Raw Materials. The Second Export Administration was split
into the Main Administrations for the Export of Industrial Equipment; Transportation, Road-Building
and Agricultural Machinery; and Manufactured and
Consumer Goods. The First Import Administration was
broken along ideological lines into the Main Administrations for the Import of Machines and Equipment
from Capitalist Countries and from Socialist Countries. The Second Import Administration became the
Main Administration for the Import of Industrial Raw
Materials, Food, and Manufactured Goods.[38]

One of the main functions of the export and import administrations is to exercise control over the
foreign trade organizations handling their class of
goods. For example, the Main Administration for the
Export of Transportation, Road-Building, and Agri-

cultural Machinery controls the operations of the
monopoly foreign trade corporations Aviaexport, Avtoexport, Traktoroexport, and Zapchastsexport. Similarly, the monopoly foreign trade corporations Dalintorg, Lenfintorg, Prodintorg, Raznoimport, Soyuzplodimport, and Vostokintorg are under the Main Administration for the Import of Industrial Raw Materials,
Food, and Manufactured Goods.

Other functions of these administrations are pa
participation in the preparation of export and import
plans, controlling fulfillment of these plans, conducting negotiations with foreign representatives on
matters of exports and imports, the issuance of export and import permits, and arranging for the display
of goods at international fairs.[39]

Regional Administrations

A more significant result of the 1953 reorganization was the establishment of trade-political or regional administrations. Prior to World War II practically all the trade of the Soviet Union was with
Western countries. As a result the operations of the
entire ministry were geared for this trade; and an
Eastern Administration handled the privileged but
insignificant trade with the Eastern border states
of Mongolia, Tanna Tuva, Sinkiang, Afghanistan, Iran,
and Turkey. By 1953 this picture was reversed. In
1955 fully 80 percent of Soviet trade was with socialist countries, another 5 percent was with developing countries, and only 15 percent was with the
developed countries of the West.[40] As a result new
organizational forms were needed to insure that
proper attention was paid to trade with all regions.

In the early postwar years the ministry had established an Administration for Trade with Eastern
European Countries, a Germany Office, and an Administration for Soviet Property Abroad. At the time
it appeared that this was an ad hoc arrangement reflecting an unusual and impermanent focusing of attention on trade with this part of the world. By
1953, however, Bulgaria, Czechoslovakia, the German
Democratic Republic, Hungary, Poland, and Rumania
had "people's democratic" governments; and the ad hoc

TABLE 9

Distribution of Trade Handled by Regional Administrations, 1970

	Million Rubles	Share (in percent)
Administration for Trade with European Socialist Countries	13,617.8	63.8
Eastern Administration	791.9	3.7
Administration for Trade with Countries of Southeast Asia and Near East	1,171.7	5.5
Administration for Trade with Countries of Africa	1,004.5	4.7
Administration for Trade with Western Countries	4,766.8	22.3
(Europe)	(3,668.7)	(17.2)
(Japan, North America, Australia)	(1,019.9)	(4.8)
(Latin America)	(78.2)	(0.4)
Total all regions	21,352.7[a]	100.0

[a]Official total of 22,085.2 cannot be verified from individual country figures.

Source: Compiled from official trade statistics in Foreign Trade, No. 5 (1971), pp. 57-58.*

arrangement had every appearance of permanence. As
a result the Administration for Trade with Eastern
European Countries and the Germany Office were combined to form the Administration for Trade with European Socialist Countries. Like its predecessor,
this administration had special offices for each
country; the only real change was the elimination of
the Austria and Finland Offices.[41] Today this administration is involved in the trade with the bloc
countries of Eastern Europe, Yugoslavia, and Cuba.
In 1970 this represented 63.8 percent of all Soviet
trade.

The Main Administration for Soviet Property
Abroad was originally included in the 1953 reorganization. During 1954 and 1955 this property was both
given and sold to the respective countries. Evidently all of it was disposed of, and by 1958 the
Main Administration had been liquidated.[42]

Formation of the People's Democratic Republics
of China, Korea, and Vietnam created a need for a
special office for the trade with these countries
and Mongolia. At first Soviet trade with these countries was carried on through the Eastern Administration. In the 1953 reorganization it was decided to
change the Eastern Administration from an organ dealing with Eastern border states into an organ dealing
only with the socialist countries in the East. In
1957 this administration had a China Division, a
Mongolia Division, and one other division that probably directed trade with Vietnam. The China Division
also controlled trade with the Korean People's Republic, and it is believed that after 1960 the name
was changed to the China-Korea Division.[43] In 1955
trade supervised by this administration represented
a substantial 39 percent of all Soviet trade. This
trade peaked in ruble value in 1959, but by then the
Eastern socialist countries accounted for only 22
percent of Soviet trade. The Sino-Soviet rift then
brought this trade down to minimal levels. In 1970
only 3.7 percent of all Soviet trade was with China,
Mongolia, North Korea, and North Vietnam.

In 1953 the Soviet Union had very little trade
with the developing countries of Southeast Asia and
the Near East. But now Soviet interest in these nations was growing; and, since the Eastern Administra-

tion had been converted to an organ dealing only
with socialist states, a new organization was needed.
As a result an Administration for Trade with Countries of Southeast Asia and the Near East was established. It appears that at this time Egypt was considered as being in the Near East. No information
has been made available on the organization of this
administration, but it apparently has special divisions or offices for each of the most important countries and for the several areas of the region. In
essence the Administration for Trade with Countries
of Southeast Asia and the Near East is an expanded
successor to the Eastern Administration, which handled
trade with the underdeveloped border states. In
1955 trade with this region (including Egypt) totaled
only 146.7 million rubles ($163 million), or 2.5 per-
cent of total Soviet trade. By 1970 this trade (excluding the United Arab Republic) had multiplied to
1.2 billion rubles ($1.3 billion), or 5.5 percent of
Soviet trade. It is interesting to note that 60
percent of this trade was with one country--India.

A fourth regional administration established by
the 1953 reorganization was the Administration for
Trade with Western Countries. This administration
regulates trade with the nonsocialist countries of
Europe, North America, Latin America, Australiasia,
and Japan. Since most African countries were still
controlled by major European powers, this administration originally supervised all trade with African
nations. As was true with the last administration,
little has been published about the organizational
structure of this administration. In 1957 it was
known to have special offices for trade with South-
west Europe, Central Europe, and northern countries.[44]
It may be surmised, however, that there are now special offices for such major trading partners as Japan,
Great Britain, West Germany, France, and Italy, as
well as offices for other European countries, North
America, South America, and Australasia. When this
administration was organized in 1953, trade volume
with the West was quite low because of restrictions
imposed by the Battle Act and similar regulations.
In 1955 trade with these countries totaled 1.0 billion rubles ($1.1 billion), or 17.2 percent of Soviet
trade. By 1970 this trade had risen to 4.8 billion

rubles ($5.3 billion), or 22.3 percent of total trade.
Over three-fourths of this 1970 trade was with Western Europe and half was with only four countries--
Great Britain, West Germany, France, and Italy. For
the first time Japan was the Soviet Union's largest
single nonsocialist trading partner.

In 1953 Egypt, Ethiopia, Libya, and Liberia
were the only countries in Africa that could be considered independent (excluding the Union of South
Africa). Between 1955 and 1958 Morocco, Sudan,
Tunisia, Ghana, and Guinea gained their independence
and 15 countries in Black Africa were just a step
away from the year of mass independence--1960. Realizing the import of this transition, the Ministry of
Foreign Trade in 1959 organized an Administration
for Trade with Countries of Africa.[45] Defining the
term literally, the countries of Africa include the
United Arab Republic, the Arab countries of North
Africa, and the countries of Black Africa. (The
Soviet Union conducts no trade with Rhodesia or the
Republic of South Africa.) To set up this administration the United Arab Republic was transferred
from the Administration for Trade with Countries of
Southeast Asia and the Near East and the other countries were transferred from the Administration for
Trade with Western Countries. In 1955 trade with Af-
rican countries was a scant 38.5 million rubles
($42.8 million), or 0.6 percent of total Soviet trade.
By 1970 this trade had exploded to 1.0 billion rubles
($1.1 billion) and 4.7 percent of Soviet trade. At
all times the United Arab Republic (Egypt) accounted
for about two-thirds of this trade.

This regional departmentalization of the Ministry of Foreign Trade is a radical departure from the
prewar organization and reflects the changed conditions in Soviet trade. Now foreign trade is regulated and controlled by both product-oriented import-
export administrations and by geographical-political-
oriented regional administrations. The five trade-
political or regional administrations work with all
countries within their regions. One of the most important functions of these administrations is the
control over the trade delegations assigned to the
countries in their region and the coordination of
the activities of all Soviet foreign trade organiza-

tions in the field of trade relations. Other functions include the study of the economies, foreign
trade, and economic policies of their countries; the
development of better economic relations with these
countries; and negotiation with official delegations
from countries in the region.[46]

Functional-Staff Administrations

To provide unified guidance and support for its
varied operations, the Ministry of Foreign Trade
utilizes a number of functional-staff administrations.
Some of these administrations date back to 1920; the
most recent addition, the State Inspectorate for
Quality of Exports, was established in 1949.

The Agreements-Legal Administration prepares
trade agreements, treaties, and protocols and helps
prepare standardized contracts for the purchase and
sale of goods. It also proposes laws for the USSR
related to trade. This administration has Legal,
Contract, and Translation Departments.[47]

The Plan-Economics Administration has a Planning
Department that participates in the preparation of
and controls the fulfillment of the various foreign
trade plans. These plans include an import plan, a
plan for the distribution of imports, an export plan,
a plan for the supply of export goods, a currency
plan, a foreign trade transport plan, and income and
expense plans for the monopoly foreign trade corporations. This department works with all the ministry
administrations and also coordinates the activities
of the planning offices in the export and import administrations and the plan-economics offices in the
monopoly foreign trade corporations. An Economics
Department conducts worldwide economic and foreign
trade analyses, and the Statistics Department prepares and publishes the official foreign trade statistics of the Soviet Union.[48]

The Currency Administration works with the State
Planning Office (Gosplan), the Ministry of Finance,
and the Plan-Economics Administration in preparing
and controlling the fulfillment of the currency plan.
It also sets up payments and credit balances by currency and by country, supervises the fulfillment of

payment agreements and the clearing of accounts with
other countries, issues permits for the payment for
exports, and controls the foreign currency accounts
of the monopoly foreign trade corporations.[49]

The Transport Administration plans for the rail-
road, river, and sea transport of goods in foreign
trade and sees that transport goals are met. In carrying out its functions, this administration works
closely with the Ministry of Railways, the Ministry
of the Merchant Marine and its monopoly foreign trade
corporation Sovfrakht, and other transport authorities. It also works with similar organizations to
coordinate the transport of foreign trade goods with
other socialist countries. The Transport Administration has separate departments handling rail transportation and water transportation, and a department
for planning and accounting. This administration
also controls the activities of the monopoly foreign
trade corporation Soyuzvneshtrans.[50]

The functions of the Main Customs Administration
were spelled out in the tariff law of May 5, 1964.
These functions include the development of tariff
policies, preparing and publishing tariff rates and
regulations, supervision of customs activities
throughout the USSR, participation in international
tariff conferences, and supervision of antismuggling
activities.[51]

The State Inspectorate for Quality of Export
Goods is an autonomous administration. It is charged
with inspecting export goods and insuring that they
meet various technical or contractual standards.
This inspectorate has inspectors at factories, at
ports, and at points en route. When required, these
inspectors issue quality certificates.[52]

The Scientific-Research Economic Institute handles the foreign trade intelligence activities of
the Ministry of Foreign Trade. To carry out this
work it has several specialized offices. Offices
for the study of the economies of capitalist and
socialist countries study the economic and foreign
trade activities of specific countries, searching
for the possibilities for developing trade relations.
Offices for machines and equipment, manufactured
goods, and agricultural goods study foreign markets
for prices, the organization of foreign trade, and

for possibilities of Soviet exports and imports. A
price office analyzes price trends in internal markets abroad. A firms office studies the activities
of foreign firms that are of special interest to the
Ministry of Foreign Trade. A foreign commercial information office studies technical data regarding
goods and freight markets and publishes a <u>Bulletin
of Foreign Commercial Information</u>.[53]

In addition to these functional-staff offices,
there are a number of other staff offices handling
such mundane functions as personnel, central accounting, general administration, archives and library,
and protocol.

COUNCIL OF MINISTERS OF THE USSR

Prior to 1957 the Ministry of Foreign Trade was
the sole agency charged with foreign trade operations
and control. In that year, however, the Main Administration for Economic Relations with Countries of
the People's Democracy of the Ministry of Foreign
Trade became the State Committee for Foreign Economic
Relations, reporting to the Council of Ministers of
the USSR. In addition to managing the activities
of the foreign aid corporations, this committee proposes technical development projects to the Council
of Ministers, works with other organizations to provide in-plant training and other technical assistance,
proposes foreign aid study projects for the various
ministries, participates in international conferences
on economic collaboration, and negotiates and works
with the Ministry of Foreign Trade, the Ministry of
Finance, and the State Bank in carrying out its functions. In setting up this committee the Council of
Ministers retained some of the control functions that
had previously been held exclusively by the Ministry
of Foreign Trade.[54]

Between 1962 and 1964 three additional state committees were organized under the Council of Ministers,
and several ministries were granted the right to deal
abroad. As a result of these changes, the Council
of Ministers assumed more direct control over foreign
trade. Specifically, the Council of Ministers appoints the minister of foreign trade and the heads

of the several state committees; supervises the Ministry of Foreign Trade, the State Committee for Foreign Economic Relations, and the foreign trade activities of the other state committees and ministries; takes whatever measures are needed to fulfill the foreign trade plans; and provides leadership in such matters as relations with foreign governments.[55] Further, the Council of Ministers determines which organizations can engage in direct foreign trade operations, resolves the most important questions of the state direction of foreign trade, and coordinates day-to-day and long-term activities of the various ministries, state committees, and other agencies operating in the sphere of foreign trade.[56] The term "monopoly of foreign trade" can best be interpreted as a monopoly of state control over foreign trade-- a monopoly now held by the Council of Ministers.

AUTHORIZED LOCAL REPRESENTATIVES

To control foreign trade activities within the Soviet Union, the Ministry of Foreign Trade utilizes a network of authorized local representatives. These representatives are charged with controlling the local activities of all organizations involved in foreign trade and supervising all Ministry of Foreign Trade organizations in their territory. Some of the specific duties of these representatives are to seek out goods for export; assist the monopoly foreign trade corporations, quality control inspectors, and port and border stations; supervise fulfillment of the plan; and receive and negotiate with foreign trade delegates.[57] To carry out these functions the authorized local representatives must rely on their powers of persuasion, for they have no legal power to enforce their orders. This is usually no problem, since the representatives can always call upon the Ministry of Foreign Trade, which does have such powers. The first authorized local representatives were assigned in 1922, and it is interesting to note that their functions have remained essentially the same.[58]

The chain of command from the functional-staff and other administrations of the ministry to the

authorized local representatives is not very clear.
In the early organization there was a clear distinction, in that the local representatives reported to
a central Local Authorized Representatives Administration, which then coordinated with the central
staff.[59] In 1930 the heavy export orientation of
these representatives was reflected by the conversion
of this administration into the Local Representatives
Sector of the Export Administration.[60] There is no
mention of such a section in the current organization,
but it must be assumed that the four export administrations collectively control the activities of the
authorized local representatives and that communications with these representatives are through the export administrations.

In May 1957 the Soviet Union reorganized its
industrial system. In each republic a Council of
National Economy (Sovnarkhoz) was established to administer all industry and construction in the republic.[61] To conform with this pattern the Ministry of
Foreign Trade assigned local authorized representatives to the Council of Ministers of each republic.[62]
In doing so the ministry reverted to a pattern followed prior to World War II but abandoned during the
war.

At the end of 1958, the Council of Ministers of
the USSR approved a plan for the establishment of
Committees for the Promotion of Exports in each of
the republics. The authorized local representatives
assigned to the republics represented the Ministry
of Foreign Trade on these committees. Other members
were representatives of the State Planning Commission,
the Ministry of Finance, the Council of National Economy of the republic, cooperatives, and other organizations. Each of these committees was charged with
developing exports and increasing the interest of
local organs in widening the availability of goods
for export.[63] Because of the emphasis on promotion
rather than control, these committees are quite different from the Export Conferences attached to each
republic's Council of Ministers in 1931. This earlier organization had wide control powers, since the
chairman of the Council of People's Commissars of
the republic was always the chairman and, in addition
to the authorized local representative, the other

members were the directors of local organs of power
that were interested in export work.

TRADE DELEGATIONS ABROAD

A distinctive feature of Soviet foreign trade
is the trade representative or trade delegation
abroad. Like commercial attachés and trade missions
of capitalist countries, the trade delegation is an
official organ of the Soviet government and is part
of the diplomatic mission in the country of assign-
ment. The trade delegation conducts market and economic intelligence studies, issues import permits,
and carries out other trade-supportive functions.

The main function of the trade delegation is to
carry out direct commercial operations as an agent
of the monopoly foreign trade corporations. The
trade delegation seeks out buyers and suppliers,
transacts business, and concludes contracts. To carry
out this last function individual members of the
delegation are authorized to sign contracts for one
or more monopoly foreign trade corporations. In some
cases such delegates are specialists assigned from
the corporation involved. In other cases a delegate
is a generalist dealing with diverse products and
corporations.

In addition to its commercial operations the
trade delegation has various regulatory functions.
It regulates Soviet trade with the country of assign-
ment, supervises the activities of Soviet organizations operating independently in foreign markets,
and guarantees the fulfillment of contracts. Other
functions of the trade delegation are to represent
the Soviet Union in the area of foreign trade, promote expansion of Soviet foreign trade, issue permits
for transit of goods, and issue bills of exchange.[64]

The staff and internal structure of the trade
delegation vary from country to country, based on
the trade volume with the country, the importance of
this trade, and other factors. In larger trade delegations the functions are divided into such offices
as export, import, and economic; and in some instances the export-import offices are further subdivided by product areas.[65]

In certain countries the Soviet Union does not have trade delegations. In such cases the functions are usually carried out by trade counselors or trade attachés. Frequently this is a transitional stage, and the trade counselor or attaché is soon replaced by a trade delegation. In the United States, however, the legal status and diplomatic immunity of the trade delegation have never been palatable. As a result the trading functions in the United States are carried out by Amtorg Inc., which is incorporated in New York; and the regulatory and other functions are conducted by a commercial counselor attached to the Soviet Embassy in Washington, D.C.

Prior to World War II trade representatives or delegations were assigned only to the countries of the West. Central control over these delegations was exercised by a separate Trade Representative Office. Following the war the Ministry of Foreign Trade set up five regional administrations, and control over the trade delegations was shifted to these administrations.

SUMMARY

When foreign trade was nationalized in 1918, a Foreign Trade Council was established to exercise control over this trade. In 1920 the blockade of Soviet Russia was ended, and a People's Commissariat of Foreign Trade replaced the Foreign Trade Council. This commissariat, now called the Ministry of Foreign Trade, has been continued to the present time. During Stalin's reign the Ministry of Foreign Trade exercised an absolute monopoly of foreign trade control. Beginning in 1957 the Council of Ministers of the USSR displaced the Ministry of Foreign Trade as the chief executor of the monopoly of foreign trade, although most of this control is still exercised through the Ministry of Foreign Trade.

Foreign trade control is exercised by three arms of the Ministry of Foreign Trade: the central office of the ministry, the authorized local representatives, and the trade delegations abroad. The authorized local representatives are assigned to each of the union republics and, under the guidance of the

export administrations, control all foreign trade
activities within the republic. The trade delegations abroad are assigned to the countries with which
the Soviet Union maintains trade relations. The
trade delegations, which are supervised by five regional administrations, control all trade operations
between the Soviet Union and the countries of assign-
ment and carry on direct commercial operations. The
organization and duties of the authorized local representatives and the trade delegations abroad have
changed relatively little since the 1920's.

The central office of the Ministry of Foreign
Trade, however, has undergone a series of changes.
Prior to World War II most of these changes were at-
tributable to a growing volume of trade. In the
postwar period the major changes were a result of
the Soviet extension of its influence over Eastern
Europe and a reorientation of Soviet trade patterns.
Whereas the prewar central office was geared for
trade with the developed countries of the West, this
situation was reversed after the war. At the same
time Soviet trade volume and diversity expanded
dramatically. As a result the operations areas of
the ministry were reorganized into a series of regional administrations and a series of export and
import administrations. It can be expected that this
structure will continue to change to accommodate
changes in Soviet economic and political policies.

4

SOVIET FOREIGN
TRADE FINANCING

Financing is absolutely essential to foreign trade. This chapter will discuss the unique character of the Soviet financing of foreign trade activities. The first section will discuss the origins, nature, and foreign trade functions of such organizations as the Moscow Narodny Bank, Ltd., the Bank for Russian Trade, Ltd., the State Bank, the Foreign Trade Bank, the International Bank for Economic Cooperation, and the International Investment Bank. The next section discusses the development of the Soviet ruble, the unique nature of this currency, and its importance to Soviet foreign trade. The last section covers foreign credits to the Soviet Union, their place in Soviet trade, and the special problems created by the renunciation of Tsarist debts. Soviet credits to other countries constitute another aspect of Soviet foreign trade financing, but they are discussed in detail in later chapters.

ORGANIZATIONS FOR FINANCING
FOREIGN TRADE

In the initial days of Soviet rule, banks were considered to be an unnecessary capitalistic insti-

tution. For this reason the Bolsheviks abolished
all banks and banking facilities. In 1921, however,
a State Bank (Gosbank) was established and was followed shortly by several other banks. The most important of these subsequent banks began as a private
bank on a concession basis, but shortly thereafter
it was nationalized and converted into a State Foreign Trade Bank. Another of these banks was one
that had been organized by the cooperative associations prior to the Revolution and was reestablished
by the Soviets in 1922. Following World War II
there was a movement toward a unified Soviet bloc
bank. This movement finally resulted in the organization of two banks--one for commercial transactions
and one for economic development credits. Each of
these banks and its relationship to foreign trade
will be discussed below.

Bank for Russian Trade, Ltd.

Soviet foreign trade began in 1920 with the establishment of the trading firm Arcos Ltd. in England. For the first three years of its operations,
Arcos Ltd. carried on its own financing functions
with funds it had deposited in British banks. The
development of a multitude of Russian trading organizations during 1923 resulted in a rapid growth of
these financing functions. Ultimately these functions became quite numerous and broad; and on July
5, 1923, a separate Arcos Banking Corporation was
founded. All Soviet funds in England, except those
in the Moscow Narodny Bank, Ltd., were transferred
from various British banks to this single repository.[1]
The exact functions of this bank are not known, but
it appears that its main purpose was to serve as an
intermediary between the Soviets and foreign banks.
Being located in London, the world's banking capital,
it was ideally situated for this purpose.

In 1926 the name of the Arcos Banking Corporation was changed to the Bank for Russian Trade, Ltd.[2]
It appears that with the establishment of the monopoly export-import corporations in 1930 and the credit
reform of the same year, the Bank for Russian Trade,
Ltd. was found unnecessary and was liquidated. From

that date on all Soviet banking activities in England
have been carried out by the surviving Moscow Narodny
Bank, Ltd.

Moscow Narodny Bank, Ltd.

Prior to World War I the cooperatives of Russia
banded together and founded the Moscow Narodny Bank
as a cooperative institution. This institution provided all the credit facilities needed by the pre-
revolutionary cooperatives, both for internal operations and for foreign trade.

When the Bolsheviks came to power, they liquidated the home office of the Moscow Narodny Bank
along with all other banks. After being admitted to
the International Congress of Cooperatives in 1921,
Soviet cooperatives entered the foreign markets. It
was soon realized that a special type of banking
facility to serve the needs of the cooperatives was
again required. As a result the All-Cooperative
Bank (Vsekobank) was founded by the decree of December 2, 1922.[3]

The All-Cooperative Bank concentrated its efforts on the internal financing of cooperatives.
Although it provided some special short-term credits,
most of the export financing for cooperatives was
provided by two subsidiary organizations--the Moscow
Narodny Bank, Ltd. in London and the Cooperative
Transit Bank in Riga, Latvia.[4]

In 1916 the pre-Revolution Moscow Narodny Bank
opened a branch in London.[5] In 1919 Russian emigrés
operating this London branch incorporated it as the
Moscow Narodny Bank, Ltd. When trade relations were
reopened with England, the Soviets challenged the
ownership of the bank; and in 1923 the All-Cooperative Bank won a controlling interest. The financial
resources of the bank were transferred to Moscow,
and the Moscow Narodny Bank, Ltd. began financing
the foreign trade activities of Soviet cooperatives.[6]

The principal aim of the Moscow Narodny Bank,
Ltd. was to finance the import and export operations
of the cooperatives trading in England and elsewhere.
The major commodities so financed were dairy products,
flax, hemp, bristles, horsehair, furs, skins, and

hides.[7] It also assisted cooperatives by issuing
credit guarantees so that credits could be obtained
from other sources.[8] To help finance certain transit trade, the Moscow Narodny Bank, Ltd. set up a
subsidiary Cooperative Transit Bank in Riga, Latvia.
The latter bank made advances against goods in transit; attracted foreign capital by rediscounting
bills, credits, and guarantees; issued guarantees to
foreign firms; and facilitated all financial and
foreign exchange operations of Soviet cooperatives
in Latvia.[9]

With the organization of monopoly foreign trade
corporations in 1930, the cooperatives ceased active
operations abroad. By this time, however, the Moscow Narodny Bank, Ltd. and the Cooperative Transit
Bank were financing more foreign trade activities of
state and public organizations than of cooperatives.[10]
As a result of the credit reform of 1930, the Bank
for Russian Trade, Ltd. in London was liquidated and
the Moscow Narodny Bank, Ltd. continued as the sole
Soviet bank in England.

Following World War II the Moscow Narodny Bank,
Ltd. continued to serve as the London banker for the
Soviet foreign trade organizations. It also carries
on a banking business on behalf of some of the other
Communist countries of Eastern Europe.[11]

The original Soviet "owners" of the Moscow
Narodny Bank, Ltd. were the All-Cooperative Bank and
three cooperative subsidiaries domiciled in England.
Although all of these organizations were liquidated,
the assets were evidently transferred to some other
agency and bank operations continued. In 1963 it
was announced that the Foreign Trade Bank (Vneshtorg-
bank) was buying the shares of the Moscow Narodny
Bank, Lts. for £700,000 sterling.[12]

The State Bank (Gosbank)

The State Bank of the Russian Socialist Federated Soviet Republic was established in October 1921.
When it was established, it was intended that it
should have a complete monopoly over all of the
credit transactions of the republic.[13] During 1922
the All-Cooperative Bank, the Industrial Bank, and

the Moscow Municipal Bank were opened; and within
the next two years the Electro Bank and the Foreign
Trade Bank were founded.[14] Now the credit responsibilities were in several hands, but the State Bank
remained the most important and the largest credit
institution.

In the spring of 1922 the State Bank opened its
first credit specifically aimed at foreign trade.
This credit was for 46 million rubles, "of which 36
millions was used to buy goods destined for export."[15]
The operations of the State Bank in foreign trade
assumed a more important nature during the following
year (1922/23), when it started financing timber exports, which required the investment of large sums.
From this time the State Bank restricted its foreign
trade financing to bulk products such as timber,
grain, and petroleum, which accounted for a high percentage of Soviet trade value.[16] These products were
controlled by relatively few organizations; thus, the
problem of control over the loans was diminished.
At first the State Bank refrained from granting
credit facilities for imports, in view of the absence
of adequate foreign exchange resources and the lack
of connections with foreign banks. This picture
soon changed, and by 1925 the State Bank was the dominant financer of imports.[17]

To handle this increased volume of financing of
foreign trade, a Foreign Department was established
as one of the main divisions of the Central Administration of the State Bank. This Foreign Department
dealt with general matters of policy, relations with
foreign banks, and similar matters. The actual
mechanics of a foreign trade credit were carried out
by the regular banking division or by the Foreign
Trade Bank, which was situated in the same building
and in many ways could be considered the executive
side of the Gosbank's foreign department.[18]

During the period of the New Economic Policy,
the State Bank retained its dominant position in
foreign trade financing. The centralization and
added control made necessary by the Five-Year Plans
soon called for a modification of the Soviet credit
system, both internal and external. This modification came in the form of the credit reform of January
30, 1930.

Internally, this reform eliminated all vestiges of commercial credit and replaced it with bank credit. To insure centralization and control over all credit, all transactions between firms within the Soviet Union were required to pass through the State Bank.[19] The State Bank now also became the accounting headquarters for the Soviet Union.

The monopoly export and import corporations usually maintained several accounts with the State Bank. These accounts were for transactions with foreign firms, suppliers, buyers, banks, the state budget, and transport and insurance organizations.[20]

In external matters the State Bank became the single center through which all of the international accounts of the Soviet Union were required to pass.[21] As will be described below, it became the buffer between an isolated Soviet ruble and the currencies of the world. When an export corporation sold goods abroad, it received English pounds sterling, American dollars, or German marks in payment. These currencies were paid directly to the State Bank, and the corporation received an equivalent ruble credit. Conversely, an import corporation paid the State Bank in rubles and the foreign supplier was paid in his own currency.

Following World War II the State Bank became quite active in the development of trade with the Soviet bloc countries. In 1957 the State Bank's paramount position in this trade was confirmed when a Comecon agreement created a central clearinghouse within the State Bank.[22] This clearinghouse was continued until the International Bank for Economic Cooperation was organized in 1963.

The State Bank's other functions remained fairly constant and the bank maintained its dominant position in Soviet foreign trade financing until 1961. During the postwar period Soviet trade increased sharply, the number of countries with which the Soviet Union traded grew dramatically, and the State Bank began corresponding with an increasing number of foreign banks. As a result it was felt that all operations involving foreign exchange settlements should be concentrated in a single specialized bank.[23] This bank was the Foreign Trade Bank, which was reorganized in 1962 for this purpose. Since that time

the State Bank's role in foreign trade financing appears to have been one of supervision and guidance
and not actual operations.

Foreign Trade Bank
(Vneshtorgbank)

Under the New Economic Policy the Soviet government sought various means of injecting capital into
the economic bloodstream of the country. On August
18, 1922, the Council of Labor and Defense found a
new means when it approved the concession agreement
of the Russian Commercial Bank, which was founded
by the Swedish consortium Svenska Economiaktiebolaget.[24]

The Russian Commercial Bank had as its objectives the promotion of trade and industry all over
the USSR and the development of foreign operations.
To carry out these objectives, the bank was divided
into a series of departments handling domestic finance and a special Foreign Department.[25] Although
it was charged with the development of foreign trade
operations, the Russian Commercial Bank was primarily
interested in the more profitable domestic market.
As a result a vacuum developed in certain areas of
foreign trade financing. The Industrial Bank provided a partial and temporary solution when it set
up a Foreign Department to finance the trade of industrial enterprises and to provide credit facilities
for mixed companies.[26]

On April 1, 1924, the Russian Commercial Bank
was nationalized and converted into the Foreign Trade
Bank. Since it was a joint stock company, 50 percent
of this bank was originally owned by organizations
under the Commissariat of Internal Trade, 20 percent
by the Commissariat of Foreign Trade, and 30 percent
by various foreign trade organizations.[27]

The charter of the new Foreign Trade Bank stated
that its objectives were "to develop the commercial
turnover of the U.S.S.R. in foreign trade and to assist internal trade and industry connected with export and import."[28] It is interesting to note that
the objectives did not include a monopoly of all
foreign trade financing. The State Bank maintained

its control over credit on the larger transactions,
such as the export of wheat, timber, and similar
items, which in the aggregate accounted for almost
two-thirds of Soviet foreign trade. The Foreign
Trade Bank was assigned two fields of responsibility
--the financing of nonbulk trade and the financing
of trade with the countries of the East.[29]

The Foreign Trade Bank devoted a good deal of
its attention to Soviet trade with the border states
of the Near and Far East. When the Russian Commercial Bank was nationalized, the Foreign Trade Bank
acquired control over the Far Eastern Bank with its
branches in Harbin, Manchuria; Shanghai, China; and
several Soviet Far Eastern port cities. At the same
time it acquired control of the Russo-Persian Bank,
which had been opened in Teheran on September 5, 1923,
by the Russian Commercial Bank.[30]

On June 2, 1924, the Council of People's Commissars, together with the puppet Mongolian government,
founded the Mongolian Trading and Industrial Bank,
the first credit institution in Mongolia.[31] The
Soviet shares in this bank were turned over to the
Far Eastern Bank and thus were controlled by the
Foreign Trade Bank. "The primary objects and aims
of the bank as set forth in the statutes [were] to
further the development of economic relations between
Mongolia and the U.S.S.R."[32] Similarly, the Foreign
Trade Bank was involved in the establishment of the
Tuvan Trade-Industry Bank in 1924 in then independent
Tanna Tuva.[33] The Foreign Trade Bank opened a branch
in Constantinople in 1925.[34] Thus, by 1925 the Soviet
Union was operating banks in all of the Asian border
nations with the exception of Afghanistan.

In addition to its banks in the East, the Foreign
Trade Bank also owned, in part or in whole, several
banks in Europe. In 1925 it purchased the Banque
Commerciale pour l'Europe du Nord in Paris.[35] Other
such banks were the Garantie und Kredit Bank für den
Osten in Berlin, the Nordiske Kreditaktieselskab in
Copenhagen, and the Svenska Economiaktiebolaget in
Stockholm.[36] It is not known when and under what
conditions the latter bank came under Soviet control,
since it was the organization that first established
the Russian Commercial Bank in 1922. Furthermore,
the Garantie und Kredit Bank für den Osten was one

of the first banks to make loans to the Soviet Union
in 1921.

Following World War II the Foreign Trade Bank
played a significant role in the economic integration
of the Soviet bloc. The Garantie und Kredit Bank
für den Osten was last reported in 1941. In 1945 or
1946, however, the Soviet occupation authorities established (or reestablished) a Garantie und Kredit-
bank. This bank reportedly had the function of financing all transactions in the Soviet-occupied zone
of Germany and was apparently under the control of
the Foreign Trade Bank. Later this bank was converted into the national bank of the German Democratic Republic.[37] In Rumania a mixed Soviet-Rumanian
Bank (Sovrombank) was established, with the Foreign
Trade Bank representing Soviet interests. In May
1948 all of the important banks in Rumania were
merged with the Sovrombank, which was later converted
into the Rumanian State Bank.[38] In Hungary the Russians obtained a 16 percent share of the Hungarian
General Credit Bank as reparations and another 40
percent by means of a "special" agreement. Again,
control was exercised by the Foreign Trade Bank;
this bank later became the Hungarian State Bank.[39]
There is no information available on the amount or
type of compensation, if any, made to the Soviet
Union when these banks became the central banks of
the respective countries.

In the Far East the picture was slightly different. In Mongolia the Far Eastern Bank had already
participated in the establishment of a central bank.
In Soviet-occupied North Korea, the Foreign Trade
Bank set up a branch.[40] Although it was not reported,
it is assumed that this branch later became the cen-
tral bank of the Korean People's Democratic Republic.
The Far Eastern Bank operated as the central bank in
Manchuria during the period of Soviet occupation.[41]
There is no evidence, however, that this bank had
any effect on the financial structure of the People's
Republic of China.

Up to the end of 1960, the State Bank conducted
most of the Soviet Union's foreign banking operations.
The Foreign Trade Bank was restricted to certain settlement and foreign exchange operations. In August
1962, however, the Foreign Trade Bank was reorganized

and given control over all foreign exchange settlement and credit operations. The accounts of the
monopoly foreign trade corporations that had been
handled by the State Bank were now transferred to
the Foreign Trade Bank.[42] Today the Foreign Trade
Bank performs the operations normally conducted by
international commercial banks. These functions
include the crediting of foreign trade, foreign exchange operations, and settlements for commodity exports and imports. To carry out these functions
the Foreign Trade Bank has established correspondent
relations with almost a thousand foreign banks.[43]

    The Foreign Trade Bank continues as a joint
stock company. The "owners" in 1964 were the State
Bank, the Ministry of Finance, Ingostrakh, the Central Union of Consumers Cooperatives, and various
monopoly foreign trade corporations.[44]

    Today the Foreign Trade Bank's major operations
abroad are the Banque Commerciale pour l'Europe du
Nord in Paris and the Moscow Narodny Bank, Ltd. in
London. The Banque Commerciale specializes in financial transactions between the Soviet Union and
France, and the Moscow Narodny Bank, Ltd. provides
full-line banking services for many countries.[45]
In 1958 the Soviet Union established the insurance
firm Garant Versicherungs AG in Vienna.[46] At that
time it was reported that the Soviets wanted to expand this into a full bank so that banking services
could be provided to non-NATO countries. In 1966
this aim was achieved with the establishment of the
Woschod Handelsbank as a commercial bank in Switzer-
land.[47]

                    International Bank for
                     Economic Cooperation

    Strict adherence to a policy of bilateral trade
agreements between the Soviet Union and the countries
of Eastern Europe, and between these countries themselves, created a problem of clearing accounts. To
avoid this problem, in 1958 the Soviet Union proposed
that the Council for Mutual Economic Assistance
(Comecon) establish a joint bank and multilateral
clearing system.[48] This Soviet bloc bank was to be

supported by deposits from the member national banks.
The headquarters of the bank was to be in Moscow,
and branches were to be located in all of the important trading centers. In June 1958 the directors of
the national banks of all the people's democracies
met in Prague, Czechoslovakia, to discuss the proposed bank. Although the proposal had been made by
the Soviet Union, the directors of the national banks
did not adopt the idea at this time.[49]

As intrabloc trade increased, the limitations
of bilateral payments agreements became more and more
obvious. As one Soviet author put it, this growth
"demanded a new organization of commodity and monetary relationships among the socialist countries,
and a greater role for money not only as a means of
payment, but as a measure of value and a means of
accumulating currency reserves."[50] Toward these
ends a Comecon conference was held in June 1962 to
lay the groundwork for a revised system of intrabloc
economic relationships. In December 1962 the Executive Committee of Comecon accepted the conference's
proposal and concrete plans were prepared. In October 1963, five years after being proposed by the
Soviet Union, the International Bank for Economic
Cooperation was established by the members of Comecon. It began operations in January 1964.[51]

Although the charter of the International Bank
for Economic Cooperation states that other countries
may associate themselves, membership is in fact
limited to member countries of Comecon--Bulgaria,
Czechoslovakia, East Germany, Hungary, Mongolia (a
Comecon member since 1962), Poland, Rumania, and
the USSR.[52] Other socialist countries--China, North
Korea, North Vietnam, Cuba, and Yugoslavia--have
never become members of either Comecon or the International Bank for Economic Cooperation. Control
over the bank's operations is reportedly on a democratic basis. Each member has only one vote in the
council, and each country is represented on the
bank's executive board.[53] Despite this apparent
democracy the International Bank for Economic Cooperation is headquartered in Moscow and in many ways
operates as an intrabloc subsidiary of the Foreign
Trade Bank.

The International Bank for Economic Cooperation
has two major functions--the multilateral clearing
of intrabloc accounts and the provision of seasonal
and short-term commercial credits. The clearing
function of the bank eliminates the need for bilateral
balancing of trade accounts. Now a member country
need only maintain a balance collectively with all
member nations. If there is a positive balance, the
member accumulates reserves of transferable rubles;
if the balance is negative, the member receives a
credit from the bank. It should be noted that a 1957
Comecon agreement had created a central clearinghouse
within the State Bank in Moscow. This clearing operation, however, was for certain limited transactions
over and above the bilateral agreements and in no
way affected the latter.[54] The majority of the
credits apparently are provided to counter seasonal
trade imbalances and usually peak in midsummer.[55]
Credits up to 2.5 percent of the borrowing country's
trade turnover are interest-free. All other seasonal
credits are at the rate of 1.5 percent per annum.
Nonseasonal, short-term credits to cover short-term
imbalances are provided at a rate of 2.0 percent
per annum.[56] By 1969 a total of 8.8 billion rubles
in short-term credits had been granted by the bank,
with 2 billion rubles of this total in 1968.[57]

To carry out its operations the International
Bank for Economic Cooperation has fixed and reserve
capital, special funds, assets on current account,
and deposits. The fixed capital was originally set
at 300 million 1961 rubles ($333 million) and was to
be contributed by members in proportion to the volume
of exports. These contributions were to be made in
gold, freely convertible currencies, or a new transferable ruble. The contribution quotas in millions
of transferable rubles were USSR, 116; East Germany,
55; Czechoslovakia, 45; Poland, 27; Hungary, 21; Bulgaria, 17; Rumania, 16; and Mongolia, 3. In all of
its transactions, the International Bank for Economic
Cooperation uses the transferable ruble. If a member
country accumulates a surplus with the bank, this
surplus will be in transferable rubles, which can be
used only within Comecon. As a surplus-producing
country, Poland unsuccessfully argued that all deposits should be made in gold or convertible curren-

cies and that all surpluses should be paid in gold
or convertible currencies, which can be utilized
anywhere.[58]

The International Bank for Economic Cooperation
has apparently served its purpose quite well. In
1970 one Soviet writer claimed: "The credit and
clearing operations in transferable rubles contributes
to the development of foreign trade and other economic
activities between the countries which are members
of the IBEC. . . . "[59] To put it in other terms,
the International Bank for Economic Cooperation represents one of the final steps in total economic integration of Comecon.

International Investment Bank

A last bank involved in the financing of Soviet
foreign trade is the International Investment Bank.
Founded in 1970, its main function is to make medium-
term (up to 5 years) and long-term (up to 15 years)
credits for the purchase of complete plants, industrial equipment, and technical assistance.[60]

Like the International Bank for Economic Cooperation, the International Investment Bank is technically
a creation of Comecon. Its initial capital was 1
billion rubles ($1.1 billion), of which 70 percent
was to be in transferable rubles and 30 percent was
to be in gold or convertible currency. Contributions
of capital in millions of rubles were USSR, 399;
East Germany, 176; Czechoslovakia, 130; Poland, 121;
Bulgaria, 85; Hungary, 84; and Mongolia, 4.5. It is
interesting to note that Rumania, while remaining in
Comecon, refused to participate in the International
Investment Bank.[61]

Although at first glance this bank might appear
to be nothing more than an internationalization of
the Soviet Union's aid program to the bloc, the real
purpose is total economic integration of Comecon.
This can be seen by the fact that the bank emerged
from the 23rd (Special) Session of Comecon, which
was called to investigate means of developing economic
integration of the socialist countries.[62] Konstantinov states this purpose very clearly when he says:
"The main prerequisite for establishing the I.I.B.

has been the further development of socialist economic
integration, above all, through the expansion of cooperation in the sphere of material production, on
the basis of co-ordination of the national economic
plans and extension of specialization and cooperation
of production."[63]

SOVIET MONEY AND FOREIGN TRADE

There have been several distinct stages in the
development of the Soviet ruble. For five years
following the Revolution the ruble was a printing
press currency. In 1922 a gold ruble was introduced;
and there was a short period of dual currency that
ended in 1924, when the gold ruble emerged as the
Soviet Union's single currency. Two years later the
Soviet ruble went off the gold standard and became
isolated from world foreign exchange, making exchange
values almost meaningless. Following World War II
the Soviets returned to a nominal gold standard, but
the ruble remained isolated. An exception to this
isolation was the use of the ruble in intrabloc
trade, and in 1963 this use became formalized with
the creation of a so-called transferable ruble.

Post-Revolution Inflation

The foreign trade transactions of Tsarist Russia
were financed in much the same manner as in other
countries. The basic unit of exchange was the gold
ruble, which contained 11.95 grains of pure gold.[64]
In accord with regular gold standard practices, the
ruble was freely convertible with gold and all other
currencies based on gold. Immediately after the
declaration of World War I, however, the State Bank
stopped exchanging bank notes for gold. As a result
all gold and silver money was hoarded, and inflation
became the rule during the war. This inflation was
further intensified by the Bolshevik Revolution of
1917. To cover any budget deficits the People's
Commissariat of Finance merely printed new paper
money called Soviet notes or Sovnotes.[65]

The extent of the inflation that followed can
be seen from three subsequent devaluations. On
November 3, 1921, a new Sovnote ruble equal to
10,000 of the preceding Sovnote rubles was issued.
The value of the ruble continued to slip; and on
October 24, 1922, a new Sovnote ruble was decreed
as equivalent to 100 of the rubles of November 3,
1921. Finally, on February 14, 1924, the issuance
of Sovnote rubles was stopped; and on March 7, 1924,
a redemption rate of one gold ruble for each 50,000
of the October 24, 1922, rubles was established.
As a result of these revaluations, the gold ruble of
1924 was worth 50 billion 1917 Sovnote rubles.[66]

The rapid depreciation of the Sovnote ruble made
this currency almost useless for foreign trade purposes. To correct this situation a new ruble con-
taining 11.95 grains of gold (identical to the prewar ruble) was issued on October 11, 1922. Based
on the gold standard, this new currency was completely
convertible and became the basic currency for foreign
trade purposes. When the gold ruble was first issued, there was no exchange rate between this ruble
and the Sovnote ruble. As a result for about 17
months the Soviet Union had two separate currencies--
one for internal purposes and one solely for foreign
trade. Finally, on March 7, 1924, the Sovnote ruble
was eliminated and the Soviet Union regained a single,
convertible currency based on the gold standard and
used both within the country and abroad.

Following the introduction of the gold ruble in
1922, the exports of the Soviet Union were mainly determined, as was the case in other countries, by the
level of prices. The state export organizations
were, in general, guided by the consideration of
whether the foreign exchange obtained for their exports, when converted into rubles at the current
rate of exchange, yielded a profit over the original
ruble cost plus freight and other charges.[67] The
direct relationship between internal price levels,
rates of exchange, and gold movements, which is
typical in the capitalist economy, was clearly of
importance to the Soviets at this time. In 1925 it
was reported that "the [gold ruble] maintains its
value in the same way as any other currency, vis.,

through the trade requirements for money, through the positive balance of the U.S.S.R. in its transactions with other countries."[68] Despite this braggadocio, A. V. Baikalov reported that after the monetary "reform in 1923-24 no official rates of exchange were regularly quoted for the rouble abroad; and unofficial rates continuously fell. Thereupon increasing quantities of roubles were offered in foreign countries, and the financial interests of the Soviet Government suffered."[69] It is probable, however, that the relative stabilization resulting from the introduction of the gold ruble prevented a much more serious exchange situation from developing out of the Sovnote inflation.

The Isolated Ruble

On July 9, 1926, the Soviet Union forbade the export of Soviet currency and foreign exchange.[70] This decree was followed by the resolution of the Central Executive Committee and the Council of People's Commissars of March 21, 1928, which stated:

. . . . .

3.   It is hereby forbidden to send or take abroad bank-notes of the U.S.S.R. State Bank, State-Treasury-Notes and metallic currency of the U.S.S.R. or bills made out in the currency of the U.S.S.R.

. . . . .

6.   Bank-notes of the State Bank of the U.S.S.R., State-Treasury-Notes and metallic currency of the U.S.S.R., and bills in the currency of the U.S.S.R. may only be brought into the U.S.S.R. from abroad on condition that proof is furnished as to their having been taken out of the U.S.S.R. before August 1st, 1926.[71]

. . . . .

By these actions the Soviet ruble was entirely isolated from the world currencies and became a strictly national currency. No longer was the ruble quoted on international markets.[72] The only exchange

rate was that established by the State Bank, and it
was based on a nominal gold content. Since this
rate was based on the parity of 1926 and did not
change with changes in the value of gold, it soon
became unreal; and all of the foreign trade of the
Soviet Union was carried out entirely in foreign currencies. The only purpose served by the official
rate of exchange was to afford a certain basis for
an estimation of the value of imports and exports.
No longer did exporting for profit in the traditional
sense exist. In its place was a system of exporting
merely to obtain the means of paying for the planned
imports. The actual rates of exchange were relatively
unimportant; what was important was the marginal
utility of both the exports and the imports. Thus,
those commodities having the least marginal utility
in the Soviet Union would be exchanged abroad for
those commodities having a high marginal utility.[73]

As a result of the rise in internal prices and
the complete isolation of the ruble from other currencies, it became impossible to determine whether
the prices obtained for Soviet exports represented
a loss or a profit on internal prices or production
costs. As an example let us assume an exchange rate
of one ruble to $1.11 (the "official" rate from
January 1961 to April 1972). Let us further assume
that Raznoimport buys 10 metric tons of aluminum at
an internal price of 10,000 rubles ($11,000) and
sells it abroad at the world price of $6,400. Stanko-
import then buys a piece of equipment for the $6,400
and sells it at an internal price of 12,000 rubles
($13,330). Obviously the official exchange rate
overvalues the ruble. This overvaluation differs,
however, from commodity to commodity, depending on
its planned utility. By keeping the ruble completely
isolated from world currencies, internal economic
development can be held closer to the plan. The
Soviets found no real need to have any other type of
exchange, since all their foreign transactions were
carried on in foreign currencies.

Thus, by 1928 the Soviet Union had attained the
position outlined by Fichte some 127 years earlier
in his Der Geschossene Handelstaat.[74] It is not
clear, however, whether this change was a direct
adoption of Fichte's ideas or an opportunistic solu-

tion to the external financial difficulties mentioned
above that merely coincided with Fichte's propositions.

In April 1936 the nominal gold value of the
ruble was ended and the ruble was made equal to three
French francs.[75] By this means the Soviets avoided
the necessity of establishing arbitrary exchange
rates that had little or no meaning. For foreign
trade purposes the ruble now fluctuated on the world
market in direct proportion to the fluctuations of
the French franc. In following months, however,
the French franc was devalued; and on October 1,
1936, the Soviet government established an exchange
rate of one ruble to 4.25 French francs. The French
franc continued to lose value; and on July 19, 1937,
the ruble was pegged to the U.S. dollar at the rate
of one dollar equal to 5 rubles 30 kopeks.[76] Since
all foreign trade was conducted in foreign exchange
at rates of exchange based on the dollar-ruble exchange rate, Soviet trade data in rubles could be
easily converted into dollars.

On March 1, 1950, the Soviet Union ended the
direct relationship between the ruble and the dollar
and revalued the ruble in terms of gold.[77] The new
ruble was made equivalent to 0.222168 grams of pure
gold. Since the U.S. dollar was equivalent to
0.888671 grams of gold, the exchange rate became
one dollar equal to four rubles. One Soviet author
claimed: "The decision regarding the increased exchange rate of the ruble was carried out because the
purchasing power of the ruble was increased as a result of lowering prices in the USSR."[78] Since there
is no relationship between the internal and the foreign exchange ruble, this statement is patently
false. The change had no effect whatsoever on trade
with the West, so the real reason seems to have been
to give the appearance that the ruble was truly an
independent currency.

Cold war politics resulted in yet another revaluation of the ruble on January 1, 1961. At that
time the gold value of the ruble was increased to
0.987412 grams.[79] The nominal value of the ruble
thus became US $1.11. The Soviets made much ado about
this change, claiming that the ruble was the most
stable and the strongest currency in the world. In
actual fact there was no net effect. The first real

change in the exchange rate came on April 3, 1972,
when President Nixon signed the bill devaluing the
U.S. dollar in terms of gold and all other currencies.[80] Following this dollar devaluation the ruble
has a nominal value of US$1.21.

The Transferable Ruble

In the post-World War II period there has been
a definite trend toward making the ruble an important
currency in its own right. For the first few years
after the war, the U.S. dollar was used for all
trading accounts and commercial loans to the countries of Eastern Europe. In April 1949, however,
trade with Poland was referred to in terms of ruble
values; and in the following months bilateral agreements specified that the ruble would henceforth be
used for all trade between the Soviet Union and the
Eastern European countries.[81]

Initially intrabloc trade not involving the
Soviet Union was carried out in local currencies.
New arrangements soon evolved; and by 1955 "the
Soviet ruble [was] used not only for accounts of
the Soviet Union with countries of the people's democracies, but also for international accounts between the countries of the democratic camp."[82] M. K.
Bednarik has suggested that the reason for this
change was instability of the bloc currencies.[83]
Instability could have been corrected by other means,
and in fact since 1958 all clearing agreements have
included a gold clause tying all values to gold and
calling for adjustments if the ruble is revalued.
It is more likely that these arrangements were planned
by the Soviet Union as a step toward a unified bloc
currency and total economic integration of this area.

Although the ruble was used as a measure for
all intrabloc trade, it was not transferable. Trade
was conducted according to bilateral trade and payments agreements, and by definition each pair of
bloc countries was required to have an exact balancing of trade accounts. In accordance with a 1957
Comecon agreement, a central clearinghouse was established within the State Bank in Moscow. The accounts handled by this clearinghouse were supplemental

to the bilateral agreements and were rather insignificant, and imbalances were cleared in convertible
currencies or gold.[84]

In 1963, with the establishment of the International Bank for Economic Cooperation, the Comecon
countries switched to a closed system of multilateral
payments. To facilitate this change a new transferable ruble was created. Now, if Poland had a trade
surplus with Bulgaria, Poland would accumulate ruble
credits that could be transferred and used in any of
the other Comecon countries. The transferable ruble
has the same nominal gold value as the internal
ruble, but like the internal ruble it is not convertible and can be used only within the closed system
of Comecon.[85]

The transferable ruble is not the national currency of the USSR and is not issued by the State
Bank. Essentially it is an accounting device used
for clearing trade balances, making industrial investment credits, and conducting other intrabloc financial transactions. A transferable ruble is created
when payment for an export is recorded by the International Bank for Economic Cooperation, and it is
eliminated when payment for an import is recorded.
The value of the transferable ruble is based on the
prices of imports and exports of the bloc countries.
As these prices approach the goal of a single bloc
price, the value of the transferable ruble will approach the value of the internal ruble.

In late 1970 one Soviet author referred to the
transferable ruble as "the collective currency of
the socialist countries."[86] With uniform conditions
of trade, a trend toward uniform prices, multilateral
payments, bloc banks for commercial and investment
credits, and a general move toward total economic
integration, it is quite probable that the current
trend of the ruble will lead to a uniform currency
for all the countries of Comecon. It is expected
that this action would be accelerated by any similar
move on the part of the European Economic Community
(the Common Market). A further possibility is that
such a currency would be made convertible.

FOREIGN CREDITS IN SOVIET TRADE

One of the first actions of the Bolsheviks after coming to power was to renounce all debts that had been incurred by the Tsarist and Kerensky governments.[87] This decision placed Soviet foreign trade at a serious disadvantage that is only now being overcome. The immediate reaction of creditor nations was to place all trade with Russia on a strictly cash basis.[88] In 1921 some limited short-term commercial credits were made. These were followed by government-guaranteed short-term credits (1926-33), limited long-term credits (1934-40), wartime lend-lease financing (1941-46), an almost total cold war credit freeze (1946-58), and expanding long-term credits on fairly normal terms (1958-71). Each of these developments and the special position of the United States in Soviet foreign trade financing will be discussed below.

Short-Term Commercial
Credits (1921-27)

The first break in the credit front occurred in 1921, when a Swedish industrial and banking consortium agreed to extend to the Soviet Union commercial credits for periods up to 18 months. To protect themselves, the consortium required a deposit of gold as collateral for the credit.[89] Several months later the Garantie und Kredit Bank fur den Osten (which later became a subsidiary of the Soviet Foreign Trade Bank) made a similar credit.[90]

During the next several years the Soviet Union was able to obtain varying amounts of short-term commercial credit from abroad. In England, Arcos Ltd. was able to obtain some commercial credits that it used or passed on to Soviet importing organizations.[91] In the United States various firms extended credits of from six months' to two years' duration.[92] As late as 1927 a consortium of Austrian banks extended a credit of 100 million schillings.[93] All of

these credits, however, were very limited and quite
insignificant. Further, short-term credits in no
way satisfied the Soviet's pressing need for medium-
and long-term financing.

Government-Guaranteed Short-Term
Credits (1926-33)

The Soviets realized that commercial short-term
credits were not a satisfactory answer, and in their
trade negotiations they sought both longer credit
terms and some form of governmental guarantee. The
first success along this line was the trade treaty
with Germany of October 12, 1925, which provided for
up to two-year government guarantees on credits of
up to 60 percent (later 70 percent) of purchase
value.[94] The Soviets claimed that one immediate result of this credit was a switching of trade from
England to Germany.[95] Trade with England did not
actually drop, but trade with Germany did increase
at a more rapid rate. Despite Soviet objections to
a high (up to 12.9 percent) interest rate and other
facets, this guarantee program was evidently quite
successful, since it was renewed and expanded annually through 1935.[96] In 1933 the Germans extended
their credit terms to a maximum of four years.[97]
Thus, Germany became the first country to offer
medium-term credits--terms twice as long as those
offered by Great Britain or the United States.
It wasn't until 1930 that other nations followed
Germany's lead and agreed to guarantee commercial
credits. In the treaty that resumed trade with Great
Britain in 1930, the British agreed to provide such
guarantees. At first these guarantees were for one
year only, but in 1931 they were increased to two
years.[98] Italy followed suit, and immediately trade
with Italy tripled and continued to grow. These
credits were so successful that they were extended
and expanded in 1931 and again in 1933.[99] Short-
term credit agreements were also signed with Norway,
Denmark, Japan, Austria, Poland, Czechoslovakia,
Latvia, and Finland.[100] The terms offered by these
countries varied; but in general they were very
short, usually only from 6 to 18 months. The

Russians had succeeded in getting guarantees but not long terms.

Long-Term Credits (1934-40)

The Soviet Union was dissatisfied with short-term credits and sought longer terms. When making important purchases the trade representatives always asked for longer-term credits--for periods of at least three, four, or five years.[101] When such loans became available, however, Soviet foreign trade conditions had changed; and as often as not the Soviet Union turned down the credits. Essentially the Soviet Union no longer felt that it had to buy great quantities of goods. Imports were severely curtailed, and the Soviet Union became quite autarkic. If a country did not have commodities the Russians considered essential, there was no reason for the Soviet Union to accept credits merely because they were offered.[102]

The first such rejection, in 1934, was a Swedish government loan of 100 million kroner at 5.5 percent for eight years. Not only was this the first bank loan and the first medium- to long-term credit offered the Soviet Union but also it was offered at an interest rate that was about half the existing discount rate on Soviet paper. The loan was to be secured by Soviet government bonds--another first. Despite all of these concessions to Soviet demands, the Soviet Union at first refused this loan. The loan was finally accepted in 1940, but at an interest rate of only 4.5 percent.[103]

Whereas there was no reason to accept unneeded loans, there was every reason to continue efforts to obtain better credit terms from those countries supplying items considered essential. In this vein, in December 1934, the Soviet government notified the German and British governments that the USSR would "refuse to place volume orders in cases where interest and other charges exceed 5 percent annually."[104] Although credit to other countries was at 5 percent, credits to the Soviet Union were usually at 8 to 10 percent.[105] At this time a German loan at 6.5 percent was rejected because the interest

was considered excessive. A year later, however,
Germany offered a five-year bank credit at 5 percent,
and it was immediately accepted.[106] Similarly, a
July 1936 British offer of a five-year credit was
accepted even though the interest was at 5.5 percent.[107] Thus, by 1936 commercial credit had been
replaced to a great extent by financial credit. It
was not completely done away with, however; and in
1935 France offered a three-year commercial credit
at 7 percent, and Italy continued its guarantee program for commercial credits.[108]

The higher rate of interest forced upon the
Soviet Union prior to 1935 was a direct result of
the repudiation of Tsarist debts in 1918. As a
debtor nation the Soviet Union had an excellent record and was rarely delinquent on any repayments. It
took almost 20 years of near-perfect repayment plus
a depression to force the interest rates offered the
Soviet Union down to a more normal range.

Lend-Lease (1941-46)

During World War II the Soviet Union received
large credits and loans from the United States,
Canada, and Great Britain. The first such assistance
was a £10 million British credit for military equipment extended on August 16, 1941.[109] This credit,
which was later expanded, had an interest rate of
3 percent. The only loan from Canada during the war
was for 10 million Canadian dollars for the purchase
of foodstuffs.[110]

The United States, under its lend-lease program,
was the primary financer of Soviet trade during the
war years. Even before deliveries under lend-lease
had begun, the United States advanced between 50 million and 100 million dollars to Amtorg for the purchase of strategic materials.[111] In October 1941
the United States agreed to include the Soviet Union
in the lend-lease program; and on June 11, 1942, a
lend-lease agreement was signed. Credits granted
under this program, when terminated on September 30,
1946, totaled $11.3 billion.[112] Half of the ship-
ments under these credits were in the form of weapons
and military equipment. The remaining half was com-

posed of industrial raw materials, consumer supplies, oil products, and other raw materials.[113] Most of these credits were interest-free and were to be repaid over a 10-year period starting five years after the war. An October 1945 extension bore an interest rate of 2.375 percent and had a 30-year repayment period. The Soviets subsequently claimed, however, that the materials obtained under these credits were "converted into supplies for mutual assistance not subject to repayment."[114] As a result the Soviets have not made any repayments, nor have they completed negotiations for a settlement.

Cold War Credit Freeze
(1946-58)

Although the Soviet Union badly needed financial help for reconstruction and development, the Soviets effectively cut themselves off from the major sources of credit funds in the early postwar period. In late 1945 they refused to negotiate a planned $1 billion credit from the United States. At the same time they refused to participate in the newly formed International Bank for Reconstruction and Development. In 1947 the Soviet Union refused Marshall Plan assistance from the United States. The reasons for these refusals were apparently more political than economic, as was evidenced by Zhdanov's statement in September 1947, after the Soviet Union had turned down Marshall Plan aid:

> The Soviet Government has never objected to receiving foreign, and especially American, credits as a means of accelerating the process of economic reconstruction. However, the Soviet Union maintains that the conditions of the credits must not be of a one-sided character and must not lead to economic and political enslavement of the debtor nation by the creditor nation.[115]

In 1946 the Soviet Union turned first to Great Britain and then to Sweden for assistance. The

English, however, were not in a favorable position
to provide credits and negotiations there were fruit-
less. The Swedish government did agree to a $280
million credit on terms of 3 percent interest and
15-year repayment. Until the thaw of 1958, this was
the only postwar credit received by the Soviet
Union.[116]

During the next few years political relations
between the Soviet Union and the West deteriorated
into the cold war. In response to Soviet actions in
Eastern Europe, the Western nations, at the request
of the United States, imposed economic restrictions--
including a prohibition of long-term credits--on
trade with the Soviet Union. This ban was formalized
in 1952 by the Battle Act, which coerced other nations to follow American anti-Soviet policy on penalty
of cancellation of foreign aid. Until 1958 this
pressure was quite effective, and no credits were extended to the Soviet Union.

Expanding Long-Term Credits
(1958-71)

Following the success of the Sputniks and in the
face of a world recession, the Soviet Union in 1958
launched an extensive campaign to obtain medium- and
long-term credits to finance expanded imports. Although these efforts failed in the United States, a
thaw in the credit freeze was achieved in Great
Britain. The first break was a five-year credit in
1958 for the machines and equipment included in the
Courtaulds agreement for a cellulose-acetate spinning
mill. A year later a German bank extended a five-
year credit to the Soviet State Bank to finance an
order for fishing boats. Soon five-year credits became quite common, and the East-West credit restrictions imposed by NATO specified a five-year limit.[117]

By 1964 the credit freeze was totally impotent
in Europe. In that year French banks broke the five-
year NATO limit and extended credits totaling $322
million on 10-year terms. The British followed suit
and provided $278 million of credit on 15-year terms
for the purchase of complete plants. Italy went
even farther. In 1965 the Italian government extended

a $110 million, 10-year credit for general purchases.
In 1966 the state finance organization, Instituto
Mobiliare Italiano, agreed to a $367 million credit
to finance the construction of a Fiat plant in the
USSR. This credit was for 14 years with an interest
rate of 5.9 percent.[118]

Also in 1966 Japanese companies provided eight-
year credits at 5.5 percent interest for a polyvinyl
chloride plant. More recently there have been credit
differences between Japan and the USSR that have resulted in a reduction of ship purchases there. In
general, however, other countries appear to have no
hesitation in providing medium- or long-term credit
to the Soviet Union. Although American financing of
the planned Kama truck plant is prohibited, a consortium of European banks has indicated its interest
in financing this project--even if the bulk of the
goods and services were to be supplied by American
firms.[119]

U.S. Credits

Prior to World War II, Soviet trade with the
United States was on a basically cash basis. The
only major exception was a $4 million, 5 percent loan
by the Reconstruction Finance Corporation in 1933 for
the purchase of American cotton. This loan, which
was for a period of one year only, was secured by
notes issued by Amtorg and unconditionally guaranteed
by the State Bank of the USSR.[120] After this initial
success, and after recognition of the Soviet Union
by the United States, Amtorg sought further loans on
longer terms and at an interest rate below 5 percent.[121]
To handle this larger trade with the Soviet Union,
the U.S. government established the Export-Import
Bank and authorized it to finance up to $100 million
of trade. In 1934, however, the Johnson Act prohibited long-term private credits to any country in
default on the payments of any obligation to the
United States. The Soviet Union was declared a de-
faulting nation because of its repudiation of pre-
Revolution debts, and as a result this new bank was
never permitted to serve its original purpose.[122]

During World War II, as discussed above, the United States financed most of the Soviet Union's import needs through lend-lease. As the war drew to an end, the Soviet Union sought additional financial assistance for reconstruction. In January 1945 the Soviet Union was reported to be seeking credits from the United States totaling $6 billion on very long terms and at a low rate of interest.[123] Although Stalin apparently thought that the United States had agreed to provide such a credit, no request was ever officially submitted and no credit was ever issued.[124] In November 1945 the Congressional Committee on Postwar Economic Policy recommended financial aid to the Soviet Union, provided she opened her doors to the outside world, revealed her armaments, and fulfilled her political obligations as other governments do.[125] As a result of these recommendations, the State Department invited the Soviets to discuss American credit assistance, and the Export-Import Bank earmarked $1 billion for credits to the Soviet Union.[126] The Soviet Union did not accept the invitation, and no action was taken on this loan. Similarly, the Soviets rejected Marshall Plan aid offered in 1947.

Since World War II, American credits to the Soviet Union have been restricted to 90-day commercial loans, a restriction imposed by the Johnson Act of 1934 and the Battle Act of 1952. The Johnson Act restrictions were invoked not only because of the default on pre-Revolution obligations but also because of the failure of the Soviet Union to repay its lend-lease debts. When lend-lease negotiations were suspended in 1951, the United States was asking for repayment of only $800 million and was willing to accept payment over a 30-year period at 2 percent interest. The Soviets agreed to the 2 percent interest but wanted to repay only $300 million over a 50-year period. Although Khrushchev agreed in 1959 to reopen these negotiations, nothing has been resolved.[127] The Battle Act has prohibited any government loans to the Soviet Union on the basis that the latter is a threat to American security.

In 1958 and 1959 the Soviet Union sought expanded credits from all countries. In a letter to President Eisenhower in June 1958, Khrushchev hinted broadly that the Soviet Union would like to obtain

large-scale credits from the United States.[128]   On
his visit to the United States in January 1959,
Anastas Mikoyan specifically brought up the question
of credits.[129] There were high expectations and
some movement toward relaxation of the Johnson and
Battle Act restrictions at that time, but no changes
were made. Current (1972) efforts may be more successful, but it is believed that Congress will be
very reluctant to change these laws unless and until
the Soviet Union agrees to some form of negotiated
settlement on lend-lease and some measure of military
détente.

SUMMARY

     In addition to organizations for conducting and
controlling foreign trade operations, a trading nation requires some form of organization to facilitate
the financing of this trade, an acceptable currency,
and adequate credit resources. At the time the Soviet Union began trading operations, it had none of
these.
     A State Bank was established in 1921 to handle
all forms of financing in Soviet Russia. Subsequently other banks were organized, including a Foreign Trade Bank. The State Bank retained a dominant
position in foreign trade finance until 1962, when
the Foreign Trade Bank was reorganized to handle all
of these functions. As part of the economic integration of Eastern Europe, an International Bank for
Economic Cooperation was set up in 1963 to facilitate
multilateral trade and an International Investment
Bank was established in 1970 to direct industrial investments within the Soviet bloc.
     The Soviet ruble started as a printing press
currency. A unified currency based on the gold standard was achieved in 1924, but two years later the
ruble became a currency totally isolated from other
world currencies. For a number of years this isolated
currency was valued in terms of the French franc or
the American dollar. In 1950 the ruble was supposedly
"freed" from the dollar and given a nominal gold
value. A comparison with the dollar continued to
be made, and in 1961 the gold value was changed so

that the ruble appeared more valuable than the dollar.   The ruble has remained isolated from most world currencies, but it has become the trade currency of the Soviet bloc.   This position was confirmed in 1963 by the creation of a new transferable ruble, which is usable only within the bloc.

Foreign credits have always been important to the Soviet Union.   Because of the repudiation of Tsarist debts, however, such credits were difficult to obtain and usually were for short periods and at high interest rates.   There was some improvement during the Depression, but this was short-lived.   The United States financed shipments to the Soviet Union during World War II through the lend-lease program. Following the war the Soviet Union refused American credits on political grounds.   Then, as a result of Soviet actions in Eastern Europe, the United States placed a politically based ban on credits to the Soviet Union.   The first break in this ban was made by England in 1958.   By 1964 European countries were willingly providing the Soviet Union with medium- and long-term credits, and today the United States stands alone as the one country that will not provide such credit facilities.

5

SOVIET FOREIGN
TRADE PROMOTION

To assist the operations of the foreign trade organizations described earlier,
the Soviet Union has established various
auxiliary organizations, has participated
in international trade fairs, and has
sponsored and participated in various foreign trade conferences and exchanges of
visits. This chapter begins with a brief
reference to the Scientific-Research Economic Institute and the foreign trade
schools, about which little is known.
Then it will discuss the origins, development, nature, and functions of the All-
Union Chamber of Commerce and its subsidiaries, the Foreign Trade Arbitration Commission, the Maritime Arbitration Commission, and the Average Adjusters Bureau.
The nature and purpose of the affiliated
chambers of commerce abroad will also be
considered. A discussion of international
trade fairs will cover Soviet participation
in fairs and exhibitions abroad, fairs and
exhibitions within the Soviet Union, and
the responsibility for organizing and managing Soviet exhibits. The final part of
this chapter will describe Soviet participation in and sponsorship of various conferences regarding foreign trade and eco-

nomic matters and the Soviet use of trade
missions and visits of ranking Soviet per-
sonalities to promote foreign trade.

AUXILIARY FOREIGN TRADE
ORGANIZATIONS

In previous chapters we have discussed the organizations responsible for Soviet foreign trade
operations, control, and finance. Other foreign
trade activities have been assigned to several additional organizations. These are the Scientific-
Research Economic Institute, the All-Union Academy
of Foreign Trade, the Institute of Foreign Trade,
the All-Union Chamber of Commerce, and mixed chambers
of commerce.

Research and Educational
Organizations

Research in the field of foreign trade is handled by the Scientific-Research Economic Institute
of the Ministry of Foreign Trade. This institute
studies problems of Soviet and world foreign trade,
the situation of world markets, and the trade policies of foreign governments. To handle this work
the institute is organized into a number of special
research offices. The Office for the Study of the
Economies of Capitalist Countries studies the economic and foreign trade activities of individual
capitalist countries and the possibilities for developing trade relations and other types of economic
collaboration with these countries. The Office for
the Study of the Economies of Socialist Countries
handles the same type of studies for socialist countries. Individual product offices for machines and
equipment, manufactured goods, agricultural goods,
and foodstuffs investigate foreign markets to determine possibilities for exports and imports. The
Price Office involves itself with studies of prices
for various products on the internal markets abroad.
The Foreign Commercial Information Office handles
product technical studies and publishes the Bulletin

of Foreign Commercial Information. There is also an
office that develops intelligence on the activities
of foreign firms that are of special interest to the
Ministry of Foreign Trade.[1] The Scientific-Research
Economic Institute also prepares texts and other materials used in the foreign trade schools.[2] In general this institute serves as the research division
of the Ministry of Foreign Trade. It is, however,
treated as an autonomous organization, and thus its
research activities are separated from the stresses
and strains of day-to-day trading activities. An
English writer suggests that the Scientific-Research
Economic Institute also works closely with the Soviet
central intelligence organizations.[3] Since this institute is little publicized, it is difficult either
to substantiate or to refute this claim.

To insure an adequate supply of qualified foreign trade personnel, the Ministry of Foreign Trade
organized two specialized educational institutions.
The All-Union Academy of Foreign Trade was established by the decree of May 5, 1931, and was followed
by the Institute of Foreign Trade on June 17, 1931.
The All-Union Academy of Foreign Trade provides
technical-vocational training in specialized areas
of foreign trade, such as petroleum export, import
of high-technology equipment, foreign trade finance,
and foreign transport. The Institute of Foreign
Trade teaches courses at the university level.[4] Both
of these schools apparently are still operating; but
there is no detailed information available on the
curricula, standards, operations, or success of these
two institutions.

All-Union Chamber of Commerce

A fourth supplementary organization in the
field of foreign trade is the All-Union Chamber of
Commerce. This organization was established in 1932
with the amalgamation of the All-Union Western Cham-
ber of Commerce and the All-Union Eastern Chamber of
Commerce into a single body.[5] The All-Union Western
Chamber of Commerce was founded in November 1921 at
Leningrad for the specific purpose of promoting trade

between the Soviet Union and the countries of the
West.[6] The immediate tasks of this early organization were to distribute information concerning foreign
markets, prices, tariffs, and similar topics within
the USSR; to maintain relations with the chambers of
commerce in the countries of Western Europe, the
Americas, and Japan; and to disseminate information
about Soviet economic life through these channels.
It also arranged for the participation of Soviet organizations in foreign trade fairs and exhibits
abroad.[7]

The background and functions of the All-Union
Eastern Chamber of Commerce were much more varied
and much more interesting. Organized in 1922 as the
Russo-Eastern Chamber of Commerce, its basic function
was "to assist in the economic bringing together of
Russia with the Soviet Republics [in Transcaucasia
and Central Asia], and also with the foreign countries
of the East--Persia [Iran], Turkey, Afghanistan,
Mongolia, China, and Japan on the basis of commercial
interests."[8] At the time of its founding, five major
tasks were assigned the Russo-Eastern Chamber of Commerce: to sponsor trade exhibits in the USSR and in
the Eastern countries; to open Russian banks in these
countries; to establish favorable conditions of trade
with the countries of the East; to establish customs,
transit privileges, and taxes that favor trade with
the East; and to publish a journal dealing with
questions bearing on such trade.[9] A document published in The Times of London, which was ostensibly
the translation of a circular note of the Politburo
of the Russian Communist Party of November 25, 1922,
indicates that the chamber was charged with a sixth
major task--directing propaganda among the Eastern
peoples.[10]

The All-Union Chamber of Commerce was established
on May 28, 1932, as "a public organization for aid-
ing the development and strengthening of the economic
relations of the U.S.S.R. abroad."[11] The active members of the chamber were required to be representatives of state, cooperative, and public establish-
ments, institutions, and organizations. These members form the General Assembly of the Chamber of
Commerce. From this assembly the Council is elected
to handle policy questions. A smaller Presidium is

elected from the members of the Council to direct
the day-to-day operations of the chamber.[12] The
chamber is divided into a number of special sections,
such as the Legal Section, the Section of Merchant
Shipping and Maritime Law, and sections to handle
the specific functions discussed below.

The specific responsibilities of the All-Union
Chamber of Commerce have evolved into a wide range
of foreign trade promotion areas. Today these areas
include contact, research, promotion, exhibitions,
patents, and special services.[13] In the contact
area the All-Union Chamber sets up and develops contacts with national, regional, and international
chambers of commerce and other economic organizations.
It also handles the exchange of specialized trade
missions and general economic delegations with foreign countries. The All-Union Chamber also acts as
a central clearinghouse assisting foreign firms and
organizations in establishing business contacts with
Soviet foreign trade organizations. In this regard
it also acts as a buffer, filtering out any unwanted
contacts with the monopoly corporations.

In the area of research, the All-Union Chamber
of Commerce conducts some research on the economies
of various countries; but for the most part it limits
its research to the activities of chambers of commerce and other organizations promoting international
trade and economic relations in these countries. It
prepares a variety of promotional materials on the
Soviet economy and its trade and economic relations
with other countries. In fulfilling its promotional
responsibilities it disseminates this material to
other countries, issues a magazine, and publishes as-
sorted bulletins and reference materials on foreign
trade subjects.

The sponsoring and organizing of various types
of exhibitions is probably the most important, and
definitely the most active, of the responsibilities
of the All-Union Chamber of Commerce. It sponsors
Soviet trade and industrial exhibitions abroad and
works with Soviet organizations in preparing for
such exhibits. It also organizes international exhibitions in the USSR and supervises trade, industrial, and specialized exhibitions of other countries
in the USSR. This function will be discussed in more
detail in a later section.

One function of the All-Union Chamber that has
become more important in recent years is arranging
for foreign patents and trademarks for Soviet products and organizations and handling Soviet patent
and trademark registration for foreign organizations.
For many years Western suppliers have been reluctant
to sell some items to the Soviet Union because they
have felt that in doing so they endangered their
property rights. To counteract this impression the
Soviet Union has been trying to improve its patent
relationships. In July 1965 they finally adhered to
the Paris Convention on the Protection of Industrial
Property, and in December 1965 the All-Union Chamber
set up a Section for the Protection of Industrial
Property.[14] In this area the chamber works closely
with Litsenzintorg, the monopoly corporation established in 1962 to buy and sell patent rights and
licenses.

In its last area of responsibility, the All-
Union Chamber of Commerce provides a number of special services to both Soviet and foreign organizations. One of these services is the issuance of
certificates of origin for Soviet exports--a function
usually performed by consulates in other countries.
Similarly, the chamber provides various services normally handled by private surveyor firms in capitalist
countries. These services include the inspection and
certification of quality and quantity of exports,
certification of force majeure conditions, and certification of trade and port customs. Although the
All-Union Chamber of Commerce is officially classified
as a "public" organization, there is some question
of its independence in carrying out these certification and inspection functions. It also provides
translation services for foreign trade materials and
coordinates the activities of republic chambers of
commerce.

Arbitration Commissions

Other important functions are handled by the
Maritime Arbitration Commission, the Average Adjusters Bureau, and the Foreign Trade Arbitration Commission, which operate under the auspices of the All-

Union Chamber of Commerce.[15] The Maritime Arbitration Commission was established as a part of the All-
Union Western Chamber of Commerce by the decree of
December 13, 1930. Its job is to handle arbitration
of disputes concerning compensation for the salvage
and the rendering of assistance at sea and disputes
arising from maritime agreements, such as charter
party contracts.[16] The Average Adjusters Bureau was
apparently set up in the early 1960's to handle the
specialized area of settling claims for particular
and general average resulting from damages of goods
at sea. The Foreign Trade Arbitration Commission
was established by the decree of June 17, 1932. It
handles arbitration of disputes arising from foreign
trade agreements, whether these agreements are between Soviet organizations or between a Soviet organization and a foreign firm. The Foreign Trade Arbitration Commission consists of 15 members who are
considered specialists in particular spheres of foreign trade.[17] Each party to a dispute selects one
arbiter from among these 15 members. The arbiters
selected then choose a chief arbiter. The three arbiters are then responsible for producing a workable
and binding solution.[18] Following the decree of
1935, which permitted the monopoly corporations to
make contracts within the Soviet Union, contracts
almost universally included a clause that stipulated
arbitration in the Soviet Union. More recently two
other arbitration clauses have been available. If
desired, a clause can be substituted that provides
arbitration in the country of the claimant or in a
third country (usually Sweden).[19] In all three instances the clause stipulates that the decision of
the arbitration commission used will be binding on
all parties. Soviet-type foreign trade arbitration
organizations have been established within the chambers of commerce of the countries of Eastern Europe,
and arbitration agreements between the Soviet Union
and these countries specify in which country arbitration will be held under various circumstances.[20]
The decisions made by the Foreign Trade Arbitration
Commission apparently have been quite fair to all
concerned, since there is no evidence of any com-
plaints by Western firms or individuals.

Affiliated Chambers of
Commerce Abroad

One of the functions of the All-Union Chamber
of Commerce has been the maintenance of relations
with similar organizations in other countries. It
appears, however, that such relationships have been
restricted to special chambers of commerce established to promote trade between a particular country
and the Soviet Union. Although the members of these
chambers were generally outstanding men of the particular country, the operations of these organizations seem to indicate that they served as chosen
instruments of the Soviet Union.

Prior to World War II there were a number of
these special or mixed chambers of commerce. The
American-Russian Chamber of Commerce is a good example. This chamber was founded in 1925 as a reorganization of an earlier American-Russian Chamber of
Commerce that had promoted trade with Tsarist Russia.[21]
The basic policy of this chamber was to promote trade
with the Soviet Union while remaining clear of all
political matters. The functions of the American-
Russian Chamber of Commerce were to compile figures,
give advice, clear transactions, keep abreast of
trade opportunities, play host to various Russian
trade delegations, facilitate the granting of visas,
and form a liaison between Amtorg and American
firms.[22] This chamber opened a branch in Moscow
that collaborated with the American section of the
All-Union Chamber of Commerce in attempting to develop
better and closer commercial ties between the United
States and the Soviet Union.[23] Because of a sharp
curtailment in Soviet-American commercial trade at
the beginning of World War II, the Moscow office of
this chamber was closed early in 1940.[24] The New
York office continued to operate; but, after the
United States imposed restrictions on Soviet trade
in 1948, it had little to do and was last heard of
in 1949.[25] Similar joint chambers of commerce were
organized in England, Estonia, Czechoslovakia, and
Germany; and a network of correspondent chambers was
set up in the countries of the East.[26]

Following World War II the All-Union Chamber of
Commerce reestablished the Russian-British and Czecho-

slovak-Soviet joint chambers of commerce and established new Finnish-Soviet and Hungarian-Soviet chambers.[27] It is interesting to note that joint chambers of commerce were not established in other Comecon
countries, yet the Czechoslovak-Soviet Chamber of
Commerce has continued to operate and the Hungarian-
Soviet Chamber operates today as the Hungarian "Section." As late as 1962 these four joint chambers
were the only ones in operation.[28] In the mid-1960's
Soviet relations with France, Italy, and Japan improved considerably; and Italo-Soviet and Franco-
Soviet joint chambers of commerce and a Soviet-
Japanese Economic Committee were organized.[29] In
October 1971 the communiqué issued at the end of
Premier Kosygin's visit to Canada called for the establishment of a Soviet-Canadian Commission on Trade
Consultations, and at the same time North Vietnam
announced the creation of a similar Soviet-North
Vietnamese Committee. That these organizations are
not limited to normal chamber of commerce operations
can be seen from the fact that at the fourth meeting
of the Soviet-Japanese Economic Committee in February
1970 it was agreed that the Japanese would build a
port near Nakhodka in the Soviet Far East.

TRADE FAIRS AND EXHIBITIONS

Trade Fairs and Exhibitions
Abroad

Soviet leaders have long appreciated the advantages of propaganda. In the field of foreign trade,
one of the most effective propaganda weapons has
long been the international trade fair or exhibition.
The first participation in such an exhibit by the
Soviets was at the Baltic Fair held in Riga, Latvia,
in September 1921. At this fair "the first lot of
goods manufactured under the Bolshevist regime ever
officially exhibited in a foreign land" was shown.[30]
Most of the goods exhibited were of the wooden handi-
craft type, a commodity that could not serve as the
foundation of a healthy mutual trade. Actually a
good deal of the space of the exhibit was used to

tell the fair visitors about the economic progress
that had been made in the Soviet Union.[31]

In the ensuing years the Soviets participated
in various trade fairs in Europe and in the Near and
Middle East. In all of these fairs and exhibitions,
trade appeared to be secondary to propaganda. An exhibit of raw materials in Turkey in 1924 was accom-
panied by lectures "on the latest successes of Soviet
industry and on the significance of the exhibition
in the establishment of close economic relations between Turkey and the Soviet Union."[32] At the Lyons
Fair in France in 1925, fully half of the space was
devoted to industrial products, although the industry
of the Soviet Union was not yet reconstructed. One-
third of the space was used for exhibits of industrial raw materials, food products, and other items;
and the remaining space was used for other purposes.[33]
The heavy emphasis on industrial goods was a classic
example of propaganda aimed at convincing people that
the Soviet Union was an industrial power. This type
of exhibit was used extensively by the USSR, and in
more recent years the People's Republic of China
has adopted this technique.* It is likely that this
emphasis on direct and indirect propaganda was the
reason for the refusal of the Brussels Commercial
Fair to allow Soviet participation in 1923.[34]

When the world economic crisis worsened in 1930,
the Soviet Union intensified its trade fair activities. At the Milan Fair in 1931 the Russians exhibited, as one visitor described it, every conceiva-
ble commodity; and, although prices were not mentioned at the fair, these commodities were being offered at prices nobody could meet. As an example of
the intensity of Soviet propaganda at the Milan Fair,
in Italy--considered the home of pasta--the Russians
displayed no fewer than 14 types of macaroni.[35] The
following year the Soviet Union participated as
grandly in the Leipzig Fair, the Paris Fair, and the

_____

*The exhibit of the People's Republic of China
at the Damascus International Trade Fair in 1956 emphasized heavy industry, although none of the equipment shown was for sale. In many cases the goods
exhibited were believed to be of Russian manufacture.

Levant Fair held in Palestine.[36] By 1935 this activity had so developed that in that year the Soviets participated in a "whole series of fairs and
exhibitions."[37] The purpose of this Soviet participation was twofold. On the one hand, the lavish
exhibits were propaganda designed to convince fair
goers that the Soviet economy was indeed immune to
depressions and was growing rapidly. On the other
hand, these exhibits served a true commercial purpose
of trying to increase exports in order to pay for
needed imports.

International trade fairs and exhibits became
even more important after World War II. The first
postwar Soviet exhibit was at the fair in Helsinki,
Finland, in 1946. Although the Soviet Union had not
yet recovered from the effects of the war, it "participated in the fair as an industrial power which
exports the products of heavy industry (machines,
lathes, etc.) and various raw materials."[38] Although
in 1947 the Soviets claimed to have received invita-
tions to participate in international fairs and exhibitions from 15 countries, the Soviet Union took
part in between three and six exhibits each year
prior to 1954.[39] Most of these exhibits were held
in the countries of Eastern Europe--Poland, Bulgaria,
Czechoslovakia, Rumania, Hungary, and the German
Democratic Republic. The most important of these
was the annual exhibit at the Leipzig Fair. This
fair was reopened by the Russians in 1946. The Soviet Union did not participate in the fair until 1950,
at which time it became the meeting place for a large
amount of East-West trade.[40]

In addition to the exhibits in Eastern Europe
during this period, the Soviet Union participated in
several exhibits in other countries. The most interesting of these was the Bombay International Industries Fair in 1952, which was attended mainly by the
Soviet Union and the people's democracies.[41] At this
fair M. V. Nesterov, president of the All-Union Chamber of Commerce, attempted to convince the Indians
that because of the Korean War the West would not supply the machinery needed by the Asians and that the
Soviet Union, which was not involved in the Korean
War, could supply this machinery and wanted to trade
with the underdeveloped countries.[42] To strengthen

this argument the Soviet Union offered to sell industrial equipment for rupees or any other soft currency.[43] To intensify the propaganda effect of this
fair, the Soviet Union at the same time held an art
exhibition in New Delhi, participated in India's International Film Festival, and conducted a cultural
exchange program with India.[44] The importance of
this exhibit is that it was held in 1952, prior to
Stalin's death, indicating that plans were already
being laid for a trade expansion program in Southeast
Asia. It would also seem to indicate that the reasons for this program were at least partially economic, since there had not yet been a change in other
Soviet policies in regard to India. Despite all
these efforts Indian businessmen found little need
for trade with the Soviet Union, and in general the
fair was a failure.

The Soviet trade fair program was expanded
rapidly following Stalin's death in March 1953.
From the previous level of three to six fairs or exhibits per year, there was a sudden jump to 11 in
1954, 18 in 1955, and a peak of 30 in 1961.[45] Subsequently this participation leveled off at a lower
level. In 1966 the Soviet Union participated in 15
exhibitions abroad, and in 1969 and 1970 it exhibited
at about 20 fairs and exhibitions.[46]

There was also a major change in orientation of
this participation. First, participation was no
longer restricted to the people's democracies. Initially the Soviet Union was most interested in promoting trade with the West, and in 1954 six of the
eleven fairs in which the Soviets participated were
in the West.[47] As trade with the West developed,
however, Soviet participation in Western trade fairs
and exhibitions was cut back to a minimum. This minimum included the periodic world's fairs at Brussels
(1958), New York (1964), Montreal (1967), and Osaka
(1970). In 1966 this minimum included an exhibition
at Utrecht and, as part of the Soviet drive to increase trade with Japan, the first Soviet Trade Fair
in that country. In 1969 it included only an exhibition at Sydney, Australia.

On the other hand, Soviet participation in fairs
and exhibitions in the underdeveloped countries has
increased constantly as trade with these countries

has developed. In 1954 the Soviet Union participated
in fairs at Izmir, Turkey; Damascus, Syria; and
Jakarta, Indonesia. By 1969 the Soviets were involved with fairs and exhibitions in nine underdeveloped countries in Africa, the Middle East, Southeast Asia, and South America. Furthermore, it is believed that funds devoted to individual trade fairs
in the underdeveloped areas exceeded those devoted
to the Soviet exhibits in Europe.[48] Thus, trade
fairs and exhibits had become an important tool in
trying to win the peoples of the underdeveloped
countries to the Soviet side.

     The Indian Industries Fair held at New Delhi in
1955 is an excellent example of techniques used in
the fairs in underdeveloped countries. This fair
climaxed a successful four-year drive to gain entry
into the Indian market. Scheduled to follow the
signing of the agreement to construct the Bhilai
steel mill, the opening of the Soviet exhibit was
timed to coincide with the arrival of Bulganin and
Khrushchev, who were making state visits to certain
countries of Southeast Asia.[49] To give the display
some additional atmosphere and to attract the general
public, the Soviet Union introduced several noncom-
mercial features, such as an illuminated panel of
the Kuibyshev hydroelectric station, a large plant
on the Volga River then still under construction; a
working model of a blast furnace similar to the unit
to be erected in India by Soviet technicians; and a
television camera in operation. The size and lavish-
ness of the Soviet exhibit, as well as the wide pub-
licity it received, could easily have conveyed the
impression that the Soviet Union and its allies
played an important role in India's foreign trade.
Actually in 1955 the Soviet Union and all of the people's democracies accounted for only 1.7 percent of
India's imports and 2.1 percent of its exports.[50]

     As one Soviet author stated, trade "fairs and
exhibits appear as a convincing means of showing economic achievements and export possibilities."[51] At
the same time they were proven vehicles for propaganda. For this reason all Soviet exhibits have
been designed primarily to attract the public. To
do this the exhibits of all the socialist countries
are usually grouped together to give an impression

of large size, and the Soviet and other pavilions
are lavishly designed. At the International Fair at
Damascus, Syria, in 1956, for example, the Soviet
pavilion was located close to those of the Chinese
People's Republic, the German Democratic Republic,
Czechoslovakia, and Yugoslavia. Since each of these
exhibits was about as large as that of the United
States, an observer could easily receive the impression that this bloc of countries held an industrial
and commercial superiority over the United States
and the other Western countries.

The As in the prewar exhibits, the Soviet pavilion
today is designed to show the great advances made
by the Soviets in industry as well as in other fields.
The Soviet pavilion at a fair in Western Europe is a
good example. An illuminated reproduction of Moscow's Red Square dominated the entrance. On either
side were charts showing great increases in the output of minerals, steel, and power. Much display was
given to alleged expenditures on public health in
the Soviet Union. Light classical music was played
on the upright and grand pianos on display. The
overall theme appeared to be that of an expanding
peacetime economy devoted to satisfying consumer
wants.[52]

The commodities displayed in the Soviet exhibits
are usually designed to impress the observer and are
not intended for sale. During the 1954 fairs it
became apparent that the exhibitors were generally
unable or reluctant to furnish information on prices,
specifications, delivery schedules, replacement parts,
local agents, and distributors.[53] At the 1955 fairs
this situation was changed somewhat; and, at the 1956
exhibit at Damascus, sales orders were being taken
at the Soviet pavilion and small objets d'art and
handicrafts were sold directly to the public. In
1965 the monopoly corporation Novoexport was set up
to handle sales of handicrafts and other objects--
mainly at international fairs and exhibitions. Propaganda continues to be one of the primary aims of
the Soviet exhibits. Pamphlets are distributed in
the Soviet pavilion and speeches are made urging the
Soviet version of "peaceful coexistence," "relaxation
of world tensions," "reunification of East and West
Germany," and the "removal of trade embargoes." To

add drama and magnetism, special propaganda themes
are also used. In 1955 the Soviets played up the
theme of peaceful use of atomic energy. At the
Brussels World's Fair in 1958 space satellites were
successfully used as a theme. Cosmonauts Gagarin
and Titov were exploited at fairs in 1962; and in
1971 the high spots were displays of proton acceler-
ators, laser installations, and microphototypesetting
machines.

The Soviet Union began displaying planes at
various fairs and exhibitions in 1960.[54] In 1965
they participated for the first time in the Paris
Air Show. At this first exhibit the Soviets showed
passenger jets, turboprop planes, an assortment of
helicopters, and a metal glider.[55] The display also
included a Vostok satellite. At the next Paris Air
Show, in 1967, the USSR showed a model of the TU-144
supersonic transport plane, and for the 1971 show
it flew in the TU-144 to share SST honors with the
Anglo-French Concorde.[56] In each of these exhibits,
the Soviet Union has stressed its superiority in
aircraft design as well as in space and aircraft
metallurgy. The advanced technology reflected in
the TU-144 and space vehicles shows a marked contrast
with the early trade fairs, where the Soviets boasted
of their technology but could not deliver. At the
Paris Air Shows the Soviets definitely could deliver
and had their order books always at the ready.

Trade Fairs and Exhibitions
Within the Soviet Union

Prior to World War II there were two distinctly
different types of trade fairs and exhibitions in
the Soviet Union. In 1922 the Russo-Eastern Chamber
of Commerce arranged for the reopening of the Baku
and Nizhni Novgorod fairs. These were trade fairs
in the ancient sense of the term. Merchants from
Persia, Turkey, Afghanistan, Mongolia, and China
brought their goods to these fairs, sold what they
could, bought what they needed, and returned home.
A good proportion of the trade with Eastern countries
was handled by these fairs. In 1930, however, these
fairs were closed and trade with the East was handled
by monopoly corporations.[57]

The second type included various temporary and
permanent exhibitions of foreign goods--mostly from
Western countries. The first such exhibit was an
agricultural exhibition that opened in Moscow on
August 19, 1923. Reportedly there were exhibits by
all of the major countries. Some of the more permanent exhibits at which at least some foreign goods
were shown were the Exhibition of Imported Machinery,
Orgametal Exhibition of Machinery for Heavy Industry,
the Workers and Peasants Inspection Exhibition of
Office Equipment in Moscow, the Ukrainian Import Exhibition of Imported Machinery, and the Exhibition
of Office Equipment at Kharkov.[58]

Following World War II there was a resumption
of industrial and trade exhibits in the Soviet Union.
The first of these exhibits was the Finnish Industrial Exhibit at Moscow in August 1946. With the
exception of this exhibit and an Indian handicrafts
exhibit in 1955, however, these exhibits were sponsored primarily by Czechoslovakia, Hungary, and
Poland--the industrialized people's democracies.[59]

In more recent years these exhibitions of foreign
goods have become points of contact bringing together
foreign suppliers and managers and engineers from
all over the Soviet Union. In the summer of 1959
the United States sponsored a large exhibit in Sokolniki Park in Moscow. Since that time there have
been a considerable number of exhibits. In 1966,
for example, the All-Union Chamber of Commerce organized a Rumanian exhibit, the second British International Exhibition, the first Swiss Industrial Exhibition, seven international exhibitions, and 73
separate specialized exhibits.[60] One of the international exhibitions was Interorgtekhnika 66, an
international exposition on mechanization with exhibits from 1,000 firms from 18 countries. The specialized exhibits are for a specific product area
and a single country. Examples in 1966 were a Danish
exhibit of electronic measuring instruments and an
exhibit of vacuum equipment by the firm Balzers of
Lichtenstein.

B. A. Borisov, president of the All-Union Chamber of Commerce, in 1972 reported that "in the last
five years, $4-billion worth of contracts have been
concluded during exhibitions."[61] Even though U.S.

trade with the Soviet Union has been somewhat restricted, American firms have been active in these
exhibits. In 1971 IBM not only displayed a 360-50
computer at a trade fair in Leningrad but sold the
machine to the Ministry of Chemicals. In May 1972
the American data processing industry put on its own
exhibit at Sokolniki Park in Moscow. The machine
tool makers of the United States have planned a show
for 1973, and the All-Union Chamber of Commerce has
laid the groundwork for an exhibit of American oil-
field equipment.[62]

Responsibility for Fairs
and Exhibitions

In the early years, according to Zhirmunski,
there was little organizational character in the
fairs and exhibitions. Since the interested economic
organizations usually had no part whatsoever in the
planning, the exhibits lacked preparation and thought
and were relatively ineffective. As a result in
1927 the task of conducting Soviet fairs and exhibitions was assigned to the All-Union Western Chamber
of Commerce. From this year the fairs were coordinated and subjected to a rigorous plan.[63] Each year
the Chamber of Commerce draws up a plan for Soviet
participation in international fairs and submits
this plan to the commissariat (ministry) for approval.
Today the All-Union Chamber of Commerce has full
responsibility for all matters regarding trade fairs
and exhibitions abroad and in the Soviet Union, including construction, operation, and dismantling of
the exhibits. In carrying out this responsibility
the chamber works closely with the monopoly corporations that supply the goods and personnel for the
exhibitions abroad.[64]

CONFERENCES AND VISITS

Moscow Economic Conference

In April 1952 a so-called International Economic
Conference was held in Moscow. This conference was

attended by 471 persons unofficially representing
49 countries. In addition to representatives from
all of the people's democracies and 17 European
countries, there were representatives from Burma,
Egypt, Indonesia, Iran, Lebanon, Pakistan, Ceylon,
Israel, Iceland, Argentina, Brazil, Chile, Mexico,
Uruguay, and Venezuela.[65] Although the conference
was ostensibly sponsored by a group of businessmen
who just happened to meet at Copenhagen in February
1952, the real sponsor was the World Peace Council,
which is known to be Communist-oriented.[66]

The stated aim of the Moscow International Economic Conference was the development of foreign trade
on the basis of equality and mutual profitability.[67]
At this time the Soviets announced that their foreign
trade organizations

> . . . could buy in the countries of
> Western Europe, America, South-East Asia,
> the Middle East, Africa and Australia reg-
> ularly exported goods and sell to these
> countries goods they want of Soviet manu-
> facture in such volume that the general
> trade turnover of the USSR with these coun-
> tries in the next 2 to 3 years would amount
> to 30-40 billion rubles or from 10 to 15
> billion rubles a year, compared to the max-
> imum postwar turnover of 5 billion rubles
> in 1948.[68]

At the same time it was announced that the Soviet
Union would purchase various consumer goods during
this period.

The primary aim of the Moscow International Economic Conference appears to have been the abolition
of restrictions placed on the trade of the participating countries with the Soviet Union. As a result
the conference was basically political although based
on definite economic needs of the Soviet Union. In
the spring of 1951 the United States had tightened
the trade embargo on the Soviet Union by the inaugura-
tion of the Battle Act, which required that American
aid be cut off from any country shipping certain
commodities to the Soviet Union or the people's
democracies. This embargo had apparently proved

somewhat effective, and the Soviet Union sought its
end. To achieve this goal all Soviet offers to buy
nonstrategic items were linked with demands for
needed items on the strategic list. Furthermore, by
dealing with private citizens the Soviets apparently
believed that pressures could be generated in the
Western countries for the relaxation of security
controls. At the same time European producers were
offered an "easy" solution to their problems of
shortages, unemployment, rising prices, and reces-
sions.[69] The governments of the West remained firm,
however, and thus the conference produced no results
in the form of increased trade or reduced barriers--
although several front organizations, such as the
British Council for the Promotion of International
Trade and the French organization COFRAC, were set
up to continue the work of fighting against the
trade embargo.[70]

Other Conferences

Following World War II the Soviet Union became
a member of various economic commissions of the
United Nations. At that time it was hoped that the
Soviets would participate actively in the conferences
held by these commissions. The first such conference
was one held by the Economic and Social Council
(ECOSOC) in 1945 to lay the groundwork for an International Trade Organization. The Soviet Union accepted an invitation to this conference; shortly
thereafter, however, it refused to participate in
the activities and began attacking the International
Trade Organization as an American imperialist tool.[71]
At the East-West trade talks held by the Economic Commission for Europe in August 1951, the Russians expressed a willingness to expand trade and to
go ahead with a formal trade conference.[72] A special
conference was called during the following months;
but in August 1952 Gunnar Myrdal, executive secretary
of the commission, announced that despite repeated
queries the Soviet Union had refused to answer the
commission's invitation.[73]
Following Stalin's death the Soviet Union participated in the activities of all of the commissions.

In April 1954 the Soviets proposed a special ECOSOC
conference to debate the "removal of obstacles to
international trade."[74] In 1955 the Soviet Union
announced its interest in joining the International
Trade Organization.[75] When they were informed that
this organization had never passed the formative
stage, the Soviets, in November 1956, proposed a
special international trade agency to be formed
within the United Nations on the basis of the experience of the Economic Commissions for Europe, Asia
and the Far East, and Latin America.[76] At the same
time the Soviet Union proposed a "world economic
conference, for the purpose of developing international trade and economic cooperation."[77] In 1957
various proposals made by the Soviet Union regarding
European economic cooperation were rebuffed by the
Economic Commission for Europe.[78] At a meeting of
the Economic Commission for Europe in 1958 the Soviets unsuccessfully called for a meeting of all
trade ministers to discuss ways and means of developing trade, the development of trade on a long-term
basis (at least eight years), the exchange of technical information on a commercial basis, and the exchange of patents and agreements for production licenses.[79] Apparently smarting from these rebuffs,
the Soviet Union in 1961 charged that ECOSOC and
its auxiliary organizations were controlled by the
West and should be reorganized into instruments for
peaceful coexistence.[80] Failing once again, the
Soviets then assumed a passive stance, participating
at a minimum level in matters relating to the developed parts of the world.

In the Far East the Soviet Union was even more
active, but in a different manner. At the Singapore
conference of the Economic Commission for Asia and
the Far East (ECAFE) in October 1951, the Soviet
Union announced that it was "prepared to enter the
Far Eastern and Pacific trade on a large scale, offering industrial and electrical equipment and agricultural machinery in exchange for jute, rubber,
shellac, rice, copra, spices, tea, tin, and quinine."[81]
In 1953, at the UN Trade Promotion Conference in
Manila, the Soviets announced that they were ready to

discuss "concrete queries and offers for the purchase
and sale of goods."[82] At all of the ECAFE meetings
thereafter the Soviets repeated their proposals and
emphasized that they were following a policy of business only.[83]

Soviet activities in this area were not restricted to conferences sponsored by the United Nations. In April 1955 Soviet trade proposals were
repeated to delegates from Southeast Asia at the International Conference of Asian Countries in New
Delhi, India, and at the Bandung Conference in Indonesia.[84] In 1957 the Afro-Asian People's Solidarity Conference provided the Soviets an opportunity
to present their offers to representatives of Asia,
the Middle East, and Africa.[85]

At the first UN Trade and Development Conference at Geneva in 1964, the Soviet Union made a major
effort to play a dominant role and win the support
of developing nations. Khrushchev sent a message
to the conference charging the West with imperialist
exploitation of the underdeveloped countries and
calling for an elimination of all artificial obstacles to trade. He also sent personal messages to
the delegates in a bid for the goodwill of the newly
industrializing Asian and African countries. The
emphasis placed on this conference can be seen by
the fact that Minister of Foreign Trade Patolichev
personally headed the Soviet delegation. In a speech
to the conference, Patolichev not only promised more
aid and trade but also proposed a new world organization to deal with international trade problems--
especially those of the underdeveloped countries.
Capping this effort, the Soviet Union announced that
it would do away with all tariffs on goods from the
developing countries at the end of 1964--a promise
that was fulfilled by the proclamation of the liberalized tariff for developing countries.[86] At the
second UN Trade and Development Conference at New
Delhi in February 1968, and the third conference in
October 1970, the Soviets played a rather passive
role, allowing the conference to develop as a trade
and economic confrontation between the developing
nations and the industrialized nations of the West.[87]

Delegations and Visits

Prior to 1954 very few groups, with the exception of certain labor delegations, were allowed to visit the Soviet Union. In 1954 various groups were invited to visit the USSR. Among these were official and unofficial trade delegations from France, Great Britain, Finland, Indonesia, Pakistan, Burma, Austria, India, and Japan.[88] The most important of these was a delegation of 33 businessmen from Great Britain. This delegation was given orders for 3 billion rubles of ships and equipment and 1.5 billion rubles of raw materials and other commodities, but as the Soviets themselves admitted:

> The British companies, however, though they very much wanted to get the Soviet orders, could not accept orders for many types of ships, equipment and other goods because they were classified as "strategic" and their export to the Soviet Union was prohibited. As a consequence the programme was put through only to an insignificant degree and the British firms lost profitable orders.[89]

This trade delegation proved to the Soviets' advantage, however, for later that same month Prime Minister Churchill spoke out for fewer trade restrictions and during the summer of 1954 revisions were made in the strategic lists.[90] Also, since 1954 trade missions from Western and developing countries to the Soviet Union have become regular occurrences.

During 1954 and 1955 Soviet trade and technical delegations were dispatched to various countries; and in the summer of 1955 Dmitri Shepilov, then president of the Foreign Affairs Committee of the Supreme Soviet, visited Egypt to discuss trade and aid. In November and December 1955, Bulganin and Khrushchev made a tour of India, Burma, and Afghanistan. Ostensibly this tour was for purposes of goodwill, but the joint communiqué issued at the time of these visits indicated that the actual purpose was the promotion of trade in these areas so as to influence the so-called neutral nations.[91] In March 1956,

Anastas Mikoyan visited New Delhi and announced that
the Soviet Union was willing to accept Indian goods
and raw materials in exchange for Soviet goods.[92]
In April 1956 Bulganin and Khrushchev visited London,
where Bulganin announced that the first objective of
their visit was the expansion of British-Soviet
trade.[93]

In 1959 this use of important personages to promote trade was aimed at the United States. In January, Anastas Mikoyan made unofficial contacts with
American businessmen in Cleveland, Detroit, Chicago,
San Francisco, Los Angeles, New York, and Washington,
D.C. First Deputy Premier Frol Kozlov followed in
June to open a Soviet exhibition in New York and to
lay the groundwork for negotiations by a team of
trade officials. Vice-President Nixon reciprocated
by opening the U.S. exhibition in Moscow in July--
at which time he had the famous "kitchen debate"
with Khrushchev. In September, Khrushchev himself
visited the United States. The pressures were clear,
as were the objectives, which were to loosen or eliminate barriers on trade, to renew most-favored-nation
treatment for the Soviet Union, and to eliminate obstacles to the extension of credit to the Soviet
Union. Although hopes were high, not much came of
these visits.[94]

The next year Khrushchev pledged support for developing countries in their struggle to overcome economic backwardness during visits to India, Burma,
Indonesia, and Afghanistan; visited France; and approved Finland's participation in EFTA on a visit to
that country. Just prior to his resignation in 1964
he toured Denmark, Sweden, and Norway to discuss
trade and to expand existing trade agreements. After
taking office in 1964, Premier Kosygin continued the
trend by covering trade and aid matters on visits to
the United Arab Republic, Finland, Turkey, France,
the United States, India, Iran, Pakistan, Algeria,
and Canada between February 1965 and October 1971.
The communiqué issued after Kosygin's visit to Canada
in October 1971 called for a broad expansion of trade
and the establishment of a joint commission on trade
consultations.

Other high Soviet officials also made trips
abroad in support of trade expansion. Anastas Mikoyan

atten·led an industrial fair in Iraq in 1960; and, at
a trade fair on his first trip to Japan in 1961, he
offered a 10-year agreement to exchange oil, coal,
and iron ore for needed Japanese goods. On his second visit to Japan in 1964, Mikoyan presented a list
of $350 million of goods that the Soviets wanted to
buy on long-term credits. First Deputy Premier Polyan-
sky discussed trade and signed an air agreement on a
visit to Canada in 1966. Foreign Minister Gromyko
helped finalize the Fiat deal on a trip to Italy in
April 1966; and several months later, in Tokyo, he
discussed possibilities of Japanese cooperation in
the economic development of Siberia. Even President
Podgorny was pressed into service with a trip to
Austria in November 1966 to broaden trade ties and
warn this country against any ties with the Common
Market. On a visit to Italy in January 1967, he discussed ways to further strengthen economic ties.

The use of such high personnel as the premier,
the first deputy premier, the foreign minister, and
the president for the promotion of trade indicates
the importance placed on this activity by the Soviet
Union. If this trade were primarily for political
reasons, this would be completely understandable.
However, there is evidence to indicate that economics
is important in the trade with Southeast Asia; and,
in the case of England and the United States, the
economic need for high-technology equipment appears
paramount--politics are involved only to the extent
of overcoming the trade embargo.

SUMMARY

In addition to the organizations discussed in
earlier chapters, various foreign trade activities
in the Soviet Union are conducted by the Scientific-
Research Economic Institute, the All-Union Academy
of Foreign Trade, the Institute of Foreign Trade,
the All-Union Chamber of Commerce, and mixed chambers
of commerce. The first three organizations conduct
research and educational activities. The All-Union
Chamber of Commerce, which was formed by combining
the All-Union Western and Eastern Chambers in 1932,
is the Soviet organ charged primarily with trade

promotion. Its major activities in this field include the preparation of Soviet exhibits at international trade fairs and coordination with joint chambers of commerce established in various countries.
In addition to its promotion activities, the All-
Union Chamber of Commerce issues certificates of
origin, registers patents, and provides miscellaneous
services. Under the Chamber of Commerce are a Foreign Trade Arbitration Commission, a Maritime Arbitration Commission, and an Average Adjusters Bureau.

The major Soviet foreign trade promotional activity has been participation in trade fairs. Immediately after World War II these exhibits were held
mainly in the people's democracies; but since Stalin's
death these exhibits have been held in other countries, especially in the underdeveloped areas. Other
promotional activities have included exhibits held
in the Soviet Union, the Moscow International Economic
Conference in 1952, participation in UN and other
economic conferences, the reception of foreign trade
delegations, and the visit by Soviet dignitaries to
various countries for trade purposes.

6

SOVIET TRADE WITH
SOCIALIST COUNTRIES

In the previous chapters the discussions have referred to Soviet foreign trade
in general and specifically to trade with
the capitalist countries of the West. Following World War II the Soviet Union set up
an entirely new type of trading system in
what the Soviets came to call the socialist
world. This socialist world is composed of
the member countries of Comecon, the people's democracies of the East, and other
socialist countries. This chapter covers
the direct and indirect actions taken by
the Soviet Union in developing trade relations with Comecon countries. These actions include the use of reparations payments, trade agreements, Soviet credits,
and help in reorganizing the organs of
foreign trade in these countries. It then
discusses Soviet efforts to integrate the
economies of Comecon and the short-lived
experiment in a market economy. The rise
and fall of trade relations with the People's Republic of China are then covered,
as is the nature of trade relations with
North Korea and North Vietnam. The chapter closes with a discussion of trade relations with two special situation coun-
tries--Yugoslavia and Cuba.

The most significant factor in the foreign trade
of the Soviet Union in the period following World
War II has been the marked reorientation of Soviet
markets. Prior to the war, trade with the countries
that now compose the "socialist world" was relatively
unimportant. Immediately following the war Soviet
trade with these countries expanded rapidly until it
accounted for 82 percent of all Soviet trade in 1952-
54. After 1954 this trade continued to expand each
year; but, as trade with nonsocialist countries increased more rapidly, the socialist percentage of
Soviet trade dropped consistently until it was 65 percent in 1969 and 1970. At the same time, and as a
direct result of Soviet pressures, the trade patterns
of each of the socialist countries were altered so
that most of this trade was between countries of the
socialist world. In referring to this change in 1952
Stalin stated:

> China and the other People's Democratic
> countries in Europe fell out of the capital-
> ist system and formed, together with the
> Soviet Union, the unified and powerful so-
> cialist camp which is opposed to the camp
> of capitalism. The economic result of the
> existence of two opposing camps was that
> the single international market fell apart
> in result of which we now have two parallel
> world markets which are opposed one to the
> other.[1]

TRADE WITH COMECON COUNTRIES

Both prior to and during World War II the economies of the countries of Eastern Europe were closely
linked to, if not integrated with, the military program of Germany. As a result there was a trend toward
greater industrialization; and in Czechoslovakia,
Poland, and Hungary there was a definite shift toward
the development of heavy industry.[2] The collapse of
Germany in 1945 eliminated the major market for and
supplier of these countries and produced an economic
void. Inasmuch as the area was cut off from Western
Europe at this time, Soviet occupation troops were

stationed in these countries; and, since the Soviet
Union urgently needed capital equipment for rehabil-
itation purposes, it was only natural that the Soviet
Union replace Germany in the foreign trade of Eastern
Europe--at least temporarily.

Reparations

    At the Potsdam Conference it was agreed that
"reparations claims of the U.S.S.R. shall be met by
removals from the zone of Germany occupied by the
U.S.S.R. and from appropriate German external assets."[3] As a result of this agreement, the Soviet
Union confiscated German assets in Bulgaria, Hungary,
Rumania, and Germany. It removed these assets to
the Soviet Union, converted them into Soviet-owned
companies, or invested them in Soviet-local mixed
companies. (See Chapter 2.) These companies, which
represented a sizable sector of these economies, conducted their own foreign trade operations; and,
since they were partially or wholly owned by the
Soviets, it was only natural that this trade was directed toward the Soviet Union.
    A one-way flow of goods to the Soviet Union
also resulted from reparations levied on the Soviet
Union's former enemies, Hungary and Rumania. In accordance with their armistice agreements, these
countries were required to supply the Soviet Union
with about $1 billion of goods over a six-year period.[4]
Poland, although not an enemy, was required to supply
the Soviet Union with about 6.5 million tons of coal
as "political" exports--at a price far below world
market.[5]
    The immediate effect of these reparations pay-
ments was an almost total reorientation of the trade
of these countries toward the Soviet Union. The
long-range effects were debilitating but, once realized, led to new tactics of control on the part of
the Soviets. By 1954 other means of controlling
the trade of Eastern Europe had been devised, and
direct control over companies in these countries
and their trade was found unnecessary. As a result
of this change and the unrest in Eastern Europe in
1953, reparations payments were canceled in 1954;

and during 1954 and 1955 the Soviet-owned and mixed companies were transferred to local ownership.[6]

Trade Agreements

A second means of gaining control over the foreign trade of Eastern Europe was the use of trade agreements. Even before the war in Europe had ended, the Soviet Union began negotiating trade agreements with both the conquered and the liberated countries of this area. Initially these agreements were all short-term, running from a period of several months to as long as 18 months. Because of their limited scope and short-term nature, these agreements apparently were not as effective as the Soviets desired; and during this period the Soviet share of Eastern European trade dropped from 100 percent in 1945 to only 25 percent in 1947.[7]

To counteract this trend the Soviets switched to long-term, comprehensive, bilateral trade agreements. The first of these agreements were signed with Hungary, Czechoslovakia, and Poland in 1947 as part of a package in which these countries received Molotov Plan aid in compensation for staying out of the Marshall Plan.[8] Agreements with other Eastern European countries followed and, with the exception of Bulgaria, were standard by 1951.[9] That this tactic was successful can be seen in the fact that the Soviet share in Eastern European trade immediately doubled in 1948 and continued to expand until it was 82 percent in 1952-54.

The long-term, bilateral trade agreements, which are still in use today, cover all aspects of trade between the contracting parties but do not include references to the volume of trade for a given period. The setting of trade volume is done by means of annual protocols to the agreement. In this manner the quantity of trade and the prices to be paid are determined not in diplomatic negotiations but in administrative talks. The primary purpose of these long-term agreements is to regulate the distribution of goods within the entire Soviet sphere of influence. Government control of production and distribution frees this trade from the economic effects of market conditions, prices, customs duties, freight costs, and the like. As a result these treaties are designed not to regulate normal commercial trade but to give direct administrative control and management to state trading activities. Furthermore, since the terms of the trade agreements, and especially the protocols, are heavily influenced and possibly dictated by the Soviets, a measure of control and management of this trade is in the hands of the Soviet Union.

Soviet influence and control are not limited to the agreements between the Soviet Union and the countries of Eastern Europe but extend to trade agreements made by these countries with each other. Although trade among these countries had been insignificant before the war, a new pattern emerged in the postwar period. Some short-term bilateral agreements between Eastern European countries were signed as early as 1945. With Soviet urging, long-term agreements were concluded beginning in 1947, and by 1951 the bloc operated a network of such agreements. Prior to 1949 the Soviet Union had no formal, direct control over any of these agreements. As will be discussed later, the Council for Mutual Economic Assistance, established in January 1949, was assigned the definite task of coordinating trade agreements and trade relations in general. The Soviet Union's preeminent role in Comecon resulted in this organization's becoming a vehicle for Soviet influence and control over bloc trade.[10]

Credits

Another means of gaining control over the trade of Comecon countries has been the granting of credits for the purchase of machines, equipment, and food from the Soviet Union. This tool was first used in 1947, when the "Molotov Plan" was inaugurated with credits to participating countries as one of its cornerstones.[11] These credits were clearly political and were intended to further alienate Eastern Europe from the West and to bind this area to the Soviet Union. The Soviet share of the trade of Eastern Europe had rapidly diminished, and these countries--

particularly Poland and Czechoslovakia--had indicated
a strong interest in Marshall Plan aid. To counter
this trend the Soviet Union provided credits and in
return obligated recipient countries to enter into
long-term trade agreements that directed their trade
toward the Soviet Union. Most of these credits were
granted in 1947 and 1948 and the last was issued in
1950, indicating that by this time the initial credits
had served their limited purpose of redirecting and
gaining control over the trade of Eastern Europe.
It should be noted that despite these credits there
was a continuing net flow of capital out of Eastern
Europe toward the Soviet Union.[12]

This outflow of capital was accentuated by certain "loans" made by the Soviet Union following the
death of Stalin. After the riots in East Germany in
1953, the Soviets found it politically expedient to
liquidate their assets in Eastern Europe. They did
this by selling Soviet companies and the Soviet share
of mixed companies to the local governments. To facilitate such sales the Soviet Union set up paper
loans that were to be repaid by the shipment of goods
from Eastern Europe to the Soviet Union. Since the
Soviet Union determined the goods, the quantities,
and the prices involved in the repayments, these
loans expanded Soviet control over the foreign trade
of these countries. The loans covered the sale of
assets that had been seized as reparations, so the
Soviets gained this control at little or no cost to
themselves.

The Polish and Hungarian uprisings in 1956
forced the Soviet Union to reappraise its economic
relations with the countries of Eastern Europe. The
first result was a politically oriented series of
credits in 1956 and 1957, totaling $1.2 billion, and
an equally political cancellation of $1.5 billion of
debts--particularly reparations payments and repayments of the loans to pay for the purchase of Soviet
assets.[13] Credits were granted to all the bloc
countries; but, as a direct result of the upheavals
in Poland and Hungary, half of the credits and debt
cancellations went to these two countries.

In 1959 the Soviet aid program for the bloc
changed in direction, tempo, and purpose. Credits
were now used to develop additional markets for com-

plete plants and equipment and as a vehicle to
achieve the socialist division of labor. In 1959
there was a dramatic (66 percent) increase in shipments of complete plants to Eastern Europe. This
trade continued to increase by about 20 percent per
year through 1963 and about 10 percent per year
thereafter. From a total of $43 million in 1957,
these shipments grew to $271 million, or 5 percent
of Soviet exports to these countries, in 1968. As
this credit-based trade increased, it was quickly
redirected toward Bulgaria and Rumania, the less-
developed countries of Eastern Europe. In 1968,
for example, 60 percent of these shipments went to
Bulgaria and another 13 percent went to Rumania.
These shipments represented 22 percent of Soviet exports to these countries. The more developed Eastern European countries had less need for either
credit or Soviet technology, and shipments of complete plants accounted for only 2 percent of Soviet
exports to these countries.[14]

The credits granted the bloc members are generally on very favorable terms. Usually the deliveries under these credits are spread over a number
of years and repayment begins in the year following
the first deliveries. Most of these credits are for
a period of five years, and the interest rate is
never above 2 percent.[15]

It is important to note that almost all Soviet
aid to Eastern Europe has been in the form of credits
or tied loans, and not cash grants or loans. These
credits are made for specific ruble values and are
limited to the purchase of specific Soviet goods.
Furthermore, the repayment of these credits must be
in the form of specifically listed goods. In this
manner the Soviet Union uses credits to help control
the trade, industry, and planning of the countries
of the bloc. As A. M. Smirnov stated:

> Credits of the USSR to the countries
> of the People's Democracies represent in
> themselves a new form of foreign credits
> not found in the credit relations between
> capitalist countries. The tying of cred-
> its and their repayment to particular
> goods makes it possible for the creditor

and debtor countries to link the giving of
credit, its use, and its repayment with national economic plans.[16]

With the establishment of the International Investment Bank in 1970, the Soviet Union had a means
of internationalizing its credit operations. The
principal function of this bank is the extension of
medium-term (up to 5 years(and long-term (up to 15
years) credits to member countries. Its significance
is that it provides the Soviet Union with a vehicle
for expanding its bilateral control-through-credit
policy to a multilateral one. Credits that would
have been made by Poland, Czechoslovakia, Hungary,
or the German Democratic Republic to other bloc countries can now be made through the International Investment Bank. Since the bank is a supranational
organization essentially controlled by the Soviet
Union, its lending practices follow those of the
Soviet Union. Although the credits have the appearance of cash loans repayable in transferable rubles,
they are designed to further the cause of integration;
and for this reason both the goods to be purchased
and the means of repayment are spelled out prior to
the granting of credit.[17] It is interesting to note
that Rumania, one of the major recipients of credit
from the Soviet Union, refused to join this bank.

Reorganization of Foreign
Trade Organizations

In the early postwar years the Soviet Union
gained a measure of control over Eastern European
foreign trade by remolding the foreign trade organizations and policies of these countries along Soviet
lines. Before World War II the foreign trade operations of these countries were conducted by private
traders and controlled by economic factors. By 1950
practically all of this trade was conducted by state
monopoly foreign trade corporations similar to those
in the Soviet Union, and the plan had replaced market economics. Since the Soviet Union controlled
the governments of Eastern Europe, this conversion
gave the Soviets stronger control over the nature and

direction of the trade activities of these countries
than would have been possible had private trading
been retained. The method of this conversion varied
from country to country but followed a basic pattern
that had been established as early as 1920 in trade
with the countries of the East. Foreign trade companies were established by the state to compete with
private traders. Since these companies received certain privileges and benefits, they soon squeezed out
more and more private traders. Finally foreign trade
was nationalized and the state foreign trade companies were given monopoly rights.

The Soviet Union also forced through a conversion from Western-style ministries of foreign trade
to Soviet-style ministries that completely regulated
and controlled all foreign trade. By means of various pressures on the bloc governments, the Soviet
Union was now able to control the trade of each of
the countries of Eastern Europe. In this manner it
was able to redirect the trade of Eastern Europe so
that most of this trade was with the Soviet Union
and other countries of Eastern Europe, whereas this
trade had been unimportant before the war.

Similarly, the Soviet Union helped the Eastern
European countries reorganize their trade promotion
activities. The most significant of these activities
as regards Soviet foreign trade has been participation in trade fairs. Generally speaking, the exhibits of these countries adopt the themes and general techniques used by the Soviet Union. By following this process of similarity, the bloc countries
give the impression of being not a group of independent countries but a single massive power. Furthermore, even if the Soviet Union does not participate
in a particular fair, the presence of one or more
exhibits from other bloc countries provides representation for the Soviet Union.

Integration

As discussed in Chapter 1, integration of the
economies of Eastern Europe has been a primary strategic goal of the Soviet Union since the end of
World War II. The most important step in this inte-

gration was the formation in January 1949 of the
Council for Mutual Economic Assistance (Comecon),
with Bulgaria, Czechoslovakia, Hungary, Poland, Rumania, and the Soviet Union as founding members.[18]
It was declared that this was not a closed organization but was open to all countries agreeing with
the principles of the council. Albania became a member in February 1949, and the newly formed German
Democratic Republic was admitted in September 1950.[19]
It is interesting to note that China, North Korea,
North Vietnam, and Cuba have not become members.
Following the Sino-Soviet rift, Albania dropped out
of Comecon and, as will be discussed later, Mongolia
joined it.

The avowed purpose of the council was the "exchange of economic experience, the rendering to each
other of technical assistance, the rendering of mutual assistance in raw materials, foodstuffs, machines,
equipment, etc."[20] The most important functions of
Comecon, however, appear to be the coordination of
the economic plans of member countries and the coordination and direction of foreign trade activities
both within the bloc and with other countries. In
carrying out these functions Comecon has become, in
effect, a supranational organization guided and controlled by the Soviet Union.

As one Soviet author stated, "Trade between the
Socialist countries is conducted in conformity with
the needs of their planned economies. This is done
by the co-ordination of economic plans, taking into
account the international socialist division of labour."[21] Although some Comecon members, particularly
Rumania, have objected to centralized planning,
there has been a definite trend in this direction.
In 1971 the great emphasis placed on integration gave
centralized economic planning a dominating role. Jan
Stankovsky suggests that as a result the planning
authority of the individual countries is being transferred bit by bit to Comecon, which exercises more
and more supranational powers.[22] Comecon has already
established standardized planning methods, and it
coordinates long-term economic plans and investments.
It has also established joint planning offices for
individual branches of industry and is developing a
unified planning center that will have power to issue

instructions. In line with its other activities,
Comecon now coordinates the joint construction of
important projects. Common prices within the bloc
are being developed, and Comecon has announced that
it plans to make the transferable ruble into a true
bloc currency. It is expected that Comecon will
then work toward common wage and tax structures and,
finally, a common bloc budget. When these goals
have been achieved, it will be more proper to refer
to bloc trade as intraregional rather than international.

Comecon also directly coordinates the foreign
trade activities of member countries. All trade
agreements and import-export plans of the member
countries must be submitted to the council in Moscow
before being put into operation.[23] The council apparently constructs a master plan for all of the member countries and approves country plans and agreements only if they agree with the master plan. In
making this master trade plan, top priority is given
to the requirements of the Soviet Union; and member
countries are required to give one another preferen-
tial treatment in trade activities.

In addition to coordinating overall trade between member countries, Comecon has been active in
formulating uniform trade practices within the bloc.
In 1951 the council issued a "General Unification of
Commerical Conditions of Contract in the Mutual Supplying of Goods to Countries Participating in the
Council for Economic Mutual Assistance." These "General Conditions" were voluntary and, as such, were
not effective. As a result new "General Conditions,"
effective January 1, 1958, were made obligatory on
all members and a single multilateral agreement was
concluded. The 1958 "General Conditions" contain 74
articles, including form of concluding contracts,
basis for supply, terms of supply, quality of goods,
quantity of goods, packing and marking, technical
documentation, shipping instructions, form of payment, and the manner of settling disputes in arbitration.[24] In 1954 Comecon issued a Unified Tariff
Nomenclautre for the foreign trade of all member
countries. This nomenclature, which is based on the
Soviet classification of goods, is used for planning,
accounting, and foreign trade statistical purposes.[25]

Following the split with China in 1960, the Soviet Union intensified its efforts to integrate Eastern Europe through the medium of Comecon. In 1962 a Comecon conference agreed to new guidelines for intrabloc economic relationships.[26] The next year the International Bank for Economic Cooperation, which the Soviets had sought since 1958, was established through Comecon to handle multilateral clearing of trade accounts and to provide short-term and seasonal trade credits. At the same time Comecon introduced the transferable ruble as a clearing currency. After the Czechoslovak invasion of 1968, the Soviet Union again added pressure for integration through Comecon. The first result was the International Investment Bank, created in 1970 to provide medium- and long-term development loans to member countries. In July 1971 Comecon announced agreement on a 15- to 20-year plan for socialist economic integration.[27] The Soviets apparently wanted a mandatory system of integration but were stymied in these efforts by Rumania, which would agree only to a loose though ambitious alliance of equals.

The end result of this trade, plan, and financial coordination is that the Soviet Union now not only controls its own foreign trade but also heavily influences the foreign trade activities of all the East European countries. By setting up standard procedures and supranational organizations, the Soviets have simplfied intrabloc trade, almost converting it from international to intraregional trade. That the Soviet Union does not have absolute control over this trade, however, can be seen in the continued resistance of Rumania to any plan that seems to impinge on its sovereignty.

Economic Reform and
Foreign Trade

After Stalin's death Soviet economist Yevsey Liberman proposed that the control of production be transferred from central planning authorities to plant managers who, through an emphasis on profitability rather than plan fulfillment, would improve total economic output. In 1965 the Soviet Union, in

an attempt to correct some of its economic woes, decided to introduce some aspects of this more market-
oriented socialism. The plan was not abandoned, and
in fact it appears that improved management within
the detailed plan was the immediate goal. As a result these reforms had little, if any, effect on
Soviet foreign trade. Some of the countries of
Eastern Europe placed a different interpretation on
these policies, however; and the result was a radical
reorganization of their foreign trade.

Czechoslovakia was the first bloc country to
undertake reforms in 1966, and the new system of
economic management that developed brought with it a
reorganization of Czechoslovakia's foreign trade.
The most noticeable change was the new role of producing enterprises in foreign trade transactions.
In some cases, particularly in the capital-goods sector, the producing enterprises completely replaced
the monopoly foreign trade corporations and began
carrying out their own foreign trade operations.
The foreign trade corporation Skodaexport, for example, became the foreign trade subsidiary of Skoda
Heavy Engineering. Similarly, Tekhnoexport was absorbed by the chemical engineering firm Chepos, part
of Strojexport was taken over by CKD Praja, and
Jablonex was transferred to the Jablonec Costume
Jewelry Enterprise.[28]

Further reflecting this new role of producing
enterprises, a new type of export corporation was
established. Each of these new trading firms specializes in the exports of a single industrial enterprise and is formed as a joint venture between this
industrial enterprise and a monopoly foreign trade
corporation. Examples of these joint trading companies are Glassexport, Czechoslovak Ceramics, Centro-
tex (textiles), Chemapol (chemicals), Kovo (precision
engineering), and Motokov (vehicles). Other industrial enterprises have not yet set up foreign trade
organizations. These firms continue to deal through
the monopoly foreign trade corporations, but now they
participate directly in the trade negotiations.

Dramatic as they are, these changes are being
introduced only gradually; and the majority of trade
reamins in the hands of the monopoly foreign trade
corporations. It should be noted, however, that the

pressures for change are strong and that the new
forms of foreign trade organization have survived
the invasion of Czechoslovakia in 1968, the subsequent crackdown on the Czech government, and continued
Soviet pressures for more integration. Furthermore,
various new foreign trade organizations have been
developed in all other Comecon countries except the
Soviet Union.[29] In some cases these have even included joint ventures with capitalist countries.

According to V. Bernasek and A. Neustadt, the
new economic system also called for an abolition of
the privileged position of the monopoly foreign trade
corporations. These corporations would then have to
justify their existence by offering a true economic
advantage. Further, importing and exporting companies would have to decide on an economic basis
whether they wanted to handle their own foreign trade
or deal through specialized trading companies or
some other form of organization. Although such an
economic choice may be in the offing, the producing
firms in Comecon today still have only a limited
choice in this area.[30]

More important than the organizational changes,
however, has been the increased market orientation
of foreign trade. According to R. Selucky:

> [Czech enterprises] are beginning to
> show an interest in buying only those means
> of production that have suitable delivery
> periods, technical quality, and good opera-
> tional characteristics, ie, purchase of ma-
> chines and equipment that raise the effec-
> tiveness of their operation, elevate their
> technical level, contribute to making the
> output of the enterprise correspond in both
> its magnitude and price to the demands of
> both the domestic and the foreign markets,
> and make the enterprise capable of meeting
> competition. In contrast to earlier peri-
> ods, Czechoslovak enterprises now have the
> right to refuse to purchase products that
> cannot contribute to increasing the effec-
> tiveness of their operation.[31]

This new market orientation calls for new approaches to the plan, prices, currency control, and

tariff policy; and it is in these areas that the
new economics of Comecon would appear to be in conflict with current Soviet policy. The Soviet Union,
for example, continues to support a system of detailed
plans; but the Comecon nations seem to prefer a
looser budget approach to planning. As Jan Pleva
succinctly put it, "What should be decisive is no
longer physical volume but economic calculus."[32]
Further, whereas the Soviets have been pushing for a
common currency for Comecon (the ruble), Czechoslovakia
in 1967 and 1968 was quite vocal about the need for
full convertibility of the Czech crown.[33] Similarly,
although the Soviet Union is striving for common non-
market prices throughout Comecon, the other member
countries have been trying to develop market prices
that could be used to measure the true economic effectiveness of producing enterprises.[34] This move
toward market pricing has also led to a reevaluation
of tariff policies and ways of making tariffs effective.[35]

It is difficult to determine the effects of
these recent changes on Soviet trade with Comecon
countries; but, if they were to be expanded, it is
likely that at least the mechanics of this trade
would be adversely affected. It is also difficult
to accurately forecast the future path of these new
economics. However, it should be noted that the
grand integration plan announced by Comecon in July
1971 would appear to echo Soviet policies and run
counter to an expanded market orientation.

Trade with Mongolia

The Mongolian People's Republic became a member
of Comecon in 1962. It is, however, an anomaly; and
Soviet trade relations with this country are distinctly different from such relations with other
Comecon countries. Whereas trade with the other members is regulated by the Main Administration for
Trade with European Socialist Countries, the trade
with Mongolia comes under the Eastern Administration
of the Ministry of Foreign Trade. Further, instead
of the specialized foreign trade corporations, all
nonaid trade with Mongolia is handled by the Eastern

Trading Corporation (Vostokintorg). In most ways,
in fact, Mongolia can be considered as one of the
people's democracies of the East. However, because
of its political significance as a buffer state between the USSR and China it has, since the Sino-
Soviet rift, been given special attention, including
membership in Comecon, the International Bank for
Economic Cooperation, and the International Investment Bank.

Soviet trade relations with Mongolia began in
1923, when it was agreed that "Russian experts and
advisors shall be entrusted with the exploitation
of the national resources of the country and the development of trade and industry."[36] With this agreement, a Soviet-prepared constitution that called for
a monopoly of foreign trade, and credits made available by the Soviet-financed Mongolian Trading and
Industrial Bank, the Soviets were well-armed to replace the Chinese influence in Mongolian foreign
trade. As a result Soviet trade increased rapidly
from relatively no trade before 1924 to 16 percent
in that year, 29 percent in 1926, and 100 percent
shortly thereafter.[37] At first this trade was conducted mainly by such Soviet firms as the Wool Corporation (Sherst) and the Leather Syndicate (Kozhsyndikat). Later, trade functions within Mongolia were
turned over to Mongolian or joint Soviet-Mongolian
organizations, and similar functions within the Soviet
Union were conducted by a specialized monopoly corporation.* After Mongolia and its foreign trade
were firmly controlled by the Soviet Union, Mongolia
was treated with benign neglect; and by 1938 trade
between these countries totaled only $20 million.

In 1949 the Soviet Union established several
joint Soviet-Mongolian companies. The most important

---

*Actually a series of corporations including the
Corporation for Trade of the USSR with Mongolia
(Stormong), 1927-30; the Eastern Trading Corporation
(Vostgostorg), 1930-31; the Soviet-Mongolia-Tanna
Tuva Trading Corporation (Sovmongtuvtorg), 1931-45;
the Soviet-Mongolia Trading Corporation (Sovmongol-
torg), 1945-51; and the Eastern Trading Corporation
(Vostokintorg), 1951-present.

of these firms were the Mongolian Petroleum Company
(Mongolneft), the Soviet-Mongolia Metal Company (Sovmongolmetal), and the Ulan Bator Railway Company.
Several minor joint companies were liquidated in
1953, apparently on a gift basis. In 1956 the Ulan
Bator Railway was given to Mongolia, as was Mongolneft in 1957. Sovmongolmetal was liquidated in 1957,
but in this case Mongolia was required to pay for
the Soviet share. To cover this purchase the Soviets
provided a 30-year loan with repayment delayed until
1962.

Following the death of Stalin, there was a renewed interest in all aspects of Mongolian economic
relations. In addition to the liquidation of joint
companies, there was a change in the volume and composition of the trade between the Soviet Union and
Mongolia. Imports remained fairly constant and from
1955 to 1970 fluctuated narrowly between $47 million
and $62 million. Throughout this period wool and
cattle accounted for fully three-fourths of Soviet
imports from Mongolia.

Exports, on the other hand, have changed markedly. In 1955 only 23 percent of the exports to
Mongolia were machines and equipment, including only
2 percent in the form of complete plants. The Soviet
Union began an industrial development program in
Mongolia in 1956-57 with a $50 million credit.[38]
When the Sino-Soviet rift occurred in 1960, the Soviet Union evidently felt that Mongolia needed even
more special attention, in order to prevent any possibility of defection. One aspect of this attention
was a promise of $500 million in credits for the
period 1961-65. Exports to Mongolia began rising
rapidly, from a low of $65 million in 1958 to a
high of almost $200 million in 1970. The industriali-
zation program continued; and, by 1968, 60 percent
of Soviet exports were machines and equipment. Complete plants were emphasized, and in 1968 these accounted for two-thirds of all machinery exports and
42 percent of all exports. Subsequently the Soviet
Union promised credits and grants totaling $733 mil-
lion for the 1965-70 Five-Year Plan. The severe imbalance of trade that favors Mongolia reflects this
Soviet financing of Mongolia's development at a current rate of about $140 million per year.[39]

Mongolia's special status was emphasized by its election to membership in Comecon in 1962. As an underdeveloped country it has little to offer this association, but it has much to gain in the way of increased aid. In 1970 Mongolia joined the International Investment Bank with a contribution of $5 million. This investment will be repaid many times over by the long-term credits it will receive. That this is the case can be seen in the Comecon pledges to pay special attention to the economic development of Mongolia in the grand integration plan announced in 1971.[40]

TRADE WITH THE PEOPLE'S
DEMOCRACIES OF THE EAST

Although the Soviet Union had a great interest in the countries of the East prior to World War II, it had essentially no trade relations with the areas now referred to as the people's democracies of the East. Since Japan controlled Chosen (Korea) and Manchuko (Manchuria), France ruled Indochina, and various Western powers influenced the activities of China, these were considered to be countries of the West and not of the East and were thus of no trade interest to the Soviets. An exception was Chinese Turkestan (the semiautonomous Sinkiang Province of western China). In 1925 the Soviet Union and Sinkiang concluded a formal trade agreement without any deference to the central Chinese government.[41] Another exception was Soviet operation of the Chinese Eastern and South Manchurian Railways from 1924 until these lines were sold to Manchuko in 1935. Following the war the People's Republic of China, the Korean People's Democratic Republic, and the Democratic Republic of Vietnam were organized, and the Soviet Union established trade relations with these new countries.

The People's Republic
of China

In the last days of World War II, the Soviet Union invaded Manchuria, defeated the Japanese troops

stationed there, and set up an army of occupation.
Clearly the Soviets considered Manchuria as Japanese
and not Chinese; and, because of its participation
in the defeat of Japan, it was entitled to certain
long-term privileges in Manchura. According to the
Yalta Agreement, the Chinese Eastern and South Manchurian Railways were taken over by a joint Soviet-
Nationalist Chinese Changchun Railway Company. Similarly, joint companies were set up to administer
Port Arthur and Dairen, two concessions the Russians
had lost to the Japanese in 1905. As if this were
not enough, the Soviet Union demanded that joint
Soviet-Chinese companies be set up to manage all industrial property in Manchuria; and, when the Chinese
refused, this property was declared war booty and
either removed to the Soviet Union or converted into
Soviet companies. According to an official U.S.
study, these removals amounted to at least $900 mil-
lion, although the Soviets admitted to taking only
about $97 million of such equipment.[42]

When the People's Republic of China came into
power in 1949, the Soviet Union turned over to it [43]
factories and some 276 other pieces of property it
had seized in Manchuria.[43] In 1950 it also gave its
share of the Chinese Changchun Railway to the new
government without charge. The other joint companies
were continued, however; and in March 1950 two new
joint companies were established for operations in
Sinkiang. These firms were the Soviet-Chinese Metals
Company (Sovkitmetal), which prospected for and
mined uranium and other metals, and the Soviet-Chinese
Petroleum Company (Sovkitneft), which drilled for oil.
A Soviet-Chinese airline (SKOGA) was also established,
and the next year the Soviet-Chinese Ship Construction Company (Sovkitsudostroi) was organized in Dairen.
As was the case in the Comecon countries, the Soviet
contribution to these joint companies was limited to
a few airplanes and the property seized from Japan.[44]

The Chinese soon became disillusioned with these
joint operations, partially for economic reasons and
partially because operation of these companies gave
the Soviets a base of influence in Sinkiang and Manchuria. When Khrushchev visited Peking in October
1954, he answered Chinese demands that the joint companies be turned over to China by agreeing to sell

China the Soviet share of these companies. To facilitate this transfer the Soviet Union provided paper
credits totaling $820 million, to be repaid in Chi-
nese goods.[45] Unlike the situation in Comecon, repayment of these credits was never forgiven; and by
1966 the Soviet Union was apparently paid the entire
$820 million. One immediate result of this transfer
was a reduction, if not elimination, of Soviet influence in Manchuria and the newly formed Sinkiang-
Uighur Autonomous Region.

The years 1949-55 can be characterized as a period of great Sino-Soviet friendship and cooperation.
It was also a period of massive Soviet financial assistance to China. In February 1950 the Soviet Union
granted China a $300 million credit for Soviet goods
to be delivered between 1950 and 1954. In 1954 this
credit was extended by another $130 million.[46]
These credits were used mainly for the purchase of
plants and equipment needed to rehabilitate the
Chinese economy and were most important to China's
First Five-Year Plan. The terms of these credits
called for repayment in Chinese goods over a 10-year
period. During this same period the Soviets extended
the Chinese People's Republic special Korean War
credits totaling $809 million.[47] No details are
available on these war credits, but it is assumed
that they covered civilian goods and support supplies.
In any case they contributed to rapidly expanding
trade between Russia and China. Although the Soviet
Union had never played a significant role in the
Chinese trade of earlier years, these credits and
other actions resulted in the Soviet Union's controlling 50 percent of this trade in 1952. (Comecon
nations, incidentally, controlled another 20 percent.)
By 1955 Soviet trade with China totaled $1.4 billion.
As a direct result of the $1.2 billion of credits,
Soviet exports to China during this period exceeded
imports from China by about $1 billion.[48]

The Soviet foreign aid program in China picked
up momentum during the period 1956-60. In accordance
with several agreements, the Soviet Union was involved
with the construction of 336 complete plants; and
during this period Soviet shipments of complete
plants to China totaled $1.3 billion. Furthermore,
the Soviet Union trained 8,000 Chinese engineers in

Russian schools and factories, invited 7,000 Chinese
students to study at Soviet universities, and assigned
some 11,000 Soviet specialists to work on the development projects in China.[49] There is no evidence,
however, to indicate that this aid was provided on
either a grant or a long-term credit basis. On the
contrary, no new credits were announced; and it
would appear that this aid was provided on a strictly
pay-as-you-go basis. While Soviet shipments increased markedly, so did Chinese exports to the Soviet Union. In fact, during this period Chinese
shipments to Russia each year exceeded their receipts
from that country. For the years 1956-60 this excess
amounted to $650 million.[50] This excess would
strongly suggest that not only was aid to China on a
cash basis but also the Soviets were insisting on
repayment in full and on time for the $2 billion of
credit already extended.*

During the late 1950's Sino-Soviet relations
began to deteriorate. At first this change had no
visible effect on economic relations, and trade
peaked in 1959. In July 1960, however, the Soviet
Union, without any warning, pulled all of its technicians out of China within a period of a few weeks,
leaving a large number of projects only partially
completed. Over the next five years the Soviet Union
continued to ship complete plants and equipment to
China, but at a sharply restricted rate. From a
high of $400 million in 1959 these shipments plum-
meted to $80 million in 1961, $15 million in 1963,
and only $4 million in 1965.[51] Chinese shipments
to the Soviet Union were also drastically curtailed,
but as in the previous period the Chinese exported
more to the Soviet Union than they received. For
the five-year period this excess totaled $900 million
--further evidence that the Soviets were insisting
on repayment of earlier credits. As a result of the
economic crisis caused by the failure of the Great
Leap Forward, the Soviet Union sold China $45 mil-
lion of Cuban sugar on credit terms and extended a

---

*Includes trade credits of $430 million, Korean
War credits of $809 million, and credits of $820 million to finance the purchase of joint companies.

$320 million credit. This latter sum, however, was
not a new trade credit but a refinancing of the un-
paid balances of earlier credits.[52]

In early 1966 the Chinese announced that the
People's Republic of China had repaid all its foreign
obligations.[53] Now there was no longer any necessity
to trade with the Soviet Union, and trade turnover
continued its precipitous decline. Soviet shipments
of complete plants became insignificant in this period and amounted to only $330,000 in 1968. Total
turnover dropped to $318 million in 1966, $96 million in 1968, and a meager $47 million in 1970.
With the repayment of Soviet credits, the 10-year
chain of excess shipments to the Soviet Union was
broken; and during this period the Chinese enjoyed
a small import surplus. In 1970 the Soviet Union
signed a trade agreement with the People's Republic
of China that called for a tripling of trade.[54] To
finance this trade the Soviets apparently extended
China $60 million of credits in 1970 and another $100
million in 1971.[55] Considering current political
disagreements, it is unlikely that this agreement
will significantly alter Sino-Soviet trade.

Korean People's Democratic Republic

As in Manchuria, the Soviet Union, in the last
days of World War II, invaded the Japanese colony of
Chosen (Korea) and, as agreed with the allies, oc-
cupied the territory north of the 38th parallel. The
Soviets immediately seized plants, mines, and other
productive property as reparations and set up Soviet
companies to operate these facilities.[56] The Soviet
Union also established a branch of the Foreign Trade
Bank, which then operated as the central bank for
North Korea.[57] After the Korean People's Democratic
Republic (KPDR) was established in 1948, the Soviet
Union apparently turned over most of the seized assets to the new government. Some of these assets,
however, were converted into joint Soviet-Korean
companies in 1949. These companies included the
Soviet-Korean Airline (SOKAO), a maritime transport
firm, and a company to process petroleum products.[58]

In 1955 the Soviets sold their shares in these joint companies and a year later converted this sale into a gift.

Soviet economic relations with the KPDR would appear to be based primarily on political considerations, and for this reason financial aid has been mostly on a grant basis. Prior to the Korean War there was one trade credit for $53 million. Immediately after the war, in 1953, the Soviet Union provided the KPDR a grant of $250 million in the form of machinery, equipment, and raw materials needed for the rehabilitation of heavy industry and agriculture. There appear to have been several loans or credits during this same period, for in 1960 the Soviet Union canceled a $190 million loan and postponed a $35 million one. Another loan or credit of $75 million was made in 1956, and by 1964 the Soviets claimed that postwar financial assistance to Korea had totaled $550 million.[59]

Between 1955 and 1967 the trade turnover between the USSR and the KPDR was fairly well balanced, indicating that there was little if any financial assistance provided during this period. In June 1966, however, the USSR and the KPDR signed a new economic and technical collaboration treaty for the period 1967-70.[60] Soviet exports to Korea climbed rapidly from $85 million in 1966 to $110 million in 1967, $172 million in 1968, $202 million in 1969, and $230 million in 1970. Korean exports also increased sharply; but during the period 1968-70 the Soviet Union exported almost $200 million more to Korea than it received in return, indicating that the 1966 agreement provided extensive new credits.[61] It should be noted that this was the period of the Cultural Revolution in China, and this aid may have been provided to protect North Korea from the chaos in China. At the same time it was intended to counter some of the disaffection that had been developing in Korea and to reorient this country toward the Soviet Union.

Democratic Republic of Vietnam

Soviet trade relations with the Democratic Republic of Vietnam (DRVN) are quite different from

such relations with other socialist countries and
can be characterized as mainly political in nature.
As in the case of other socialist countries, the
Soviet Union developed export sales to the DRVN by
providing generous long-term credits. The first of
these credits, $100 million for 25 specific projects,
was granted in 1955. Further credits of $87 million
for the food-processing industry and $107 million for
a large number of small projects were extended in
1960.[62] As a direct result of these credits, the
Soviet Union exported $272 million of goods to Viet-
nam during the 1955-64 decade. The Vietnamese increased their shipments to Russia, reaching a peak
of about $35 million a year in 1963 and 1964; but
this was not enough to repay the credits and a deficit of $93 million accumulated.[63]

As the war gained in tempo in 1965, Soviet non-
armament exports to the DRVN increased markedly,
while Vietnamese shipments to the USSR were reduced.
In 1966 a new economic assistance agreement including
a new $800 million credit was concluded.[64] Imme-
diately Soviet shipments to Vietnam more than doubled
from $68 million in 1966 to $148 million in 1967, and
by 1969 these shipments reached $190 million.* Since
the Vietnamese had precious little to offer the Soviet
Union, their exports continued to drop from the
1963-64 peak of $35 million to a 1969 low of less
than $17 million.[65] Because of this imbalance in
trade, a deficit of $700 million was accumulated in
1965-70, raising the total deficit to almost $800
million--the amount of the 1966 credit. Since the
DRVN exports to the Soviet Union in the 16-year period from 1955 to 1970 totaled a little over $300
million, it is unlikely that the credits extended
by the Soviet Union will ever be repaid. That such
repayment is probably not expected can be inferred
from the fact that a new economic aid and trade
agreement providing still more credits was concluded
in October 1971.

---

*These figures do not include military shipments,
which were quite extensive.

TRADE WITH OTHER SOCIALIST
COUNTRIES

Yugoslavia

Soviet trade relations with Yugoslavia fall into
four distinct periods. During the first period (1945-
48) Yugoslavia reoriented its trade toward the Soviet
Union and Eastern Europe, reorganized its foreign
trade operations and control organizations along Soviet lines, and joined the Soviet Union in two joint
companies. Unlike the countries of Eastern Europe,
which made these changes under duress, Yugoslavia
converted to socialism voluntarily. To help develop
its trade with the USSR, the latter between 1945 and
1948 extended Yugoslavia $200 million of credits.[66]
In 1948, however, the Yugoslavs publicly showed their
dissatisfaction with the Soviet-Yugoslav joint companies and other Soviet economic exploitation and
for their efforts were expelled from the Cominform,
which then formally represented the socialist world.
For the next five years Yugoslavia conducted no trade
whatsoever with the Soviet Union, and in 1954 this
trade was at only a token level.

The third period (1955-61) was one of semirap-
prochement. Yugoslavia's success in developing trade
relations with the West during the period of excom-
munication apparently galled Soviet leaders. As
Khrushchev put it: "There was naturally a lot of
resentment in the Soviet Union against Yugoslavia because of the amount of trade it did with the West.
This resentment was based more on jealousy than
ideology."[67] It was mainly for this reason that
Khrushchev, Mikoyan, and others visited Yugoslavia
in 1955 to invite Tito to rejoin the socialist world.
To sweeten the invitation the Soviets canceled $90
million of previous debts and agreed to a $194 mil-
lion new credit. Trade was renewed; and from practically no trade in 1954 and a $34 million turnover
in 1955, trade more than tripled to $119 million in
1956. However, Soviet actions in quelling the Hungarian revolt in 1956 once again strained Soviet-
Yugoslav relations. The new credit was canceled but
trade was not seriously affected, continuing to
fluctuate around $100 million per year.

Full rapprochement with the Soviet Union came in the fourth and current period (1962-71). As a result of the Sino-Soviet rift, the Soviet Union increased its efforts to bring Yugoslavia back into the socialist fold. These efforts reached a crescendo level in 1962, with a series of high-level state visits between the two countries. One immediate result was a sharp increase in trade. From $118 million in 1962, turnover climbed rapidly to $580 million in 1970. Although Khrushchev refused to grant Yugoslavia massive aid in 1963, a cumulative trade deficit of $235 million between 1966 and 1970 would suggest that such aid was included in the 1966 trade agreement.

Yugoslavia has also been included in the Soviet Union's plans for integration of the economies of Eastern Europe. In 1963 Yugoslavia was granted observer status in Comecon. A year later it was elevated to affiliate status, allowing participation without obligation in the activities of the various standing commissions. In 1965 Yugoslavia joined Intermetall, the Comecon affiliate charged with integrating the steel industry of the bloc. Finally, in 1971 Yugoslavia attended the Comecon integration meeting at Bucharest and agreed to participate in the new integration plan at least in some respects.

Republic of Cuba

The Republic of Cuba can be considered a special situation as regards Soviet trade relations. Trade with Cuba began in 1955 because of an increasing Soviet need for sugar. After Castro came to power in 1959, politics replaced sugar in importance and trade was greatly expanded. In February 1960, while on his trade promotion visit to the United States, Anastas Mikoyan went to Havana to open a trade exhibit and sign a 12-year, $100 million aid agreement.[68] In return for oil and industrial equipment, the Soviets agreed to take one million tons of sugar at the world price of 3¢ per pound in each of the next five years. Further fanning the fires of discord between the United States and Cuba, the Soviets in December 1960 announced that, if the United States boycotted Cuban sugar, the Soviet Union would take 2.7 million

tons at a price of 4¢ per pound. In fact, Soviet
imports of sugar from Cuba were 1.5 million tons in
1960 and 3.3 million tons in 1961--far exceeding the
agreed-upon amounts and providing Cuba with a trade
surplus in these two years. In October 1961 the
Soviets further upped the ante and said that they
would take 3.2 million tons of sugar each year through
1965 and committed other bloc countries to an additional 1.7 million tons per year.[69]

Over the next three years (1962-64), however,
Castro's purposeful neglect of the sugar industry
resulted in a decline in the sugar harvest from over
6 million tons in 1961 to 3.7 million tons in 1964.
The Soviets increased the price they paid to 6¢ per
pound and allowed Cuba to redirect some sugar to
world markets. Since sugar is almost the sole basis
for Cuban trade and its ability to repay foreign
credits, in January 1964 the Soviet Union and Cuba
signed a sugar supply agreement. The Soviets agreed
to buy 24 million tons of sugar at 6¢ per pound over
a seven-year period, and in return Cuba agreed to
accept Soviet assistance in reorienting the Cuban
economy back to sugar. The goal of this agreement
was a sugar output of 10 million tons per year by
1970. In May 1967 both countries agreed to go on
with the second phase of the reconstruction project.
By 1971, however, production had increased to only
5.9 million tons--some 5 percent below the level of
1961.

In addition to the 1960 credit of $100 million,
Marshall I. Goldman refers to credits of $403 mil-
lion in 1963, $159 million in 1964, and $89 million
in 1966.[70] The sugar reconstruction programs also
included large amounts of long-term credit. However,
these announced credits fall far short of the $1.7
billion trade deficit with the Soviet Union that
Cuba has accumulated since 1961.[71] Further, there
has been a considerable amount of military aid to
Cuba, even after the missile crisis of 1962. It can
only be assumed that these credits have all been
made primarily for political reasons and that the Soviet Union does not expect compensation in full.

SUMMARY

Prior to World War II only a small amount of Soviet foreign trade was conducted with those countries now composing the socialist world. Today 55 percent of Soviet trade is with the member countries of Comecon and another 10 percent is with other socialist countries. Furthermore, the Soviet Union exercises a degree of control over the foreign trade activities of the other Comecon countries. To obtain this control the Soviet Union used various means, including reparations payments, trade agreements, reorganization of the foreign trade activities of these countries, and the institution of such superstate organizations as the Council for Economic Mutual Assistance, the International Bank for Economic Cooperation, and the International Investment Bank. Recent actions appear to indicate that the Soviet goal in this area is total integration of the economies of all Comecon countries with that of the Soviet Union.

Soviet control of foreign trade was less than complete in the case of socialist countries outside Comecon. Trade relations with China and Yugoslavia began on a note of warmth and friendship. Soon, however, political and economic differences came to the fore. Trade and aid to China grew rapidly from 1949 to 1959; but, following the political schism in 1960, this trade dwindled to almost nothing. Yugoslavia's differences resulted in its banishment from the socialist world from 1948 to 1954. Rapprochement began in 1955, and after 1962 relations improved considerably.

Trade with the smaller socialist countries would appear to be based mainly on political considerations; and in Korea, Vietnam, and Cuba the Soviet Union has sustained a growing trade surplus that in all likelihood will never be paid for.

SOVIET TRADE WITH
DEVELOPING COUNTRIES

Since World War II the developing countries of Asia, Africa, the Middle East, and
Latin America have been developed as important suppliers of industrial raw materials
and foodstuffs to the Soviet Union and as
customers for Soviet machines and equipment.
This chapter begins with a discussion of
the development of this trade in the early
postwar years, the decline in trade ending
in 1950, and the subsequent revival of Soviet trade with the developing countries.
The basic economic reasons for this trade--
the need for industrial raw materials and
the need for foodstuffs--are then considered. This discussion is divided by commodity, and an analysis is made of each of
the major products imported by the Soviet
union from the developing countries. An
examination is then made of the supply, political, and financial considerations in
selecting specific developing countries as
sources of supply. The chapter ends with
a discussion of the long-term credits that
are the backbone of the Soviet foreign aid
program.

Soviet interest in the developing countries of
the world has varied considerably. During the 1920's

the Soviets displayed a great interest in the peoples
of the independent states bordering the Soviet Union.
At that time little or no attention was paid to the
areas that were under some form of foreign domination,
such as India, Egypt, the Arab countries, and China
proper. This great interest of the 1920's turned to
a hardening of the Comintern line in the 1930's, and
with the Soviet purges of 1937 there came a total
eclipse of all interest in the Orient.[1] The Comintern turned its attention to Latin America in 1927,
at which time a Soviet trading corporation was established in Argentina. In 1931 this corporation
was forced to move to Uruguay because of its political
activities, and in 1935 it was closed by the Uruguayan
government for a similar reason. Since that time it
appears that the Soviets have lost interest in this
area also.

THE BEGINNING OF SOVIET TRADE
WITH DEVELOPING COUNTRIES

In 1947 the well-known Soviet economist Yevgeni
Varga proposed that the creation of an independent
India constituted a new political fact of real importance. Such a proposal would imply the adoption
of a special policy for trade with the newly independent countries of the East. Varga, however, was up-
braided for his proposal; and it was officially announced that there would be no change whatsoever.[2]
That there was no change can be seen by the fact
that, although the Soviet Union imported large quantities of needed raw materials from the developing
countries in 1947 and 1948, this trade, like that
with all nonbloc countries, was reduced to a low
volume in 1950. Articles in the official journal
Foreign Trade further emphasized the absence of any
change in foreign trade policy. In February 1950 an
article was entitled "Expansion of American Monopolies
in Countries of the Near and Middle East." In September of the same year there was published "Expansion of American Imperialism in South-East Asia," and
in July 1951 "English and American Monopolies in
India and Pakistan."[3] During 1952 an indication of
a change in policy toward Southeast Asia appeared

first in articles concerning the Bombay Industrial
Exhibit in January and later in an article entitled
"Several Problems of the Foreign Trade of the Countries of South-East Asia."[4] This latter article ob-
jectively pointed out the marketing problems faced
by the one-crop countries of Southeast Asia and was
free from the usual vindictiveness.

At the UN Economic Commission for Asia and the
Far East (ECAFE) Conference at Singapore in October
1951, the Soviet Union announced an interest in
trading industrial and electrical equipment for such
raw materials produced in Southeast Asia as jute,
rubber, rice, copra, tea, and tin.[5] In January 1952
the Soviet Union, together with several other Eastern
European countries, participated in a lavish industrial exhibit at Bombay. Three months later, at the
Moscow Economic Conference, the underdeveloped countries not only of Southeast Asia but also of South
America and the Near East were singled out for special
attention. All of these actions indicated a definite
intention to reenter the markets of the developing
countries primarily as buyer of raw materials but
also as supplier of industrial equipment. Immediately
Soviet imports from the less-developed countries increased sharply. Imports of cotton from Egypt increased from $7.2 million in 1951 to $28.8 million
in 1952. Cocoa imports from Ghana (the Gold Coast)
rose from $9.5 million to $12.0 million. Oranges
to the value of $1.2 million were imported from Israel.
Imports from Pakistan, presumably jute, jumped from
$4.2 million in 1951 to $15.4 million in 1952. On
the other hand, trade with Iran and Turkey remained
stable, while imports of rubber from Malaya and imports of tea and jute from India dropped sharply.[6]

At the time of these increased imports, exports
to Egypt, Iran, and Pakistan increased sharply to
cover the cost of the imports. Despite this increase
in exports, the Soviet trade deficit for Southeast
Asia and the Near East increased from $29 million in
1951 to $32 million in 1952. To cover this deficit
it was necessary for the Soviet Union to increase
sales elsewhere. It is the opinion of this writer
that this chronic trade deficit with the underdeveloped countries was the basic reason for the subsequent changes in Soviet policies regarding trade with

these countries, particularly the selling of complete
factories on long-term credits.

Through 1956 Soviet trade with the developing
countries was on essentially a straight commercial
basis, with no aid or special financing provided by
the Soviet Union. Between 1952 and 1956 Soviet
trade with all nonbloc countries increased 67 percent.
Throughout most of this period, trade with the underdeveloped countries grew at about the same rate and
accounted for a fairly constant 18 percent of Soviet
trade with the nonbloc countries and 5.5 percent of
all Soviet trade.[7] Although the developing countries
accounted for 17 percent of total world trade in
1956, Soviet trade with these countries represented
only 0.14 percent of total world trade.[8] Despite
the small size of this trade, imports from Southeast
Asia, the Near East, and Africa in 1956 accounted
for 100 percent of Soviet imports of hides, rubber,
and cocoa; 97 percent of cotton; 74 percent of dried
fruit; at least 50 percent of wool, citrus, and tea;
37 percent of spices; and 28 percent of rice.[9]
Furthermore, Soviet purchases in 1956 accounted for
12 percent of Iran's trade, 17 percent of Turkey's,
and over 20 percent of the trade of Afghanistan,
Egypt, and Iceland.[10]

After 1956 Soviet trade with the developing
countries expanded rapidly and by 1970 had grown sixfold. This rapid growth rate was not met in the other
nonbloc countries, and as a result by 1970 this trade
grew to 13 percent of all Soviet trade and 39 percent
of trade with nonbloc countries.

REASONS FOR SOVIET TRADE WITH
DEVELOPING COUNTRIES

In recent years various spokesmen for the West
have described Soviet trade with underdeveloped countries as an economic offensive that is based completely on political reasons. A publication of the
U.S. House of Representatives stated: "During the
years since Stalin's death . . . the Sino-Soviet bloc
has unleashed a powerful new offensive. This offensive . . . consists of economic and military assistance and of expanded commercial activity in pursuit

of political goals. It is directed toward the ultimate goal of political domination of the underdeveloped world through economic means."[11] Such an explanation fits into the historical trend of Soviet
relations with the countries of the East. It also
fits into the pattern of Soviet-agitated political
unrest that has been observed in the developing countries in the years following World War II. This explanation assumes, however, that economic reasons
are of no importance whatsoever or are of strictly
secondary importance. If this were true, the Soviet
Union would not be limited in the type of goods imported but would import anything that provided a
political advantage. Furthermore, such an explanation would be valid only if the trade in question
was developed solely during the period of the offensive. In the following sections it will be shown
that the Soviet Union's choice of commodities was
indeed limited by economic factors and that, for
the most part, the trade in these particular commodities existed prior to 1953. Under these conditions
an explanation limited to political reasons is in-
complete and misleading. On the other hand, an analysis of political reasons for this trade will also
be made, since an explanation based solely on economics would be equally erroneous.

                        Soviet Need for
                        Raw Materials

     As Soviet industry has developed, so have its
demands for industrial raw materials. Following a
policy of autarky, the Soviet Union has tried wherever
possible to supply these goods from internal sources.
Adequate supplies of some goods, however, could not
be produced internally and had to be imported. Since
many of these goods were produced mainly or solely in
the underdeveloped countries, the Soviets had little
or no economic choice but to trade with these countries. An analysis of Soviet trade statistics indicates that such industrial raw materials accounted
for an average of about 66 percent of the imports
from developing countries during the 1952-72 period.
The primary raw materials imported from these coun-

tries are cotton, wool, rubber, hides, and jute; and
it is interesting to note that the Soviet Union has
always been an importer of these items. Furthermore,
the prewar peak import level for cotton was not
equaled until 1959 and jute did not reach such a level
until 1963.[12]

The Soviet Union began importing cotton shortly
after the Revolution. By 1927/28 these imports
reached a peak of 145,000 tons, dropping to 115,000
tons in 1929. Then, following a policy of autarky,
cotton-growing in Soviet Central Asia increased
rapidly after 1929 and imports were sharply reduced.
During the 1920's the major suppliers of cotton were
Egypt, Iran, and the United States. In 1937 the Soviet Union imported only 22,000 tons of cotton,
mainly from Iran.[13]

Immediately following World War II, Soviet cotton production reportedly dropped below previous
levels.[14] During this same period Soviet demand for
cotton apparently exceeded the available internal
supply. To meet this demand and to obtain types of
cotton not grown in the USSR, the Soviets found it
necessary to rely on imports. These imports were,
as before the war, rather erratic. In 1948 Soviet
imports from Egypt, presumably all cotton, amounted
to $49.8 million (approximately 40,000 tons). They
then dropped to $28.8 million (approximately 20,000
tons) in 1952, $7.2 million in 1951, $11.9 million
in 1953, and only $5.4 million in 1954.

The consumer-goods movement that followed the
death of Stalin resulted in a rapidly rising demand
for cotton that was reflected in even more rapidly
increasing imports. Since cotton had traditionally
been imported from Egypt, it was only logical to look
upon this country as a prime source. In 1955 the
Soviet Union imported 10,300 tons of cotton from
Egypt. These imports then grew tenfold to 111,000
tons in 1960. This trade was not without its politics. Both before and after the Suez crisis of 1956,
the Soviets supplied Egypt with military equipment
in exchange for cotton. In 1958 the Soviet Union
agreed to build the Aswan Dam, with repayment naturally to be in cotton. The politics of this aid, however, cannot explain the increased Soviet demand for
imported cotton. In fact Egypt (later the United

Arab Republic) could not supply the USSR's cotton
needs, and in most of the years since 1958 it has
supplied less than half of Soviet cotton imports.
To meet its increased needs the Soviet Union turned
to all other cotton-producing countries except the
United States. By 1968 the Soviets were importing
cotton from Afghanistan, Iran, Pakistan, the Sudan,
Syria, Mali, and Brazil. Between 1959 and 1962 the
People's Republic of China was also a major supplier.

Whereas the Soviet Union has become a heavy importer of cotton, it is even a heavier exporter of
this commodity. Some writers see in this a political
explanation for all cotton imports. However, it
must be remembered that cotton comes in different
types and different qualities. To obtain the proper
mix, the Soviets must import long staple cotton from
Egypt and other countries. Further, there have been
many charges of Soviet reexporting of imported cotton. In this regard it should be noted that almost
80 percent of all Soviet cotton exports have been to
the socialist countries--particularly the members of
Comecon. Also, these exports remained fairly constant between 1955 and 1964, while imports grew
rapidly. Further, between 1965 and 1968, when cotton
imports dropped some 25 percent, to a point below
the prewar peak, cotton exports from the Soviet Union
increased about 40 percent.[15]

Rubber is the second most important raw material
imported from the developing countries and can be
obtained only from such countries. Rubber first became important in the Soviet Union during the First
Five-Year Plan, and imports during this period rose
rapidly before leveling off at somewhat above 30,000
tons per year.[16]

Immediately after World War II the Soviet Union
satisfied its rubber needs by importing from Malaya.
In 1948 these imports amounted to $47.4 million, or
about 70,000 tons. In 1951, however, under the terms
of the Battle Act, rubber was declared a strategic
commodity; and shipments by all rubber-producing
countries to the Soviet Union and other socialist
states were terminated. On December 10, 1952, Ceylon,
which was bound by neither the Battle Act nor the
China Embargo, signed a five-year agreement to supply
China with rubber in exchange for needed rice.[17]

Most, if not all, of this rubber was subsequently delivered to the Soviet Union.

In 1955 Malaya and Indonesia relaxed their bans on rubber shipments and supplied the Soviet Union with 33,700 tons of rubber. Imports from Malaya then grew extremely rapidly until they reached a peak of 280,200 tons in 1962 and have continued at a rate of over 200,000 tons per year since then. These imports have caused the Soviets special problems because the Malaysians have found precious little to buy from Russia in exchange. As discussed in Chapter 1, this imbalance led to the so-called dumping of aluminum in 1956 and 1957. However, since the demand for rubber is so strong, the Soviet Union has been willing to continue an imbalanced trade relationship. Rubber imports from Indonesia also increased rapidly until they peaked at 60,000 tons in 1962. Here the Soviet Union was more successful in developing barter trade. With the ouster of Sukarno in 1966, Soviet aid shipments to Indonesia were sharply curtailed but purchases of rubber continued strong. Ceylon has been a regular though smaller supplier of rubber. From 1953 to 1960 most of these shipments were made through China on a three-sided barter arrangement. Direct shipments from Ceylon began in 1958 and, following the split with China in 1960, all of these shipments became direct. Thailand has been an on-and-off source, as has Burma; and Nigeria and Cameroun have supplied minor amounts.[18]

During the war and postwar period, the Soviet demand for rubber has grown at a rapid pace. At the same time the Soviets apparently have not developed the production of synthetic rubber to the extent that the United States has. As a result the Soviet Union is dependent on supplies of natural rubber obtained from Malaysia, Indonesia, and Ceylon, the major rubber-producing countries. Until the Soviets have developed an adequate synthetic rubber industry, it is likely that large imports of natural rubber from the developing countries will continue.

That the importation of leather and hides has long been significant can be seen in the fact that the Leather Syndicate (Kozhsyndikat) was formed in 1922. Today this commodity is the third most important raw material imported from the developing coun-

tries. A small quantity of large hides is imported
almost equally from the United States and Argentina.
The bulk of the hides imported, however, are small
ones and India has provided over 50 percent of the
Soviet Union'a need for small hides. In 1967 these
imports from India peaked at 18,300 tons, or 73 percent of total imports; and since 1965 India has regularly captured about two-thirds of this market.
The remainder of these imports is spread over a number of countries, including Afghanistan, Brazil,
Greece, Indonesia, Iran, Lebanon, Mongolia, and
Ethiopia--all developing countries. China was also
a source until 1960. After that year imports from
China continued, but at a sharply reduced rate, until
they were eliminated in 1966.

Wool has always been a major import of the Soviet
Union. Prior to World War II, Mongolia, the Sinkiang
Province of China, Iran, and Afghanistan were the
primary suppliers. Australia, also a major supplier,
in the late 1930's was replaced by Turkey. Imports
of wool reached a peak of 39,200 tons in 1929. Although imports declined in subsequent years, they
could not be done without and thus remained at about
30,000 tons per year.[19]

Following World War II the Soviet demand for
wool once again required imports. Since Australia
is the world's major producer of wool, the Soviet
Union turned to this country and in 1948 purchased
$34.5 million, or approximately 15,000 tons, of wool
from Australia.[20] Mongolia and Sinkiang then revived
their wool trade; and, since these sources were within
the Soviet family, purchases from Australia were
eliminated. Soviet demand for wool, however, exceeded
the amounts available from Mongolia and China (Sinkiang); and in 1953 Australia again became Russia's
major wool supplier. This trade was short-lived,
however, for in 1955 the Soviet Union severed its
trade ties with Australia because of the Petrov spy
case. (Petrov, an MVD officer, defected and exposed
the Soviet espionage network to the Australian government.)

This political action had no effect on Soviet
wool needs; and as a result New Zealand, the Union
of South Africa, Uruguay, Argentina, Afghanistan,
and India became important suppliers of wool. Other

sources in the Third World included Iran, Pakistan, Syria, Iraq, Lebanon, Turkey, Libya, Morocco, and Tunisia. The most important source during this period was China. When the Sino-Soviet split occurred in 1960, the scenario was reversed. The Petrov incident was forgotten, and Australia resumed its position as major wool supplier to the Soviet Union. This time, however, the newly developed sources (with the exception of white South Africa) were retained. In 1968 Australia and New Zealand supplied 47 percent of Soviet wool imports, Mongolia furnished another 14 percent, and the developing countries accounted for a record 27,200 tons, or 39 percent, of this market.

Current economic plans for Mongolia seem to emphasize industrial development. As a result it is unlikely that wool production will be greatly increased, and shipments to the Soviet Union will probably remain around the historic 10-11,000-ton level. As the Soviet demand for wool continues to increase, the Soviet Union has no economic choice but to continue to use whatever foreign sources are available. Australia and New Zealand will most likely remain the prime suppliers, but it is expected that the Soviets will continue their drive to buy wool from Argentina and Uruguay and the various countries of the Near East and Southeast Asia.

Jute and jute bags constitute the fourth major raw material imported from the less-developed countries. Prior to World War II the Soviet Union usually imported somewhat over 20,000 tons of jute per year, mainly from what is now Bangladesh. In 1948 this trade was resumed, and in that year the Soviet Union imported $13.4 million of jute from Pakistan. In accordance with the wheat barter agreements of 1949 and 1951, the Soviet Union also obtained jute from India. In 1952 jute imports from Pakistan amounted to $15.4 million, but by 1955 this trade had become nonexistent. To meet its needs for jute in 1955 and 1956, the Soviet Union imported 20,000 tons of it from China. Since jute is not grown in China, these shipments were undoubtedly reexports of Pakistani jute. With the signing of a trade agreement with Pakistan in 1956, this trade dropped to only 5,000 tons in 1957; the difference was made up by a sharp increase, to 11,400 tons, of jute imported directly from Pakistan.[21]

In 1958 the Soviet Union began importing jute bags from India, and by 1964 the value of these bags was greater than total imports of raw jute. Since the Indians had the facilities to make these bags, it was to the Soviets' advantage to buy the finished product and not use their capital resources to expand their own jute mills. Equally significant was Pakistan's swing toward China in 1963. The demand for jute had increased markedly in the Soviet Union, and to meet this demand imports were begun from India. Pakistan continued to supply jute to Russia, but India now became the prime supplier. In 1968 India provided 85 percent of Soviet imports of jute and jute products. Statistics are not yet available, but it is assumed that since the formation of independent Bangladesh (formerly East Pakistan) the Soviets have switched back to this source because of the superior quality of jute available there.

From the above discussion it can be seen that a primary objective of the Soviet Union in its trade with the developing countries is the obtaining of industrial raw materials needed by the expanding Soviet industry. It can also be seen that the Soviet Union did not purchase any industrial raw materials for which it did not have an urgent need, even though such imports might have been to its political advantage. The demand for certain industrial raw materials became evident as early as 1948, at which time large purchases of these commodities were made by the Soviet Union. Subsequently, as a result of restrictions applied in the cold war and of restrictions in accordance with a strict policy of autarky, the imports of these items were kept at abnormally low levels. As the restrictions on both sides have been lifted, trade in these commodities has expanded on the basis of need. In some cases, such as cotton and wool, internal or controlled sources of supply have been inadequate and either imports or excessive capital expenditures have been required. In other cases, such as jute and rubber, the Soviet Union has no internal supplies and must rely on the primary producing countries until substitutes can be found. If the Soviet Union reverts to a policy of complete autarky, it will increase internal production of needed commodities and develop substitutes for others. If such a policy is not followed, it is to be expected that imports of these items will increase from year to year.

Soviet Need for Foodstuffs

The remaining third of Soviet imports from the developing countries is limited to a few food items highly desired by the Soviet people, primarily cocoa, nuts, rice, tea, fruit, spirits, and coffee. Sugar was also in this group before Cuba became a socialist state. The primary purpose of these imports appears to have been the need to match the monetary incentives paid the Soviet citizens with items that they could buy.

Imports of raw sugar from Cuba accounted for one-third of all the food imports from the underdeveloped countries in 1957. Prior to the war the Soviet Union had always been an exporter of sugar. In the years following the war, the demand for sugar in the Soviet Union apparently increased rapidly; and imports of refined sugar from the countries of Eastern Europe were begun. In 1955 these imports from Czechoslovakia, Hungary, East Germany, and Poland dropped to 351,100 tons. To meet the demand the Soviets imported 235,600 tons of refined and 205,600 tons of raw sugar from Cuba in 1955. As a result of the political unrest in Eastern Europe in 1956, imports from Hungary, East Germany, and Poland were discontinued. As a result in 1957 the importation of raw sugar from Cuba was sharply increased to 350,900 tons, and 60,300 tons of refined sugar were imported from Italy.[22] It should be noted that Soviet purchases of sugar from Batista's Cuba in no way helped Castro to gain power. Further, although sugar imports from socialist Cuba subsequently grew even larger, they were begun because of a Soviet need for sugar and not for some subversive political purpose.

Chocolate is considered a very desirable luxury in the Soviet Union. After the First Five-Year Plan was completed in 1932, imports of cocoa beans from the Gold Coast (Ghana) were begun. From a low of 300 tons in 1932, these imports quickly grew to 11,000 tons in 1937.[23] Immediately after the war the

Soviets resumed the importation of cocoa at about the
1937 level. In 1948 these imports amounted to $10.1
million. In 1951, 1952, and 1953, cocoa imports
were valued at $9.5, $12.0, and $10.1 million, re-
spectively. As a result of Malenkov's incentive program, cocoa imports doubled to $20.4 million in 1954;
but these imports dropped to $11.5 million, or 14,100
tons, in 1955.[24] In 1957 Ghana received its independence, and in that year cocoa imports from that country tripled from 12,200 tons in 1956 to 37,600 tons
in 1957. (Imports from unidentified sources resulted
in total imports of 16,400 tons in 1956 and 44,100
tons in 1957.) Ghana remained the Soviet Union's
prime supplier of cocoa, providing two-thirds of
almost all cocoa imported by the USSR. In 1965 these
imports from Ghana peaked at 66,600 tons. After the
ouster of Nkrumah and a cooling of relations in 1966,
these imports dropped to 38,100 tons, or 35 percent
of Soviet imports, in 1968. Despite these shifts in
politics, the demand for cocoa remained high. From
a peak of 88,800 tons in 1965 (75 percent from
Ghana) imports dropped to 56,500 tons in 1966 (96
percent from Ghana). Subsequently, despite reduced
imports from Ghana, total cocoa imports rose to a
new peak of 109,000 tons in 1968 (only 35 percent
from Ghana). To meet this increased demand, the Soviet Union developed additional sources in Brazil,
Cameroun, Congo, Togo, the Ivory Coast, Ceylon, and
Nigeria. The latter country has been the most developed, and in 1968 Nigeria supplied 32 percent of
Soviet cocoa imports--almost as much as Ghana.

Various types of nuts are also much desired in
Russia, and in the 1930's attempts were made to grow
almonds and other nuts in Central Asia. Despite
these efforts the Soviets found it necessary to import
1,700 tons of nuts in 1938. Following World War II
nut imports were resumed. Initially these imports
were limited to almonds from Afghanistan and Iran,
walnuts from Afghanistan and China, and pine nuts
from Mongolia. In 1958 the Soviet Union imported
5,100 tons of these nuts. Since 1960 China has been
eliminated as a supplier of walnuts; but, as the demand increased sharply, these orders were merely
shifted to Afghanistan. For some unexplained reason,
imports of pine nuts from Mongolia were eliminated

and no imports of these nuts were made from other countries.

Today two other nuts--cashews from India and filberts from Turkey--account for almost three-fourths of Soviet nut imports. Although Goldman states that there is little evidence of domestic consumption of cashew nuts in the USSR, these nuts have been imported in increasing quantities since 1958.[25] In 1958 the Soviet Union imported 4,800 tons of cashews, and by 1968 this import volume had grown to 16,300 tons. There have been many charges that Soviet purchases of cashews were frequently diverted to the United States. It should be noted, however, that Soviet import statistics seem to be in general agreement with Indian export statistics, indicating that these nuts actually arrived in the Soviet Union. Further, Soviet import policy frowns on the import of unneeded goods. Thus, it must be assumed that the cashews satisfied a latent demand for nuts. Filberts were first imported from Turkey in 1964, shortly after Soviet-Turkish relations took a turn toward détente. These imports increased from a minimal 500 tons in 1964 to 12,100 tons in 1968. Although politics was of some importance in the timing, and possibly the magnitude, of the imports of both cashews and filberts, it was not the sole controlling factor; this trade has a solid foundation in economic need, comparative advantage, and consumer preference.

Rice is another item that is considered a luxury by many Russians, and for many others it is a staple food item. Prior to World War II the importation of rice varied considerably, but in many years it exceeded 50,000 tons. Practically all of this rice was imported from Iran.[26] Immediately after the war it appears that China supplied the Soviet Union with all its rice needs. Although statistical verification is not available, it is quite possible that, as in the case of sugar from Eastern Europe, China cut its shipments of rice to the USSR in 1955, necessitating the development of other sources to meet the existing demand. In any case, on July 1, 1955, the Soviet Union signed a three-year rice barter agreement with Burma.[27] Under the terms of this agreement, the Soviets imported 150,700 tons of rice from

Burma in 1955. In the same year they imported 19,400
tons from Egypt. In the next two years imports from
Burma were reduced while imports from Egypt were increased, so that imports from these two countries
were 180,000 tons in 1956 and 189,400 tons in 1957.
Between 1958 and 1960, however, these imports were
sharply curtailed because shipments from China were
resumed at a high level. During the entire postwar
period China remained the Soviet Union's primary
source of rice, and between 1958 and 1960 China supplied over 90 percent of Soviet rice imports.[28]

Following the break with China in 1960, rice
imports from China were cut off almost overnight.
In 1961 Soviet rice imports totaled a minimal 20,000
tons. Arrangements were quickly made to resume rice
imports from both Burma and the United Arab Republic
(Egypt); and new sources were developed in Cambodia,
North Korea, Pakistan, Brazil, and even in the United
States and Mexico. The most important of these
sources has been the United Arab Republic (UAR),
which in 1968 supplied 143,000 tons, or 55 percent,
of Soviet rice imports.[29] The development of these
new sources and the continued high volume of rice
imports indicate that there is a strong, persistent,
and otherwise unsatisfied demand for rice in the
Soviet Union. For this reason it can be concluded
that the primary basis for Soviet rice imports is
economic and not political, but the selection of
the particular source may well be politically determined.

Oranges are considered an ultimate in luxury in
the Soviet Union. Prior to World War II orange imports were severely restricted, but even so they
amounted to over 20,000 tons in 1937 and 1938. As
part of the trade expansion program in 1952, oranges
valued at $1.2 million were imported from Israel.
These imports were increased to $3.8 million in
1954.[30] In 1955, in addition to 12,400 tons of
oranges from Israel, the Soviet Union imported
10,700 tons from Morocco, 3,000 tons from Lebanon,
400 tons from Greece, and 4,800 tons from Italy. As
a result of the Suez crisis of 1956, the Soviets canceled all orange imports from Israel and sought new
sources. Imports from Morocco and Lebanon were
sharply increased to a total of 25,000 tons in 1957.

More significant, however, is the fact that imports
from Italy jumped to 13,000 tons, Greece supplied
4,900 tons, and the Union of South Africa entered
the market with 2,500 tons.[31] This sharp increase
in these latter countries, which occurred despite
higher prices, would indicate that there was a definite increase in demand for oranges.

In subsequent years the importation of oranges
continued to increase, reaching a peak of 193,400
tons in 1968. In 1963 the Soviet Union and Morocco
began an oil-for-oranges barter, and orange imports
from that country doubled. By 1968 Morocco was supplying 101,700 tons of oranges, about 52 percent of
Soviet imports. The UAR is now the second largest
supplier, followed by Algeria. Greece has remained
a significant factor in this market. It is interesting to note that, despite the break with China in
1960, the latter has continued to supply oranges and
mandarin oranges to the Soviet Union.

The consumer-goods drive following Stalin's
death has also resulted in increasing imports of
other fruits--both dried and fresh. The most important of these has been raisins. In 1968 the Soviet
Union imported 18,000 tons of raisins from Afghanistan, 17,300 tons from Turkey, 12,300 tons from Iran,
and 3,400 tons from Cyprus. Date imports from Iraq
in 1968 totaled 20,000 tons, and 3,600 tons of dried
apricots were imported from Iran and Afghanistan.
Most other fruits were obtained from the Comecon
countries, but bananas were also imported from Vietnam and Guinea and apples were purchased from Lebanon.

Tea is Russia's national drink and, despite
efforts to grow adequate amounts in the Caucasus,
has always been imported. In 1938 these imports
totaled 16,700 tons. After the war China supplied
all of Soviet tea imports until 1955. India became
a second source in 1956, and by 1960 Soviet imports
were divided equally between China and India. Following the split in 1960, almost the entire tea market was switched to India. Since Soviet imports of
22,700 tons of tea in 1968 are not much larger than
1938 imports, it is possible that many Russians have
switched to coffee. In 1938 coffee imports were a
scant 1,200 tons. By 1968 these imports had grown
to 31,400 tons. As a result of the 1960 coffee-for-

manufactured-goods agreement with Brazil, coffee imports from Brazil grew rapidly to a peak of 23,300
tons in 1963. Subsequently Brazilian coffee shipments dropped to half this level, and India and Colombia became major suppliers. In 1968 the Soviets imported 12,000 tons of coffee from Brazil, 8,700 tons
from India, 4,100 tons from Colombia, and 5,400 tons
from Indonesia, Ethiopia, Yemen, Cameroun, and Guinea.

From the above discussion it can be seen that
there were sound economic reasons for much of the
foodstuff imports from the developing countries. In
the case of sugar, rice, and tea the underdeveloped
countries were developed as alternative sources after
imports from Soviet bloc countries were reduced. On
the other hand, cocoa, nuts, and fruit were imported
to make financial incentive plans more effective;
and purchases were made from the developing countries
primarily because they are the major producers of
these commodities. In all cases the items imported
are highly desired by the Soviet people.

Independence and National Liberation

One of the most significant political changes
in the postwar period was the dissolution of the major
European empires. The British started this process
by granting India and Pakistan their independence in
1947 and Burma and Ceylon theirs in 1948. The Dutch
followed suit by making Indonesia fully independent
in 1949, and under UN auspices Libya gained total independence from Italy in 1951. In 1954 French Indochina was split into independent Cambodia, Laos, and
the two Vietnams. In the next several years the
French gave up Morocco, Tunisia, and Guinea and the
British freed Ghana and Malaya. Then in 1960, in
one explosive movement, Nigeria got its independence
from England, Belgium gave up its sovereignty over
the Congo, and French Equatorial and West Africa were
splintered into a number of independent countries.
The last wave of independence, between 1961 and 1963,
saw Algeria gaining its independence from France and
Britain transferring sovereignty to local governments
in Tanganyika, Uganda, and Kenya.

As mentioned earlier, the Soviets at first ignored this change. Although purchases were made from India, Pakistan, Burma, and Ceylon in 1947 and 1948, they were made for strictly economic reasons. For some reason the Soviets continued to think of these countries as British colonies and thus outside their sphere of interest. As the cold war forced the Soviet Union to return to a policy of autarky, these imports quickly dropped to very low levels.

Following the death of Stalin in 1953, the Soviet Union hurriedly developed trade ties with the newly independent countries, including India, Pakistan, Burma, Indonesia, and Israel. Subsequently, as other countries gained their independence, the Soviets quickly increased their trade with each of them, so that today they have trade relations with almost all of the developing countries. It is most likely that these trade ties were developed for the economic reasons discussed in the preceding sections, but it is also possible that the Russians were heeding Lenin's injunction that the road to London and Paris lies through Asia and Africa and were developing trade relations for political reasons. In an environment of anti-Communist hysteria, all economic explanations were ignored; and each new trade action was seen solely as another phase in a trade-political offensive that had subversion as its major goal.

A calmer view would seem to indicate that the Soviets handled political subversion and trade quite separately. Although the Soviet Union supported national liberation movements in various countries, it did not use trade for this purpose. On the other hand, the Soviets were quite opportunistic; and when trade offered a specific political advantage, it was utilized. Thus, they were quick to buy up depressed commodities--such as coffee, sugar, and cocoa--and immediately use the purchases to further ingratiate themselves with the selling country. Also, when a country's relations with the West began to sour, as happened in Cuba and Turkey, the Soviets quickly moved in and increased trade. Generally, however, the increased trade involved only a shifting of sources for commodities needed and already being purchased by the Soviet Union from other developing countries. Furthermore, the Soviet Union has had some of its worst experiences in countries where trade and politics were closely entwined. In Indonesia and Ghana, for example, the Soviets suffered major setbacks when their political protégés were ousted. In India politics have been much subdued, and Soviet trade and aid relations have been quite effective in winning friends. In short, the Soviets have come to a realization that socialist revolutions in the Third World are far off. To further their cause, they now accept existing governments as they are and try to develop lasting, friendly relations. Trade obviously is an ideal medium for reaching this end, and thus further expansion of trade with the developing countries can be expected.

SELECTION OF SOURCES
OF SUPPLY

The first step in Soviet foreign trade planning is the determination of the goods to be imported. Once this has been done, the foreign trade corporations must select the source or sources of supply. In making such a selection, these corporations must consider various factors: which countries produce the commodity in the volume needed, what are the political relationships between the Soviet Union and the producing countries, and what arrangements must be made in order to pay for the needed imports. Each of these considerations is of great importance to the Soviet planner and will be discussed below in relation to the commodities imported from the under-developed countries.

Supply and Political
Considerations

Following a policy of Soviet bloc autarky as described in Chapter 1, the Soviet Union, after World War II, utilized bloc sources in preference to all others whenever possible. In the case of wool and hides, Mongolia and China became the primary suppliers. Sugar was imported from Czechoslovakia, Hungary, East Germany, and Poland. China became the sole supplier

of tea and rice. It appears that in 1955 a combination of increased demand in the Soviet Union and reduced shipments by the bloc countries forced the Soviet Union to seek additional sources outside the
bloc. Similar and stronger pressures to find new
nonsocialist sources were also generated in 1960 by
the Sino-Soviet split. Adequate supplies of other
commodities, such as rubber, cocoa, and oranges,
could be obtained mainly or only from nonbloc sources,
particularly from the underdeveloped countries of
Asia and Africa. When political relations with these
countries turned sour, as happened in Ghana, Indonesia, and Australia, the Soviet Union was again
forced to seek alternative sources.

In seeking additional sources for the few items
they wished to import, the Soviets were limited by
the small number of countries producing the commodities in adequate volume.[32] Thus, when the Eastern
European countries reduced their shipments of sugar
to the Soviet Union, it was only logical that the
Soviets should turn to the world's primary exporter,
Cuba, for all of their needs. It should be noted
that availability of adequate supplies of sugar was
the sole determining factor in this choice. There
is no evidence of any political involvement by the
Soviet Union during Batista's reign. Soviet political involvement came only after Castro's takeover in
1960, long after Cuba was selected as Russia's prime
source of sugar. After that time it can be assumed
that the volume of sugar imported was determined
partly on the basis of Soviet needs and partly on
the basis of political expediency.

Soviet economic and political relations with
China had a significant effect on the determination
of specific sources of supply. In the postwar period
the Soviet Union, for the most part, limited its tea
and rice imports to China. By 1955, however, Sino-
Soviet economic relations showed signs of strain;
and the Chinese became unwilling or unable to meet
the Soviet demand for these commodities. As a result
the Soviet Union was forced to develop new sources.
For tea the Soviets turned mainly to India, the
world's largest producing country, and also purchased
small amounts of tea from Ceylon and North Korea.
Similarly, Burma, the leading rice exporter outside

the bloc, was developed as an additional source of
rice. Egypt also became a supplier of rice under the
terms of the 1955 arms-for-commodities barter agreement. Following the Sino-Soviet split in 1960, the
Soviet Union eliminated China as a source for rice,
tea, walnuts, and hides. Since the demand for these
items continued strong, the Soviets converted their
alternative sources for tea and rice into primary
sources and developed additional sources. Initially
Burma and the UAR split the rice market. Gradually,
however, Burma was phased out and the UAR became the
major supplier of rice; Spain, North Korea, and Pakistan became substantial suppliers. India now became
almost the sole source of tea, although small amounts
continued to be imported from Ceylon and North Vietnam. In the same manner, walnut imports were shifted
from China to Afghanistan, and India replaced China
as the major supplier of hides.

Another example of the effect of Chinese relations on source selection can be seen in the case of
jute. Jute is produced in quantity only in Bangladesh (formerly East Pakistan) and India. To meet
their needs for jute, it was necessary for the Soviets
to trade with either of these countries or to obtain
the jute from another country that purchased it from
Pakistan or India. Pakistan was initially chosen as
the prime source of supply because of the superior
quality of jute grown in East Bengal. At first this
jute came through China on a three-sided barter arrangement, but after 1956 imports were made directly
from Pakistan. To Russia's chagrin, Pakistan aligned
itself with China in 1963. In retaliation the Soviets immediately shifted most of their jute purchases
to India, and in 1968 almost 85 percent of Soviet
imports of jute and jute products was from India.
In 1971 the Soviet Union supported the independence
movement in East Pakistan and was one of the first
countries to recognize newly independent Bangladesh.
Since the jute from Bangladesh is superior to that
from India, it is assumed that the Soviet Union has
once again shifted its source of supply. It is likely,
however, that some of this jute will be shipped
through India, where it will be made into jute bags
and other products.

Western restrictions on trade with the Soviet Union affected source determination in at least one case--rubber. Malaya and Indonesia are the biggest producers and exporters of natural rubber and were Russia's prime sources of supply prior to World War II. After the war this trade was resumed, and these countries were the Soviet Union's only sources of rubber until restrictions were placed on this trade by the West. Since Ceylon was not affected by these restrictions, it, through China, became the Soviets' only source of rubber. When restrictions on the trade of rubber were lifted, Indonesia and Malaya again became prime suppliers of rubber and Ceylon was continued as a minor supplier.

The nature and degree of Soviet relations with the developing countries has also determined the source of supply, as can be seen in the case of Ghana and cocoa. Ghana is the leading producer and exporter of cocoa. Since the Soviet Union had purchased cocoa from the Gold Coast before the war, it was only natural that they return to this source in the postwar period. Between 1955 and 1966 Ghana supplied about 75 percent of the Soviet Union's imports of cocoa. In 1958 and 1959, however, the Russians seemed not to be ready to deal with independent African nations; and in these two years Ghana supplied only a little over a fourth of Soviet cocoa needs. After Nkrumah was ousted in 1966 and relations with the Soviet Union cooled drastically, the Soviets shifted their cocoa purchases to Nigeria, Brazil, and Cameroun; and Ghana's share of the Soviet cocoa market dropped to only 35 percent in 1968.

Immediately after Ghana got its independence in 1957, the Soviets shifted their major cocoa purchases to not yet independent Nigeria and Cameroun. This shift is not fully explained, but it appears that the Russians preferred to conduct this trade with proven colonial sources and not involve themselves with the newly independent state of Ghana. In 1960 the Soviet Union offered Nkrumah aid and immediately shifted its cocoa trade back to Ghana. For several years Nigeria and Cameroun were seemingly ignored. To meet a growing demand for cocoa, the Soviets again returned to Nigeria in 1964 and, as a result of cool-

ing relations with Ghana in 1966, by 1968 the Russians
were buying almost as much cocoa from Nigeria as
from Ghana. Cocoa purchases from Cameroun were resumed in 1968, because of the ouster of Nkrumah. Although Nigeria and Cameroun were ignored as sources
in 1961, Brazil became a significant supplier in that
year. Although the original purchase was possibly
in return for Brazil's granting of diplomatic recognition, it should be noted that Brazil has continued
to supply the Soviet Union with a substantial amount
of cocoa.

As in the case of cocoa, a combination of economic and political considerations have been involved
in determining sources for such products as wool and
oranges. Following the war Mongolia and China were
the Soviet Union's only suppliers of wool. The demand for wool, however, continued to grow--especially
after the death of Stalin. Mongolia and China were
unable to keep up with this demand, and in 1953 and
1954 the Soviets purchased $33.1 million and $32.3
million, respectively, of wool from Australia. Then
in 1955, because of the Petrov espionage case, the
Soviet Union severed all ties with Australia and
hurriedly sought replacement sources to meet its wool
needs. Other than Australia, the major wool suppliers
were New Zealand, Argentina, the Union of South Africa,
and Uruguay. As a result of this political action,
the Soviet Union met its economic needs by switching
its Australian trade to these countries. Subsequently India, Afghanistan, Iran, Syria, and Turkey
were developed as minor sources of wool. Politics
again entered the picture in 1960 in two ways.
First, because a number of countries in Black Africa
gained their independence that year, the Soviets
found it expedient to cut off all trade with apartheid-
minded South Africa. Second, as a result of the
Sino-Soviet split, China ceased to be a supplier of
wool to the Soviet Union. Australia once again became the USSR's prime source of wool, and since that
time there have been no other changes in sources.

Orange imports present a similar situation. Although oranges are grown in the United States, Mexico,
India, and Japan, the primary exporters of oranges
are those countries surrounding the Mediterranean.
When the Soviet Union began importing oranges in 1952,

its sole source was Israel, one of the leading exporting countries. By 1955 orange imports from Israel
amounted to 12,400 tons, Morocco supplied 10,700 tons,
Italy was the source of 4,800 tons, and Lebanon furnished 3,000 tons. Up to this time availability of
supply appears to have been the primary criterion in
the selection of sources. At the time of the Suez
crisis in October 1956, however, the Soviet Union
sided with the Arabs; as a result the Soviets terminated all purchases of oranges from Israel. To meet
a growing demand for oranges, it was necessary for
the Soviet Union either to increase imports from
other current sources or to develop new sources. Imports from Morocco sharply increased; and, although
Italian oranges were almost twice as expensive as
those from other sources, these two countries together supplied two-thirds of Soviet orange imports
in 1957. The next year Spain suffered from depressed
prices and the Soviets immediately switched their
purchases from Italy and Morocco so as to reduce the
cost of badly wanted orange imports. Morocco regained its position as leading orange supplier in
1960; and subsequently the UAR, Cyprus, and Algeria
have been added as sources. Since 1965 no imports
have been made from either Italy or Lebanon.

The above discussion indicates that the primary
criterion in selecting a source of supply has been
the availability of the needed commodities and not
some political factor. This, however, does not eliminate the possibilities of political influence in
the choice of sources. This has been pointed out
particularly in the case of the Sino-Soviet schism,
the Suez crisis, and African independence. In the
smaller countries, particularly in Africa, some token
purchases may have been made to politically influence
the citizenry; but in general such influence was more
an opportunistic by-product of such trade and not a
planned campaign of politics through trade.

Arrangements for Paying
for Imports

One of the most severe problems faced by the
Soviet Union in its procurement of needed raw materials

and foodstuffs is the generation of the foreign exchange needed to pay for these goods. During the
1950's this problem was most acute in the sterling
bloc. Despite its large purchases of rubber from
Malaya, cocoa from Ghana, and wool from New Zealand
and the Union of South Africa, the Soviet Union was
not able to sell these countries anything. As a result the Soviet Union incurred a growing trade deficit in pounds sterling that was mitigated in 1957
only by greatly increased sales of aluminum, tin,
petroleum, timber, manganese, and ferroalloys on the
British market. Similarly, sugar imports from Cuba
in the 1950's were not balanced by any Cuban purchases
of Soviet goods, and the Soviet Union was forced to
sell goods in other markets to raise the exchange
needed to pay Cuba.

To avoid this situation the Soviet Union has
tried to develop a compensatory market for Soviet
goods in all countries from which it buys. In doing
so it has relied heavily on bilateral barter and
trade agreements. As early as 1949 the Soviet Union
signed a barter agreement with India that provided
India with badly needed wheat in exchange for jute,
tea, and castor oil. A similar arrangement was made
in 1951, but in 1953 a barter agreement could not be
reached because India at that time had an adequate
wheat reserve.[33] In 1950 the Soviet Union proposed
a barter of unlimited amounts of Thailand rice for
Soviet machinery, paper, and fertilizer.[34] The Thais,
however, turned down this offer. On July 1, 1955,
the Soviet Union and Burma signed a three-year barter
agreement under which Burmese rice was exchanged for
rice mill equipment, textile mills, textiles, trucks,
cement, and other items.[35] Since Burma was suffering
from an unmarketable surplus of rice, this agreement
was warmly received. Subsequently the rice market
firmed, and prices rose above those in the long-term
agreement with the Soviet Union. As a result Burma
asked for relief from the Soviet Union, and shipments
of rice to the latter were cut back.[36]

In the Near East the Soviet Union signed a barter agreement with Egypt in March 1948. In exchange
for 38,000 tons of cotton, the Soviet Union supplied
Egypt with 216,000 tons of wheat and 19,000 tons of
corn. Another barter agreement was concluded in

August 1953, providing for the exchange of cotton
for oil and war materials. On March 6, 1954, an
Egyptian economic delegation, including the Egyptian
deputy minister of war, went to Moscow to discuss
trade. Later that month an agreement for the exchange
of $14.4 million of goods was signed. The following
year, in April 1955, another barter agreement was
signed for the exchange of cotton for oil. Against
this background of barter agreements, Egypt on September 23, 1955, announced that it had made a long-term,
barter-credit arrangement whereby Egypt would exchange
cotton for arms. It has frequently been alleged that
the Soviet purpose behind this barter arrangement was
to stir up trouble in the Near East. This may in
fact be true. It must be remembered, however, that
the Egyptians had long sought weapons from the West
to protect themselves from a possible attack by Israel.
In addition it was not the Egyptians who started the
fighting in the Suez crisis but Israel, Great Britain,
and France. Furthermore, the barter arrangement was
evidently to the satisfaction of both the Soviet
Union and Egypt, since Egypt disposed of its cotton
and obtained the arms it wanted and the USSR obtained
needed cotton in exchange for obsolescent military
equipment and not scarce foreign exchange.[37]

From this discussion it can be seen that the use
of barter agreements opened or widened sources of
supply that did not require the utilization of foreign
exchange. Since the Soviet Union's supply of foreign
exchange was quite limited, such a consideration became very important in determining the selection of
a source.

Soviet Long-Term Credits
to Developing Countries*

In trying to develop trade with the less-
developed countries, the Soviet Union faced several
very severe problems. One was that as former colonies

----

*A complete analysis of the Soviet foreign aid
program is beyond the scope of this work. For read-
ers interested in this subject, M. I. Goldman, Soviet

these countries were oriented mainly toward the West.
Another was that these countries, for the most part,
had an adequate and growing market willing and able
to pay in convertible currency or in pounds sterling,
which were convertible within the sterling bloc.
These countries were usually more than willing to
sell their products to the Soviets for cash--provided
it was cash they could use. But in general these
countries had little interest in buying from the Soviet Union. To counter this lack of interest and to
develop adequate means of financing Soviet purchases,
the Soviets increased their selling efforts in the
underdeveloped areas. This, in fact, was one of the
primary reasons for the sharp increase in Soviet participation in trade fairs in this area. In September
1953, Mikhail Menshikov, former minister of foreign
trade, was appointed Soviet ambassador to India.
Upon arriving in India in November 1953, Menshikov
offered to sell India complete factories. This offer
was rejected, but in December 1953 an agreement calling for increased trade through private Indian merchants was signed by India and the Soviet Union.[38]
Subsequently trade agreements were signed with various
other countries in Southeast Asia and the Near East.
As a result of these agreements and the increased
selling effort in India and other developing countries,
sales to this area increased sharply. Despite these
increases, sales did not keep pace with purchases;
and the Soviet trade deficit with the underdeveloped
countries grew from $32 million in 1952 to $54 million in 1954 and $174 million in 1957.

Soviet demand for industrial raw materials and
foodstuffs continued to increase, making it impera-
tive that a new means be found to penetrate the markets of the less-developed countries. Since the
governments of the developing countries are almost
universally dedicated to a program of rapid industrialization, and since the Soviet Union has a comparative
advantage in industrial equipment, the answer lay in

Foreign Aid (New York: Frederick A. Praeger, 1967),
and B. R. Stokke, Soviet and Eastern European Trade
and Aid in Africa (New York: Frederick A. Praeger,
1967), are recommended.

assisting these countries in their economic development programs. The solution was the sale of complete
plants, other industrial equipment, and technical
assistance on long-term credits. After experimenting
in Afghanistan, the Soviets came up with a development
credit system in 1955 that became the standard for
all of its subsequent "aid" programs. These credits
are repayable in local currencies or commodities
over a 12-year period and bear a very attractive interest rate of only 2.5 percent.

These credits have often been referred to as
Soviet economic aid, but this is possibly a misnomer.
Although the countries received new facilities, there
is little evidence that the credits were designed
primarily to aid the economy of the recipient countries; and in some cases, Guinea for example, the
"aid" actually hurt the economy. The primary purpose of the Soviet Union appears to have been an attempt to generate within the underdeveloped countries
the foreign exchange equivalent needed to pay for
Soviet purchases from these countries. The use of
these credits has enabled the Soviets to increase
their imports from the developing countries to an
extent that would not have been possible without
them. Since these imports appear to be needed by
the Soviet Union, it would seem that the credit program has been very successful. That the Soviets
viewed their "aid" in pragmatic business terms can be
seen in Khrushchev's recollections of the Aswan Dam
credits, in which he said he

> . . . instructed our economists at the State
> Planning Commission to study the Egyptian
> proposal carefully. They did so and some
> time later gave us a projection of what the
> dam would yield in the way of an economic
> as well as political return on our invest-
> ment. We were interested in determining
> whether it would be a profitable business
> transaction. Naturally we would be glad to
> have an opportunity to bolster the economy
> of our friends and in so doing to strengthen
> our relations with them. But that was a
> political consideration, and we had also to
> make sure that we wouldn't simply be giving

our money away. We had to make sure that
the Egyptians could repay us in regular deliveries of their best long-fiber cotton,
rice, and other goods.[39]

It is interesting to note that the credit program is in complete accord with the basic foreign
trade policies of the Soviet Union. The basic import
and export policies call for the import of needed
goods and the export of those items needed to pay
for the imports. Generally speaking, the exported
goods should be those least needed or those in which
the Soviet Union has the highest comparative advantage. In all of these agreements, the materials sent
by the Soviet Union were of an industrial nature, in
which the Soviets hold a comparative advantage. It
may be argued that the Soviet Union can use the steel
mills for its own purposes. This is quite probably
correct. However, the Soviet Union also needs certain
commodities. In granting credits to a country such
as India, Soviet foreign trade planners must balance
the gains from Indian raw materials and the gains
from additional steel capacity. If it is determined
that the raw materials or other commodities are of
more importance, then the steel capacity must be
sacrificed. In most of the credit agreements, the
Soviet Union is not faced with this problem; and the
products imported by the Soviets definitely provide
an advantage over the goods exported. Being human,
however, the Russians have made mistakes, particularly
in the rush to help the multitude of newly independent
countries.
Despite the success of the long-term credits in
various countries, the Soviet Union has not been able
to completely eliminate its trade deficits with the
developing countries. There is no such program in
Malaysia, and by 1970 the cumulative trade deficit
with this country totaled $1.7 billion. Further, de-
spite much talk of Soviet economic activities, the
Soviet Union has a cumulative trade deficit of $245
million in Black Africa (especially Ghana) and $470
million in Latin America (Argentina and Brazil). In
these cases the Soviets have several alternatives.
They can reduce their purchases despite their needs.
They can develop sales of Soviet goods in these areas.

They can generate foreign exchange by selling goods elsewhere for hard currency. Or they can utilize their gold resources. Obviously the most attractive alternative would be to increase trade, and it appears that this is the choice currently being pursued by the Soviets.

SUMMARY

Soviet foreign trade with the developing countries in the years following Stalin's death has frequently been referred to as an economic offensive for political purposes. By analyzing the content and nature of this trade, this chapter attempts to show that this trade was motivated primarily by economic factors.

The Soviet need for such raw materials as cotton, wool, rubber, hides, and jute has accounted for about 66 percent of Soviet trade with the underdeveloped countries. The remaining third of this trade has consisted of such foodstuffs as sugar, cocoa, rice, oranges, nuts, and tea, which are highly desired by the Soviet citizens. The demand for these products was evident as early as 1948, when large quantities of these commodities were purchased from the less-developed countries. Such a demand is also indicated by the fact that large quantities of certain of these commodities were also imported from the members of the socialist world. For various reasons the demand in the Soviet Union exceeded available internal or controlled supplies, and imports had to be relied on.

In selecting sources for the few items they wished to buy, the Soviets were limited in their choice of sources primarily by the availability of the needed commodities. For this reason imports of sugar, rice, cocoa, and tea were made from the primary producing countries of each of these products. Likewise, jute was imported from its two sources, India and Bangladesh (East Pakistan); and rubber was imported from the three major producing countries, Indonesia, Malaysia, and Ceylon. Wool was at first purchased from Australia, and oranges were imported mainly from Israel. When for political reasons there was a hiatus in trade with Australia, trade

with Israel was severed, and trade with China was cut
to a nominal level, the Soviet Union was required to
rely on the limited number of alternative sources.

One of the major problems faced by the Soviet
Union in the procurement of needed commodities was a
lack of the foreign exchange needed to pay for them.
To counter this problem, the Soviets at first utilized
barter arrangements to exchange various commodities
for the items they desired to import. At the same
time the selling efforts of Soviet corporations were
increased in the underdeveloped countries. Despite
these efforts the Soviet trade deficit with the developing countries grew, requiring new methods of
financing imports. Beginning in 1954 and 1955, the
Soviet Union sold complete factories and other installations to the less-developed countries on long-
term credit. The repayment of these credits was to
be in local goods or local currency. In this manner
the Soviet Union has been able to step up its purchases from the developing countries. As the Soviet
demand for various commodities increases, it is likely
that the use of such credits will be continued.

The fact that Soviet trade with the developing
countries has been motivated primarily by economic
factors does not eliminate the importance of political factors. Once trade has been established, the
Soviets undoubtedly exploit it for whatever political
advantage can be obtained. Although constructed for
financial reasons, the Bhilai and Bokaro steel mills
in India and the Aswan Dam in the UAR have served
the Soviet Union as ideal tools with which to convince the peoples of the underdeveloped countries
that the Soviet Union is interested in their economic
welfare. Furthermore, by exploiting the fact that
they are buying commodities currently in surplus as
a result of cuts in Western purchases, the Soviets
are able to convince some people that the Soviet
Union is their benefactor. Possibly more important
is the potential danger to a country's freedom that
can result if the country becomes heavily indebted
to the Soviet Union. But the Soviet Union has also
had its political misfortunes, as exemplified by the
ousters of Sukarno and Nkrumah; and India and the
UAR have consistently resisted domination by the
Soviet Union.

8

WESTERN RESTRICTIONS ON TRADE WITH THE SOVIET UNION

To complete this study of Soviet foreign trade, it is necessary to consider the
various restrictions placed on it by the
countries of the West. This chapter begins
with a discussion of the restrictions applied during the interwar years from 1918
to 1940. These restrictions include the
Allied blockade from 1918 to 1920, the
antidumping measures of 1930 and 1931, and
limitations on Soviet trade imposed at the
beginning of World War II. A discussion
of the strategic trade controls applied by
the West following World War II concludes
the chapter. This discussion includes the
reasons for such controls, the methods of
control, the relative effectiveness of the
controls, and recent steps taken to reduce
the amount of control over trade with the
Soviet bloc.

Since 1918 the trade of the Soviet Union has,
at almost all times, been subject to some form of restriction or discrimination by the nations of the
West. For the first 20 years this discrimination was
mainly in the form of higher interest rates, which
resulted from a mistrust of the Soviets following the
annulment of all Tsarist debts. (This discrimination
has been discussed in Chapter 4.) In addition to

such discrimination by private individuals and firms,
definite discrimination against trade with the Soviet Union has been applied by various Western governments on four specific occasions: the blockade
of Russia from 1918 to 1920, embargoes in 1930 and
1931 to counteract dumping, failure to issue export
licenses in 1940, and the various restrictions on
trade with the Soviet Union and other bloc countries
dating from 1948.

INTERWAR PERIOD RESTRICTIONS
(1918-41)

Blockade of the Soviet Union
(1918-20)

During World War I the British and French instituted a naval blockade to prevent the neutral nations from trading with Germany. After the Russians
signed a separate peace treaty at Brest-Litovsk in
March 1918, the blockade was extended to cover trade
with Russia. When the Supreme War Council in Paris
lifted the naval blockade from Germany on July 12,
1919, it officially established a new blockade on
Soviet Russia.[1] The objective of this new blockade
was to prevent neutral nations from trading with
Russia, so that the Bolsheviks would be forced into
submission. To insure effectiveness, other countries
were asked to join Britain and France in insuring
that no trade got through.[2] The United States announced that it would not participate in a naval
blockade, for such an action would be against traditional American policy. The United States also let
it be known that it approved the action and that it
would cooperate by refusing clearance for ships bound
to Soviet Russia.[3]

As a result of this blockade, trade with Soviet
Russia was completely severed. A small amount of
trade continued in the areas controlled by the White
Guard, but no trade whatsoever was conducted with
Bolshevik-held territory. By November 1919, however,
it had become evident that the Soviet government has
control of the Civil War; and it was unlikely that

this government was going to collapse because of internal weakness. Under these circumstances the blockade no longer served a useful purpose; and on January 16, 1920, the Allied Supreme Council lifted the blockade.[4]

Antidumping Discrimination
(1930-31)

As mentioned previously, the Soviet adherence to a balance of imports with exports and the world depression combined to result in alleged Soviet dumping in 1930 and 1931. Usual measures to counteract dumping were to no avail, so it was felt that more drastic measures were called for. Within a period of months France, Belgium, Hungary, Rumania, Yugoslavia, and Canada imposed special antidumping restrictions that applied only to the Soviet Union.[5] The United States applied a prohibitive tariff on Soviet matches and demanded certificates stating that Soviet timber had not been processed by forced labor.[6]

All of these restrictions were clearly discriminatory, for they applied only to the trade of the Soviet Union. Being very sensitive to any form of discrimination, the Soviets reacted immediately by adopting a policy of counterattack. On October 20, 1930, the Council of People's Commissars passed a resolution banning imports and the use of ships and harbors of countries discriminating against the Soviet Union.[7] The next day the Commissariat of Foreign Trade cut off all trade with France, Canada, and certain other countries.[8] On July 11, 1931, the French lifted their embargo, and on the same day the counterembargo was lifted by the Soviets.[9] The Canadian embargo and counterembargo were lifted on February 27, 1935.[10]

This action, at a time when the Soviets were striving to complete their First Five-Year Plan in the face of a world economic crisis, would at first appear daring. Actually the trade with these particular countries amounted to very little, and the counterembargo was a grand bluff that worked. If it had been its major suppliers that had applied this embargo, it is most likely that the Soviet Union

would have backed down. By 1933 the First Five-Year
Plan had been completed, and the Soviets felt more
independent of even their major suppliers. In that
year two engineers from the British Vickers firm
were arrested as spies by the Russians. When these
men were given prison sentences, the British applied
an embargo on 80 percent of the imports from the Soviet Union.[11] The Soviets immediately applied a
counterembargo identical to the one they had earlier
applied to France.[12] Although the Soviets felt more
independent, they evidently still needed the goods
from England. As a result, after only two and one-
half months the Russians backed down, released the
engineers, and ended the counterembargo.[13]

Wartime Discrimination
(1940-41)

The Soviet Union and Germany concluded a nonaggression pact on August 23, 1939. One week later
Poland was invaded, and World War II was officially
begun. Because of the nonaggression pact, the Allies
considered the Soviet Union an unfriendly nation and
immediately clamped restrictions on trade with that
country.

The U.S. Department of Commerce placed restrictions on the issuance of export and reexport licenses
for goods destined to the Soviet Union. Up to this
time the Soviet Union had purchased various commodities, including wool, on the American exchanges. In
May 1940 a cargo of wool that was purchased on the
San Francisco exchange and shipped from Peru was refused a reexport license.[14] During 1940 the United
States, through a "gentlemen's agreement," placed an
absolute embargo on copper and aviation gasoline.[15]
Subsequently other items were included in this embargo for national defense reasons. In May 1941 export licenses for machinery valued at $5 million were
refused 24 hours before shipment.[16]

Since the countries of Europe were devoting all
production facilities to military needs, the actions
of the United States at this time resulted in an almost complete embargo on Soviet trade. With the invasion of Russia in June 1941, however, the situation

was reversed; and as an ally the Soviet Union was supplied its needs by the United States, Canada, and Great Britain.

STRATEGIC CONTROLS ON TRADE WITH
THE USSR (1948-   )

In the early postwar years it was hoped that the Soviet Union would abandon its policy of autarky and rejoin the world economy as a full member. By 1947 the seizure of control of the Eastern European countries and other actions by the Soviets convinced the countries of the West that the Soviet Union was determined to sabotage Western Europe's economic recovery and at the same time to strengthen its own war potential. The Berlin blockade and the Korean War intensified these feelings and raised fears of further Soviet military actions. To counteract this threat, the United States and other countries of the West initiated various collective actions, including coordinated control over the trade of strategic items with the Soviet Union and the members of the Soviet bloc.

Initial U.S. Controls

In December 1947 the U.S. House of Representatives passed a resolution calling on the Department of Commerce to show cause why any more material of potential military significance should be exported to the Soviet Union. In accordance with this resolution, the Department of Commerce made a study of such trade; and on March 1, 1948, it placed most exports to the Soviet Union and the bloc under mandatory licensing control.[17] At this time the decision as to which commodities would or would not be given an export license was strictly administrative, and the Department of Commerce was responsible for making the decisions. This system of mandatory licensing control was confirmed by the Export Control Act of 1949, which remained in force for 20 years.

On March 24, 1948, the Economic Cooperation Act of 1948 was amended, and section 117(d) directed the economic cooperation administrator:

> to refuse delivery in so far as practicable
> to participating countries of commodities
> which go into the production of any commod-
> ity for delivery to any non-participating
> European country which commodity would be
> refused export licenses to those countries
> by the United States in the interests of
> national security.[18]

Since the list of goods ineligible for export licenses from the United States was quite lengthy,
this amendment placed a considerable amount of control over the trade of the recipient nations with
the Soviet Union in the hands of the economic cooperation administrator.

Soviet support, if not sponsorship, of the Korean War added new pressures to the cold war; and
more extensive measures of control over trade with
the Soviet bloc were given to the economic cooperation administrator by the Cannon Amendment to the
Economic Cooperation Act on September 27, 1950, and
by the Kem Amendment, a rider to the 1951 Appropria-
tions Act, on June 2, 1951.[19] According to the Cannon Amendment, aid was to be cut off from any country whose trade with the Soviet bloc was found to be
detrimental to U.S. security. Under these conditions
American exports to the Soviet Union were controlled
by the Department of Commerce, and the trade of most
other countries with the Soviet bloc was placed under
the surveillance of the economic cooperation administrator.

At this time pressures were also applied to imports from the Soviet Union. In January 1951 the
Treasury Department (Customs) banned all imports of
Soviet crabmeat. It was alleged that this crabmeat
was being processed by Japanese POWs, and under section 307 of the Tariff Act of 1930 the import of any
goods made by forced labor is prohibited. In June
1951, Congress, in an amendment to the Reciprocal
Trade Agreement Extension Act, forbade the administration to extend to the Soviet Union any tariff or
other concession negotiated with other countries.
Following through, President Truman on August 1,
1951, proclaimed that as of September 1, 1951 all
most-favored-nation (MFN) privileges previously

granted the Soviet Union were canceled. By this action imports from the Soviet Union became subject to
the exceedingly high duties of the 1930 Smoot-Hawley
Tariff--duties as much as 10 times those charged imports from other countries. Furthermore, a rider to
the Extension Act eliminated a good part of the traditional imports of Soviet furs by invoking an embargo on imports of mink, ermine, marten, kolinsky,
weasel, fox, and muskrat furs.[20]

The Battle Act

On January 24, 1952, the Mutual Defense Assistance Control Act of 1951 went into effect. This act
specifically declared:

> . . . it to be the policy of the United
> States to apply an embargo on the shipment
> of arms, ammunition, and implements of war,
> atomic energy materials, petroleum, trans-
> portation materials of strategic value, and
> items of primary strategic significance
> used in the production of arms, ammunition,
> and implements of war to any nation or com-
> bination of nations threatening the secur-
> ity of the United States, including the
> Union of Soviet Socialist Republics and
> all countries under its domination.
>   It is further declared to be the pol-
> icy of the United States that no military,
> economic, or financial assistance shall be
> supplied to any nation unless it applies
> an embargo on such shipments to any nation
> or combination of nations threatening the
> security of the United States, including
> the Union of Soviet Socialist Republics
> and all countries under its domination.[21]

According to the Mutual Defense Assistance Control Act, usually referred to as the Battle Act,
goods of primary strategic significance were defined
as those that "exports in any quantity would contribute significantly to Soviet war potential." In addi-

tion to arms, ammunition, and implements of war,
goods in this category included all commodities
"(1) designed for the production or development of
arms, ammunition, and implements of war; (2) used
for that purpose even if not specifically designed
therefor; (3) representative of significant technological advances of strategic value, particularly in
the field of industrial high-precision work and mass
production in support of military potential; or (4)
so deficient in the Soviet bloc as to represent an
important obstacle in the maintenance or increase of
the military potential of that area."[22] To insure
uniformity in the application of this act, specific
lists of items were made up. These Battle Act lists
specified all types of arms, ammunition, and atomic
energy materials and 10 broad fields of commodities,
including metalworking machinery; chemical and petroleum equipment; electrical and power-generating equipment; general industrial equipment; transportation
equipment; electronic and precision instruments;
metals; minerals and their manufactures; chemicals;
petroleum products; and rubber and rubber products.
In addition to these goods, the Battle Act called for
quantitative controls on those goods deemed to be of
secondary strategic importance (i.e., goods whose
strategic value is related primarily to quantities
shipped.) Other items not included on the Battle
Act lists were subject to mandatory licensing control under the Export Control Act of 1949. As a result practically all capital goods produced in the
West were placed under some form of restriction.

The Coordinating Committee
(COCOM)

During 1948 the United States held a series of
discussion with the major Marshall Plan countries in
Western Europe to outline bilateral strategic trade
control practices. At this time the only control
exerted by the United States was that which prevented
American aid from being used to produce goods for
trade with the bloc. Because of the threat of possible aggression, however, several of the European
governments adopted some form of control over strate-

gic trade. During this period it was found that effective control of such trade required coordination
between all the countries producing a particular
commodity. As a result a consultative group with
representatives from 15 countries was organized in
Paris in November 1949. To carry out the day-to-day
problems of implementing the decisions of the consultative group, the Coordinating Committee, or
COCOM, was established.[23]

At regular meetings of the consultative group
and the Coordinating Committee, the participating
countries jointly prepared lists of items of primary
strategic importance and developed strict levels of
exports for lengthy lists of goods deemed to be of
secondary strategic importance. As a result, by
January 1952 most of these countries already had restrictions as broad as those called for in the Battle
Act.

Subsequently, however, various participating
countries, especially Great Britain, called for an
easing of the restrictions on trade with the bloc.
On February 25, 1954, immediately following the return of a delegation of British businessmen from
Moscow, Winston Churchill spoke for all Europe in
urging more trade with the bloc, stating:

> I do not suggest that at the present
> time there should be any traffic in mili-
> tary equipment, including certain machine
> tools such as those capable only or mainly
> of making weapons and heavy weapons. But
> a substantial relaxation of the regulations
> affecting manufactured goods, raw mate-
> rials, and shipping--which, it must be re-
> membered, were made 3 or 4 years ago in
> circumstances which we can all feel were
> different from those which prevail--a sub-
> stantial relaxation would undoubtedly be
> beneficial in its proper setting, bearing
> in mind the military and other arguments
> adduced.[24]

The Coordinating Committee went over the entire
list of controls between April 27 and June 17, 1954,
and recommended various changes. In general the

United States was opposed to much relaxation of controls; but on July 21, 1954, the Consultative Committee agreed to a new, smaller list of items to be
controlled.[25] The controls agreed upon at that time
lasted four years. In July 1958 the Consultative
Committee announced a further substantial easing of
restrictions on trade with the bloc. At this time
many items, such as machine tools, oil tankers, factory ships, refrigerator ships, transportation equipment, and electronic equipment were cut off the restrictions.[26] Whereas the 1954 embargo list included 190 items that were embargoed completely, 25
items that had quantity controls, and 67 that were
kept under surveillance, the 1958 list contained
only 120 items that were totally embargoed and 35
others that were to be kept under watch.[27] Although
the joint control lists were cut to a minimum, the
Battle Act control list remained quite extensive; and
the easing of restrictions in 1958 merely cut the
list from 950 to 700 items.[28] Furthermore, there
was no change in the mandatory license controls,
which were enforced as stringently as ever.

Soviet Reaction to Strategic
Trade Controls

At no time was there a total embargo on trade
with the Soviet Union and the European members of
the bloc. In fact a majority of the items involved
in the trade with this area as a whole before the
war were not placed on the restricted lists.[29] Consumer items, for example, were never included on any
of the lists. These lists did, however, include
many, if not most, categories of machine tools and
other capital goods. In the prewar period the primary imports of the Soviet Union were capital goods
of all types. Since the Soviet Union exerted complete control over the countries of Eastern Europe
in the early postwar period, it was only logical that
the same pattern be applied in these countries. Under these circumstances the restrictions placed on
trade with the bloc actually prohibited a major part
of the trade that was to be expected. For these restrictions to have had no effect on trade, the Soviet

Union would have had to reverse its basic policies of
of limiting consumer goods and importing capital
goods. Since such a reversal was not to be expected,
the restrictions of the West served as a partial embargo.

When the security controls on trade with the
Soviet Union were first imposed in 1948, the Soviet
Union put up a bold barrage of indifference. Even
as late as June 5, 1951, the Soviet representative
to the Economic Commission for Europe declared, "If
the ruling circles of the United States want to ima-
gine that they can hurt the Soviet Union by banning
trade in various ways, they are welcome, as far as
we are concerned, to go on imagining this."[30]

Despite this mask of indifference, the trade
restrictions apparently were very effective; and the
Soviet Union went to great lengths to circumvent the
control procedures and to pressure for a removal of
these restrictions. To obtain vitally needed items,
Soviet agents frequently paid three, four, and even
as much as ten times the market value for such
items.[31] With such an impetus unscrupulous businessmen in the West were easily persuaded to forge export
certificates, misrepresent cargoes, ship goods to
false addressees, and utilize various methods of
diversion.[32] Many honest businessmen were also
tricked into sending apparently legitimate shipments
that were subsequently routed through free ports to
a bloc country. As a result an unknown quantity of
goods on the restricted lists found its way behind
the iron curtain.

The effectiveness of the restrictions can also
be seen in the pressures generated to abolish all restrictions on East-West trade. As mentioned earlier,
the Moscow Economic Conference and the visit of British businessmen to Moscow in 1954 had the creating
of such pressures as a primary goal. So did the
visits of Bulganin and Khrushchev to London and of
Mikoyan to the United States. Soviet speeches at
various UN conferences decried Western restrictions.
Propaganda was constantly aimed at individual European countries, in an attempt to convince the people
that other European countries were trading with the
bloc and that their country was losing out because of
American restrictions.[33] Negotiations for trade

treaties frequently began with a Soviet demand for
items on the strategic list tied to the purchase of
items not on the list. In short, the Soviet Union at
every opportunity attempted to create pressures from
within to have the trade restrictions removed. Although the restrictions were reduced, it is impossible to estimate the effect these various pressures
had on the final decisions.

Trade Restrictions in a
Decade of Change

Anastas Mikoyan's widely publicized unofficial
visit to the United States in January 1959 was made
primarily to seek an end to trade barriers. During
this visit Mikoyan talked with groups of businessmen
in Cleveland, Detroit, Chicago, San Francisco, Los
Angeles, New York, and Washington, D.C.[34] The apparent purpose of these talks was to convince American
businessmen to apply pressures on Washington to ease
trade restrictions, so that Soviet-American trade
would be increased. In Washington at the end of his
visit, Mikoyan asked the State Department specifically for reassurances that the United States would
loosen barriers on trade, reapply the MFN treatment
to the Soviet Union, and eliminate obstacles to the
extension of credit to the Soviet Union. The State
Department rebuffed Mikoyan on all three points.[35]
In September 1959, Krushchev urged the same changes
during his visit with President Eisenhower at Camp
David. In the "spirit of Camp David" that prevailed
after this meeting, the administration began "to consider the mechanics of dismantling some of the barriers to trade with Russia erected during 10 years
of cold war."[36] These efforts continued until May
1960, when the U-2 incident not only made a fiasco
out of the summit conference but also ended all hopes
for an immediate rapprochement.
During the next several years the United States
became, if anything, more restrictive in matters of
trade with the Soviet Union. In 1962, for example,
mandatory license controls were extended to include
anything that the president considered a significant
contribution to the economic potential of the USSR

and the bloc. As a result the Commerce Department
licensed fewer shipments to the Soviet bloc in 1962
than in any year since 1958. In the same year the
Trade Expansion Act of 1962 reiterated Congress'
stand on MFN treatment for the Soviet Union.[37] Although its European friends were desirous of selling
everything short of actual weapons, the United States
forced through a stiffening of COCOM restrictions.
By 1964 the COCOM list, which had been pared to 120
items in 1958, had been expanded to 146 items. Most
of the additions were in new fields of technology,
and electronics accounted for 37 percent of the expanded list.[38] In 1963, when a bad crop forced the
Soviet Union to buy wheat from the United States,
President Kennedy, bowing to the demands of the long-
shoremen and the maritime industry, initiated a new
restriction that required that 50 percent of the
wheat shipments be made in American ships. The only
liberalization during this period was a lifting of
the ban on Soviet crabmeat on March 25, 1961, when
the Treasury Department finally agreed that there
were no Japanese POWs in the crab-processing industry.

    In 1964 a new liberalization movement began. In
that year a special study mission to Europe reported
to the House Committee on Foreign Affairs that the
Battle Act restrictions

> . . . impose additional restrictions on
> American exporters attempting to do busi-
> ness in that part of the world. Most of
> those restrictions now fail to accomplish
> their original purpose. They no longer
> deny the Soviet Union and Eastern Europe
> access to goods embodying advanced indus-
> trial technology, obtainable at one time
> only in the United States. Today such
> goods are generally available to Soviet
> and Eastern European buyers in Western
> Europe and in Japan.[39]

During the same year the U.S. Chamber of Commerce
and the National Foreign Trade Council both urged
liberalizing the restrictions on trade with the
Soviet Union. In 1965 the prestigious Committee for
Economic Development completed a study on East-West
trade that concluded that " . . . the interests

of the West would be served in present circumstances
by an expansion of East-West trade brought about by
mutual East-West reductions of the obstacles to
trade. . . "40

The administration then took the initiative,
and on February 16, 1965, President Johnson appointed
a Special Committee on U.S. Trade Relations with
Eastern European Countries and the Soviet Union.
This committee, which was composed of leaders from
business, unions, and the academic world, submitted
a report on April 29, 1965, that called for flexible
trade policies to replace the existing rigid ones.
In May 1966 the administration submitted a proposal
for an East-West Trade Relations Act of 1966 (S. 3363,
H.R. 15212) that was based on this committee's recom-
mendations. Despite such potential advantages as
trade profits, improved negotiating position, and an
opportunity to influence the development of Eastern
Europe, these bills died in committee.[41]

Undaunted by congressional refusal to act on the
East-West Trade Relations Act, President Johnson
moved ahead on his own. In a speech to the National
Editors Conference on October 7, 1966, the president
announced seven steps he was taking to improve East-
West trade relations. One of these steps was to reduce controls on nonstrategic exports, and on October 12, 1966, the Department of Commerce announced
a revision of the Commodity Control List that removed
400 nonstrategic commodities from mandatory license
control and permitted them to be shipped under general licenses. Two other steps were a consular convention with the USSR and a New York-Moscow air
agreement, both of which were signed in 1967. A
more controversial step was an executive order that
permitted the Export-Import Bank to finance American
exports that were going to the Fiat plant being built
in the Soviet Union. These efforts can be categor-
ized as the high-water mark in attempts to liberalize East-West trade up to that time.[42]

After reaching a high point in 1966, efforts to
liberalize East-West trade began to wane in the face
of Congressional opposition. Further, Congress appeared to be unhappy with President Johnson's do-it-
yourself liberalization, particularly the financing
of shipments to Communist countries by the Export-

Import Bank. One objection was that it was wrong
for the United States to provide any financial help
to any country that was actively supporting American
enemies in Vietnam. As a result a rider was attached
to the Export-Import Bank Extension Act of 1968 that
specified that the Export-Import Bank could not finance any shipments to a Communist country until
after the Vietnam was was concluded. Then, following the invasion of Czechoslovakia, the administration reviewed all U.S. economic and other relations
with Russia. The Department of Commerce once again
tightened its license controls, increasing the number of items that might adversely affect the national
security of the United States if exported to the Soviet Union.[43]

The Nixon Trade Decontrol
Program

The Nixon phase of East-West trade liberalization began with the enactment of the Export Administration Act of 1969, which replaced the Export Control Act of 1949. The most significant features of
this new law are a congressional endorsement of a
policy favoring expansion of peaceful trade with the
USSR and specific instructions to the Department of
Commerce to lift controls on commodities and proces-
ses freely available to Communist countries from non-
American sources. As a result of this act, the Department of Commerce has removed hundreds of items
from control lists since January 1970. This delist-
ing has included chemicals, iron and steel products,
telephone and telegraph equipment, tractors, radio
and television studio equipment, semiconductors, electric motors, and centrifugal casting machines. In
making these decontrol decisions, the Department of
Commerce sought the assistance of trade associations
and individual companies. The National Machine Tool
Builders Association, for example, obtained catalogs
from foreign machine toolmakers to back up assertions
that many restricted machine tools were freely available abroad.[44] In June 1971, R. H. Meyer, head of
the Office of Export Control, stated that, although
a large number of items had already been delisted,

the decontrol review was only half done and that "in the end there will be a very, very sizable shrinkage in the difference between our lists and the COCOM lists."[45]

In 1971 President Nixon created a new Council on International Economic Policy as an interagency group that he himself chaired. This council was charged with developing all types of international economic policies, but its most important responsibility was improving trade relations with the Soviet Union and with China. This responsibility was reflected in the appointment of Peter G. Peterson, former chairman of Bell and Howell, as executive secretary. Peterson had been an outspoken advocate of liberalizing trade with the Communist countries, and as executive secretary he was now in a position where he could actively influence American East-West trade policy.[46] In April 1971, President Nixon issued a proclamation that ended the shipping restrictions on grain exports that had been imposed by President Kennedy in 1963, and in November the United States sold 3 million tons of feed grains that could now be shipped by any carrier. Congress also did its part by changing the Fino Amendment to remove the proscription against Export-Import Bank financing of shipments to the Soviet Union.[47]

The administration has also been actively encouraging American businesses to develop trade relations with the Soviet Union. In both 1970 and 1971 the Department of Commerce sponsored trade missions for the depressed machine tool industry. During the same period American participation in Soviet trade fairs was expanded, and for the first time IBM was allowed to display its 360-50 computer in Leningrad.

In 1971 the Department of Commerce also began loosening its controls on strategic items not included on the COCOM list. The first major breakthrough was approval for export of $88 million of machine tools for the gigantic truck plant the Russians are building on the Kama River. By the end of the year, the Department of Commerce had licensed proposals for over $1 billion of automotive equipment for the Kama project. In addition to giving the machine tool industry a needed shot in the arm, such approvals showed that the administration strongly

backed this project and was moving ahead at full
speed to eliminate unneeded trade barriers. At the
same time these approvals were a sign to the Soviets
that steps toward settlement of political differences, such as the SALT talks, would lead to an
easing of trade restrictions and that the United
States was not going to increase trade with China
at Russia's expense.[48]

In addition to the Kama plant, the Soviets also
proposed a long-term agreement to buy about $200 mil-
lion of grain annually; and in April 1972 Secretary
of Agriculture Earl Butz went to Moscow to discuss
such a possibility.[49] Both the Kama project and the
grain deal have one problem in common--money. To pay
for these purchases, the Soviet Union needs credit
and an improved opportunity to sell in the United
States. It was hoped that these matters might be
resolved at the summit meeting in May 1972. Soviet
Minister of Foreign Trade Patolichev and Peter G.
Peterson, now Secretary of Commerce, worked around
the clock to reach an agreement that could be announced at that meeting, but they were not successful. There was, however, an agreement to improve
shipping relations between the two countries. Of
more significance was the establishment of a joint
American-Soviet commission that will negotiate an
overall agreement to promote trade.[50] Two major
features expected in this agreement are MFN treatment for Soviet imports and Export-Import Bank credits to finance sales of equipment and technology by
U.S. firms. A prerequisite to any credit agreement
would be some sort of settlement of the World War II
lend-lease debts. MFN treatment will require action
by Congress, as would any special arrangements to be
made on grain sales by the Commodity Credit Corporation and any imports of natural gas. It would appear
that the political climate is ripe for such changes,
and 1973 may be the year of the final breakthrough
on Soviet-American trade relations.

SUMMARY

During its existence the Soviet Union has four
times been faced with discriminatory trade restric-

tions. Three of these occasions were the naval
blockade imposed by Great Britain and France between
1918 and 1920; antidumping embargoes imposed by
France, Canada, and other countries in 1930 and 1931;
and the de facto embargo that was a reaction to the
Soviet-German nonaggression pact of 1939.

The most extensive and longest-lasting of the
restrictions were those placed against trade with the
entire Soviet bloc by all of the countries of the
West beginning in 1948. These restrictions, based
on the premise that the Soviet Union threatened ag-
gressive action, prevented the sale of a long list
of goods and placed quantitative restrictions on
others. In 1954 these restrictions were substantially
reduced, and in 1958 a further reduction in the international restrictions was made.

Between 1958 and 1968 there were increasing
pressures to liberalize East-West trade. At the
same time there were such negative factors as the
U-2 incident, the building of the Berlin Wall, Cuba,
the Vietnam war, and the invasion of Czechoslovakia.
As a result there were contradictory moves toward
trade rapprochement and moves toward increased restrictions. Since 1969 there has been a positive
and continual movement toward improved trade with
the Soviet Union and a dismantling of the trade restrictions system. This movement, moreover, has been
a joint effort of both Congress and the administration. Decontrol reached a high point in 1971 and
paved the way for a discussion of trade issues at
the May 1972 summit in Moscow. Although the summit
talks did not result in a trade agreement, a joint
U.S.-Soviet commission was established to negotiate
such an agreement, hopefully by the end of 1972.

9

PROSPECTS FOR SOVIET FOREIGN TRADE

Various aspects of Soviet foreign trade have been discussed in the previous chapters. These aspects include policy, organization for operations and control, finance, promotion, trade with socialist and developing countries, and Western restrictions on Soviet foreign trade. In this chapter the author has extrapolated the data presented in these discussions and has forecast possible future actions. These forecasts are grouped into five categories: organizations, finance, promotion, trade with specific areas, and policy. Within each category recent trends are discussed, and possible changes forecast for the next few years are outlined. In the next chapter the author will discuss suggested possible actions to be taken by the United States on the basis of forecast trends of Soviet foreign trade.

In recent years various writers and speakers have warned the people of America and other countries of the West concerning the growing threat of the Soviet economic offensive. Nikita Khrushchev added fuel to the fire in November 1957 by announcing: "We declare war upon you--excuse me for using such

273

an expression--in the peaceful field of trade. We
declare war. We will win over the United States.
The threat to the United States is not the ICBM, but
in the field of peaceful production. We are relent-
less in this, and it will prove the superiority of
our system."[1]

In the preceding chapters the nature and volume
of Soviet foreign trade during various historical
periods have been described. An analysis of the data
presented in these chapters indicates that, although
the methods of organization and operation of Soviet
foreign trade hold a potential danger to capitalist
trade, the threat of an economic offensive has been
grossly exaggerated. It is quite true that Soviet
trade has increased dramatically since the late
1940's. It is also true, however, that total world
trade has increased greatly during this same period.
In 1931 Soviet imports accounted for 2.7 percent of
total world imports, and in 1932 Soviet exports
reached a peak of 2.3 percent of world exports. Subsequently this trade was sharply curtailed. Despite
the rapid increase of Soviet trade with nonsocialist
countries beginning in 1951, this trade accounted for
only 1.2 percent of total world trade in 1958 and remained at the same low level over the next 10 years.

What, then, are the prospects for Soviet foreign
trade in the years to come? In answering this question, five topical fields will be given consideration: organization, finance, promotion, trade with
specific areas, and policy. Within each field an
attempt will be made to forecast future trends.
Where desirable, alternative lines of action will be
discussed.

ORGANIZATION

During the period of the New Economic Policy,
the Soviet Union experimented with a wide range of
organizations in the field of foreign trade operations. These organizations included the State Export-Import Offices, cooperative organizations, Soviet companies abroad, Soviet-foreign mixed companies,
foreign companies on a concession basis, specialized
corporations, and syndicates of manufacturing organi-

zations. Beginning in 1925 more and more of the
activities were concentrated in the hands of the
specialized corporations, and in 1930 the various
organizations were replaced by a series of specialized monopoly foreign trade corporations. Since
then these organizations have adequately served the
foreign trade needs of the Soviet Union.

In recent years there have been several developments that might presage a change in at least some
of the monopoly corporations. These developments
include the transfer of some corporations from the
Ministry of Foreign Trade to other ministries and
state committees, the establishment of foreign servicing companies (zagranpostavki), and the adoption
of the new socialist economics in Czechoslovakia and
other Comecon countries. In Czechoslovakia some
monopoly trade corporations have become subsidiaries
of the organizations producing the goods they handle.
In the Soviet Union there has been a similar combining of related functions but in a different manner. As a result all merchant marine matters are
now under the control of the Ministry of Merchant
Marine, including operations of Sovfrakht, which
handles shipping operations, and Sovinflot, which
services vessels. Although the Soviets may not want
to follow the Czechoslovak example, it seems likely
that production ministries will gain more control
over foreign trade activities. As an example the
Ministry of the Automobile Industry might well take
over Avtoexport, which exports cars and trucks; Zapchastsexport, which exports parts; and Avtopromimport, which imports complete plants and equipment
for the production of cars and trucks. Similarly,
the Ministry of the Aircraft Industry, which now
operates the Aviation Foreign Servicing Company,
could well take over Aviaexport, so that all matters
relating to aircraft production, sales, and service
would be under one central control.

Although such a reorganization would be beneficial in a number of production areas, it would not
be possible or advantageous in all cases. In any
event such changes will probably come slowly, and
most of the foreign trade operations organizations
will continue as they are now. It is likely, however, that the nature and scope of operations of

some of these corporations will undergo changes in the future.

The concept of regional foreign trade corporations seems ripe for a change. Today there are three such corporations: Vostokintorg, Lenfintorg, and Dalintorg. Vostokintorg handles trade with the border states of Sinkiang, Mongolia, Afghanistan, Iran, and Turkey. In recent years the economic and trade conditions of these countries have changed. The foreign aid corporations have taken over an increasing proportion of the trade and economic relations with these countries. Furthermore, as a result of other growing needs, the specialized monopoly trade corporations began operations in this area. It would appear that Vostokintorg is an anachronism that will soon be replaced by these other organizations. Lenfintorg would seem to have even less reason for continued existence, for the goods it deals in are also handled by other monopoly corporations. Dalintorg, on the other hand, was formed in 1964 for the distinct purpose of developing trade relations with Japan. These relations have been so well developed that in 1970 Japan was Russia's largest capitalist trading partner. Now that its original goal has been attained, it would seem logical to assume that Dalintorg will be phased out in the near future.

There is every reason to believe that the Soviet economy will continue to expand, even if at a slower pace. As a result of this expansion, there will probably be a further shift from agriculture to industry. New goods will be produced, output of other products will be increased, and the need for industrial raw materials, machines, and equipment will be expanded. To meet these changes the Soviets will probably reorganize existing foreign trade corporations and establish new corporations to handle new lines of goods. In this vein it should be noted that almost half of the existing monopoly trade and aid corporations have been formed since the early 1960's.

Increasing attention is being paid to the needs of the Soviet consumer. Events since the death of Stalin indicate a growing pressure for more satisfaction of consumer wants. As a result the Soviet Union is currently planning the construction of consumer-goods industries. When these industries are in operation, it is quite possible that there will be an increased exchange of consumer goods between the Soviet Union and other countries. Initially such an exchange would be handled by Raznoexport and Raznoimport, which deal in miscellaneous goods; but eventually it is likely that a special corporation or corporations dealing with consumer goods will be established.

A radical departure that is a distinct possibility is some form of joint-venture operation. At the present time joint operations are limited to production contracts under which Soviet production facilities are used to produce goods for Western firms. General Electric is now negotiating a joint operation in which GE would supply turbine rotors with epoxy blades, the Soviet firm Electrosila would build the turbines, and GE or some joint firm would sell the completed turbines in international markets.[2] Since 1966 the Japanese have been talking with the Soviets about possible joint economic development of Siberia. Now there is an excellent possibility that Soviet natural gas reserves will be developed for export to the United States. This project, which has a price tag of over $4 billion, could well work out as a joint venture of Tenneco, El Paso Natural Gas, Japanese interests, and appropriate Soviet organizations.[3] The form that these joint organizations will take is not yet decided, but with American participants it is certain that they will not be the same as the mixed companies of the early postwar years.

Changes in the foreign trade control organizations are much more difficult to forecast. The local authorized representatives within the country and the trade representatives abroad have served their respective control functions in almost the same manner since the 1930's. At this time there is no reason whatsoever to expect any changes in these institutions. The control organization of the Ministry of Foreign Trade, however, has undergone various changes over the years and will probably be changed somewhat in the future.

FINANCE

In the field of foreign trade finance, several
major developments are to be expected in the years
to come. One of these is a single bloc currency for
the member countries of Comecon. Recently there has
been a definite trend toward the use of the ruble as
a single intrabloc currency. Prior to 1950 the U.S.
dollar was used in all relations with the bloc countries. In 1950 the ruble was revalued and placed on
a gold basis. Immediately thereafter it was adopted
as a measure for all foreign trade operations between
the Soviet Union and the bloc countries and between
these countries themselves. At this time the ruble
itself was not convertible or transferable and accounts were balanced in kind, not cash. In 1963 the
transferable ruble was created as a separate collective bloc currency for intrabloc transactions. Thus,
today these countries use a national currency for
internal operations, the transferable ruble for intrabloc trade and investments, and foreign exchange for
all other foreign trade. But the transferable ruble
is essentially a clearing currency, and there is
still no convertibility between the national currencies and the transferable ruble. It is likely, however, that the grandiose bloc integration program
announced in 1971 will lead to full intrabloc convertibility in the near future. After this convertibility has been attained, it would be only a short
step to converting all national currencies into a
single bloc currency--the Soviet ruble. The Soviet
Union has announced that such a conversion is its
goal, but the strength of national pride in the Comecon countries may delay such an action for a while.

Convertibility of the internal ruble with other
world currencies is also a distinct possibility.
Since 1926 the ruble has served solely as an internal
currency. Foreign trade with bloc countries since
1963 has been cleared in transferable rubles, which
are separate from the Russian ruble. Further, foreign trade with nonbloc countries has always been
carried on in foreign exchange and not the ruble.
In the postwar period the Soviet Union has become
one of the two leading world powers. The use of

other currencies for purposes of foreign trade has
apparently piqued the pride of the Soviets, and it
was evidently for this reason that the ruble was
changed from a dollar base to a gold base in 1950
and revalued upward to "outvalue" the dollar in 1961.
There would appear to be no economic need for convertibility of the internal ruble since the arbitrary
exchange rates have, in effect, provided convertibility. For political purposes, and for purposes of
pride, convertibility of the internal ruble could
prove advantageous. Such an action, however, would
require a revision of Soviet fiscal policy so that
either prices would fluctuate with exchange rates
(Liberman economics) or they would be insulated in
some new manner from erratic fluctuations of foreign exchange. As a result convertibility of the
internal ruble will probably not occur for several
years.

Another development to be expected in the field
of foreign trade finance is a renewal of American
credits to the Soviet Union. In recent years the
major European countries and Japan have provided extensive credits for various periods of time. The
largest of these was in relation to the Fiat plant
constructed in the Soviet Union. The Japanese have
recently been particularly lenient. Whereas they
usually demand repayment in yen, they have been so
eager to get certain machine tool orders that they
have accepted repayment in dollars. Although President Johnson planned to use Export-Import Bank financing for American shipments for the Fiat plant, there
have been no American credits since lend-lease days.
The Kama project, the long-term grain agreement, and
various other transactions currently being negotiated
hinge on some form of credit; and since the United
States is eager for this business it is expected that
some arrangement will be made. A necessary first
step for any such credit will be a settlement of
outstanding lend-lease debts. Such a settlement was
apparently discussed by Nixon and Brezhnev at the
May 1972 summit meeting, but the matter was not resolved. It is expected that such a settlement will
be made as a result of the negotiations of the joint
American-Soviet trade commission. Such a settlement
will satisfy Johnson Act requirements and make long-

term private credits a possibility. Congressional
action will be needed to modify the Battle Act prohibition against government credits to the Soviet
Union; and, considering the current mood of Congress,
a settlement of the lend-lease debts would probably
trigger such a change. For the grain agreement the
Soviet Union is seeking very low interest rates,
such as 2.5 percent and 3 percent. Since the cost
of money is at least twice this amount, such special
interest rates are not very likely.

PROMOTION

In the field of foreign trade promotion, there
is little reason to expect much if any change. Foreign trade fairs will probably remain the primary
means of trade promotion. It is possible, however,
that fairs and exhibits in the developing countries
might be cut back somewhat, so that more efforts can
be expended on fairs and exhibits in the developed
countries. One reason for such a change in emphasis
is a Soviet realization that Communist revolutions
are far off and possibly not to the advantage of the
USSR. Another reason is the need to improve sales
in the developed countries, in order to pay for advanced technology imports so badly needed in the
Soviet Union. Participation in the fairs and exhibitions, as in past years, will be supplemented by
visits of trade delegations and of Soviet personali-
ties. Trade missions from the developed countries,
especially the United States, will also increase in
number and type. The All-Union Chamber of Commerce
has remained relatively unchanged since its formation
in 1932, and there is no evidence of any forthcoming
changes in it. It is possible, however, that there
will be an increased use of joint chambers of commerce
and a new Soviet-American Chamber of Commerce is a
distinct possibility.

TRADE WITH SPECIFIC AREAS

Socialist World

During the years following World War II, the
Soviet Union converted the foreign trade activities

of the countries of Eastern Europe into a basically intrabloc pattern. Furthermore, by various means, including the use of mixed companies, Soviet-owned companies, and political pressures, the Soviet Union has become the major trading partner of each of these countries. Recent events in the Soviet bloc indicate two contradictory trends. On the one hand, an application of Liberman economics in Czechoslovakia and other Comecon countries has led to a decentralization of foreign trade control. At its extreme this decentralization resembles capitalism in that the plan serves as a broad budget, and foreign trade activities are carried out by producing organizations on a strict profit-loss basis. The other trend is integration of the economies of the Comecon countries. If carried through as planned by the Soviets, this trend would result in a single monolithic bloc operating under a single detailed plan. The integration trend is much stronger, as evidenced by the establishment of the International Bank for Economic Cooperation and the International Investment Bank and the 1971 adoption of the Comecon integration plan. It is expected that initially this trend will prevail and the Soviet Union will gain further control over bloc trade by such means as a central Comecon plan, a Comecon currency, and standard Comecon prices. Once this control is secure, it is expected that more attention will be paid to increased efficiency through decentralization--possibly along the lines recently observed in Czechoslovakia.

The volume of bloc trade with the Soviet Union will undoubtedly remain quite large. However, as Soviet trade with nonsocialist countries increases, it is expected that the bloc percentage of Soviet trade will continue to decrease. Despite this decrease it is likely that the socialist countries will remain the Soviet Union's primary trading partners. Soviet trade with China is currently at minimal levels. One effect of President Nixon's visit to Peking in early 1972 could be to force the Soviet Union to reappraise its relations with China. It is possible that arm's-length relations will be resumed in order to insure that the United States does not ally itself too closely with China.

Developing Countries

Soviet trade with the developing countries in
the postwar period has developed primarily because
of an economic need for the industrial raw materials
and foodstuffs produced by these countries. As the
economy of the Soviet Union develops, it is evident
that its needs for raw materials will likewise increase. Furthermore, the relaxation of totalitarian
controls following Stalin's death and the development
of a new, sophisticated, highly educated, and highly
paid elite have released strong and increasing pressures for the import of various consumer items, including desired foodstuffs. Since this elite is
growing in size and importance, it is expected that
these pressures will continue to grow in the years to
come. As a result Soviet purchases from the underdeveloped countries with which they are now trading
should increase, and new countries will be added to
the list of suppliers to the Soviet Union, especially
Latin American countries.

To pay for these increased imports from the less-
developed countries, the Soviet Union will have to
find methods of obtaining the necessary foreign exchange. Direct sale or barter of goods will be used
wherever possible and an increasing variety of goods,
including oil products, will be offered. In an increasing number of instances, however, the Soviet
Union will probably generate foreign exchange equiva-
lence by selling complete plants, equipment, and
technical assistance on long-term credits. The repayment of these credits will be in cash or goods,
and in either manner the Soviet Union will be able to
obtain the goods it needs. Because of the strain on
the Soviet economy caused by such giant projects as
the Aswan Dam and the Bhilai and Bokaro steel mills,
it is expected that the Soviet Union will limit its
offers mainly to medium-size operations. It is expected that some form of development assistance will
be offered particularly to Malaysia, where the Soviet
Union has consistently run an extremely high trade
deficit. It is possible that surplus commodities
could be sold in the West to earn the exchange needed
to cover this deficit, but such sales are also urgently needed to pay for necessary high-technology
imports.

As described earlier, the primary purpose of this trade is economic. At the same time, however, the Soviets will utilize it to the utmost for political purposes. When the trade volume with any particular country becomes large enough, the Soviet Union may well attempt to use this trade, or the credits facilitating it, as a lever for obtaining political concessions. In this regard, however, it is well to remember that the Soviets have not been overwhelmingly successful, as was shown by the changed relations with Ghana after the ouster of Nkrumah and problems faced in Indonesia after the fall of Sukarno.

Developed Countries of
the West

Soviet trade with the developed countries of the West has grown rapidly in the postwar years; but, because of various restrictions imposed by the West, this trade has always been a minor part of overall Soviet trade. After the relaxation of restrictions in 1958, there was an immediate upsurge in the purchase of complete plants. In 1959, for example, the Soviets ordered a complete $6.3 million chemical plant from Vickers-Armstrong (Engineers), Ltd.; and Courtaulds, Ltd., a large British producer of rayon, signed a $42 million contract to build several synthetic fiber plants in the Soviet Union.[4] Since then such purchases have been rather commonplace. After Khrushchev's involuntary retirement in 1964, the abrasiveness went out of the Soviet trade drive; and there has been a continued increase in trade since then. Whereas imports from the West never exceeded 20 percent of total Soviet imports during Khrushchev's reign, these imports had jumped to 25 percent by 1969. Since the Soviets have acknowledged their technological deficiencies, there has been a constant pressure to increase imports of high-technology equipment and facilities from the West. The Kama project is one example of the type of imports to be expected in future years. Another would be cryogenic equipment needed for the natural gas project. Other examples are computers, laser equipment, automated (computerized) production facilities, and advanced electronic gear.

Trade relations with other Western countries
are already warm and cordial. The Nixon-Brezhnev
summit meeting of May 1972 seems to have gone a long
way toward improving Soviet-American relations. The
signing of the arms limitation agreement shows that
the Soviets are sincerely interested in improving
these relations. Should the Soviet Union actively in-
tervene to bring about an end to the Vietnam war, it
can be expected that Soviet-American trade relations
will improve even further; and Congress will be very
disposed toward dismantling many of the remaining
trade restrictions. Since this trade will require
expanded credits, it is also expected that there
will be efforts to make such credits available. As
mentioned earlier, there is a strong possibility
that some form of joint-venture arrangements will be
made with the Soviet Union. Of immediate interest
is the development of Siberian natural gas for export
to the United States. It is quite possible that
other joint ventures will be developed as a means of
paying for increased high-technology imports from
the developed countries of the West.

POLICY

Since 1918 the Soviet Union has followed two
basic policies--a monopoly of foreign trade and autarky. With the exception of possible joint-venture
operations, there is no evidence at this time to indicate any change in the monopoly of foreign trade
operations or control in the Soviet Union. Socialism
has been and is the basis upon which the Soviet Union
was founded. Any abandonment of the monopoly of
foreign trade would require at least a partial relaxation of this socialism. Within the Soviet Union it
appears that changes are taking place in the practice
of socialism. It is possible that these changes will
result in a decentralization of Soviet foreign trade
operations. This decentralization has already begun
with the transfer of certain foreign trade corporations to other ministries and state committees. It
is expected that this trend will continue.

The policy of autarky is less significant and
definitely subject to change. Immediately following

World War II the Soviet Union reverted to a policy
of autarky. As a result Soviet trade reached a low
point in 1950 and 1951. Subsequently this policy
has been gradually relaxed, and foreign trade has increased. With the present realization of the need
for advanced technology, it is to be expected that
this autarky will be even further reduced. During
the 1930's the Soviets imported Western technology
but never gave up their autarkic policies. At the
present time, however, the level of development in
the Soviet Union and an improvement in overall relations would seem to augur well for an abandonment of
autarky in favor of international interdependence.

It is likely that the Soviet policy of importing
only that which is considered necessary and limiting
exports to those needed to pay for imports will be
continued, since import needs far exceed export
capabilities. However, the interpretation of what
is necessary probably will be broadened considerably.
Furthermore, it is quite probable that the principles
of comparative advantage and international division
of labor (not just the socialist division of labor)
will gain more attention as the production costs of
Soviet raw materials continue to rise. Also to be
considered is the new type of relationship that has
grown up between the Soviet Union as a buying nation
and the underdeveloped countries as suppliers. Since
the Soviet Union is economically and politically
stronger than these nations, it is not likely that
the Soviets will feel the necessity of cutting themselves off from dependence on these sources. Still
another consideration is the trend toward a higher
standard of living in the Soviet Union. The policy
of autarky is usually associated with a policy of
austerity, a policy of doing without. In recent
years this policy of austerity has gradually been
eased, and recent developments in the Soviet Union
indicate that a reinstitution of severe austerity
would be very difficult to accomplish. In consideration of these factors, it is believed unlikely that
the Soviet Union will revert to a policy of almost
total autarky unless it is forced to do so by Western
actions.

Another possible change in Soviet policy might
be an increased use of the profit concept in foreign

trade operations. Such a change has already occurred
in Czechoslovakia, and quality has apparently replaced quantity as a measure of economic success.
The Soviets have been slow in adapting the ideas of
Soviet economist Liberman to foreign trade areas,
but it is possible that these ideas will find further
application in the years to come.

SUMMARY

    An analysis of the data in the preceding chap-
ters indicates the probability of several developments in Soviet foreign trade. In the field of organization it is expected that there will be few
changes in form but various changes in scope. These
changes will result from altered economic conditions
in the Eastern countries, expansion of the Soviet
economy, more interest in consumer demands, and
Soviet entry into other phases of international business. Major changes expected would be further transfer of monopoly trade corporations to production
ministries and the establishment of joint-venture
firms with the developed countries of the West. In
the area of finance, intrabloc convertibility, a
bloc currency, and full convertibility of the internal ruble are all foreseen, as are American credits
to the Soviet Union. No major changes are anticipated
in the field of foreign trade promotion, and current
methods and procedures will probably continue in the
future.
    Trade with the Comecon countries presents two
conflicting trends. On the one hand, the Eastern
European countries have moved toward decentralized
control and operations, whereas the Soviet Union has
pushed bloc integration. It is expected that integration will win out initially. Trade with China
can be expected, mainly to counteract inroads of the
United States in Chinese affairs.
    The basic policy of the monopoly of foreign
trade is likely to remain unchanged. A broader interpretation will probably be made of the import and
export policies. Although these policies will remain
constant, there are indications that the Soviet Union
will not resort to total autarky, as it did during
the period of the Five-Year Plans.

10

SUGGESTED ACTIONS
TO BE TAKEN
BY THE WEST

In the last chapter a forecast was made of possible future trends in Soviet foreign trade. This chapter concludes the study with suggestions of actions to be taken by the United States and the West under various conditions. These suggestions have been divided into four groups--actions to preserve competitive position, actions to avoid the dangers inherent in state trading, actions to strengthen capitalism in the developing countries, and actions to encourage increased East-West trade. In the field of competition, consideration is given first to the world competitive situation. Specific actions to be taken by businesses and by the government are then suggested. Three dangers inherent in state trading are considered, and specific preventive actions are recommended. These dangers are the political use of foreign trade, use of a socialist pricing system, and the use of pressures based on a monopoly trading position. After discussion of the possibility of socialism in the developing countries, actions to prevent such an occurrence are suggested. The chapter concludes with a discussion of steps that could and should be taken by the United States to increase

East-West trade and commercial interdependence.

The analysis presented in the last chapter indicates that there is no economic threat to the United States and other Western countries from present and future Soviet foreign trade. There are, however, three situations for which the West must be prepared: intensified trade competition, the potential dangers inherent in state trading, and the possibility that the developing countries might adopt Soviet methods to fulfill their development programs.

FOREIGN TRADE COMPETITION

A discussion of competition on the world markets in the postwar period is beyond the scope of this work. It bears repeating, however, that this competition has been growing very intense in recent years. Following the war U.S. foreign trade increased sharply, but from 1957 to 1969 the American share of total foreign trade dropped from 16 percent to 13.5 percent. Great Britain has also been losing its share of trade, dropping from 10 percent in 1957 to only 6.5 percent in 1969. German industry made a remarkable recovery after the war; and by 1957 Germany was the third largest world trader, handling 7 percent of total world trade. With the initiation of the European Common Market in 1959, Germany became the nucleus of a trading bloc that controlled 15 percent of world trade. In the decade that followed, Germany climbed to second place with 10 percent of world trade; and the Common Market almost doubled its share to 27 percent. Similarly Japan rose from practically no trade in 1950 to fourth place, or 5.6 percent of world trade, by 1969. During this period the Soviet Union has suffered a cut in its share of total trade. In 1958 this share was 4.3 percent, but in 1969 it had dropped to 3.9 percent--with only 1.4 percent being trade with nonsocialist countries. From these data it can be seen that the major competitive factors on the world market are, and for some time will be, the United States, Europe (including Great Britain), and Japan. If competition can be considered a threat rather than

an incentive, the major economic threat to any of
these three powers would, therefore, come from the
other two powers and not from the Soviet Union. On
this basis it can be said that the power most likely
to encroach on American markets abroad is the expanded European Common Market.

At the present time Soviet trade with nonsocialist countries accounts for only 1.4 percent of world
trade. Recently there have been a number of moves
to increase this trade over the next few years. Such
an increase would be based on the needs of the Soviet
Union, and imports would still be limited by the import policy. If, on the other hand, the Soviet Union
were to abandon its restrictions and begin conducting trade on the basis of international economics,
it is quite likely that its trade would increase at
an even faster pace. Today the Soviet Union is the
second largest industrial power in the world. On
this basis alone it would seem that Soviet adoption
of free trade policies would result in the Soviet
Union's conducting approximately 10 percent of world
trade (the share now held by Germany). In increasing
its share to such a level, the Soviet Union could
indeed present a strong competitive threat to the
United States (an increased Soviet share would neces-
sitate a reduced share for somebody, and that somebody is usually the market leader). At this time
adoption of free trade by the Soviet Union appears
very unlikely. It is possible, however, that the
Soviet Union will make more use of the theories of
comparative advantage and international division of
labor in the future. Trade and competition, therefore, can be expected to increase. The amount of
such trade is impossible to forecast; however, it
would appear that the limits of such trade might
well be the 3.9 percent of world trade reached in 1969
and the 10 percent that might be expected from Russia's position as the number two industrial power.

Assuming increased competition in foreign trade
from the Soviet Union as well as from an expanded
Common Market and Japan, what actions should be taken
by the United States to protect its competitive position? The actions suggested can be divided into two
categories--actions to be taken by business and actions to be taken by the government. Those to be

taken by business are by far the more important if
the United States is to maintain a capitalist system.

Marketing Methods

The world is no longer a seller's market; it is
now definitely a buyer's market. As a result it is
necessary that American businesses adapt the modern
marketing concept to their foreign operations. One
aspect of this marketing concept is the proper use
of marketing intelligence, including market research
techniques. In many cases only the most elementary
of these techniques are required. This can be seen
by recent Russian activities in the developing countries, where the Soviets merely ask the people what
they want and then sell it to them. In other cases
more refined techniques will be required. All too
often in the past, American businesses have exported
their domestic products with little or no modification to meet local needs. To retain these markets
it will be necessary to find out what local needs are
and attempt to satisfy them. If this is not done, a
competitor nation, possibly the Soviet Union, may
well find a way to meet these needs and capture the
entire market.
Marketing techniques used in foreign markets
must also be improved. Local conditions in various
countries dictate the use of different methods of
marketing. It is necessary that American firms determine what these methods are and model their operations accordingly. At the same time it is becoming
increasingly necessary to select for foreign operations personnel who can adapt to varying conditions.
The training of these personnel must also be improved,
so that they become more aware of local conditions.
Language training and an introduction to the culture
of the area in which they are to operate are absolute
necessities. It has been noted that members of Soviet
trade delegations invariably speak the language and
are familiar with the customs of the area in which
they serve. As a result a certain rapport can be established. If the American trader remains aloof and
clings to English as his sole language, he will be
severely handicapped in business operations and will

lose the initiative to competitor nations that make
the extra effort.

Investment Abroad

The investment of American capital abroad must
be increased to counteract any decreases in direct
trading operations. With its reduced internal customs duties the expanded European Common Market provides a competitive advantage to plants operating
within this market. At the same time, inclusion of
Great Britain and other EFTA countries in the Common
Market eliminates the need for two European operations and makes a single, more economical plant even
more attractive. In the underdeveloped countries the
great desire for economic development will lead to
the establishment of various industries. The net effect of these actions will be decreased trade in certain commodities. To maintain their position in foreign markets, the producers of these commodities will
have to establish operations abroad. As a result of
these investments the economies of the various countries should be improved and the total volume of
trade between the United States and these countries
should increase proportionally. If American investments are not made, especially in the developing countries, it is likely that the Soviet Union will sell
these countries the factories they need on long-term
credits. In this manner it is possible that the Soviet Union could redirect the trade of these countries
from the West to the Soviet bloc.

Cost Reduction

At home it is vitally important that producers
find additional methods of reducing production costs.
Improved technology and new equipment in European and
Japanese factories have lessened the competitive advantage once held by the United States. It is possible that advances in automation and new technology
will again provide some measure of advantage. An example would be advances in solid state microcircuitry
that have made American-made electronic calculating

machines very competitive with Japanese models. The
recent financial crisis that ended with a devaluation
of the dollar indicates that the more immediate problem is the wage/productivity squeeze. If American
industries cannot increase their productivity, American products will continue to be priced out of the
market. Although strongly objected to by American
unions, an increased use of overseas assembly and
packaging plants provides one possible means of reducing various production and shipping costs. At
the same time such operations provide employment for
local nationals and are thus a form of private foreign aid. It should be noted that Sony of Japan,
among others, is adopting this practice and will be
assembling in Mexico for the U.S. market. Improved
packaging methods and new techniques of freight handling now available can also be used to reduce costs
in the transportation of goods. Increased attention
must be paid to reducing marketing costs and to improving marketing cost accounting.

Increased Imports

Increased imports by American businesses are of
importance to many countries. Many American businessmen look upon foreign trade as a one-way affair involving American exports. To maintain high levels
of exports, it is necessary that the importing nation
obtain dollars. The basic method is by selling commodities to the United States. The United States
cannot hope for increased exports if it continues to
apply restrictions such as those on the importation
of oil, peanuts, and meat.

Government Aid

The actions to be taken by the government are
basically those that would facilitate and encourage
the activities of the businessman. To encourage
trade in general, for example, it will be necessary
for the government to continue its program of reducing
barriers to world trade, especially in the field of
tariffs. In doing so the government now has the added

task of convincing a growing protectionist movement
of the necessity for such actions. The operations
of the Export-Import Bank should be continued, and
possibly expanded, to provide more credit facilities
for foreign trade. At the same time Export-Import
Bank procedures should be simplified, so that American businessmen can arrange credit quickly and thus
be able to react rapidly in a changing world market-
place.

To encourage overseas operations and investments,
two specific actions are recommended. First, the
tax laws should be amended so that an extra incentive
is added to this type of operation. A modest beginning along this line would be to refrain from taxing
foreign earnings until they are repatriated. More
extreme, and possibly more effective, proposals would
call for a complete exemption from taxes for a period
of five years for new overseas investments and consideration of a separate, lower rate of corporate
tax for foreign earnings--particularly earnings generated in developing countries. It is realized that
these actions are contrary to present efforts to ease
the balance-of-payments situation; but it is felt
that such actions are, in the long run, best for American business and the American economy. Second, the
government investment insurance program should be
made much more attractive. It should be broadened
to cover most risks other than normal business risks
(i.e., convertibility, repatriation of profits, currency revaluation, expropriation, nationalization,
and internal disturbances). Also, the price of this
insurance should be reduced to a marketable level.
By these means overseas operations will become attractive to more and more businesses, and American companies will be encouraged to make investments in relatively unstable and backward areas.

American aid in the economic development of underdeveloped countries must be continued. However,
more use should be made of loan funds that are available to businesses in the aided areas. At the present time a majority of American aid--what is left of
it--goes for public works projects on a government-
to-government basis. It should be recalled that the
Soviet Union has provided technical assistance on a
strictly loan basis on a government-to-government

basis, and one result is a series of state-owned factories in the developing areas. If America wants to
encourage private industry, it must provide private
businessmen in the less-developed countries with the
means of developing such industry. The Development
Loan Fund set up in 1957 was a step in the right direction, as was the Overseas Private Investment Corporation established in 1970. However, if these organizations are to serve the purpose desired, their
activities must be greatly expanded and broadened.

Direct government assistance to businesses de-
siring to operate overseas is another area that could
use much improvement. For the most part the only
assistance provided by the U.S. government is information. Often a firm needs more than information.
Management often needs direct assistance in locating
distributors, joint-venture partners, advertising
agencies, accounting services, and other commercial
contacts. It may also need help in dealing with
local governmental bodies, such as customs, licensing
agencies, and taxing authorities. Large companies
can surmount many of these problems by having a man
on the spot. For smaller companies a man in each
market area is not feasible. One solution would be
to broaden the functions of our commercial attachés
and similar representatives abroad beyond the present
data-collecting and reporting areas, so that they
can actively help American businesses overseas.
Other countries have been willing to supply such services to their nationals, but the American Foreign
Service has actively avoided involvement in actual
business affairs.

A last action that could be taken by the government would involve the use of subsidies in two types
of situations. In past years there have been a number of cases of American industry's seeking increased
protection on the basis that it was war-essential.
One of the most famous of these cases was the Swiss
watch tariff, which resulted in an increase in tariffs on watches. If these industries are truly war-
essential, and if their business is significantly hurt
by imports, a subsidy might prove more beneficial
than would increased tariffs or quotas. A subsidy
would protect the American industry and at the same
time would allow the importation of foreign commodities.

As a result all concerned would be better off. It
is interesting to note that, although our traditional
jeweled-movement watch industry suffered from declining sales, it very successfully diversified into the
electronics field; and Timex established an entirely
new watch industry based on the pin-lever watch.
The increased tariffs did not protect American industry; they merely accelerated Timex's growth at the
expense of more costly watches and a long-overdue
diversification of the older watch industry.

The other possible use of the subsidy would be
to meet the Soviet price competition that was forcing
American products out of the market. If the price
competition were fair competition according to capitalist standards, such a subsidy would not be required. However, if the price competition were determined to be unfair (i.e., sales below cost), subsidies would be the best method available to protect
American business interests abroad. Subsidies should
be used with extreme caution to avoid unnecessary
costs. At the same time their use must be flexible,
so that maneuvers of the Soviet Union could be adequately met. Determining fairness could prove very
difficult, as can be seen in the case of Soviet oil
sales to India. The Anglo-American oil oligopoly in
India claimed that the Soviet price was indeed unfair competition. Further examination suggests,
however, that the oligopoly had artificially inflated
its prices and that the Soviet sale was quite fair--
by capitalist standards. The British Board of Trade
apparently came to the same conclusion regarding
aluminum prices in 1958.

STATE TRADING

Since 1918 considerable attention has been paid
to the potential dangers inherent in the Soviet system of monopoly state trading. In the previous chapters, however, it has been shown that, with the exception of the dumping of 1930 and 1931, none of these
dangers has gone beyond the potential stage. Specifically, the dangers that are possible under such
a system are the political use of foreign trade,
adoption of a pricing policy that is not compatible

with the methods used in capitalist countries, and
the exertion of undue influence as a result of a
monopoly position.

Political Use of Foreign Trade

In recent years the foreign trade activities of
the Soviet Union in the developing countries have
been based primarily on economic factors. Although
political activities usually accompany such trade,
there is little evidence that these trade activities
are being carried out for strictly political purposes.
It is entirely possible, however, that in the future
the Soviet Union may conduct trade with a specific
country for no other purpose than political gain.
What actions can be taken by the United States or
other countries of the West in such an event?

The best action that could be taken by the West
would be one that would prevent such an event from
occurring, not one taken after the fact as a correc-
tive measure. For this reason it is necessary that
the economic vulnerabilities of each country be determined and action be taken to strengthen weak
spots. The most common vulnerability in the developing countries is the existence of commodity surpluses,
especially in one-commodity nations. Some method
must be devised for disposing of these commodity surpluses. One possible method is the use of an international version of the Commodity Credit Corporation.
Created within the framework of the United Nations,
such an organization would be able to profit from the
experience of the various UN economic commissions,
the International Bank for Reconstruction and Development, the Food and Agriculture Organization, and
similar organizations. As a UN organization it would
also have the advantage of being apolitical. The
basic purpose of this organization would be to purchase commodity surpluses and dispose of them so as
to support the world market prices of these commodities. In coordination with the other UN organizations,
this Commodity Credit Corporation would make studies
of the economies of various countries and would recom-
mend changes in economic direction as dictated by
changes in the international market situation. To

insure against continued production of commodities
no longer needed by the world markets, this organization could place levels on the volume of various surpluses that would be covered over a certain period
of time. The primary goal of this organization would
be to afford the producing countries an alternative
method of disposing of their surplus goods. In this
way a major vulnerability would be removed, and it
would be more difficult for the Soviet Union to force
a country into a trading arrangement designed primarily
for political purposes.

Pricing

Although Marxian socialism calls for a pricing
system based primarily on labor value, the Soviet
Union has relied almost exclusively on world market
prices for its foreign trade operations. Exceptions
to this rule are the dumping of 1930 and 1931, the
disposal of aluminum and tin in 1957, and certain
isolated sales of other commodities. From time to
time spokesmen for the Soviet Union have displayed
dissatisfaction with world prices as a basis for
trade and have suggested that a new Soviet foreign
trade pricing system, based on labor input, will be
forthcoming.

If the Soviet Union were to adopt a price system
that resulted in dumping by capitalist standards, it
would be necessary for other countries to take some
action, either individually or collectively, to counter this development. These actions would probably
be in the form of special antidumping tariffs and
quota systems. Collective action, possibly through
the United Nations or the General Agreement on Tariffs and Trade, would be preferable, since it would
make possible a solid front of capitalist countries.
Such collective action, however, would probably be
very difficult to obtain. One reason for this would
be the desire of various countries to purchase the
products of the Soviet Union at the lowest possible
prices. This would be especially true in the developing countries.

If the purchasing nations refuse to levy an antidumping tariff on such trade, it is quite possible

that the United States and other countries of the West
would be placed at a definite competitive disadvantage.
Under such circumstances it might be necessary, as
suggested earlier, for these countries to provide
export subsidies to their traders.

It must be pointed out, however, that the use
of a pricing policy resulting in long-term dumping
by the Soviet Union is most unlikely. Unless the
Soviet Union were able to purchase commodities on a
similar price scale, such a policy would result in a
continued drain on the Soviet economy. It is likely
that the present export and import policies will be
continued. Further, in accordance with the export
policy, exports will probably be kept at a level that
just adequately covers imports. This will require
continued use of world prices or an extensive use of
negotiated prices.

Monopoly Pressures

In capitalist foreign trade there is usually
both a competition of buyers and a competition of
sellers involved in every transaction. By the use of
monopoly trading corporations, the Soviet Union has
eliminated all competition on one side of the transaction. If a business deal is to be concluded with
the Soviet Union, it must be concluded through this
one organization and on terms agreeable to it. As a
result the capitalist buyer or seller dealing with
the Soviet Union is at a disadvantage.

To avoid such a disadvantage, it has frequently
been suggested that some form of collective action
be taken. In 1927 the Russland-Ausschuss der Deutschen
Wirtschaft was formed to represent the interests of
all German businesses in dealing with the Soviet
Union.[1] Shortly thereafter the London Chamber of
Commerce considered the possibility of a clearinghouse
for Soviet trade, and the British Softwood Buying
Corporation was set up as a syndicate controlling all
British imports of timber from Russia.[2] During the
depression in 1930 and 1931, Briand called for "an
international credit institute in Europe . . . through
which every member of the League of Nations would
pass its trade with the Soviet Union."[3] At the same

time one author called for "an accord between all
countries . . . having as its aim the establishment
in each country of a single control for all trade
with the USSR."[4]

It is possible that in the future the Soviet
Union may use its monopoly position to force through
special prices or concessions. In such a case it
may again become necessary to take some measure of
collective action. To enjoy the advantages of specialization and avoid the inflexibility of a bureaucratic organization, such action would be most effective if limited to specific industries and not carried
out on a national or international basis.

UNDERDEVELOPED COUNTRIES

Since 1918 the Soviet Union has raised itself
from an agricultural, underdeveloped country to become one of the leading industrial powers. To do
this the Soviets have relied primarily on internal
resources and on a system of socialism. Today the
developing countries of the world seek a rapid improvement in their economic condition. To many of
these countries it might appear that capitalism is
not a fast enough means of attaining such ends. In
recent years Communist propaganda has tried mightily
to convince these people that Soviet-type socialism
holds the answer to their dreams. At first this
propaganda was not very effective, but in the last
few years it has apparently made great strides. Also,
such actions as the development of state-owned steel
mills at Bhilai and Bokaro, India, with Soviet assistance has given even more strength to Soviet arguments.

The countries of the West must find some means
of showing the less-developed countries the advantages of capitalism in a program of economic development. By promising a better life and avoiding certain
realities, propaganda may convince these people to
switch to socialism. In the past the peoples of the
underdeveloped countries have, for the most part,
seen only the bad aspects of capitalism. As a result
only concrete action will convince them that capitalism is more advantageous. A lengthy discussion of

the problems of economic development is beyond the
scope of this work. It appears, however, that a complete reappraisal of this problem is necessary. In
past years the American technical aid programs have
been based on a balanced development of the economy.
Such a development required primarily governmental
assistance in the fields of public works, agriculture,
public health, and education. Improvement in all
these fields has been essential, but it has not solved
the economic problems faced by the peoples of the
less-developed countries. It is quite possible that
an unbalanced economic development might be more advantageous. This type of development would require
emphasis on the productive factors of an economy.
As these factors were developed, pressures would grow
for improvement in the other sectors.

    To carry out an unbalanced economic development,
there must be increased participation of the business
sectors of the developed countries. New factories
must be built. Business techniques in the developing
countries must be improved. Business education must
be expanded. If the needed assistance is given on a
government-to-government basis, there will be a ten-
dency toward supporting a form of socialism. Furthermore, capitalism is an ideology personified by the
businessman, and the methods and ideas of businessmen
tend to lose some of their essential vigor when
transmitted by other agencies. Therefore, the best
means of carrying out such a program is on a business-
to-business basis As suggested earlier, American
businesses should abandon ideas of economic isolation-
ism and enter into joint arrangements with companies
abroad. Such an action should be taken even where
the venture at first may appear risky. To assist in
such an undertaking, it has been suggested that the
government make various tax concessions and offer
financial assistance and insurance against a wide
range of risks peculiar to international business.

    In the developing countries of the world the
battle is one for men's minds. Two ideologies can
be seen face-to-face. The people who are the targets
of this struggle have seen many of the bad aspects
of capitalism, and they have been told in glowing
terms of the advantages of socialism. If the West

fails in its efforts to develop contacts on a business-
to-business basis on a large scale, capitalism will
lose by default. In this case it can be expected
that government-to-government contacts between the
Soviet Union and the less-developed countries will
increase. If the volume of these contacts is suffi-
cient, it is probable that the underdeveloped countries will adopt socialism.

IMPROVED EAST-WEST TRADE

During the decade 1960-70, Soviet imports from
Japan grew almost sixfold, and Japan became the Soviet Union's major trading partner in the capitalist
world. Although it is the extreme case, this growth
is symptomatic of a change in East-West trade relations that has been going on for more than a decade.
As discussed in the last chapter, Japan and Western
Europe have long been willing and eager to sell the
Soviet Union anything short of actual arms. The
United States, on the other hand, has maintained an
extensive list of export controls on both strategic
and nonstrategic trade and has always leaned toward
restriction if there was any question. It has been
argued that these trade restrictions were designed
to deprive the Soviet Union of certain military potential. An examination of Soviet policy, however,
shows that military needs are given first priority
regardless of other availabilities. Thus, if American trade restrictions impose a hardship, they impose
this hardship on the civilian sector of the economy
and not on the military. Despite their original in-
tentions, the net effect of these restrictions has
been not a limitation of Soviet military capability
but a decreased competitive position for American industry that has resulted in sales going to Japanese
and European competitors. If Soviet-American trade
relations are to be improved, these restrictions
will have to be removed or at least severely limited.
Since the restrictions are political in nature, the
method of removal should be designed so as to result
in some compensatory benefits for the United States.

Most-Favored-Nation Treatment

Congress should immediately authorize the president to negotiate a MFN agreement with the Soviet Union. The Soviet-American commission established at the Moscow summit meeting in May 1972 is in fact negotiating such an agreement. However, any such agreement would then have to be ratified by Congress because of existing laws prohibiting such arrangements. If Congress were to grant advance authority, this would be a positive sign to the Soviets that the United States is indeed interested in developing improved trade relations and could well be the catalyst for other agreements. Opponents of such an MFN agreement argue that the United States would get no meaningful tariff concession in return and that MFN is not needed because most current imports from the Soviet Union are duty-free. These arguments are quite specious. First, it is not necessary that the Soviet concessions be limited to tariffs. The negotiations are political in nature, and the concessions could be in a totally unrelated political area. Besides, it was not for tariff purposes that the MFN privileges were withdrawn--the reasons were purely political. Second, current Soviet sales may not be a true indication of what can and would be sold. As an example, the Soviet Union could export vodka to the United States. Recently the Soviets have cut back vodka production to curb drunkenness. Instead of cutting production, they could ship this vodka to the United States. Today, however, the duty on vodka is prohibitive. Similarly, dressed furs could be imported, provided the duty were not so high. The granting of MFN could also serve as a psychological weapon. Without MFN the Soviets feel persecuted and discriminated against. Granting of MFN could ease other, unrelated tensions and improve overall Soviet-American relations.

Fur Embargo

Congress should immediately repeal the fur embargo that prohibits the importation of certain types of furs. This embargo serves no useful purpose. On

the contrary, it reduces the ability of the Soviet
Union to sell in the United States and thus earn dollars that can be used to pay for needed imports.
Further, it either deprives the American consumer of
certain furs or increases the price for these furs
because of the lack of effective competition. No
quid pro quo should be sought here. The embargo was
a unilateral action taken in a fit of political pique
and should be eliminated unilaterally.

Credits

The administration should take the initiative in
seeking a solution to the lend-lease debt impasse.
In past discussions the United States has made certain concessions but has refused to go below some
predetermined bargaining point. The end result has
always been a continued impasse and thus a continued
restriction against various credits to the Soviet
Union. In new discussions the administration should
proceed with the positive idea that an agreement will
be reached. Creative new solutions may be needed.
For example, it might be agreed that a certain sum
was to be repaid in kind and not cash--say in future
shipments of natural gas. Further, it should be remembered that repayment of the lend-lease debts is
more political than economic, and in certain instances
the United States has written off the debt for political reasons. In any case the sum to be repaid is
unimportant. What is important is that the impasse
be resolved in such a way that both sides feel they
have gained.

Presidential authority to issue Export-Import
Bank credit guarantees should be continued. In addition some thought should be given to other forms of
government or government-guaranteed credit. At the
present time the Commodity Credit Corporation is
limited to providing credit at government cost for a
maximum of three years. A subsidized credit rate is
not recommended, but congressional action to liberalize other Commodity Credit Corporation credit terms
would be strongly recommended.

It is also recommended that Congress authorize
the Export-Import Bank to make credit guarantees of

longer term--say 15 years. In all such cases proper
banking methods must be observed in the granting of
credit or guarantees. By providing such improved
credit facilities, comparable with those granted by
other Western countries, the United States would be
paving the way for much-improved Soviet-American commercial relationships. Soviet needs are currently
so great that they are now seeking massive credits
up to a reported $15 billion. It is likely that they
will receive these credits somewhere, and trade will
surely follow the credits.

                    Strategic Trade Controls

     Strategic trade controls, in one form or another,
will probably have to be retained. It would be recommended, however, that the Battle Act as such be
repealed. In its place there should be an act that
places controls on all sales of all arms to all coun-
tries--with no special discrimination against Communist countries per se. This specific discrimination
remains a constant thorn in the Soviet side. Its removal would immeasurably improve Soviet-American relations. At the same time international control on
all arms shipments would effectively limit shipments
of these items to any part of the world except with
specific governmental approval.
     More important, the definition of strategic
goods must be restated in a much more limited sense.
Actual arms, ammunition, war planes, and similar
items are by definition strategic. Other items, however, should be reviewed; and, if there is no direct
relationship, they should be reclassified as nonstrategic. Computers are a good example. While computers can be used for strategic purposes, their
main usage in the United States is for nonstrategic
business, government, academic, and scientific appli-
cations. Yet it was only in 1971 that International
Computers of England received COCOM permission to sell
its first computer to Russia. It was in the spring
of 1972 that IBM sold its first 360-50 computer to
the Soviets (after a year of delay and red tape).
     Congress has already taken the initiative in the
nonstrategic goods area and has ordered decontrol of

items freely available elsewhere. This decontrol effort should be continued and broadened. Even if certain items are not available in Europe or Japan, if
they are not strategic the United States should consider selling them to the Soviets. Preferably the
management of this decontrol procedure should remain
in the hands of the administration. Further, the
administration should have the authority to remove
(or even add) restrictions selectively whenever such
an action would be beneficial to the United States.

In short the government--both Congress and the
administration--should exert every effort to eliminate all unnecessary barriers to Soviet-American
trade. Peaceful trade that leads to eventual economic
interdependence should be actively encouraged. At
the same time general strategic controls that are
not discriminatory should protect the United States
from military adventures.

SUMMARY

Although there is no present danger to the West
from Soviet foreign trade activities, there are three
potential dangers: intensified competition, the
dangers of state trading, and the possibility that
socialism will be adopted by the developing countries.
In the field of competition, the major threat to the
United States is offered by an expanded European
Common Market and Japan. In the future it is impossible that the Soviet Union will become a strong
competitive factor. To maintain our competitive position, American business firms must apply modern marketing and marketing intelligence techniques to foreign
operations; increase foreign investments; reduce
costs of production, transportation, and marketing;
and maintain a high level of imports. At the same
time the American government should promote international business by reducing tariffs, providing financial assistance, reducing taxes on overseas operations, and redirecting but continuing its foreign aid
program. In emergency cases it should also be ready
to provide subsidies to essential American industries.

There are three potential dangers in the Soviet
use of state trading: the use of trade for political

purposes, adoption of a socialist pricing system,
and the dangers inherent in a monopoly position. To
avoid Soviet use of trade for primarily political
purposes, the West must provide adequate markets for
the commodities of the world. In this way a producing
nation would have an alternative means of disposing
of its goods and could not be forced into a Soviet
trade pattern created for political purposes. It has
been suggested that such an alternative might be an
international Commodity Credit Corporation within the
framework of the United Nations. A change in the
Soviet pricing system does not appear likely. If
such a change occurred and resulted in dumping, it
would be necessary for buying countries, individually
or collectively, to institute some means of countering this dumping. The actions suggested are the use
of antidumping tariffs and restrictive quotas. If
some nations do not apply such measures, the competitive position of countries of the West in these markets would be endangered. For such cases export
subsidies are suggested. If the Soviet Union attempts
to use its monopoly trading position to obtain unwar-
ranted price reductions or other concessions, an association of exporters would be one logical means of
countering such pressures.

For purposes of improving Soviet-American trade
relations, it is recommended that the United States
dismantle most of its trade control machinery--but
on a selective, negotiated basis. Special attention
is paid to renewing MFN status, eliminating the fur
embargo, improving credit arrangements, and eliminating most of the nonstrategic and some of the strategic
trade controls.

All works published in Russian are indicated by *.

CHAPTER 1

1. M. M. Zhirmunski, Soviet Export (Moscow: Mezhdunarodnaya Kniga, 1936), p. 32.
2. USSR, Collection of Laws and Decrees Pt. I (Moscow: Otdel Opublikovaniya Zakonov, 1918), pp. 411-12.*
3. USSR, Collection of Laws and Decrees Pt. I (Moscow: Otdel Opublikovaniya Zakonov, 1922), art. 266.*
4. "Trade Policy and Prospects," Russian Information and Review, November 4, 1922, p. 72.
5. M. Ya Kaufman, Foreign Trade and Trade Policy of the USSR (Moscow: Redaktsiono-Izdatel-skovo Otdela, NKVT, 1924), p. 6.*
6. USSR, Collection of Laws, Pt. I (1922), art. 905*; USSR, Documentation Relating to Foreign Economic Relations of the USSR, prepared for the Monetary and Economic Conference, London, June 1933 (Moscow: "International" Typographic Works, 1933), p. 42.
7. V. S. Pozdniakov, "The State Monopoly of Foreign Trade in the USSR," Soviet State and Law, No. 10 (1967), p. 42.
8. S. M. Siddiq, Indo-Russian Trade (Delhi: Indian Council of World Affairs, 1948), p. 21.
9. V. Boyeff, The Soviet Union and World Problems (Chicago: University of Chicago Press, 1935), p. 26.
10. A. P. Rosenholz, Fifteen Years of the Foreign Trade Monopoly (Moscow: Co-operative Publishing Society of Foreign Workers in the USSR, 1933), pp. 9-10.
11. Ibid., p. 6.
12. J. D. Yanson, Foreign Trade in the USSR (London: Victor Gollancz, 1934), p. 24.

13. "The Principles of Russian Foreign Trade," Russian Information and Review, October 15, 1921, p. 38.

14. A. P. Rozenholz, The USSR and the Capitalist World (Moscow: Vneshtorgizdat, 1934), p. 29.

15. M. N. Sobolev, ed., Economics and Policies of Foreign Trade (Moscow: Narkomtorga SSSR i RSFSR, 1928), p. 61.*

16. Zhirmunski, Soviet Export, p. 14.

17. Ibid., p. 8.

18. Rozenholz, The USSR, p. 3.

19. Rosenholz, Fifteen Years, pp. 13-14.

20. USSR, People's Commissariat of Foreign Trade, Foreign Trade up to the 7th Congress of the Soviet of the USSR (Moscow: Vneshtorgizdat, 1935), p. 10.*

21. Zhirmunski, Soviet Export, p. 68.

22. D. D. Mishustin, Foreign Trade and Industrialization of the USSR (Moscow: V/O Mezhdunarodnaya Kniga, 1938), p. 31.*

23. H. R. Knickerbocker, Soviet Trade and World Depression (London: John Lane-The Bodley Head Ltd., 1931), pp. 32-33.

24. The New York Times, January 17, 1958, p. 32; January 23, 1958, p. 37.

25. Ibid., March 28, 1958, p. 37.

26. Ibid., March 14, 1958, p. 36.

27. Ibid.; USSR, Ministry of Foreign Trade, Foreign Trade of the USSR for 1956 (Moscow: Vneshtorgizdat, 1958), p. 41; for 1957, p. 41.*

28. USSR, Ministry of Foreign Trade, Foreign Trade of the USSR for 1957, pp. 7-10, 41-43.*

29. "Soviets Push on Western Markets," Business Week, March 2, 1963, p. 98.

30. USSR, Ministry of Foreign Trade, Foreign Trade of the USSR for 1959-63, pp. 102-03.*

31. "U.S. Presses Allies to Stem Oil Invasion," Business Week, August 5, 1961, p. 29.

32. Foreign Trade, Official journal of the USSR Ministry of Foreign Trade, No. 12 (1964), p. 35.*

33. "Soviets Push on Western Markets," p. 98.

34. "Soviets Push Petroleum Exports," Business Week, May 7, 1960, p. 106; "Soviets Push on Western Markets," p. 95.

35. Yanson, Foreign Trade, p. 33.

36. Rozenholz, The USSR, pp. 3-4.

37. M. M. Zhirmunski, Organization and Technique of Soviet Exports (Moscow: Vneshtorgizdat, 1935), p. 13.*

38. Boyeff, The Soviet Union, p. 41.

39. Scientific-Research Institute of the Monopoly of Foreign Trade, Foreign Trade of the Soviet Union (Moscow: V/O Mezhdunarodnaya Kniga, 1938), p. 93.*

40. United States, Foreign Operations Administration, East-West Trade Trends, Mutual Defense Assistance Control Act of 1951, Fourth Report to Congress (1954), p. 5.

41. C. Douglas Dillon, "The Challenge of Soviet Economic Expansion," The Department of State Bulletin, May 25, 1959, p. 763.

42. Boyeff, The Soviet Union, p. 27.

43. I. Diumulen, "The Soviet Union in the System of International Economic Relations," World Economics and International Relations, No. 3 (1964), p. 40.

44. K. Voronov, "Current Organization of Foreign Trade of the USSR," Foreign Trade, No. 8 (1966), p. 48.*

45. Foreign Trade, No. 4 (1971), p. 5.*

46. "Foreign Embassies in the USSR," Russian Information and Review, April 26, 1924, p. 269.

47. The New York Times, April 24, 1923, p. 6.

48. "Foreign Embassies in the USSR."

49. Scientific-Research Institute of the Monopoly of Foreign Trade, Foreign Trade of the USSR for 20 Years: 1918-1937 (Moscow: V/O Mezhdunarodnaya Kniga, 1939), pp. 22-31.*

50. Jacques Doussé, La Politique Economique de l'URSS Appliquée à son Commerce Extérieur (Paris: Marcel Giard, 1933), p. 169.

51. The New York Times, May 9, 1921, p. 20.

52. B. N. Kovarsky, The Regulation of Foreign Trade (Moscow: Redaktsionno-Izdatelskovo Otdela, NKVT, 1925), p. 7*; "The Agreement with Norway," Russian Information and Review, October 1, 1921, p. 17.

53. "The Anglo-Soviet Treaties," Russian Information and Review, August 16, 1924, pp. 106-07.

54.   "Soviet Foreign Trade Policy," Russian
Information and Review, December 6, 1924, p. 355.
     55.   Doussé, La Politique Economique, pp.
169-70.
     56.   Scientific-Research Institute of the
Monopoly of Foreign Trade, Foreign Trade of the
USSR for 20 Years, pp. 27-31.*
     57.   The New York Times, September 29, 1939,
p. 8.
     58.   Ibid., October 17, 1939, p. 6; October
19, 1939, p. 7.
     59.   "Trans-Caucasian Trade," Russian Infor-
mation and Review, November 11, 1922, p. 92.
     60.   Elias Hurwicz, Die Orientpolitik der
Dritten Internationale (Berlin: Deutsche Verlagsgesellschaft fur Politik und Geschichte mbH,
1922), p. 35; USSR, People's Commissariat of Foreign Affairs, Handbook of Active Trade Agreements
and Other Economic Agreements of the USSR Concluded with Foreign Governments, I (Moscow: SSSR,
Narodnie Komissariat po Inostrannie Delam, 1935),
v*; All-Union Eastern Chamber of Commerce, Countries of the East (Moscow: Vsyesoyuznaya-
Vostochnaya Torgovaya Palata, 1929), p. 781.*
     61.   USSR, Collection of Laws and Decrees,
Pt. I (Moscow: Otdel Opublikovaniya Zakonov,
1925), p. 176.*
     62.   "Foreign Trade Conference," Russian In-
formation and Review, February 2, 1924, p. 66.
     63.   Scientific-Research Institute of the
Monopoly of Foreign Trade, Trade Relations of the
USSR with Countries of the East (Moscow: V/O
Mezhdunarodnaya Kniga, 1938), pp. 48-49*; Zhirmunski, Soviet Export, p. 22.
     64.   Foreign Trade, No. 4 (1971), p. 5.*
     65.   Leon M. Herman, "The New Soviet Posture
in World Trade," Problems of Communism, November-
December 1954, pp. 12-13.
     66.   Foreign Trade, No. 4 (1971), p. 5.*
     67.   The Wall Street Journal, August 9, 1971,
p. 15.
     68.   Michael Sapir, The New Role of the So-
viets in the World Economy (Washington, D.C.:
Committee for Economic Development, 1958), p. 27.

69. G. Smirnov, B. Zotov, and G. Shagalov, "Theory of Foreign Trade," Planned Economy, No. 8 (1964), p. 4.

70. Foreign Trade, No. 8 (1971), p. 12.*

71. A. Bergson, R. Bernaut, and L. Turgeon, "Prices of Basic Industrial Products in the USSR, 1928-1950," Journal of Political Economy, August 1956, pp. 15-19, 48-52, 323.

72. A. Stoupnitzky, Statut International de l'URSS--Etat Commerçant (Paris: Librairie Générale de Droit et de Jurisprudence, 1936), pp. 132-33.

73. USSR, Collection of Laws and Decrees, Pt. I (1922), p. 482.*

74. "The Customs Tariff," Russian Information and Review, May 24, 1924, p. 328.

75. All-Union Eastern Chamber of Commerce, Countries of the East, p. 961.*

76. "Foreign Trade Conference," Russian Information and Review, August 1, 1922, p. 497.

77. Doussé, La Politique Economique, p. 163.

78. Stoupnitzky, Statut International, pp. 133-35; Doussé, La Politique Economique, p. 162; Great Britain, Commercial Counsellor to His Majesty's Embassy in Moscow, The Organisation of Foreign Trade of the Union of Soviet Socialist Republics (London: HM Stationery Office, 1931), p. 10; USSR, Collection of Laws and Decrees, Pt. I (1926), p. 34; Pt. I (1927), p. 79.*

79. Foreign Trade, No. 9 (1966), p. 13; No. 10 (1961), p. 5.*

80. "New Customs Tariff of the USSR," supplement to Foreign Trade, No. 9 (1961), pp. 4-11.*

81. Foreign Trade, No. 9 (1966), p. 13.*

82. Ibid.

CHAPTER 2

1. B. L. Krassin, Foreign Trade and Foreign Economic Policy of the Soviet Government (Moscow: Gosudarstvennoye Izdatelstvo, 1921), p. 21.*

2. M. Ya Kaufman, Organization and Regulation of the Foreign Trade of Russia (Moscow: Ekonomicheskaya Zhizn, 1925), p. 28.*

3. Jacques Doussé, La Politique Economique de l'URSS Appliquée à son Commerce Extérieur (Paris: Marcel Giard, 1933), p. 121.

4. M. M. Zhirmunski, Soviet Export (Moscow: Mezhdunarodnaya Kniga, 1936), p. 34.

5. "Russia's Foreign Trade and the New Policy," Russian Information and Review, February 15, 1922, pp. 229-30.

6. "Gostorg," Russian Information and Review, July 1, 1922, p. 449.

7. Ibid.

8. "Foreign Trade Conference," Russian Information and Review, August 15, 1922, pp. 520-21.

9. A. L. Troyanovsky and M. Kaufman, Export, Import and Concessions of the USSR (Moscow: Gosudarstvennoi Kontorie Obyavlyenii "Dvigatel," 1926), pp. 352/66-67*; A. I. Kutuzov, ed., Foreign Trade of the USSR for 10 Years (Moscow: Narkomtorg SSSR i RSFSR, 1928), pp. 200-02*; and Encyclopedia of Soviet Exports, I (2d ed.; Berlin: Torgovovo Predstavitelstva SSSR v Germanii, Tsentrosoyuza i Gostorga, 1928), 45.*

10. Kutuzov, Foreign Trade, p. 200.*

11. "The All-Russian Import and Export Society, Ltd.," Russian Information and Review, March 15, 1922, pp. 281-82.

12. A. Stoupnitzky, Statut International de l'URSS--Etat Commerçant (Paris: Librairie Générale de Droit et de Jurisprudence, 1936), p. 87.

13. B. N. Kovarsky, The Regulation of Foreign Trade (Moscow: Redaktsionno-Izdatelskovo Otdela, NKVT, 1925), p. 56.*

14. M. M. Zhirmunski, Organization and Technique of Soviet Exports (Moscow: Vneshtorgizdat, 1935), p. 35.*

15. M. N. Sobolev, ed., Economics and Policies of Foreign Trade (Moscow: Narkomtorga SSSR i RSFSR, 1928), p. 99.*

16. Troyanovsky, Yurovsky, and Kaufman, Export, Import and Concessions, p. 512/7.*

17. Sobolev, Economics and Policies, p. 107.*

18. Zhirmunski, Soviet Export, p. 43.

19. Sobolev, Economics and Policies, p. 109.*

20. "Companies for Foreign Trade," Russian Information and Review, June 15, 1922, p. 432.

21.   Louis Segal and A. A. Santalov, Commercial Year-Book of the Soviet Union (London: George Allen and Unwin, 1925), pp. 276-86.

22.   USSR, People's Commissariat of Foreign Trade, Handbook of Active Decrees on Foreign Trade, I (Moscow: Redaktsionno-Isdatelskovo Otdela, NKVT, 1924-26), 56.*

23.   Zhirmunski, Soviet Export, p. 43.

24.   A. A. Santalov and Louis Segal, Soviet Union Year Book (London: George Allen and Unwin, 1928), pp. 239-44; (1929), p. 249; Jacques Jeramec, Le Monopole du Commerce Extérieur en Russie Sovietique (Paris: Librairie Générale de Droit et de Jurisprudence, 1928), p. 92; Great Britain, Commercial Counsellor to His Majesty's Embassy in Moscow, The Organisation of Foreign Trade of the Union of Soviet Socialist Republics (London: HM Stationery Office, 1931), p. 23; Sobolev, Economics and Policies, p. 107*; 50 Years of Soviet Foreign Trade (Moscow: Mezhdunarodnieye Otnosheniya, 1967), p. 51.*

25.   Great Britain, Commercial Counsellor to His Majesty's Embassy in Moscow, The Organisation of Foreign Trade, pp. 23-25.

26.   Krassin, Foreign Trade and Foreign Economic Policy, p. 5.*

27.   Stoupnitzky, Statut International, p. 104.

28.   Encyclopedia of Russian Exports, II (1st ed.; Berlin: Torgovovo Predstavitelstva SSSR v Germanii pri vchasti Upravleniya Upoln, NKVT na Ukraine i Tsentrosoyuza, 1925), pp. 4-7*; Noah Barou, Russian Co-operation Abroad (London: P. S. King and Son, 1930), pp. 45, 52, 63, 68.

29.   USSR, Collection of Laws and Decrees, Pt. I (Moscow: Otdel Opublikovaniya Zakonov, 1922), art. 266.*

30.   Barou, Russian Co-operation Abroad, pp. 22-23, 45, 52, 63.

31.   Encyclopedia of Russian Exports, II, p. 7.*

32.   Ibid., III, p. 466.

33.   Jeramec, Le Monopole du Commerce Extérieur, p. 98.

34.   Segal and Santalov, Commercial Year-Book, pp. 276-86; Encyclopedia of Russian Exports, II, p. 11.*

35.   Stoupnitzky, Statut International, p.
71; Doussé, La Politique Economique, pp. 131-32;
M. M. Zhirmunski, Soviet Export (Moscow: Mezhdunarodnaya Kniga, 1936), pp. 65-66; I. A. Kirillov,
The Financing of Trade (Moscow: Izdatelstvo
NKRKI, 1927), p. 77.
36.   Encyclopedia of Russian Exports, II,
p. 7.*
37.   Stoupnitzky, Statut International, p.
104.
38.   Patton D. Allen, Director, European
Division, Bureau of Foreign Commerce, U.S. Department of Commerce, Washington, D.C, Letter
dated December 9, 1958.
39.   The New York Times, June 2, 1920, p. 17.
40.   Ibid., June 19, 1920, p. 15.
41.   Encyclopedia of Russian Exports, III,
p. 466.*
42.   "New Russian Book Company in England,"
Russian Information and Review, November 10,
1923, p. 300; Jeramec, Le Monopole du Commerce
Extérieur, p. 118; Louis Segal and A. A. Santalov,
Soviet Union Year Book (London: George Allen
and Unwin, 1926), pp. 283-85.
43.   The New York Times, May 13, 1927, p. 1.
44.   Scientific-Research Institute of the
Monopoly of Foreign Trade, Foreign Trade of the
Soviet Union (Moscow: V/O Mezhdunarodnaya Kniga,
1938, pp. 84-85.*
45.   The New York Times, June 19, 1924, p. 31.
46.   American Bankers Association, Industry,
Government, Finance and Foreign Trade in Soviet
Russia (New York: American Bankers Association,
1929), pp. 22-24.
47.   Allen, Letter; Santalov and Segal,
Soviet Union Year Book (1929), p. 329.
48.   The New York Times, February 16, 1929,
p. 17.
49.   Soviet Union Information Bureau, The
Soviet Union (Washington, D.C.:   The Bureau, 1929),
p. 165.
50.   The New York Times, August 1, 1931, p.
22; October 29, 1931, p. 9.
51.   Ibid., December 4, 1935, p. 11; January
1, 1936, p. 25; January 26, 1936, p. 26.

52. Stoupnitzky, Statut International, p. 98.

53. USSR, Collection of Laws and Decrees,
Pt. I (1922), art. 266.*

54. American Bankers Association, Industry,
Government, Finance, pp. 20-21; "The Investment
of Foreign Capital," Russian Information and
Review, May 10, 1924, p. 295.

55. Troyanovsky, Yurovsky, and Kaufman, Export, Import and Concessions, p. 561.*

56. Sobolev, Economics and Policies, p. 99.*

57. Ibid.

58. Stoupnitzky, Statut International, p. 71;
Doussé, La Politique Economique, pp. 131-32;
Zhirmunski, Soviet Export, pp. 65-67.

59. "Trading Concessions," Russian Information and Review, June 9, 1923, p. 555.

60. "The Investment of Foreign Capital,"
May 17, 1924, p. 310.

61. Stoupnitzky, Statut International, p. 71;
Doussé, La Politique Economique, pp. 131-32;
Zhirmunski, Soviet Export, pp. 65-67.

62. Zhirmunski, Soviet Export, p. 46.

63. Zhirmunski, Organization and Technique,
p. 45.*

64. Scientific-Research Institute of the
Monopoly of Foreign Trade, Foreign Trade of the
Soviet Union, p. 66.*

65. Stoupnitzky, Statut International, p. 90.

66. Scientific-Research Institute of the
Monopoly of Foreign Trade, Foreign Trade of the
Soviet Union, p. 66.*

67. Zhirmunski, Organization and Technique,
p. 55.*

68. Ibid., p. 56.

69. Zhirmunski, Soviet Export, pp. 100-01.

70. Scientific-Research Institute of the
Monopoly of Foreign Trade, Foreign Trade of the
Soviet Union, p. 70.*

71. A. P. Rosengoltz, Soviet Foreign Trade--
New Developments (London: Trade Delegation of
the USSR in Great Britain, 1936), p. 20.

72. Ibid.

73. J. D. Yanson, Foreign Trade in the USSR
(London: Victor Gollancz, 1934), p. 165.

74. Scientific-Research Institute of the Monopoly of Foreign Trade, *Foreign Trade of the Soviet Union*, p. 71.*

75. *Ibid.*

76. W. W. Tarnovsky, "Banking: The First Private Bank," *Manchester Guardian Commercial*, June 26, 1924, p. 67.

77. Zhirmunski, *Organization and Technique*, p. 50.*

78. *Ibid.*, p. 45.

79. *Ibid.*, pp. 55-56.

80. Jeramec, *Le Monopole du Commerce Extérieur*, pp. 101-02.

81. Sobolev, *Economics and Policies*, p. 109.*

82. A. P. Rozengolts, *Foreign Trade of the USSR Under New Conditions* (Moscow: Sotsekiz, 1936), p. 32.*

83. Pavel A. Cherviakov, *Organization and Technique of the Foreign Trade of the USSR* (Moscow: Veneshtorgizdat, 1958), p. 29*; *Foreign Trade*, Official journal of the USSR Ministry of Foreign Trade, No. 4 (1958), p. 40.*

84. *The New York Times*, May 25, 1947, p. 6.

85. *Ibid.*, May 5, 1946, sec. III, p. 1.

86. *Foreign Trade*, No. 9 (1939), p. 42.*

87. *Ibid.*, No. 8 (1940), p. 10.

88. *Ibid.*, No. 2 (1940), p. 44.

89. A. D. Keilin, *Transport and Insurance in Foreign Trade: Legal Conditions of Foreign Trade Agreements* (Moscow: V/O Mezhdunarodnaya Kniga, 1947), p. 40.*

90. *Foreign Trade*, No. 9 (1939), p. 43.*

91. Changes announced in the Official Section of various issues of *ibid.* from July 1945 to November 1947.*

92. *Ibid.*, Nos. 9-12 (1948), Official Section.

93. *Ibid.*, No. 1 (1952), p. 44.

94. *Ibid.*, No. 9 (1951), pp. 45-46.

95. *Ibid.*, No. 5 (1952), pp. 40-41.

96. *Ibid.*, No. 11 (1956), p. 30.

97. *Ibid.*, No. 6 (1945), p. 44.

98. *Ibid.*, No. 5 (1947), p. 46.

99. *Ibid.*, No. 9 (1951), pp. 43-45.

100. *Ibid.*, No. 9 (1947), p. 46; No. 9, 1951, p. 41.

101. Keilin, Transport and Insurance, p. 37*; Foreign Trade, No. 9 (1945), pp. 46-47; No. 11-12 (1945), p. 38.*

102. Foreign Trade, No. 7 (1951), p. 47.*

103. Ibid., No. 2 (1952), p. 44.

104. The New York Times, November 16, 1946, p. 1.

105. Allen, Letter.

106. W. Barker, British Embassy, Washington, D.C., Letter dated February 20, 1959.

107. Die Neue Zeitung, April 24, 1947, as cited by Kerblay, p. 8.

108. Foreign Trade, No. 7 (1950), p. 16.*

109. A. M. Smirnov and N. N. Liubimov, Foreign Trade of the USSR (Moscow: Vneshtorgizdat, 1954), p. 254.*

110. Ibid., p. 256.

111. Die Neue Zeitung; Margaret Dewar, Soviet Trade with Eastern Europe: 1945-1949 (London: Royal Institute of International Affairs, 1951), p. 67.

112. Foreign Trade, No. 11 (1953), p. 20.*

113. Ibid., No. 10 (1955), p. 29.

114. Ibid., No. 3 (1951), pp. 1-2; United States, Foreign Operations Administration, Soviet Bloc Economic Activities in the Free World, Mutual Defense Assistance Control Act of 1951, Sixth Report to Congress, 1955, p. 5.

115. Clifford R. Barnett, Poland (New Haven, Conn.: Hraf Press, 1958), p. 295.

116. Dewar, Soviet Trade with Eastern Europe, pp. 89-91.

117. "Iran," Colliers Encyclopedia, XI (1957), 118.

118. Foreign Trade, Nos. 4-5 (1946), pp. 2-3.*

119. Ibid., No. 9 (1954), p. 7.

120. United States, Congress, House of Representatives, Select Committee on Foreign Aid, The East European Economy in Relation to the European Recovery Program, Preliminary Report 20 pursuant to H. Res. 296, a resolution creating a Special Committee on Foreign Aid, 80th Cong., 2d sess., 1948, p. 143.

121. Foreign Trade, No. 10 (1948), p. 3.*

122. Smirnov and Liubimov, Foreign Trade of the USSR, pp. 53-54.*

123. Foreign Trade, No. 5 (1950), p. 4.*

124. National Committee for a Free Europe, Economic Treaties and Agreements of the Soviet Bloc in Eastern Europe: 1945-1951 (Washington, D.C.: The Committee, 1952), p. xxix.

125. Monitorul Oficial, No. 186 (Bucharest, 1945).

126. Ibid., Nos 188, 245.

127. Rumania at the Peace Conference, as cited by National Committee for a Free Europe, Economic Treaties, p. 26.

128. Ibid.

129. Unites States, Congress, House of Representatives, Select Committee on Foreign Aid, The East European Economy, p. 140.

130. Magyar Kozlony, Hivatalos Lap, No. 82 (Budapest, 1947).

131. Magyar Kozlony, Hivatalos Lap, No. 177 (Budapest, 1946).

132. Foreign Trade, No. 4 (1947), p. 38.*

133. Ibid., No. 5 (1950), p. 9.

134. Ibid., No. 10 (1954), pp. 5-6.

135. Ibid., No. 8 (1955), p. 26; No. 10 (1955), p. 30.

136. Ibid., No. 10 (1954), pp. 5-6; No. 11 (1954), pp. 45-46; No. 12 (1954), pp. 8-9, 42, 43; No. 2 (1955), p. 4; No. 8 (1955), p. 26; No. 10 (1955), p. 30; No. 1 (1956), pp. 28, 30.

137. Ibid., No. 7 (1957), p. 35.

138. Ibid., No. 8 (1957), p. 4.

139. Smirnov and Liubimov, Foreign Trade of the USSR, pp. 77-78.*

140. Foreign Trade, No. 4 (1958), p. 40*; Pavel A. Cherviakov, Organization and Technique of the Foreign Trade of the USSR (Moscow: Vneshtorgizdat, 1962), p. 226.*

141. United States, International Cooperation Administration, Survey of East-West Trade in 1955, Mutual Defense Assistance Control Act of 1951, Eighth Report to Congress, 1956, p. 33.

142. Foreign Trade, No. 4 (1958), p. 40*; Cherviakov, Organization and Technique (1962), p. 227*; V. S. Pozdniakov, State Monopoly of Foreign Trade in the USSR (Moscow: Izdatelstvo "Mezhdunarodniye Otnosheniya," 1969), p. 96.*

143. <u>Ibid</u>.

144. Cherviakov, <u>Organization and Technique</u> (1962), p. 228.*

145. K. Voronov, "Current Organization of Foreign Trade of the USSR," <u>Foreign Trade</u>, No. 8 (1966), p. 49.*

146. Cherviakov, <u>Organization and Technique</u> (1962), p. 58*; Pozdniakov, <u>State Monopoly</u>, pp. 94-95*; Voronov, "Current Organization of Foreign Trade," p. 49.*

147. Cherviakov, <u>Organization and Technique</u>, (1962), pp. 58-59*; V. S. Pozdniakov, "The State Monopoly of Foreign Trade in the USSR," <u>Soviet State and Law</u>, No. 10 (1967), p. 44.

148. Pozdniakov, <u>State Monopoly</u>, p. 95.*

149. Cherviakov, <u>Organization and Technique</u> (1962), pp. 55, 60.*

150. <u>Foreign Trade</u>, No. 4 (1955), p. 29.*

151. <u>Ibid</u>., No. 7 (1957), pp. 37-38; No. 12 (1957), pp. 42-43.

152. Cherviakov, <u>Organization and Technique</u> (1962), pp. 229, 232, 339*; <u>Foreign Trade</u>, No. 1 (1965), pp. 49-50; No. 2 (1965), pp. 51-52; No. 8 (1969), pp. 13-14.*

153. <u>Foreign Trade</u>, No. 11 (1958), pp. 53-54.*

154. <u>Ibid</u>., Nos. 1, 4, and 10 (1956); Nos. 2 and 7 (1957), Official Section.

155. Cherviakov, <u>Organization and Technique</u> (1962), pp. 61, 272.*

156. "Russian Trade: Talk and Practice," <u>Business Week</u>, September 12, 1959, p. 40; "The Ruble Skirmish," <u>Fortune</u>, April 1959, p. 77; "Big Machinery Sale to Russia," <u>Business Week</u>, January 2, 1960, p. 69.

157. Cherviakov, <u>Organization and Technique</u> (1962), pp. 338-39.*

158. <u>Foreign Trade</u>, No. 6 (1965), pp. 54-55.*

159. <u>Ibid</u>., No. 12 (1970), pp. 57-58.

160. <u>Ibid</u>., No. 5 (1971), pp. 58-59.

161. "Car Hungry Russians . . . ," <u>Business Week</u>, June 27, 1959, p. 94.

162. Cherviakov, <u>Organization and Technique</u> (1962), p. 337.*

163. V. Golovin, "Medexport--New All-Union Association," <u>Foreign Trade</u>, No. 3 (1961), p. 26.*

164. Foreign Trade, No. 12 (1963), pp. 54-55.*

165. Ibid., No. 12 (1965), pp. 49-50.

166. Ibid., No. 9 (1970), pp. 63-64.

167. N. Okonechnikov, "The Course of Widening Specialization in the All-Union Associations," Foreign Trade, No. 9 (1966), p. 10.

168. N. V. Vasiliev, "Each Day Brings New Work," Foreign Trade, No. 10 (1960), p. 29.

169. Cherviakov, Organization and Technique (1962), p. 339.*

170. V. Vasin, "USSR Exports Airplanes," Foreign Trade, No. 8 (1962), p. 13*; Cherviakov, Organization and Technique, (1962), p. 337*; and Foreign Trade, No. 10 (1961), pp. 40-41.*

171. Foreign Trade, No. 6 (1965), pp. 19-21.*

172. Ibid., No. 7 (1966), pp. 57, 59.

173. Ibid., No. 10 (1966), p. 57.

174. Okonechnikov, "The Course of Widening Specialization," p. 11.*

175. Foreign Trade, No. 11 (1960), p. 48.*

176. Ibid., No. 3 (1965), p. 50.

177. Ibid., No. 11 (1962), p. 52; No. 1 (1963), p. 52.

178. Voronov, "Current Organization of Foreign Trade," p. 50*; Pozdniakov, State Monopoly, p. 164.*

179. Pozdniakov, State Monopoly, p. 112.*

180. Cherviakov, Organization and Technique (1962), p. 57.*

181. Alec Flegon, Soviet Foreign Trade Techniques (London: Flegon Press, 1965), p. 48.

182. Cherviakov, Organization and Technique (1962), pp. 51, 58.*

183. Ibid., p. 56.

184. "Putting a Bear in Britain's Tank," Business Week, July 20, 1968, p. 80.

185. Pozdniakov, "The State Monopoly," p. 47; Foreign Trade, No. 6 (1967), p. 24.*

186. Pozdniakov, State Monopoly, p. 98.*

187. Cherviakov, Organization and Technique (1962), p. 56.*

188. Foreign Trade, No. 7 (1965), p. 50.*

189. Cherviakov, Organization and Technique (1962), pp. 61-62*; Pozdniakov, State Monopoly, p. 102.*

190. Foreign Trade, No. 1 (1963), pp. 52-53.*

191. Pozdniakov, State Monopoly, pp. 97-99.*

192. Flegon, Soviet Foreign Trade Techniques, pp. 23-24.

193. Foreign Trade, No. 1 (1972), p. 34.*

194. Ibid., No. 9 (1971), p. 23.

195. Cherviakov, Organization and Technique (1962), p. 12*; "Soviets Build a Vienna Business on Insurance--And Sidelines," Business Week, February 10, 1962, p. 56.

196. "Reds Step up Trade with U.S.," Business Week, February 21, 1959, p. 80.

197. "Putting a Bear in Britain's Tank."

198. Edward Hughes, "The Russians Drill Deep in the Middle East," Fortune, July 1968, pp. 104.

199. Flegon, Soviet Foreign Trade Techniques, p. 49.

200. "Russia Revs up for a Car Race," Business Week, April 10, 1965, p. 48.

201. Foreign Trade, No. 9 (1971), p. 23.*

CHAPTER 3

1. A. P. Rosenholz, Fifteen Years of the Foreign Trade Monopoly (Moscow: Co-Operative Publishing Society of Foreign Workers in the USSR, 1933), p. 5.

2. The New York Times, April 3, 1918, p. 3.

3. RSFSR, Collection of Laws and Decrees of the Workers and Peasants Government, Pt. I (Moscow, 1918), pp. 411-12.*

4. M. Ya Kaufman, Organization and Regulation of the Foreign Trade of Russia (Moscow: Ekonomicheskaya Zhizn, 1925), p. 25.*

5. Ibid., p. 30.

6. RSFSR, Collection of Laws (1920), art. 235, p. 236.*

7. V. Groman, M. Kaufman, and M. Zamengof, Foreign Trade of the USSR for 1923 (Moscow: Redaktsionno-Izdatelskovo Otdela, NKVT, 1924), p. 163*; M. M. Zhirmunski, Soviet Export (Moscow: Mezhdunarodnaya Kniga, 1936), p. 37.

8. Louis Segal and A. A. Santalov, Commercial Year-Book of the Soviet Union (London: George Allen and Unwin, 1925), pp. 268-69.

9. USSR, People's Commissariat of Foreign Trade, Handbook of Active Decrees on Foreign

Trade, I (Moscow: Redaktsionno-Isdatelskovo
Otdela, NKVT, 1924-26), 21-22.*

10. RSFSR, Collection of Laws (1920), 10*;
Segal and Santalov, Commercial Year-Book, p. 12.

11. The New York Times, December 1, 1922, p. 3.

12. "Trade and Industry," Russian Information and Review, January 6, 1923, pp. 221-22.

13. USSR, Collection of Laws and Decrees, Pt.
I (Moscow: Otdel Opublikovaniya Zakonov, 1925),
art. 590, p. 1152.*

14. USSR, People's Commissariat of Foreign
Trade, Handbook of Active Decrees, III, p. 7.*

15. Scientific-Research Institute of the
Monopoly of Foreign Trade, Foreign Trade of the
Soviet Union (Moscow: V/O Mezhdunarodnaya Kniga,
1938), p. 64.*

16. Jacques Jeramec, Le Monopole du Commerce
Extérieur en Russie Sovietique (Paris: Librairie
Générale de Droit et de Jurisprudence, 1928), p.
88.

17. Ibid., p. 87.

18. Scientific-Research Institute of the
Monopoly of Foreign Trade, Foreign Trade of the
Soviet Union, p. 66*; A. P. Rozengolts, Foreign
Trade of the USSR Under New Conditions (Moscow:
Sotsekiz, 1936), p. 35*; Great Britain, Commercial
Counsellor to His Majesty's Embassy in Moscow,
The Organisation of Foreign Trade of the Union
of Soviet Socialist Republics (London: HM Sta-
tionery Office, 1931), p. 3.

19. Scientific-Research Institute of the
Monopoly of Foreign Trade, Foreign Trade of the
Soviet Union, p. 663*; M. M. Zhirmunski, Organi-
zation and Technique of Soviet Exports (Moscow:
Vneshtorgizdat, 1935), p. 48.*

20. Scientific-Research Institute of the
Monopoly of Foreign Trade, Foreign Trade of the
Soviet Union, pp. 72-73.*

21. Ibid., pp. 73-77.

22. Foreign Trade, Official journal of the
USSR Ministry of Foreign Trade, No. 4 (1958), p.
39.*

23. Ibid., No. 4 (1940), p. 42.

24. Ibid., No. 10 (1944), p. 47; No. 3
(1945), p. 47; No. 6 (1945), p. 46; No. 3 (1946),
p. 46; No. 12 (1946), p. 44; No. 6 (1947), p. 47.

25. Ibid., No. 1 (1944), p. 48.

26. Ibid., No. 1-2 (1943), p. 46; No. 3 (1945), p. 47; No. 11-12 (1945), p. 40.

27. Ibid., No. 9 (1945), p. 48; No. 10 (1945), p. 47; No. 11-12 (1945), p. 41; No. 5 (1947), p. 44; No. 9 (1947), p. 45: No. 3 (1948), p. 46; No. 10 (1951), p. 44; No. 12 (1951), p. 43; No. 1 (1952), p. 43.

28. Ibid., No. 11-12 (1945), p. 40; No. 4-5 (1946), p. 46; No. 2 (1947), p. 45.

29. Ibid., No. 4-5 (1946), p. 45; No. 6-7 (1946), pp. 43-45; No. 8 (1946), p. 46; No. 12 (1946), p. 44.

30. USSR, Collection of Laws, Pt. I (1945-46), p. 15.*

31. The New York Times, March 7, 1953, p. 3; Foreign Trade, No. 3 (1953), p. 39.*

32. The New York Times, September 15, 1953, p. 5.

33. K. Voronov, "Current Organization of Foreign Trade of the USSR," Foreign Trade, No. 8 (1966), p. 49*; V. S. Pozdniakov, State Monopoly of Foreign Trade in the USSR (Moscow: Izdatelstvo "Mezhdunarodniye Otnosheniya," 1969), p. 75*; Alec Flegon, Soviet Foreign Trade Techniques (London: Flegon Press, 1965), p. 27; V. S. Pozdniakov, "The State Monopoly of Foreign Trade in the USSR," Soviet State and Law, No. 10 (1967), p. 45.

34. Foreign Trade, No. 6 (1940), p. 37.*

35. Pavel A. Cherviakov, Organization and Technique of the Foreign Trade of the USSR (Moscow: Vneshtorgizdat, 1958), p. 36*; Pozdniakov, State Monopoly, p. 76.*

36. A. M. Smirnov and N. N. Liubimov, Foreign Trade of the USSR (Moscow: Vneshtorgizdat, 1954), pp. 77-78*; Cherviakov, Organization and Technique (1958), pp. 36-37*; Foreign Trade, No. 11 (1958), pp. 51-52*; United States, Department of State, Division of Biographical Information, Soviet Political Leaders, Biographical Directory No. 251, July 1957, pp. 53-56.

37. Pavel A. Cherviakov, Organization and Technique (1962), p. 18*; Flegon, Soviet Foreign Trade Techniques, p. 31.

38. Pozdniakov, State Monopoly, p. 80.*

39. Flegon, Soviet Foreign Trade Techniques, p. 31; Pozdniakov, State Monopoly, pp. 80, 148.*

40. USSR, Ministry of Foreign Trade, Foreign Trade of the USSR for 1959-63 (Moscow: Vnesh-torgizdat, 1965), p. 10.*

41. United States, Department of State, Division of Biographical Information, Soviet Political Leaders, pp. 53-56.

42. Cherviakov, Organization and Technique (1958), pp. 36-37*; Foreign Trade, No. 11 (1958), pp. 51-52.*

43. United States, Department of State, Division of Biographical Information, Soviet Political Leaders, pp. 53-56.

44. Ibid.

45. Cherviakov, Organization and Technique (1962), p. 37.*

46. Cherviakov, Organization and Technique (1958), p. 37*; Pozdniakov, State Monopoly, p. 78.*

47. Pozdniakov, State Monopoly, p. 79*; Flegon, Soviet Foreign Trade Techniques, p. 29.

48. Cherviakov, Organization and Technique (1962), p. 40*; Pozdniakov, State Monopoly, pp. 78, 133*; Flegon, Soviet Foreign Trade Techniques, p. 32.

49. Pozdniakov, State Monopoly, p. 79*; Flegon, Soviet Foreign Trade Techniques, pp. 32-33.

50. Ibid.

51. Pozdniakov, State Monopoly, p. 79*; Flegon, Soviet Foreign Trade Techniques, p. 33.

52. Pozdniakov, State Monopoly, p. 80*; Flegon, Soviet Foreign Trade Techniques, pp. 34-35.

53. Cherviakov, Organization and Technique (1962), p. 90.*

54. Ibid., pp. 58-59.

55. Pozdniakov, State Monopoly, p. 72.*

56. Pozdniakov, "The State Monopoly," pp. 45-46.

57. Cherviakov, Organization and Technique (1962), pp. 45-46*; Pozdniakov, State Monopoly, pp. 81-82.*

58. USSR, People's Commissariat of Foreign Trade, Handbook of Active Decrees, I, p. 24*;

Scientific-Research Institute of the Monopoly of
Foreign Trade, Foreign Trade of the Soviet Union,
p. 81*; Zhirmunski, Organization and Technique,
p. 49.*
       59. USSR, People's Commissariat of Foreign
Trade, Handbook of Active Decrees, I, p. 23.*
       60. Zhirmunski, Organization and Technique,
p. 48.*
       61. United States, Department of State,
Division of Biographical Information, Soviet Political Leaders, Supplement, p. 2; Foreign Trade,
No. 4 (1958), p. 41.*
       62. Foreign Trade, No. 11 (1958), p. 54.*
       63. Cherviakov, Organization and Technique
(1962), p. 36*; Flegon, Soviet Foreign Trade
Techniques, p. 37.
       64. Pozdniakov, State Monopoly, pp. 87-91*;
Cherviakov, Organization and Technique (1962),
p. 47*; Flegon, Soviet Foreign Trade Techniques,
p. 38.
       65. Pozdniakov, State Monopoly, p. 92.*

CHAPTER 4

       1. "Arcos Banking Corporation, Ltd.,"
Russian Information and Review, December 1, 1923,
p. 342.
       2. Louis Segal and A. A. Santalov, Soviet
Union Year Book (London: George Allen and Unwin,
1926), p. xxii.
       3. I. A. Kirillov, The Financing of Trade
(Moscow: Izdatelstvo NKRKI, 1927), p. 69.*
       4. London University, Banking and Credit
in the Soviet Union (London: School of Slavonic
and East European Studies in the University of
London, 1935), p. 61.
       5. Noah Barou, Russian Co-Operation Abroad
(London: P. S. King and Son, 1930), p. 70.
       6. "The Vsekobank in London," Russian In-
formation and Review, May 3, 1924, p. 275; Barou,
Russian Co-Operation Abroad, p. 70.
       7. Ibid.
       8. "The Moscow Narodny Bank," The Soviet
Union Review, April 18, 1925, p. 306.
       9. Barou, Russian Co-Operation Abroad, p. 84.

326 SOVIET FOREIGN TRADE

10. Kirillov, The Financing of Trade, pp. 76, 78.*

11. S. Barker, British Embassy, Washington, D.C., Letter dated February 20, 1959.

12. Foreign Trade, Official journal of the USSR Ministry of Foreign Trade, No. 6 (1963), p. 7.*

13. A. Troyanovsky, L. Yurovsky, and M. Kaufman, Export, Import and Concessions of the USSR (Moscow: Gosudarstvennoi Kontorie Obyavlyenii "Dvigatel," 1926), p. 63*; Jacques Jeramec, Le Monopole du Commerce Extérieur en Russie Sovietique (Paris: Librairie Générale de Droit et de Jurisprudence, 1928), pp. 113-14.

14. London University, Banking and Credit, p. 35.

15. Jacques Doussé, La Politique Economique de l'URSS Appliquée à son Commerce Extérieur (Paris: Marcel Giard, 1933), p. 151.

16. A. Stoupnitzky, Statut International de l'URSS--Etat Commerçant (Paris: Librairie Générale de Droit et de Jurisprudence, 1936), pp. 425-26.

17. Troyanovsky, Yurovsky, and Kaufman, Export, Import and Concessions, p. 71*; Jeramec, Le Monopole du Commerce Extérieur, pp. 114-15; Segal and Santalov, Soviet Union Year Book, p. vi.

18. London University, Banking and Credit, pp. 18-19.

19. Stoupnitzky, Statut International, pp. 425-26.

20. L. Frey et al., The Financing of Foreign Trade (Moscow: V/O Mezhdunarodnaya Kniga, 1938), p. 322.*

21. Ibid., p. 215.

22. Mojmir K. Bednarik, "The Moscow Bank: The International Bank for Economic Cooperation," American Review of Soviet and Eastern European Foreign Trade, January-February 1966, p. 4.

23. M. Poliakov, "USSR Bank for Foreign Trade," Economic Gazette, February 29, 1964, p. 64.

24. Kirillov, The Financing of Trade, p. 90*; W. W. Tarnovsky, "Banking: The First Private Bank," Manchester Guardian Commercial, June 26, 1924, p. 932.

25. _Ibid._

26. Troyanovsky, Yurovsky, and Kaufman, Export, Import and Concessions, p. 75*; "The Investment of Foreign Capital," Russian Information and Review, May 10, 1924, p. 295.

27. Kirillov, The Financing of Trade, p. 94*; Troyanovsky, Yurovsky, and Kaufman, Export, Import and Concessions, p. 73.*

28. Kirillov, The Financing of Trade, p. 91.*

29. Stoupnitzky, Statut International, p. 425.

30. "The Bank for Foreign Trade," Russian Information and Review, June 28, 1924, p. 408; "Latest News Items," Russian Information and Review, September 29, 1923, p. 196; "The Foreign Trade Bank," Russian Information and Review, November 29, 1924, p. 343.

31. All-Union Eastern Chamber of Commerce, Countries of the East (Moscow: Vsyesoyuznaya-Vostochnaya Torgovaya Palata, 1929), p. 757.*

32. "Soviet Trade with the East," The Soviet Union Review, March 14, 1925, p. 210.

33. All-Union Eastern Chamber of Commerce, Countries of the East, p. 779.*

34. "Soviet Bank at Constantinople," The Soviet Union Review, April 18, 1925, p. 305.

35. Troyanovsky, Yurovsky, and Kaufman, Export, Import and Concessions, p. 75.*

36. Stoupnitzky, Statut International, p. 428; Santalov and Segal, Soviet Union Year Book (1928), pp. 239-44.

37. Thomas C. Stave, Second Secretary of Embassy, American Embassy, Bonn, Germany, Letter dated March 26, 1959.

38. Margaret Dewar, Soviet Trade with Eastern Europe: 1945-1949 (London: Royal Institute of International Affairs, 1951), p. 80.

39. _Ibid._, p. 70.

40. Large Soviet Encyclopedia, IV (2d ed.; Moscow: Gosudarstvennoye Nauchnoe Izdatelstvo "Bolshaya Sovyetskaya Entsiklopediya," 1949-58), p. 187.*

41. United States, Foreign Operations Administration, Soviet Bloc Economic Activities in the Free World, Mutual Defense Assistance Control Act of 1951, Sixth Report to Congress, 1955, p. 5.

42. Foreign Trade, No. 3 (1963), p. 47.*
43. Poliakov, "USSR Bank for Foreign Trade,"
pp. 64-65.
44. Ibid., pp. 66-67.
45. Marion W. Worthing, First Secretary of
Embassy, American Embassy, Paris, Letter dated
March 27, 1959.
46. "Soviets Build a Vienna Business on In-
surance--And Sidelines," Business Week, February
10, 1962, p. 56.
47. "Country Notes," American Review of Soviet and Eastern European Foreign Trade, September-October 1966, p. 62.
48. The New York Times, March 2, 1958, p. 27.
49. Ibid., August 19, 1958, p. 4.
50. Foreign Trade, No. 7 (1964), p. 29.*
51. Ibid., No. 1 (1964), p. 42.
52. "Agreement Concerning Multilateral Settlements in Transferable Rubles and Organization
of the International Bank for Economic Cooperation," American Review of Soviet and Eastern European Foreign Trade, January-February 1966, pp. 9,
18.
53. K. Nazarkin, "Profitable to All," American Review of Soviet and Eastern European Foreign
Trade, May-June 1965, pp. 35, 37; "Agreement
Concerning Multilateral Settlements," January-
February 1966, pp. 21, 27.
54. Bednarik, "The Moscow Bank," p. 4.
55. Foreign Trade, No. 8 (1969), p. 27*;
"Agreement Concerning Multilateral Settlements,"
January-February 1966, p. 14.
56. Bednarik, "The Moscow Bank," p. 7.
57. Foreign Trade, No. 8 (1969), p. 27.*
58. Ibid., No. 7 (1964), p. 31; Bednarik,
"The Moscow Bank," p. 6; "Agreement Concerning
Multilateral Settlements," January-February 1966,
p. 111.
59. Foreign Trade, No. 1 (1970), p. 51.*
60. Ibid., No. 11 (1970), p. 17; No. 8
(1972), p. 14.
61. Ibid., No. 11 (1970), p. 17.
62. Ibid., p. 16.
63. Ibid., No. 8 (1972), p. 12.

64. "The History of Soviet Currency," The Soviet Union Review, January 3, 1925, p. 16.

65. Troyanovsky, Yurovsky, and Kaufman, Export, Import and Concessions, pp. 95-97.*

66. "The History of Soviet Currency," pp. 17-18.

67. London University, The Prospects of British and American Trade with the Soviet Union (London: School of Slavonic and East European Studies in the University of London, 1935), p. 4.

68. "The History of Soviet Currency," p. 30.

69. A. V. Baikalov, Money, Prices and Gold in the Soviet Union (London: School of Slavonic and East European Studies in the University of London, 1934), p. 15.

70. USSR, Collection of Laws and Decrees, Pt. I (Moscow: Otdel Opublikovaniya Zakonov, 1926), art. 348.*

71. USSR, Documentation Relating to Foreign Economic Relations of the USSR, Prepared for the Monetary and Economic Conference, London, June 1933 (Moscow: "International" Typographic Works, 1933), p. 23.

72. Frey et al., The Financing of Foreign Trade, p. 215.

73. London University, The Prospects, p. 45.

74. Doussé, La Politique Economique, p. 119.

75. USSR, Collection of Laws (1936), art. 10, p. 86.*

76. A. M. Smirnov, International Accounts and Credit Relations in the Foreign Trade of the USSR (Moscow: Vneshtorgizdat, 1953), pp. 32-33.*

77. Ibid., p. 34.

78. A. M. Smirnov and N. N. Liubimov, Foreign Trade of the USSR (Moscow: Vneshtorgizdat, 1954), p. 92.*

79. Foreign Trade, No. 1 (1961), p. 7.*

80. Riverside Press-Enterprise (Riverside, Calif.), April 3, 1972, p. 1.

81. The New York Times, April 21, 1949, p. 11; D. M. Genkin, ed., Legal Questions of Foreign Trade of the USSR with European Countries of the People's Democracy (Moscow: Vneshtorgizdat, 1955), p. 164*; Smirnov and Liubimov, Foreign Trade of the USSR, p. 107.*

82. Genkin, Legal Questions of Foreign Trade, p. 164.*

83. Bednarik, "The Moscow Bank," p. 3.

84. Foreign Trade, No. 7 (1964), pp. 28-29*; Bednarik, "The Moscow Bank," p. 4.

85. Ibid., p. 5.

86. Foreign Trade, No. 11 (1970), pp. 17-18.*

87. Stoupnitzky, Statut International, p. 32.

88. Troyanovsky, Yurovsky, and Kaufman, Export, Import and Concessions, p. 59.*

89. A. I. Kutuzov, ed., Foreign Trade of the USSR for 10 Years (Moscow: Narkomtorg SSSR i RSFSR, 1928), p. 217*; Doussé, La Politique Economique, p. 151.

90. The New York Times, December 12, 1921, p. 22.

91. Kutuzov, Foreign Trade, p. 217*; The New York Times, November 21, 1924, p. 3.

92. Ibid., February 28, 1924, p. 28; June 19, 1924, p. 31.

93. Frey et al., The Financing of Foreign Trade, pp. 271-72.*

94. W. Höffding, German Trade with the Soviet Union (London: School of Slavonic and East European Studies in the University of London, 1936), p. 6.

95. A. A. Santalov and Louis Segal, Soviet Union Year Book (London: George Allen and Unwin, 1927), p. 246.

96. I. S. Ginzburg, Foreign Trade of the USSR (Moscow: Gosudarstvennoye Sotsialno-Economicheskoye Izdatelstvo, 1937), pp. 110-11*; Frey et al., The Financing of Foreign Trade, pp. 267-69*; The New York Times, March 30, 1926, p. 4.

97. The New York Times, January 29, 1933, sec. II, p. 15.

98. Ginzburg, Foreign Trade of the USSR, p. 111*; The New York Times, April 20, 1930, p. 7.

99. Ginzburg, Foreign Trade of the USSR, p. 111*; The New York Times, December 7, 1933, p. 2.

100. USSR, Documentation, pp. 36-37; Frey et al., The Financing of Foreign Trade, pp. 274-75.*

101. Boris Eliacheff, Le Dumping Sovietique (Paris: Marcel Giard, 1931), p. 41.

102. _The New York Times_, December 24, 1934, p. 7.

103. _Ibid._, March 13, 1934, p. 17; March 15, 1934, p. 15.

104. _Ibid._, December 21, 1934, p. 36.

105. Ginzburg, _Foreign Trade of the USSR_, p. 112.*

106. A. Rozenholtz, _Foreign Trade and Economic Independence of the USSR_ (Moscow: USSR Chamber of Commerce, 1935), p. 18; _The New York Times_, April 10, 1935, p. 30; Ginzburg, _Foreign Trade of the USSR_, p. 116*; Höffding, _German Trade_, pp. 7-8.

107. Ginzburg, _Foreign Trade of the USSR_, p. 112.*

108. _The New York Times_, January 27, 1935, p. 5; June 16, 1935, p. 22.

109. Pavel A. Cherviakov, _Organization and Technique of the Foreign Trade of the USSR_ (Moscow: Vneshtorgizdat, 1958), p. 29*; _Large Soviet Encyclopedia--Union of Soviet Socialist Republics_ (Moscow: Gosudarstvennie Nauchnie Institut "Sovyetskaya Entsiklopediya," 1948), p. 1043*; Smirnov, _International Accounts and Credits_, p. 241.*

110. Smirnov and Liubimov, _Foreign Trade of the USSR_, p. 223.*

111. _The New York Times_, January 26, 1945, p. 3; Smirnov, _International Accounts and Credit_, p. 241.*

112. 23d Report to Congress on Lend-Lease Operations, as cited by B. H. Kerblay, _The Economic Relations of the U.S.S.R. with Foreign Countries During the War and in the Post-War Period_, "Bulletins on Soviet Economic Development," Bulletin No. 5. (Birmingham: Department of Economics and Institutions of the U.S.S.R., Faculty of Commerce and Social Science, University of Birmingham, March 1951), p. 4.

113. _Large Soviet Encyclopedia--Union_, p. 1043.*

114. Smirnov, _International Accounts and Credit_, p. 242.*

115. _Ibid._, p. 244.

116. _Foreign Trade_, No. 10-11 (1946), pp. 18-21*; _The New York Times_, October 9, 1946, p. 19.

117.   "Russian Trade: Talk and Practice,"
Business Week, September 12, 1959, p. 40; "Big
Machinery Sale to Russia," Business Week, January
2, 1960, p. 69; Foreign Trade, No. 12 (1964), p.
20.*

118.   Foreign Trade, No. 7 (1969), p. 8; No.
8 (1966), p. 44*; "How Fiat Sold Moscow," Business
Week, May 14, 1966, p. 106.

119.   "Country Section," American Review of
Soviet and Eastern European Foreign Trade, March-
April 1966, p. 80; Foreign Trade, No. 10 (1971),
p. 16*; "The Big Breakthrough in East-West
Trade," Business Week, June 19, 1971, p. 86.

120.   The New York Times, July 3, 1933, p. 1.

121.   Ibid., September 16, 1933, p. 1.

122.   Ibid., March 13, 1934, p. 17; May 6,
1934, p. 1.

123.   Ibid., January 26, 1945, p. 1.

124.   Ibid., March 3, 1946, p. 27.

125.   Ibid., November 13, 1945, p. 20.

126.   Ibid., March 3, 1946, p. 27; April 24,
1946, p. 4.

127.   "Breaching the Trade Barrier," Business
Week, October 10, 1959, pp. 32-34.

128.   The New York Times, June 5, 1958, p. 10.

129.   Ibid., January 20, 1959, p. 3.

CHAPTER 5

1.   Pavel A. Cherviakov, Organization and
Technique of the Foreign Trade of the USSR (Moscow: Vneshtorgizdat, 1962), p. 90.*

2.   Scientific-Research Institute of the
Monopoly of Foreign Trade, Foreign Trade of the
Soviet Union (Moscow: V/O Mezhdunarodnaya Kniga,
1938), p. 86.*

3.   Alec Flegon, Soviet Foreign Trade Techniques (London: Flegon Press, 1965), p. 35.

4.   A. Stoupnitzky, Statut International de
l'URSS--Etat Commerçant (Paris: Librairie Générale de Droit et de Jurisprudence, 1936), p.
143; Flegon, Soviet Foreign Trade Techniques, p.
35; Scientific-Research Institute of the Monopoly
of Foreign Trade, Foreign Trade of the Soviet
Union, p. 86.*

5. All-Union Eastern Chamber of Commerce,
Countries of the East (Moscow: Vsyesoyuznaya-
Vostochnaya Torgovaya Palata, 1929), p. 4*;
Violet Conolly, Soviet Economic Policy in the
East (London: Oxford University Press, 1933),
p. 151.

6. Louis Segal and A. A. Santalov, Commercial Year-Book of the Soviet Union (London:
George Allen and Unwin, 1925), pp. 202-03.

7. Large Soviet Encyclopedia, XIII (1st ed.;
Moscow: A/O "Sovyetskaya Entsiklopediya," 1926-
31), 550.*

8. All-Union Eastern Chamber of Commerce,
Countries of the East, p. 945.*

9. "Russo-Eastern Chamber of Commerce,"
Russian Information and Review, February 10, 1923,
p. 301.

10. The Times (London), January 1, 1923, p.
9.

11. M. M. Zhirmunski, Organization and Technique of Soviet Exports (Moscow: Vneshtorgizdat,
1935), p. 152.*

12. Scientific-Research Institute of the
Monopoly of Foreign Trade, Foreign Trade of the
Soviet Union, pp. 85-86.*

13. Foreign Trade, Official journal of the
USSR Ministry of Foreign Trade, No. 8 (1966), p.
51; No. 6 (1967), p. 53*; All-Union Chamber of
Commerce, Soviet Foreign Trade Organizations
(Moscow: Vneshtorgizdat, 1971), pp. 14-16.*

14. Foreign Trade, No. 3 (1967), p. 15*;
V. S. Pozdniakov, State Monopoly of Foreign Trade
in the USSR (Moscow: Izdatelstvo "Mezhdunarodniye
Otnosheniya," 1969), p. 110.*

15. All-Union Chamber of Commerce, Soviet
Foreign Trade Organizations, p. 17.*

16. Scientific-Research Institute of the
Monopoly of Foreign Trade, Foreign Trade of the
Soviet Union, p. 86*; Great Britain, Commercial
Counsellor to His Majesty's Embassy in Moscow,
The Organisation of Foreign Trade of the Union
of Soviet Socialist Republics (London: HM Sta-
tionery Office, 1931), p. 10.

17. Foreign Trade, No. 11-12 (1944), p. 40.*

18.   Zhirmunski, Organization and Technique,
p. 53*; J. D. Yanson, Foreign Trade in the USSR
(London: Victor Gollancz, 1934), p. 159; M. M.
Zhirmunski, Soviet Export (Moscow: Mezhdunarodnaya Kniga, 1936), p. 64; Scientific-Research
Institute of the Monopoly of Foreign Trade, Foreign Trade of the Soviet Union, p. 86.*

19.   James H. Giffen, The Legal and Practical
Aspects of Trade with the Soviet Union (New York:
Frederick A. Praeger, 1969), p. 191.

20.   D. M. Genkin, ed., Legal Questions of
Foreign Trade of the USSR with European Countries
of the People's Democracy (Moscow: Vneshtorgizdat,
1955), pp. 243, 252.*

21.   Soviet Union Information Bureau, The
Soviet Union (Washington, D.C.:   The Bureau,
1929), pp. 165-66; The New York Times, June 24,
1925, p. 44.

22.   Hans Heymann, We Can Do Business with
Russia (Chicago: Ziff Davis, 1945), p. 78.

23.   Soviet Union Information Bureau, The
Soviet Union, p. 167.

24.   The New York Times, March 15, 1940, p. 2.

25.   Ibid., August 21, 1949, Sec. III, p. 1.

26.   "Anglo-Russian Chamber of Commerce,"
Russian Information and Review, November 7, 1923,
p. 317; A. A. Santalov and Louis Segal, Soviet
Union Year Book (London: George Allen and Unwin,
1928), p. 327; All-Union Eastern Chamber of Commerce, Countries of the East, p. 946.*

27.   A. M. Smirnov and N. N. Liubimov, Foreign Trade of the USSR (Moscow: Vneshtorgizdat,
1954), p. 86*; Cherviakov, Organization and Technique (1958), pp. 61-62*; Foreign Trade, No. 3
(1954), pp. 43-44*; The New York Times, September
4, 1946, p. 3.

28.   Cherviakov, Organization and Technique
(1962), p. 89.*

29.   All-Union Chamber of Commerce, Soviet
Foreign Trade Organizations, p. 17.*

30.   The New York Times, September 25, 1921,
Sec. VII, p. 1.

31.   Zhirmunski, Organization and Technique,
p. 212.*

32. "Soviet Exhibition in Turkey," Russian Information and Review, May 24, 1924, p. 334.

33. "Lyons Fair and USSR," The Soviet Union Review, February 28, 1925, p. 163.

34. The New York Times, March 30, 1923, p. 13.

35. H. R. Knickerbocker, Soviet Trade and World Depression (London: John Lane-The Bodley Head Ltd., 1931), pp. 8-12.

36. Zhirmunski, Organization and Technique, p. 212*; All-Union Chamber of Commerce, Countries of the East (Moscow: Gosudarstvennoye Sotsialno-Ekonomicheskoye Izdatelstvo, 1934), p. 307.*

37. Zhirmunski, Organization and Technique, p. 211.*

38. Foreign Trade, No. 7 (1947), p. 28.*

39. M. V. Nesterov, International Trade--An Important Factor in the Strengthening of Peace (Moscow: Izdatelstvo "Znaniye," 1956), p. 23*; Foreign Trade, No. 7 (1947), p. 29.*

40. Foreign Trade, No. 5 (1950), p. 34.*

41. United States, Foreign Operations Administration, East-West Trade Trends, Mutual Defense Assistance Control Act of 1951, Fourth Report to Congress, 1954, p. 33.

42. Leon M. Herman, "The New Soviet Posture in World Trade," Problems of Communism, November-December 1954, pp. 12-13.

43. The New York Times, January 19, 1952, p. 2.

44. Ibid., March 5, 1952, p. 2.

45. Foreign Trade, No. 1 (1955), p. 2; No. 11 (1957), p. 55; No. 3 (1962), p. 15.*

46. Ibid., No. 3 (1967), p. 13; No. 7 (1971), pp. 26-27.

47. Ibid., No. 1 (1955), p. 2.

48. United States, International Cooperation Administration, Survey of East-West Trade in 1955, Mutual Defense Assistance Control Act of 1951, Eighth Report to Congress, 1956, p. 15.

49. Foreign Trade, No. 3 (1955), p. 23; No. 11 (1957), p. 57.*

50. United States, International Cooperation Administration, Survey of East-West Trade in 1955, p. 19.

51. B. D. Zotov, Foreign Trade of the European Countries of the People's Democracy in the
Work of Building Socialism (Moscow: Izdatelstvo
Akademii Nauk SSSR, 1958), p. 174.*
52. United States, Foreign Operation Administration, Soviet Bloc Economic Activities in the
Free World, Mutual Defense Assistance Control Act
of 1951, Sixth Report to Congress, 1955, pp. 7-8.
53. Ibid., p. 9.
54. Foreign Trade, No. 8 (1962), p. 13.*
55. Ibid., No. 6 (1965), p. 19.
56. Ibid., No. 5 (1967), p. 47; The Wall
Street Journal, May 14, 1971, p. 1.
57. Great Britain, Commercial Counsellor to
His Majesty's Embassy in Moscow, The Organisation
of Foreign Trade, p. 111; USSR, Collection of
Laws and Decrees, Pt. I, XVIII (Moscow: Otdel
Opublikovaniya Zakonov, 1930), art. 209, 352.*
58. "The Agricultural Exhibition," Russian
Information and Review, August 25, 1923, p. 115;
Great Britain, Commercial Counsellor to His Majesty's Embassy in Moscow, The Organisation of
Foreign Trade, pp. 11-12.
59. Foreign Trade, No. 8 (1946), p. 35;
No. 12 (1955), supplement; No. 9 (1949), pp. 28-
29; No. 10 (1949), p. 30; No. 9 (1955), p. 23*;
Margaret Dewar, Soviet Trade with Eastern Europe:
1945-1949 (London: Royal Institute of International Affairs, 1951), pp. 31-32.
60. Foreign Trade, No. 3 (1967), p. 13.*
61. "Moscow: Before the Nixon Visit," Business Week, May 6, 1972, p. 71.
62. Ibid., pp. 69-71.
63. Zhirmunski, Organization and Technique,
p. 211.*
64. Zhirmunski, Soviet Export, p. 108;
Cherviakov, Organization and Technique (1958), p.
54.*
65. Foreign Trade, No. 5 (1952), p. 1.*
66. Ibid., No. 2 (1952), p. 43*; Herman,
"The New Soviet Posture," p. 13.
67. Ibid., No. 5 (1952), pp. 4-5.*
68. Ibid., p. 9.*
69. United States, Mutual Security Agency,
A Program for the Denial of Strategic Goods to

the Soviet Bloc, Mutual Defense Assistance Control Act of 1951, First Report to Congress, 1952, pp. 27-28.

70. United States, Foreign Operations Administration, The Revision of Strategic Trade Controls, Mutual Defense Assistance Control Act of 1951, Fifth Report to Congress, 1954, pp. 6-7; and Soviet Bloc Economic Activities, p. 19.

71. The New York Times, February 13, 1946, p. 1.

72. Ibid., August 30, 1951, p. 6.

73. Ibid., August 19, 1952, p. 10.

74. Ibid., May 1, 1954, p. 4.

75. Ibid., August 3, 1955, p. 6.

76. Ibid., November 23, 1956, p. 12; February 13, 1957, p. 1.

77. V. Alkhimov and V. Mordvinov, Foreign Trade of the U.S.S.R. (London: Soviet Booklets, 1958), p. 8.

78. The New York Times, May 1, 1957, p. 16; May 16, 1957, p. 7.

79. Ibid., April 11, 1958, pp. 1-2.

80. Ibid., October 12, 1961, p. 10.

81. Ibid., October 16, 1951, p. 15.

82. Ibid., February 25, 1953, p. 3.

83. Ibid., February 18, 1954, p. 4; February 5, 1956, p. 8; March 22, 1957, p. 4; and January 23, 1958, p. 1.

84. Foreign Trade, No. 6 (1955), pp. 18-20.*

85. United States, Department of State, The Sino-Soviet Economic Offensive in the Less Developed Countries, European and British Commonwealth Series No. 51, May 1958, p. 5.

86. The New York Times, March 22, 1964, Sec. III, p. 14; March 23, 1964, p. 47; March 24, 1964, p. 1; March 27, 1964, p. 6; April 9, 1964, p. 41.

87. Ibid., February 3, 1968, p. 3; February 8, 1968, p. 71.

88. Nesterov, International Trade, p. 22.*

89. Alkhimov and Mordvinov, Foreign Trade of the U.S.S.R., p. 24.

90. United States, Foreign Operations Administration, The Revision of Strategic Trade Controls, pp. 8-9, 17-19.

91. United States, International Cooperation Administration, Survey of East-West Trade in 1955,

p. 28; United States, Department of State, The
Sino-Soviet Economic Offensive, p. 70.

92. The New York Times, March 29, 1956, p.
54.

93. Ibid., April 12, 1956, p. 1.

94. Ibid., January 25, 1959, p. 6; "Drumming
for Red Trade," Business Week, July 11, 1959, p.
31.

CHAPTER 6

1. Foreign Trade, Official journal of the
USSR Ministry of Foreign Trade, No. 10 (1952),
p. 17.*

2. Margaret Dewar, Soviet Trade with Eastern
Europe: 1945-1959 (London: Royal Institute of
International Affairs, 1951), p. 2.

3. Royal Institute of International Affairs,
Survey of International Affairs: 1947-1948 (London: Oxford University Press, 1952), p. 230.

4. National Committee for a Free Europe,
Economic Treaties and Agreements of the Soviet
Bloc in Eastern Europe: 1945-1951 (Washington,
D.C.: The Committee, 1952), pp. xxiii, xxvii.

5. Alexander Gerschenkron, "Russia's Trade
in the Postwar Years," Annals of the American
Academy of Political and Social Science, May 1949,
p. 89.

6. A. M. Smirnov and N. N. Liubimov, Foreign
Trade of the USSR (Moscow: Vneshtorgizdat, 1954),
p. 256.*

7. National Committee for a Free Europe,
Economic Treaties, pp. xxxvi, xl.

8. Foreign Trade, No. 10 (1947), pp. 32-33;
No. 4 (1948), p. 12*; Gazette of the Supreme Soviet of the USSR, Pt. I (1948), p. 9.*

9. Keesings Archiv der Gegenwart (Bremen:
Verlag Export-Edition, 1951), p. 2827; Foreign
Trade, No. 5 (1950), p. 15; No. 10 (1951), p. 44;
No. 1 (1955), p. 1*; Smirnov and Liubimov, Foreign
Trade of the USSR, p. 247.*

10. Monitorul Oficial, No. 65 (Bucharest,
1946); Keesings Archiv der Gegenwart (1945), p.
577; (1947), pp. 967, 1098; (1948-49), p. 1526;
(1950), p. 2671; Pravda, February 25, 1947*; For-

eign Trade, No. 5 (1948), p. 10; No. 3 (1952), p. 15.*

11. The New York Times, December 14, 1947, p. 10; Foreign Trade, No. 4 (1948), p. 12*; B. D. Zotov, Foreign Trade of the European Countries of the People's Democracy in the Work of Building Socialism (Moscow: Izdatelstvo Akademii Nauk SSSR, 1958), p. 123*; A. M. Smirnov, International Accounts and Credit Relations in the Foreign Trade of the USSR (Moscow: Vneshtorgizdat, 1953), p. 256.*

12. For a fuller discussion of these credits and those that followed the death of Stalin, see Marshall I. Goldman, Soviet Foreign Aid (New York: Frederick A. Praeger, 1967), pp. 23-37.

13. United States, Department of State, The Sino-Soviet Economic Offensive in the Less Developed Countries, European and British Commonwealth Series No. 51, May 1958, p. 16.

14. USSR, Ministry of Foreign Trade, Foreign Trade of the USSR for 1959-63 (Moscow: Vneshtorgizdat, 1965), pp. 96-97; for 1968 (1969), pp. 60-61.*

15. Foreign Trade, No. 9 (1961), p. 5; No. 7 (1967), p. 7.*

16. Smirnov, International Accounts and Credit, p. 258.*

17. Foreign Trade, No. 8 (1971), p. 14.*

18. The New York Times, January 26, 1949, p. 1; Foreign Trade, No. 4 (1949), pp. 4-5.*

19. Foreign Trade, No. 5 (1951), p. 1.*

20. Ibid., No. 4 (1958), p. 5.

21. V. Alkhimov and V. Mordvinov, Foreign Trade of the U.S.S.R. (London: Soviet Booklets, 1958), p. 16.

22. Jan Stankovsky, "Problems of Integration in Comecon," Soviet and Eastern European Foreign Trade, Fall-Winter 1971-72, p. 316.

23. United States, Foreign Operations Administration, East-West Trade Trends, Mutual Defense Assistance Control Act of 1951, Fourth Report to Congress, 1954, p. 6.

24. Foreign Trade, No. 12 (1958), p. 9.*

25. Ibid., No. 6 (1955), pp. 25-26.

26. Ibid., No. 7 (1964), p. 29.

27. The Wall Street Journal, August 9, 1971, p. 15.

28. Soviet and Eastern European Foreign Trade, March–April 1967, pp. 20-21; Jan Pleva, "Some Economic and Legal Aspects of Foreign Trade in Czechoslovakia," Soviet and Eastern European Foreign Trade, May–June 1967, p. 15.

29. V. Brzak and D. Marsikova, "New Methods of Management and Organization of Foreign Trade in Socialist Countries," Soviet and Eastern European Foreign Trade, Fall–Winter 1970, pp. 214-67.

30. V. Bernasek and A. Neustadt, "Changing Conceptions of the Foreign Trade Monopoly in the USSR," Soviet and Eastern European Foreign Trade, Winter 1968/69, pp. 70-71; Pleva, "Some Economic and Legal Aspects," p. 15.

31. R. Selucky, "The Impact of the Economic Reforms on the Foreign Economic Relations of the Socialist Countries," Soviet and Eastern European Foreign Trade, Fall 1968, p. 76.

32. Pleva, "Some Economic and Legal Aspects," pp. 13-14.

33. Josef Horsky, "Foreign Trade Policy," Soviet and Eastern European Foreign Trade, September–October 1967, p. 28; R. Zukal, "Currency Convertibility and External Economic Relations," Soviet and Eastern European Foreign Trade, Fall 1968, pp. 58-71.

34. Pleva, "Some Economic and Legal Aspects," pp. 14-15, 17; Ausch, Sandor, and Ferenc Bartha, "Theoretical Problems Relating to Prices in Trade Between the Comecon Countries," Soviet and Eastern European Foreign Trade, Summer 1968, pp. 35-71; Josef Horsky, "Foreign Trade Theory and Its Relation to Planning," Soviet and Eastern European Foreign Trade, Fall 1968, p. 10.

35. Horsky, "Foreign Trade Policy," p. 28; Brzak and Marsikova, "New Methods of Management," p. 240.

36. I. J. Korostovetz, Von Cinggis Khan zur Sowjetrepublik (Berlin: Walter de Gruyter, 1926), p. 333.

37.   Violet Conolly, Soviet Economic Policy in the East (London: Oxford University Press, 1933), pp. 101-02; Korostovetz, Von Cinggis Khan, p. 344.

38.   United States, Department of State, The Sino-Soviet Economic Offensive, p. 16.

39.   Compiled from data in USSR, Ministry of Foreign Trade, Foreign Trade of the USSR for 1959-63; for 1964; for 1965; for 1966; and for 1968*; Foreign Trade, No. 5 (1971), pp. 57-58.*

40.   The Wall Street Journal, August 9, 1971, p. 15.

41.   Conolly, Soviet Economic Policy, p. 28.

42.   Max Beloff, Soviet Policy in the Far East 1944-1951 (London: Oxford University Press, 1953), pp. 25-41.

43.   Questions of Economics, February 1952, p. 53.*

44.   Foreign Trade, No. 5 (1950), p. 9; No. 10 (1954), pp. 5-6.*

45.   Ernst Hagemann, "The Foreign Trade of the People's Republic of China with the Eastern European Countries 1950-1969," Soviet and Eastern European Foreign Trade, Spring 1972, p. 78.

46.   Foreign Trade, No. 3 (1950), pp. 47-48; No. 2 (1955), p. 2.*

47.   Hagemann, "The Foreign Trade," p. 78.

48.   Foreign Trade, No. 10 (1959), pp. 3, 6, 9.*

49.   Hagemann, "The Foreign Trade," pp. 63-64.

50.   Calculated from data in USSR, Ministry of Foreign Trade, Foreign Trade of the USSR for 1959-63, pp. 16-17.*

51.   Ibid., pp. 376-77; for 1965, pp. 254-55.

52.   Marshall I Goldman, Soviet Foreign Aid (New York: Frederick A. Praeger, 1967), p. 50.

53.   Hagemann, "The Foreign Trade," p. 77.

54.   Ibid., p. 80

55.   Riverside Press-Enterprise, Riverside, Calif., April 12, 1972, p. A-2.

56.   United States, Foreign Operations Administration, Soviet Bloc Economic Activities in the Free World, Mutual Defense Assistance Control Act of 1951, Sixth Report to Congress, 1955, p. 5.

57. <u>Large Soviet Encyclopedia</u>, IV (2d ed.; Moscow: Gosudarstvennoye Nauchnoe Izdatelstvo "Bolshaya Sovyetskaya Entsiklopediya," 1949-58), 187.*

58. <u>Foreign Trade</u>, No. 8 (1955), p. 26; No. 10 (1955), p. 30.*

59. Goldman, <u>Soviet Foreign Aid</u>, p. 37; <u>Foreign Trade</u>, No. 9 (1967), p. 13.*

60. <u>Foreign Trade</u>, No. 9 (1967), p. 16.*

61. USSR, Ministry of Foreign Trade, <u>Foreign Trade of the USSR for 1968</u>, p. 13*; <u>Foreign Trade</u>, No. 5 (1971), p. 57.*

62. Goldman, <u>Soviet Foreign Aid</u>, p. 38.

63. USSR, Ministry of Foreign Trade, <u>Foreign Trade of the USSR for 1959-63</u>, pp. 14-15; <u>for 1964</u>, pp. 12-13.*

64. Goldman, <u>Soviet Foreign Aid</u>, p. 38.

65. USSR, Ministry of Foreign Trade, <u>Foreign Trade of the USSR for 1966</u>, pp. 12-13; <u>for 1968</u>, pp. 12-13*; Foreign Trade, No. 5 (1971), p. 57.

66. Goldman, <u>Soviet Foreign Aid</u>, pp. 24-25, 30.

67. Nikita Khrushchev, <u>Khrushchev Remembers</u>, translated and edited by Strobe Talbott (Boston: Little, Brown, 1970), p. 383.

68. <u>Collier's Encyclopedia Yearbook</u> (New York: P. F. Collier and Son, 1960), p. 182.

69. Goldman, <u>Soviet Foreign Aid</u>, p. 163.

70. <u>Ibid.</u>, p. 165.

71. Calculated from data in USSR, Ministry of Foreign Trade, <u>Foreign Trade of the USSR for 1959-63</u>; <u>for 1964</u>; <u>for 1966</u>; and <u>for 1969</u>*; <u>Foreign Trade</u>, No. 5 (1971), p. 57.*

CHAPTER 7

1. W. Z. Laquer, "The Shifting Line in Soviet Orientology," <u>Problems of Communism</u>, March-April 1956, pp. 20-26.

2. <u>Ibid.</u>, p. 24.

3. <u>Foreign Trade</u>, Official journal of the USSR, Ministry of Foreign Trade, No. 2 (1950), pp. 27-39; No. 9 (1950), pp. 7-15; No. 7 (1951), p. 7.*

4. Ibid., No. 2 (1952), pp. 15-20; No. 4 (1952), pp. 10-13.*

5. The New York Times, October 16, 1951, p. 15.

6. Statistical data used in this chapter selected and/or calculated from data in USSR, Ministry of Foreign Trade, Foreign Trade of the USSR for 1959-63 (Moscow: Vneshtorgizdat, 1965); also for 1964, for 1965, for 1966, and for 1968* unless otherwise indicated.

7. Computed from data in United States, International Cooperation Administration, The Strategic Trade Control System: 1948-1956, Mutual Defense Assistance Control Act of 1951, Ninth Report to Congress, 1957, pp. 96-103.

8. International Monetary Fund, International Financial Statistics (April 1959), pp. 22-25.

9. Foreign Trade, No. 11 (1957), p. 65.*

10. United States, International Cooperation Administration, East-West Trade Developments: 1956-1957, Mutual Defense Assistance Control Act of 1951, 10th Report to Congress, 1958, p. 10.

11. United States, Congress, House of Representatives, Committee on Foreign Affairs, The Communist Economic Offensive, 85th Cong., 2d sess., 1958, p. 1.

12. Scientific-Research Institute of the Monopoly of Foreign Trade, Foreign Trade of the USSR for 20 Years: 1918-1937 (Moscow: V/O Mezhdunarodnaya Kniga, 1939), pp. 60-81*; USSR, Ministry of Foreign Trade, Foreign Trade of the USSR for 1957, pp. 23-24; for 1959-63, pp. 134-57; for 1968, pp. 88-105.*

13. Scientific-Research Institute of the Monopoly of Foreign Trade, Foreign Trade of the USSR for 20 Years, pp. 188-89.*

14. Alec Nove, "Soviet Trade and Soviet Aid," Lloyds Bank Review, January 1959, p. 13.

15. USSR, Ministry of Foreign Trade, Foreign Trade of the USSR for 1959-63, pp. 148-49; for 1968, p. 98.*

16. Scientific-Research Institute of the Monopoly of Foreign Trade, Foreign Trade of the USSR for 20 Years, p. 68.*

17. United States, Department of State,
The Sino-Soviet Economic Offensive in the Less
Developed Countries, European and British Common-
wealth Series No. 51, May 1958, p. 87.

18. Trade volumes from statistics in USSR,
Ministry of Foreign Trade, Foreign Trade of the
USSR for 1959-63; also for 1965, for 1966, and for
1968.*

19. Scientific-Research Institute of the
Monopoly of Foreign Trade, Foreign Trade of the
USSR for 20 Years, pp. 184-85.*

20. United States, International Cooperation
Administration, The Strategic Trade Control System, p. 104.

21. Scientific-Research Institute of the
Monopoly of Foreign Trade, Foreign Trade of the
USSR for 20 Years, pp. 188-89*; USSR, Ministry
of Foreign Trade, Foreign Trade of the USSR for
1956, pp. 30, 128; for 1957, pp. 30, 128, 145.*

22. USSR, Ministry of Foreign Trade, Foreign
Trade of the USSR for 1956, pp. 33, 57, 65, 80,
101, 153; for 1957, pp. 33, 57, 65, 80, 101, 156.*

23. Scientific-Research Institute of the
Monopoly of Foreign Trade, Foreign Trade of the
USSR for 20 Years, p. 66.*

24. United States, International Cooperation
Administration, The Strategic Trade Control System, pp. 96-104.

25. Marshall I. Goldman, Soviet Foreign Aid
(New York: Frederick A. Praeger, 1967), p. 110

26. Scientific-Research Institute of the
Monopoly of Foreign Trade, Foreign Trade of the
USSR for 20 Years, pp. 164-65.*

27. Foreign Trade, No. 9 (1955), p. 4.*

28. USSR, Ministry of Foreign Trade, Foreign
Trade of the USSR for 1959-63, pp. 152-53.*

29. USSR, Ministry of Foreign Trade, Foreign
Trade of the USSR for 1968, p. 101.*

30. United States, International Cooperation
Administration, The Strategic Trade Control System, pp. 96-104.

31. USSR, Ministry of Foreign Trade, Foreign
Trade of the USSR for 1956, pp. 70, 74, 116,
136; for 1957, pp. 70, 74, 136, 151, 152.*

32. Production data for this and following paragraphs from Food and Agricultural Organization of the United Nations, <u>Yearbook of Food and Agricultural Statistics: 1956</u> and <u>1969</u> (Rome: FAO, 1957 and 1970).

33. <u>The New York Times</u>, February 12, 1949, p. 3; June 24, 1951, p. 2; September 3, 1953, p. 3.

34. <u>Ibid.</u>, January 26, 1950, p. 3.

35. <u>Foreign Trade</u>, No. 9 (1955), p. 4.*

36. United States, Department of State, <u>The Sino-Soviet Economic Offensive</u>, p. 73.

37. <u>The New York Times</u>, March 3, 1948, p. 39; August 12, 1953, p. 12; March 28, 1954, p. 2; April 29, 1955, p. 33; <u>Foreign Trade</u>, No. 3 (1954), p. 43*; United States, Congress, House of Representatives, Committee on Foreign Affairs, <u>The Communist Economic Offensive</u>, p. 5.

38. <u>The New York Times</u>, September 3, 1953, p. 3; November 14, 1953, p. 2; <u>Foreign Trade</u>, No. 12 (1953), p. 1.*

39. Nikita Khrushchev, <u>Khrushchev Remembers</u>, translated and edited by Strobe Talbott (Boston: Little, Brown, 1970), p. 440.

CHAPTER 8

1. <u>The New York Times</u>, July 17, 1919, p. 1.

2. <u>Ibid.</u>, October 31, 1919, p. 17.

3. <u>Ibid.</u>, September 30, 1919, p. 6.

4. Xenia Eudin and Harold Fisher, <u>Soviet Russia and the West</u> (Stanford, Calif.: Stanford University Press, 1957), p. 7.

5. Boris Eliacheff, <u>Le Dumping Sovietique</u> (Paris: Marcel Giard, 1931), pp. 178, 182; <u>The New York Times</u>, October 14, 1930, p. 41; October 26, 1930, p. 27; USSR, <u>Documentation Relating to Foreign Economic Relations of the USSR</u>, Prepared for the Monetary and Economic Conference, London, June 1933 (Moscow: "International" Typographic Works, 1933), p. 17.

6. Eliacheff, <u>Le Dumping Sovietique</u>, p. 181; USSR, <u>Documentation</u>, p. 17.

7. J. M. Budish and Samuel S. Shipman, <u>Soviet Foreign Trade--Menace or Promise</u> (New York: Horace Liveright, 1931), p. 264.

8. USSR, Documentation, p. 18; The New York Times, April 20, 1931, p. 3.

9. USSR, Documentation, p. 18.

10. The New York Times, September 12, 1936, p. 6.

11. Ibid., April 20, 1933, p. 1.

12. USSR, Documentation, p. 19.

13. The New York Times, July 2, 1933, p. 1.

14. Ibid., June 1, 1940, Sec. III, p. 7.

15. Ibid., May 25, 1941, Sec. III, p. 1.

16. Ibid., May 7, 1941, p. 4.

17. United States, International Cooperation Administration, The Strategic Trade Control System: 1948-1956, Mutual Defense Assistance Control Act of 1951, Ninth Report to Congress, 1957, pp. 4-5.

18. United States, Mutual Security Agency, A Program for the Denial of Strategic Goods to the Soviet Bloc, Mutual Defense Assistance Control Act of 1951, First Report to Congress, 1952, p. 6.

19. United States, International Cooperation Administration, The Strategic Trade Control System, p. 8.

20. Keesing's Contemporary Archives (Bristol, Eng.: Keesing's Publications Limited (of London), September 8-15, 1951), p. 11696; "Breaching the Trade Barrier," Business Week, October 10, 1959, p. 34; "Red Carpet Out for Buyers," Business Week, August 11, 1962, p. 34.

21. United States, Mutual Security Agency, A Program for the Denial, p. 31.

22. Ibid., p. 43.

23. United States, Foreign Operations Administration, World-Wide Enforcement of Strategic Trade Controls, Mutual Defense Assistance Control Act of 1951, Third Report to Congress, 1953, pp. 20-21.

24. United States, Foreign Operations Administration, The Revision of Strategic Trade Controls, Mutual Defense Assistance Control Act of 1951, Fifth Report to Congress, 1954, pp. 8-9.

25. Ibid., p. 19.

26. The New York Times, July 22, 1958, p. 14; July 31, 1958, p. 7.

27. _Ibid._, August 15, 1958, p. 2.

28. _Ibid._, November 7, 1958, p. 1.

29. United States, Foreign Operations Admin-
istration, _East-West Trade Trends_, Mutual Defense
Assistance Control Act of 1951, Fourth Report to
Congress, 1954, p. 9.

30. Leon M. Herman, "The New Soviet Posture
in World Trade," _Problems of Communism_, November-
December 1954, pp. 9-16.

31. United States, Mutual Security Agency,
A Program for the Denial, p. 10.

32. United States, Foreign Operations Administration, _World-Wide Enforcement_, pp. 3-12;
United States, Mutual Security Agency, _Problems
of Economic Defense_, Mutual Defense Assistance
Control Act of 1951, Second Report to Congress,
1953, pp. 13-16.

33. United States, Foreign Operations Admin-
istration, World-Wide Enforcement, p. 27; United
States, Foreign Operations Administration, _Soviet
Bloc Economic Activities in the Free World_, Mu-
tual Defense Assistance Control Act of 1951,
Sixth Report to Congress, 1955, p. 26.

34. _The New York Times_, January 15, 1959,
p. 6.

35. _Ibid._, January 20, 1959, pp. 1, 3.

36. "Breaching the Trade Barrier," p. 32.

37. "Soviet-Bloc Market: So Big and yet so
Far," _Business Week_, October 19, 1963, p. 53;
Thomas F. Willers, "Reappraising Trade with Rus-
sia," _Duns Review_, March 1965, p. 21.

38. United States, Department of State,
Battle Act Report (1964), Mutual Defense Assistance Control Act of 1951, 17th through 24th Reports to Congress, 1965-72, p. 4.

39. United States, Department of State,
Battle Act Report (1965), p. 14.

40. _Ibid._, p. 15.

41. United States, Department of State,
Battle Act Report (1966), p. 8; James H. Giffen,
_The Legal and Practical Aspects of Trade with
the Soviet Union_ (New York: Praeger Publishers,
Inc., 1969), pp. 217-18.

42. _Public Papers of the Presidents: Lyndon
Baines Johnson_, Vol. II, _July 1-December 31, 1966_

(Washington, D.C.:   U.S. Government Printing Office, 1967); United States, Department of State, Battle Act Report (1966), p. 13; (1966), p. 9.

43.   United States, Department of State, Battle Act Report (1968), p. 14.

44.   "The Rules Ease on Trade with Russia," Business Week, June 12, 1971, p. 94; United States, Department of State, Battle Act Report (1970), p. 5.

45.   "The Rules Ease on Trade with Russia," p. 94.

46.   "The Big Breakthrough in East-West Trade," Business Week, June 19, 1971, p. 84; "Picking up Where Mack Left off," Business Week, September 25, 1971, p. 42.

47.   United States, Department of State, Battle Act Report (1971), pp. 3-4.

48.   "The Rules Ease on Trade with Russia," p. 94; United States, Department of State, Battle Act Report (1971), p. 4.

49.   The Wall Street Journal, April 5, 1972, p. 2.

50.   "A Deal Shapes up with the Soviets," Business Week, June 3, 1972, p. 17.

CHAPTER 9

1.   San Francisco Examiner, November 24, 1957, Sec. I, p. 2.

2.   "The Warmup in Russian Trade," Business Week, May 6, 1972, p. 71.

3.   The Wall Street Journal, May 18, 1972, p. 2.

4.   Business Week, May 9, 1959, p. 110; May 16, 1959, p. 67.

CHAPTER 10

1.   W. Höffding, German Trade with the Soviet Union (London: School of Slavonic and East European Studies in the University of London, 1936), p. 4.

2.   H. R. Knickerbocker, Soviet Trade and World Depression (London: John Lane-The Bodley Head Ltd., 1931), pp. 132, 165-66.

3. <u>Ibid</u>., pp. 69-70

4. Boris Eliacheff, <u>Le Dumping Sovietique</u> (Paris: Marcel Giard, 1931), pp. 189-90.

Sources in the Russian language have been translated and listed accordingly. Where appropriate, the Russian equivalent is shown in transliteration and enclosed in brackets following the English. Publishers' names are shown in transliteration only. Translations are also provided for sources other than those in Western European languages.

Public Documents

Buletinul Oficial [Rumanian Official Collection of Laws]. Bucharest, 1949.

Czechoslovakia. Sbirka Zakonu [Collection of Laws]. Prague, 1946.

Czechoslovakia, Ministerstvo Zahranicniho Obchodu [Ministry of Foreign Trade]. Czechoslovak Economic Bulletin. Prague, 1946.

Durzhaven Vestnik [Bulgarian Collection of Laws]. Sofia, 1945, 1946, 1949.

Food and Agriculture Organization of the United Nations. Yearbook of Food and Agricultural Statistics: 1956 and 1969. Rome: FAO, 1957 and 1970.

Georgia [Transcaucasian Republic]. Traité conclu le 7 Mai 1920 entre la République Démocratique de Géorgie et la République Socialiste Fédérative Sovietiste Russe et Accord de Transit et de Commerce conclu le 14 Novembre 1920 entre la République Démocratique de Géorgie d'une part et la République Socialiste Fédérative Sovietiste Russe et la République Socialiste d'Azerbaidjan d'autre part. Paris: Imprimerie P. DuPont, 1922.

Great Britain, Commercial Counsellor to His Majesty's
    Embassy in Moscow. The Organisation of Foreign
    Trade of the Union of Soviet Socialist Republics.
    London: HM Stationery Office, 1931.

Kaya, Sevket. Türkiye Maricî Ticaret Resmî Istatis-
    tiklerine [Turkish Foreign Trade Official Sta-
    tistics]. Istanbul: Güneş Matbaasi, 1940.

Magyar Kozlony, Hivatalos Lap [Hungarian Official
    Collection of Laws]. Budapest, 1946 and 1947.

Monitorul Oficial [Collection of Rumanian Laws].
    Bucharest, 1945, 1946, 1948, and 1949.

Poland. Dziennik Ustaw [Polish Official Collection
    of Laws]. Warsaw, 1945.

Public Papers of the Presidents: Lyndon Baines John-
    son. Vol. II, July 1-December 31, 1966. Washington,
    D.C.: U.S. Government Printing Office, 1967.

RSFSR. Collection of Laws and Decrees of the Workers
    and Peasants Government [Sobraniye Uzakonenii i
    Rasporyazhenii Rabochevo i Krestyanskovo Pravi-
    telstva]. Moscow, 1917-22.

República Argentina, Ministerio de Hacienda. Inter-
    cambio Comercial Argentino por Países en el año
    1953. Buenos Aires: República Argentina, 1954.
    (Also 1954, pub. 1955.)

Soviet Union Information Bureau. The Soviet Union.
    Washington, D.C.: The Bureau, 1929.

United Nations, Relief and Rehabilitation Administra-
    tion. Economic Rehabilitation in Albania.
    Operational Analysis Paper No. 46. London:
    Division of Operational Analysis, UNRRA European
    Regional Office, 1947.

_____. Industrial Rehabilitation in Czechoslovakia.
    Operational Analysis Paper No. 16. London:
    Division of Operational Analysis, UNRRA European
    Regional Office, 1947.

United States, Congress, House of Representatives,
    Committee on Foreign Affairs. The Communist
    Economic Offensive. 85th Cong., 2d sess., 1958.

United States, Congress, House of Representatives,
    Committee on Un-American Activities. Hearings,
    International Communism (The Communist Trade
    Offensive). 85th Cong., 1st sess., 1957.

United States, Congress, House of Representatives,
    Select Committee on Foreign Aid. The East Euro-
    pean Economy in Relation to the European Recov-
    ery Program. Preliminary Report 20 pursuant to
    H. Res. 296, a resolution creating a Special
    Committee on Foreign Aid. 80th Cong., 2d sess.,
    1948.

_____. The Soviet Union in 1947. Supplement to
    Preliminary Report 20 pursuant to H. Res. 296,
    a resolution creating a Special Committee on
    Foreign Aid. 80th Cong., 2d sess., 1948.

United States, Department of State. Battle Act Re-
    port (1964-71). Mutual Defense Assistance Con-
    trol Act of 1951, 17th through 24th Reports to
    Congress, 1965-72.

_____. The Sino-Soviet Economic Offensive in the
    Less Developed Countries. European and British
    Commonwealth Series No. 51, May 1958.

_____, Division of Biographical Information. Soviet
    Political Leaders. Biographical Directory No.
    251, July 1957.

United States, Foreign Operations Administration.
    East-West Trade Trends. Mutual Defense Assis-
    tance Control Act of 1951, Fourth Report to Con-
    gress, 1954.

_____. Soviet Bloc Economic Activities in the Free
    World. Mutual Defense Assistance Control Act
    of 1951, Sixth Report to Congress, 1955.

_____. The Revision of Strategic Trade Controls.
Mutual Defense Assistance Control Act of 1951,
Fifth Report to Congress, 1954.

_____. World-Wide Enforcement of Strategic Trade
Controls. Mutual Defense Assistance Control
Act of 1951, Third Report to Congress, 1953.

United States, International Cooperation Administration. East-West Trade Developments: 1956-1957.
Mutual Defense Assistance Control Act of 1951,
10th Report to Congress, 1958.

_____. Soviet Deterrents to Increased Foreign Trade.
Mutual Defense Assistance Control Act of 1951,
Seventh Report to Congress, 1956.

_____. Survey of East-West Trade in 1955. Mutual
Defense Assistance Control Act of 1951, Eighth
Report to Congress, 1956.

_____. The Strategic Trade Control System: 1948-
1956. Mutual Defense Assistance Control Act of
1951, Ninth Report to Congress, 1957.

United States, Mutual Security Agency. Problems of
Economic Defense. Mutual Defense Assistance
Control Act of 1951, Second Report to Congress,
1953.

_____. A Program for the Denial of Strategic Goods
to the Soviet Bloc. Mutual Defense Assistance
Control Act of 1951, First Report to Congress,
1952.

USSR. Collection of Laws and Decrees [Sobraniye
Zakonov i Rasporyazhenii]. Moscow: Otdel
Opublikovaniya Zakonov, 1918, 1922-30, 1936,
and 1945-46.

_____. Documentation Relating to Foreign Economic
Relations of the USSR. Prepared for the Mone-
tary and Economic Conference, London, June 1933.
Moscow: "International" Typographic Works, 1933.

USSR, Ministry of Foreign Trade [Ministerstvo Vnesh-
    nyei Torgovli]. Foreign Trade of the USSR for
    1956 [Vneshnyaya Torgovlya SSSR za 1956 God].
    Moscow: Vneshtorgizdat, 1958. (Also 1957, pub.
    1958; 1959-63, pub. 1965; 1965, pub. 1966; 1966,
    pub. 1967; and 1968, pub. 1969.)

USSR, People's Commissariat of Foreign Affairs [Narod-
    nie Komissariat po Inostrannie Delam]. Handbook
    of Active Trade Agreements and Other Economic
    Agreements of the USSR Concluded with Foreign
    Governments [Sbornik Deistvuyushchikh Torgoviekh
    Dogovorov i Iniekh Khozyaistvenniekh Soglashenii
    SSSR Zaklyuchenniekh s Inostranniemi Gosudarst-
    vami]. Moscow: SSSR, Narodnie Komissariat po
    Inostrannie Delam, 1935.

USSR, People's Commissariat of Foreign Trade [Narodnie
    Komissariat Vneshnyei Torgovli]. Foreign Trade
    up to the 7th Congress of the Soviet of the USSR
    [Vneshnyaya Torgovlya k VII Syezdu Sovyetov
    SSSR]. Moscow: Vneshtorgizdat, 1935.

_____. Handbook of Active Decrees on Foreign Trade
    [Sbornik Deistvuyushchikh Postenovlenii po
    Veneshnyei Torgovle]. Moscow: Redaktsionno-
    Isdatelskovo Otdela, NKVT, 1924-26.

USSR, Supreme Soviet [Verkhovnie Sovyet]. Gazette
    of the Supreme Soviet of the USSR [Vedomsti
    Verkhovnovo Sovyeta SSSR]. Moscow, 1948.

                            Books

Aleksandrov, D. The Struggle of the Soviet Union for
    the Broadening of Business Ties with All Coun-
    tries--A Basic Factor of Peace [Borba Sovyet-
    skovo Soyuza za Rasshireniye Deloviekh Svyazyei
    so Vsyemi Stranami--Vazhnie Faktor Mira]. Mos-
    cow: Izdatelstvo "Znaniye," 1954.

Alkhimov, V., and V. Mordvinov. Foreign Trade of
    the U.S.S.R. London: Soviet Booklets, 1958.

All-Union Chamber of Commerce [Vsyesoyuznaya Tor-
    govaya Palata]. Countries of the East [Strany
    Vostoka]. Moscow: Gosudarstvennoye Sotsialno-
    Ekonomicheskoye Izdatelstvo, 1934.

_____. Soviet Foreign Trade Organizations [Sovyet-
    skiye Vneshnetorgoviye Organizatsii]. Moscow:
    Vneshtorgizdat, 1971.

All-Union Eastern Chamber of Commerce [Vsyesoyuznaya
    Vostochnaya Torgovaya Palata]. Countries of
    the East [Strany Vostoka]. Moscow: Vsyesoyuz-
    naya-Vostochnaya Torgovaya Palata, 1929.

American Bankers Association. Industry, Government,
    Finance and Foreign Trade in Soviet Russia.
    New York: American Bankers Association, 1929.

Armstrong, John A. The Soviet Bureaucratic Elite.
    New York: Frederick A. Praeger, 1959.

Arskii, R. Industrial Position of Soviet Russia and
    Prospects of Foreign Trade. Moscow: Communist
    International, 1921.

Baikalov, A. V. Money, Prices and Gold in the Soviet
    Union. London: School of Slavonic and East
    European Studies in the University of London,
    1934.

Barnett, Clifford R. Poland. New Haven, Conn.:
    Hraf Press, 1958.

Barou, Noah. Russian Co-Operation Abroad. London:
    P. S. King and Son, 1930.

Barsegyants, Oganes B. Trade and Industry by Decree
    and Order [Torgovlya i Promieshlennosts po
    Dekretam i Rasporyazhyeniyam]. Moscow: Izdat-
    elstvo "Znaniye," 1922.

Baykov, Alexander. Soviet Foreign Trade. Princeton,
    N.J.: Princeton University Press, 1946.

Belenkii, A. Ya., I. S. Zheleznyakov, and I. P.
    Eisenberg. Finance Plan and Balance of Foreign
    Trade Corporations [Finplan i Balans Vneshnyetor-
    govovo Obyedineniya]. Moscow: V/O Mezhdunarod-
    naya Kniga, 1937.

Beloff, Max. Soviet Policy in the Far East 1944-1951.
    London: Oxford University Press, 1953.

Berliner, Joseph S. Soviet Economic Aid. New York:
    Frederick A. Praeger, 1958.

Boyeff, V. The Soviet Union and World Problems.
    Chicago: University of Chicago Press, 1935.

Bron, Saul G. Soviet Economic Development and Amer-
    ican Business. New York: Horace Liveright,
    1930.

Budish, J. M., and Samuel S. Shipman. Soviet Foreign
    Trade--Menace or Promise. New York: Horace
    Liveright, 1931.

Cherviakov, Pavel A. Organization and Technique of
    the Foreign Trade of the USSR [Organizatsia i
    Tekhnika Vneshnyei Torgovli SSSR]. Moscow:
    Vneshtorgizdat, 1958 and 1962.

Collier's Encyclopedia. 20 volumes. New York: P. F.
    Collier and Son, 1957 and 1961.

Collier's Encyclopedia Yearbook. New York: P. F.
    Collier and Son, 1958-1969.

Condoide, Mikhail V. Russian-American Trade. Colum-
    bus: The Bureau of Business Research, College
    of Commerce and Administration, The Ohio State
    University, 1946.

Conolly, Violet. Soviet Economic Policy in the East.
    London: Oxford University Press, 1933.

_____. Soviet Trade from the Pacific to the Levant.
    London: Humphrey Milford-Oxford University Press,
    1935.

Degras, Joan, ed. Soviet Documents on Foreign Policy.
    London: Oxford University Press, 1951.

Dewar, Margaret. Soviet Trade with Eastern Europe:
    1945-1949. London: Royal Institute of Interna-
    tional Affairs, 1951.

Doussé, Jacques. La Politique Economique de l'URSS
    Appliquée à son Commerce Extérieur. Paris:
    Marcel Giard, 1933.

Eliacheff, Boris. Le Dumping Sovietique. Paris:
    Marcel Giard, 1931.

Encyclopedia of Russian Exports [Entsiklopediya Russ-
    kovo Eksporta]. Vols. II and III. 1st edition.
    Berlin: Torgovovo Predstavitelstva SSSR v Ger-
    manii pri vchasti Upravleniya Upoln, NKVT na
    Ukraine i Tsentrosoyuza, 1925.

Encyclopedia of Soviet Exports [Entsiklopediya Sov-
    yetskovo Eksporta]. Vol. I. 2d edition. Ber-
    lin: Torgovovo Predstavitelstva SSSR v Germanii,
    Tsentrosoyuza i Gostorga, 1928.

Eudin, Xenia, and Harold Fisher. Soviet Russia and
    the West. Stanford, Calif.: Stanford Univer-
    sity Press, 1957.

Facts on File. New York: Person's Index, Facts on
    File, 1945-70.

50 Years of Soviet Foreign Trade [50 Let Sovyetskoy
    Vneshnyei Torgovli]. Moscow: Mezhdunarodnieye
    Otnosheniya, 1967.

Flegon, Alec. Soviet Foreign Trade Techniques. Lon-
    don: Flegon Press, 1965.

For a Lasting Peace, For a People's Democracy. Infor-
    mation Bureau of the Communist and Workers'
    Parties, November 18, 1949.

Frey, L., A. Smirnov, G. Lopatin, and I. Zheleznyakov.
    The Financing of Foreign Trade [Finansirovaniye

Vneshnyei Torgovli]. Moscow: V/O Mezhdunarodnaya Kniga, 1938.

Frumkin, M. I. National Economy and Foreign Trade
of the USSR [Narodnoye Khozyaistvo i Vneshnyaya
Torgovlya SSSR]. Moscow: Gosudarstvennoye
Izdatelstvo, 1926.

Genkin, D. M., ed. Legal Questions of Foreign Trade
of the USSR with European Countries of the People's Democracy [Pravovieye Voprosie Vneshnyei
Torgovli SSSR s Evropeiskimi Stranami Narodnoi
Demokratii]. Moscow: Vneshtorgizdat, 1955.

Gerschenkron, Alexander. Economic Relations with
the USSR. New York: The Committee on International Economic Policy, 1945.

Giffen, James H. The Legal and Practical Aspects of
Trade with the Soviet Union. New York: Frederick A. Praeger, 1969.

Ginzburg, I. S. Foreign Trade of the USSR [Vneshnyaya
Torgovlya SSSR]. Moscow: Gosudarstvennoye
Sotsialno-Economicheskoye Izdatelstvo, 1937.

Goldman, Marshall I. Soviet Foreign Aid. New York:
Frederick A. Praeger, 1967.

Groman, V., M. Kaufman, and M. Zamengof. Foreign
Trade of the USSR for 1923 [Vneshnyaya Torgovlya
SSSR za 1923 God]. Moscow: Redaktsionno-Iz-
datelskovo Otdela, NKVT, 1924.

Harper, Samuel N., and Ronald Thompson. The Government of the Soviet Union. New York: D. Van
Nostrand, 1949.

Heymann, Hans. We Can Do Business with Russia. Chicago: Ziff Davis, 1945.

Höffding, W. German Trade with the Soviet Union.
London: School of Slavonic and East European
Studies in the University of London, 1936.

Hurwicz, Elias. Die Orientpolitik der Dritten Internationale. Berlin: Deutsche Verlagsgesellschaft für Politik und Geschichte mbH, 1922.

International Monetary Fund. International Financial Statistics. April 1959.

Jeramec, Jacques. Le Monopole du Commerce Extérieur en Russie Sovietique. Paris: Librairie Générale de Droit et de Jurisprudence, 1928.

Kaufman, M. Ya. Foreign Trade and Trade Policy of the USSR [Vneshnyaya Torgovlya i Torgovaya Politika SSSR]. Moscow: Redaktsionno-Izdatelskovo Otdela, NKVT, 1924.

_____. Organization and Regulation of the Foreign Trade of Russia [Organizatsia i Regulirovaniye Vneshnyei Torgovli Rossii]. Moscow: Ekonomicheskaya Zhizn, 1925.

Keesings Archiv der Gegenwart. Bremen: Verlag Export-Edition, 1945-51.

Keesing's Contemporary Archives. Bristol, Eng.: Keesing's Publications Limited (of London), 1950-70.

Keilin, A. D. Transport and Insurance in Foreign Trade: Legal Conditions of Foreign Trade Agreements [Transport i Strakhovaniye vo Vneshnyei Torgovlye: Pravovieye Usloviya Vneshnetorgoviekh Sdelok]. Moscow: V/O Mezhdunarodnaya Kniga, 1947.

Kerblay, B. H. The Economic Relations of the U.S.S.R. with Foreign Countries During the War and in the Post-War Period. "Bulletins on Soviet Economic Development," Bulletin No. 5. Birmingham: Department of Economics and Institutions of the U.S.S.R., Faculty of Commerce and Social Science, University of Birmingham, March 1951.

Khrushchev, Nikita. Khrushchev Remembers. Translated and edited by Strobe Talbott. Boston: Little, Brown, 1970.

Kirillov, I. A. The Financing of Trade [Finansiro-
    vaniye Torgovli]. Moscow: Izdatelstvo NKRKI,
    1927.

Knickerbocker, H. R. Soviet Trade and World Depres-
    sion. London: John Lane-The Bodley Head Ltd.,
    1931.

Koort, F. Soviet Industry and Foreign Trade. Lon-
    don: Soviet News (Booklet No. 13), 1957.

Korostovetz, I. J. Von Cinggis Khan zur Sowjetrepub-
    lik. Berlin: Walter de Gruyter, 1926.

Kovarsky, B. N. The Regulation of Foreign Trade
    [Regulirovaniye Vneshnii Torgovli]. Moscow:
    Redaktsionno-Izdatelskovo Otdela, NKVT, 1925.

Krassin, B. L. Foreign Trade and Foreign Economic
    Policy of the Soviet Government [Vneshtorg i
    Vneshnyaya Ekonomicheskaya Politika Sovyetskovo
    Pravitelstva]. Moscow: Gosudarstvennoye Iz-
    datelstvo, 1921.

Kutuzov, A. I., ed. Foreign Trade of the USSR for
    10 Years [Vneshnyaya Torgovlya Soyuza SSR za X
    Let]. Moscow: Narkomtorg SSSR i RSFSR, 1928.

Large Soviet Encyclopedia [Bolshaya Sovyetskaya Ent-
    siklopediya]. 65 volumes. 1st edition. Mos-
    cow: A/O "Sovyetskaya Entsiklopediya," 1926-31.

Large Soviet Encyclopedia [Bolshaya Sovyetskaya Ent-
    siklopediya]. 51 volumes. 2d edition. Moscow:
    Gosudarstvennoye Nauchnoe Izdatelstvo "Bolshaya
    Sovyetskaya Entsiklopediya," 1949-58.

Large Soviet Encyclopedia--Union of Soviet Socialist
    Republics [Bolshaya Sovyetskaya Entsiklopediya--
    Soyuz Sovyetskikh Sotsialisticheskikh Respublik].
    Moscow: Gosudarstvennie Nauchnie Institut "Sov-
    yetskaya Entsiklopediya," 1948.

London University. Banking and Credit in the Soviet
    Union. London: School of Slavonic and East

European Studies in the University of London, 1935.

_____. The Prospects of British and American Trade with the Soviet Union. London: School of Slavonic and East European Studies in the University of London, 1935.

Middle East: 1958. 6th edition. London: Europa Publications Limited, 1958.

Mishustin, D. D. Foreign Trade and Industrialization of the USSR [Vneshnyaya Torgovlya i Industrializatsiya SSSR]. Moscow: V/O Mezhdunarodnaya Kniga, 1938.

National Committee for a Free Europe. Economic Treaties and Agreements of the Soviet Bloc in Eastern Europe: 1945-1951. Washington, D.C.: The Committee, 1952.

Nesterov, M. V. International Trade--An Important Factor in the Strengthening of Peace [Mezhdunarodnaya Torgovlya--Vazhnie Faktor Ukrepleniya Mira]. Moscow: Izdatelstvo "Znaniye," 1956.

New Customs Tariff of the USSR [Novy Tamozheny Tarif SSSR]. Supplement to Foreign Trade [Vneshnyaya Torgovlya], No. 9, 1961.

Pasvolsky, Leo. Russia in the Far East. New York: The Macmillan Company, 1922.

Pozdniakov, V. S. State Monopoly of Foreign Trade in the USSR [Gosudarstvennaya Monopoliya Vneshnyei Torgovli v SSSR]. Moscow: Izdatelstvo "Mezhdunarodniye Otnosheniya," 1969.

Rosengoltz, A. P. [Rozengolts, A. P.]. Soviet Foreign Trade--New Developments. London: Trade Delegation of the USSR in Great Britain, 1936.

Rosenholz, A. P. [Rozengolts, A. P.]. Fifteen Years of the Foreign Trade Monopoly. Moscow: Co-Operative Publishing Society of Foreign Workers in the USSR, 1933.

Royal Institute of International Affairs. Survey of
    International Affairs: 1947-1948. London:
    Oxford University Press, 1952.

Rozengolts, A. P. Foreign Trade and the Struggle for
    Techno-Economic Independence of the USSR [Vnesh-
    nyaya Torgovlya i Borba za Tekhniko-Ekonomiches-
    kuyu Nezavisimost SSSR]. Moscow: Partizdat TsK
    VKP(b), 1935.

_____. Foreign Trade of the USSR Under New Condi-
    tions [Vneshnyaya Torgovlya SSSR v Noviekh
    Usloviyakh]. Moscow: Sotsekiz, 1936.

Rozenholtz, A. [Rozengolts, A. P.]. Foreign Trade
    and Economic Independence of the USSR. Moscow:
    USSR Chamber of Commerce, 1935.

Rozenholz, A. P. [Rozengolts, A. P.]. The USSR and
    the Capitalist World. Moscow: Vneshtorgizdat,
    1934.

Santalov, A. A., and Louis Segal. Soviet Union Year
    Book. London: George Allen and Unwin, 1927-30.

Sapir, Michael. The New Role of the Soviets in the
    World Economy. Washington, D.C.: Committee
    for Economic Development, 1958.

Scientific-Research Institute of the Monopoly of For-
    eign Trade [Nauchno-Issledovatelskii Institut
    Monopolii Vneshnyei Torgovli]. Foreign Trade of
    the Soviet Union [Vneshnyaya Torgovlya Sovyetskovo
    Soyuza]. Moscow: V/O Mezhdunarodnaya Kniga,
    1938.

_____. Foreign Trade of the USSR for 20 Years:
    1918-1937 [Vneshnyaya Torgovlya SSSR za 20 Let:
    1918-1937 GG]. Moscow: V/O Mezhdunarodnaya
    Kniga, 1939.

_____. Trade Relations of the USSR with Countries
    of the East [Torgoviye Otnosheniya SSSR so
    Stranami Vostoka]. Moscow: V/O Mezhdunarodnaya
    Kniga, 1938.

Segal, Louis, and A. A. Santalov. Commercial Year-
    Book of the Soviet Union. London: George Allen
    and Unwin, 1925.

_____. Soviet Union Year Book. London: George
    Allen and Unwin, 1926.

Shtein, B. E. Russian Exports and Foreign Markets
    [Russkii Eksport i Vneshniye Rienki]. Moscow:
    Ekonomicheskaya Zhizn, 1923.

Siddiq, S. M. Indo-Russian Trade. Delhi: Indian
    Council of World Affairs, 1948.

Smirnov, A. M. International Accounts and Credit
    Relations in the Foreign Trade of the USSR
    [Mezhdunarodnieye Raschyotie i Kreditnieye Ot-
    nosheniya vo Vneshnyei Torgovlye SSSR]. Moscow:
    Vneshtorgizdat, 1953.

_____. International Accounts and the Financing of
    Foreign Trade [Mezhdunarodnieye Raschyotie i
    Finansirovaniye Vneshnyei Torgovli]. Moscow:
    V/O Mezhdunarodnaya Kniga, 1946.

Smirnov, A. M., and N. N. Liubimov. Foreign Trade
    of the USSR [Vneshnyaya Torgovlya SSSR]. Moscow:
    Vneshtorgizdat, 1954.

Sobolev, M. N., ed. Economics and Policies of Foreign
    Trade [Ekonomika i Politika Vneshnyei Torgovli].
    Moscow: Narkomtorga SSSR i RSFSR, 1928.

Stokke, Baard Richard. Soviet and Eastern European
    Trade and Aid in Africa. New York: Frederick
    A. Praeger, 1967.

Stoupnitzky, A. Statut International de l'URSS--
    Etat Commerçant. Paris: Librairie Générale de
    Droit et de Jurisprudence, 1936.

Temperley, H. W. V., ed. A History of the Peace Con-
    ference in Paris. London: Henry Frowde and
    Hodder and Stoughton, 1924.

Troyanovsky, A., L. Yurovsky, and M. Kaufman. Export,
    Import and Concessions of the USSR [Eksport,
    Import i Kontsessii Soyuza SSR]. Moscow: Go-
    sudarstvennoi Kontorie Obyavlyenii "Dvigatel,"
    1926.

USSR, Chamber of Commerce. Economic Conditions in
    the USSR. Moscow: Vneshtorgizdat, 1931.

Vilensky, V. D. Modern Mongolia [Sovremennaya Mon-
    goliya]. Kharkov: "Proletarii," 1925.

Vostokintorg. Supplement to Foreign Trade [Vnesh-
    nyaya Torgovlya], 1960.

Voznesensky, Nikolai A. The Economy of the USSR Dur-
    ing World War II. Washington, D.C.: Public
    Affairs Press, 1948.

Yanson, J. D. Foreign Trade in the USSR. London:
    Victor Gollancz, 1934.

Zhirmunski, M. M. Organization and Technique of So-
    viet Exports [Organizatsiya i Tekhnika Sovyet-
    skovo Eksporta]. Moscow: Vneshtorgizdat, 1935.

_____. Soviet Export. Moscow: Mezhdunarodnaya
    Kniga, 1936.

Zotov, B. D. Foreign Trade of the European Countries
    of the People's Democracy in the Work of Building
    Socialism [Vneshnyaya Torgovlya Evropeiskikh
    Stran Narodnoi Demokratii na Sluzhbe Stroitelstva
    Sotsializma]. Moscow: Izdatelstvo Akademii
    Nauk SSSR, 1958.

Articles and Periodicals

"Agreement Concerning Multilateral Settlements in
    Transferable Rubles and Organization of the In-
    ternational Bank for Economic Cooperations,"
    Gazette of the Supreme Soviet of the USSR [Vedo-
    mosti Verkhovnovo Sovyeta Soyuza Sovyetskikh
    Sotsialisticheskikh Respublik], No. 7 (1964).

Item 83 reprinted in American Review of Soviet and Eastern European Foreign Trade, January-February 1966, pp. 9-36.

Allen, Robert Loring. "Economic Motives in Soviet Foreign Trade Policy," The Southern Economic Journal, October 1958, pp. 189-201.

American Review of Soviet and Eastern European Foreign Trade, 1965-66.

Ausch, Sandor, and Ferenc Bartha. "Theoretical Problems Relating to Prices in Trade Between the Comecon Countries," Soviet and Eastern European Foreign Trade, Summer 1968, pp. 35-71.

Bednarik, Mojmir K. "The Moscow Bank: The International Bank for Economic Cooperation," American Review of Soviet and Eastern European Foreign Trade, January-February 1966, pp. 3-8.

Bergson, A., R. Bernaut, and L. Turgeon. "Prices of Basic Industrial Products in the USSR, 1928-1950," Journal of Political Economy, August 1956, pp. 303-28.

Bernasek, V., and A. Neustadt. "Changing Conceptions of the Foreign Trade Monopoly in the USSR," Soviet and Eastern European Foreign Trade, Winter 1968/69, pp. 62-79.

Bogomolov, O. "Problems in Production Specialization and Cooperation Among CMEA Countries," Soviet and Eastern European Foreign Trade, Spring 1968, pp. 68-90.

Bolshakov, L. "Soviet Goods on the World Market," Economic Gazette [Ekonomicheskaya Gazeta], November 25, 1960; also in Soviet Review, January 1961, pp. 61-63.

Brzak, V., and D. Marsikova. "New Methods of Management and Organization of Foreign Trade in Socialist Countries," Soviet and Eastern European Foreign Trade, Fall-Winter 1970, pp. 214-67.

Business Week. 1950-72.

Dillon, C. Douglas. "Realities of Soviet Foreign
     Economic Policies," The Department of State Bul-
     letin, February 16, 1959, pp. 237-43.

_____. "The Challenge of Soviet Economic Expansion,"
     The Department of State Bulletin, May 25, 1959,
     pp. 759-64.

_____. "The Issues Today," The Management Review,
     January 1959, pp. 6-15.

Diumulen, I. "The Soviet Union in the System of In-
     ternational Economic Relations," World Economics
     and International Relations [Mirovaya Ekonomika
     i Mezhdunarodnye Otnosheniya], No. 3, 1964; also
     in American Review of Soviet and Eastern European
     Foreign Trade, January-February 1965, pp. 39-51.

Foreign Trade [Vneshnyaya Torgovlya]. Official jour-
     nal of the USSR Ministry of Foreign Trade. 1943-
     71.

Fortune. 1959-70.

Gerschenkron, Alexander. "Russia's Trade in the
     Postwar Years," Annals of the American Academy
     of Political and Social Science, May 1949, pp.
     85-100.

Golovin, V. "Medexport--New All-Union Association,"
     Foreign Trade [Vneshnyaya Torgovlya], No. 3
     (1961), p. 26.

Hagemann, Ernst. "The Foreign Trade of the People's
     Republic of China with the Eastern European
     Countries 1950-1969," Soviet and Eastern European
     Foreign Trade, Spring 1972, pp. 56-86.

Herman, Leon M. "The New Soviet Posture in World
     Trade," Problems of Communism, November-December
     1954, pp. 9-16.

Horsky, Josef. "Foreign Trade Policy," Soviet and Eastern European Foreign Trade, September-October 1967, pp. 24-30.

_____. "Foreign Trade Theory and Its Relation to Planning," Soviet and Eastern European Foreign Trade, Fall 1968, pp. 3-21.

Hughes, Edward. "The Russians Drill Deep in the Middle East," Fortune, July 1968, pp. 102-05.

Laiks [Latvian language newspaper]. Brooklyn, New York, February 25, 1959.

Laquer, W. Z. "The Shifting Line in Soviet Orientoloty," Problems of Communism, March-April 1956, pp. 20-26.

Nazarkin, K. "Profitable to All," American Review of Soviet and Eastern European Foreign Trade, May-June 1965, pp. 35-38.

Nove, Alec. "Soviet Trade and Soviet Aid," Lloyds Bank Review, January 1959, pp. 1-19.

Okonechnikov, N. "The Course of Widening Specialization in the All-Union Associations" [Po Puti Dalneighyei Spetsializatsia Vsesoyuznikh Obedineniye], Foreign Trade [Vneshnyaya Torgovlya], No. 9 (1966), pp. 9-11.

Pleva, Jan. "Some Economic and Legal Aspects of Foreign Trade in Czechoslovakia," Soviet and Eastern European Foreign Trade, May-June 1967, pp. 3-18. Paper submitted to 4th International Symposium of Jurists and Economists, Zagreb, September 1966.

Poliakov, M. "USSR Bank for Foreign Trade," Economic Gazette [Ekonomicheskaya Gazyeta], February 29, 1964; also in American Review of Soviet and Eastern European Foreign Trade, January-February 1965, pp. 63-67.

Pozdniakov, V. S. "The State Monopoly of Foreign
    Trade in the USSR," Soviet State and Law
    [Sovetskoe Gosudarstvo i Pravo], No. 10 (1967);
    also in Soviet Review, Summer 1968, pp. 42-49.

Pravda. February 25, 1947.

Questions of Economics [Voprosy Ekonomiki], February
    1952, p. 53.

Riverside Press-Enterprise (Riverside, Calif.).
    1971-72.

Rundt, Stefan Jean. "What U.S. Business Can Do,"
    The Management Review, January 1959, pp. 32-42.

Russian Information and Review. Journal of the In-
    formation Department of the Russian Trade Dele-
    gation in London. 1921-24.

San Francisco Chronicle. March 7, 1959; May 28, 1959.

San Francisco Examiner. November 24, 1957.

Sayres, Paul W. "The New Offensive in Underdeveloped
    Countries," The Management Review, January 1959,
    pp. 16-24.

Selucky, R. "The Impact of the Economic Reforms on
    the Foreign Economic Relations of the Socialist
    Countries," Soviet and Eastern European Foreign
    Trade, Fall 1968, pp. 72-86.

Smirnov, G., B. Zotov, and G. Shagalov. "Theory of
    Foreign Trade," Planned Economy [Planovoe
    Khoziaistvo], No. 8, 1964; also in American Re-
    view of Soviet and Eastern European Foreign
    Trade, January-February 1965, pp. 3-15.

Soviet and Eastern European Foreign Trade. 1967-72.

Soviet Union Review. Journal of the Information De-
    partment of the Russian Trade Delegation in Lon-
    don. 1925.

Stankovsky, Jan.   "Problems of Integration in Come-
    con," Soviet and Eastern European Foreign Trade,
    Fall-Winter 1971/72, pp. 306-19.

Tarnovsky, W. W.   "Banking: The First Private Bank,"
    Manchester Guardian Commercial, June 26, 1924,
    p. 932.

The New York Times.   1918-59.

The Times (London).   January 1, 1923.

The Wall Street Journal.   1970-72.

Vasiliev, N. V.   "Each Day Brings New Work" [Kazhdy
    Den Vnosit v Rabotu Novoe], Foreign Trade
    [Vneshnyaya Torgovlya], No. 10 (1960), p. 29.

Vasin, V.   "USSR Exports Airplanes" [SSSR Eksporti-
    iruet Samoleti], Foreign Trade [Vneshnyaya Tor-
    govlya], No. 8 (1962), pp. 11-13.

Voronov, K.   "Current Organization of Foreign Trade
    of the USSR" [Sovremennaya Organizatsia Vnesh-
    nyei Torgovli SSSR], Foreign Trade [Vneshnyaya
    Torgovlya], No. 8 (1966), pp. 48-51.

Willers, Thomas F.   "Reappraising Trade with Russia,"
    Duns Review, March 1965, p. 21.

Zukal, R.   "Currency Convertibility and External
    Economic Relations," Soviet and Eastern European
    Foreign Trade, Fall 1968, pp. 58-71

                        Other Sources

Allen, Patton D., Director, European Division, Bureau
    of Foreign Commerce, U.S. Department of Commerce,
    Washington, D.C. Letter dated December 9, 1958.

Barker, W., British Embassy, Washington, D.C. Letter
    dated February 20, 1959.

Kearns, Henry, Assistant Secretary of Commerce for
     International Affairs.   "Soviet Trade Strategies
     and How American Business Might Meet Them."
     Address delivered to the briefing session of the
     American Management Association, Savoy-Hilton
     Hotel, New York City, November 5, 1958.

Kriessmann, Wilhelm, Austrian Trade Delegate, Los
     Angeles, Calif.   Letter dated December 22, 1958.

Stave, Thomas C., Second Secretary of Embassy, Ameri-
     can Embassy, Bonn, Germany.   Letter dated March
     26, 1959.

Worthing, Marion W., First Secretary of Embassy,
     American Embassy, Paris.   Letter dated March 27,
     1959.

In this book GLEN ALDEN SMITH has combined an unusual background in Russian area studies, international business, foreign aid, and teaching. Following undergraduate work in Russian area studies and graduate study in Russian history, Dr. Smith specialized in international business at Stanford's Graduate School of Business. Upon receiving his MBA in 1954, he joined the AID (then FOA) program as a Foreign Service Staff Officer. Following a stint in FOA's Tariffs and Trade Office, Dr. Smith was assigned as Middle East Regional Foreign Trade and Investment Adviser in Beirut, Lebanon, where he saw the Suez crisis close up. Returning to the United States in 1957, he completed his doctoral studies in international business at Stanford and then taught at the School of World Business at San Francisco State University. In 1961 Dr. Smith joined Kaiser Aluminum International. As an executive of this firm he was active in Kaiser's development in Thailand, India, and Ghana and has traveled extensively in the Far East, Southeast Asia, and Europe. In 1970 Dr. Smith left industry temporarily to serve as chairman of the Marketing Department at California State University, San Bernadino, California. At the present time Dr. Smith is vice-president of International Mill Service.